NEGIMA! 7

Ken Akamatsu

TRANSLATED BY

Toshifumi Yoshida

ADAPTED BY

T. Ledoux

LETTERING AND RETOUCH BY

Steve Palmer

BALLANTINE BOOKS · NEW YORK

A Word from the Author

The school trip over, the students of homeroom 3-A return at last to the Mahora Academy campus. Welcome to Volume 7!

In the story it's "Golden Week," putting us, calendar-wise, at the beginning of May.* What mischief awaits the students now that they're back in school? (^^;) The real question, though: Will I be able to keep up with drawing the series until their graduation ceremony?!

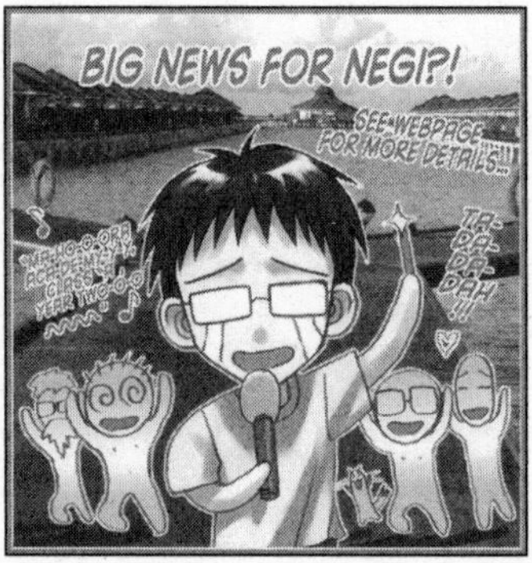
BIG NEWS FOR NEGI?!
SEE WEBPAGE FOR MORE DETAILS!!!
TA-DA-DA-DAH!!!

I'm going to be able to release some really big Negi news soon. The CD, the character merchandise, the PS2 game...the next logical development should be obvious. ("Gatchapon" toys in vending machines? No?)

Ken Akamatsu
www.ailove.net

*Golden Week is a collection of four national holidays that all occur during the same week. Most companies close down for this week.

Negima! Volume 7 is a work of fiction. Names, characters, places, and incidents are the products of the author's imagination or are used fictitiously. Any resemblance to actual events, locales, or persons, living or dead is entirely coincidental.

2005 Del Rey Books Trade Paperback Edition

Published in the United States by Del Rey Books, an imprint of The Random House Publishing Group, a division of Random House, Inc., New York.

Originally published in serial form by Shonen Magazine Comics and subsequently published in book form by Kodansha, Ltd., Tokyo in 2004, copyright © 2004 Ken Akamatsu

ISBN 0-345-47787-1
Printed in the United States of America
www.delreymanga.com

Library of Congress Control Number: 2004090830

1 2 3 4 5 6 7 8 9

Translator —Toshifumi Yoshida
Adaptor—T. Ledoux
Lettering and retouch—Steve Palmer
Cover Design—David Stevenson

Honorifics

Throughout the Del Rey Manga books, you will find Japanese honorifics left intact in the translations. For those not familiar with how the Japanese use honorifics and, more important, how they differ from American honorifics, we present this brief overview.

Politeness has always been a critical facet of Japanese culture. Ever since the feudal era, when Japan was a highly stratified society, use of honorifics—which can be defined as polite speech that indicates relationship or status—has played an essential role in the Japanese language. When addressing someone in Japanese, an honorific usually takes the form of a suffix attached to one's name (example: "Asuna-san"), or as a title at the end of one's name or in place of the name itself (example: "Negi-sensei," or simply "Sensei!").

Honorifics can be expressions of respect or endearment. In the context of manga and anime, honorifics give insight into the nature of the relationship between characters. Many translations into English leave out these important honorifics, and therefore distort the "feel" of the original Japanese. Because Japanese honorifics contain nuances that English honorifics lack, it is our policy at Del Rey not to translate them. Here, instead, is a guide to some of the honorifics you may encounter in Del Rey Manga.

-*san:* This is the most common honorific, and is equivalent to Mr., Miss, Ms., or Mrs. It is the all-purpose honorific and can be used in any situation where politeness is required.

-*sama:* This is one level higher than "-san." It is used to confer great respect.

-*dono:* This comes from the word "tono," which means "lord." It is an even higher level than "-sama," and confers utmost respect.

-*kun:*   This suffix is used at the end of boys' names to express familiarity or endearment. It is also sometimes used by men among friends, or when addressing someone younger or of lower station.

-*chan:*   This is used to express endearment, mostly toward girls. It is also used for little boys, pets, and even among lovers. It gives a sense of childish cuteness.

Bozu: This is an informal way to refer to a boy, similar to the English term "kid" or "squirt."

Sempai: This title suggests that the addressee is one's senior in a group or organization. It is most often used in a school setting, where underclassmen refer to their upperclassmen as "sempai." It can also be used in the workplace, such as when a newer employee addresses an employee who has seniority in the company.

Kohai: This is the opposite of "sempai," and is used toward underclassmen in school or newcomers in the workplace. It connotes that the addressee is of lower station.

Sensei: Literally meaning "one who has come before," this title is used for teachers, doctors, or masters of any profession or art.

-[blank]:   Usually forgotten in these lists, but perhaps the most significant difference between Japanese and English. The lack of honorific means that the speaker has permission to address the person in a very intimate way. Usually, only family, spouses, or very close friends have this kind of permission. Known as *yobisute,* it can be gratifying when someone who has earned the intimacy starts to call one by one's name without an honorific. But when that intimacy hasn't been earned, it can also be very insulting.

魔法先生 ネギま!

MAGISTER NEGI MAGI

7

Ken Akamatsu

赤松 健

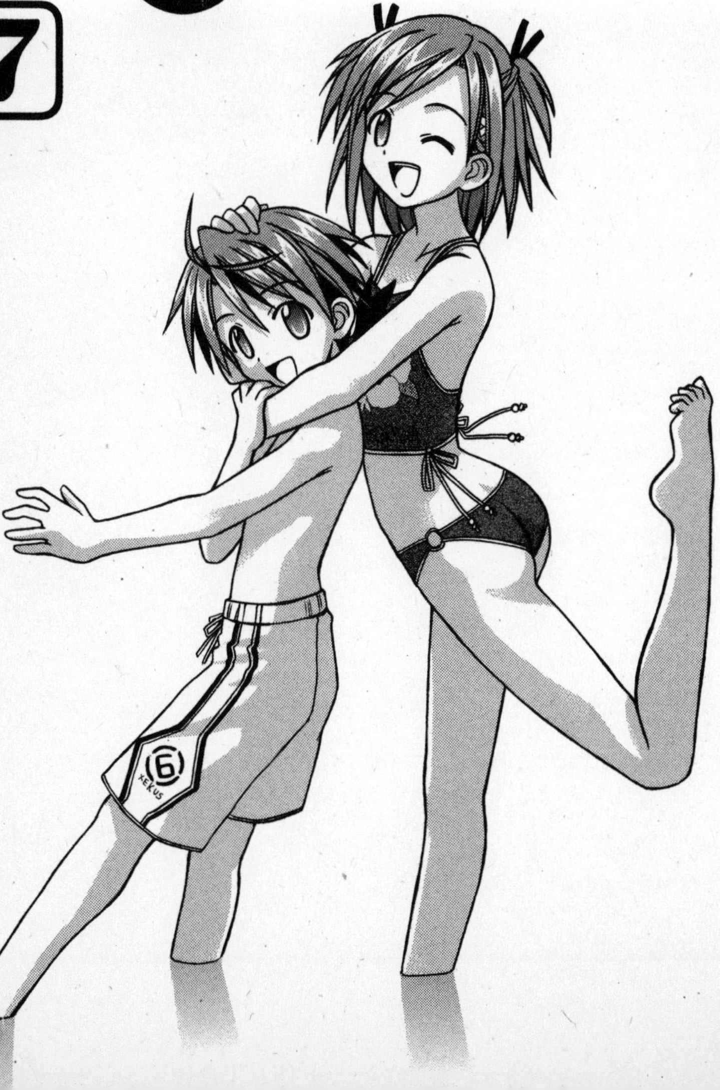

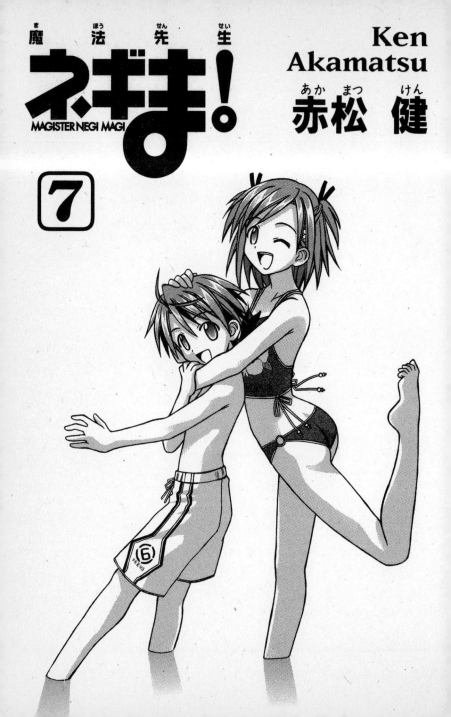

ASUNA : ?!
NOT YOUR PROBLEM...?
HOW CAN YOU SAY THAT, NEGI-BŌZU,
AFTER EVERYTHING THAT'S...?!

NEGI : HEY, HEY, WHOA, ASUNA-SAN,
YOU'RE CHOKING M—
I JUST DIDN'T WANT TO INVOLVE AN
INNOCENT BYSTANDER IN...

CONTENTS

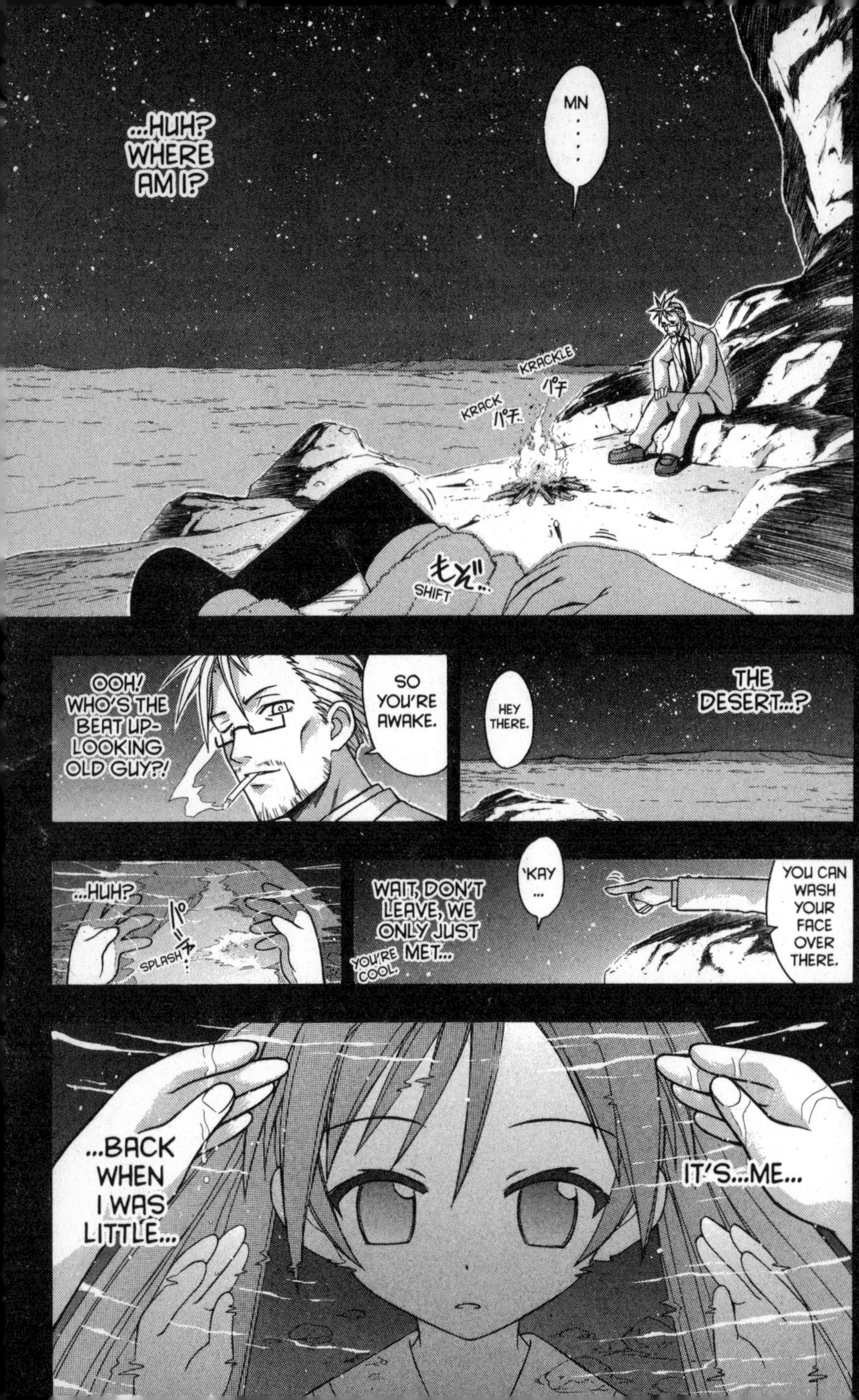
MN . . . .
...HUH? WHERE AM I?
KRACKLE パチ
KRACK パチ..
もぞ...
SHIFT
THE DESERT...?
HEY THERE.
SO YOU'RE AWAKE.
OOH! WHO'S THE BEAT UP-LOOKING OLD GUY?!
YOU CAN WASH YOUR FACE OVER THERE.
'KAY ...
WAIT, DON'T LEAVE, WE ONLY JUST MET...
YOU'RE COOL.
...HUH?
パシャ...
SPLASH
IT'S...ME...
...BACK WHEN I WAS LITTLE...

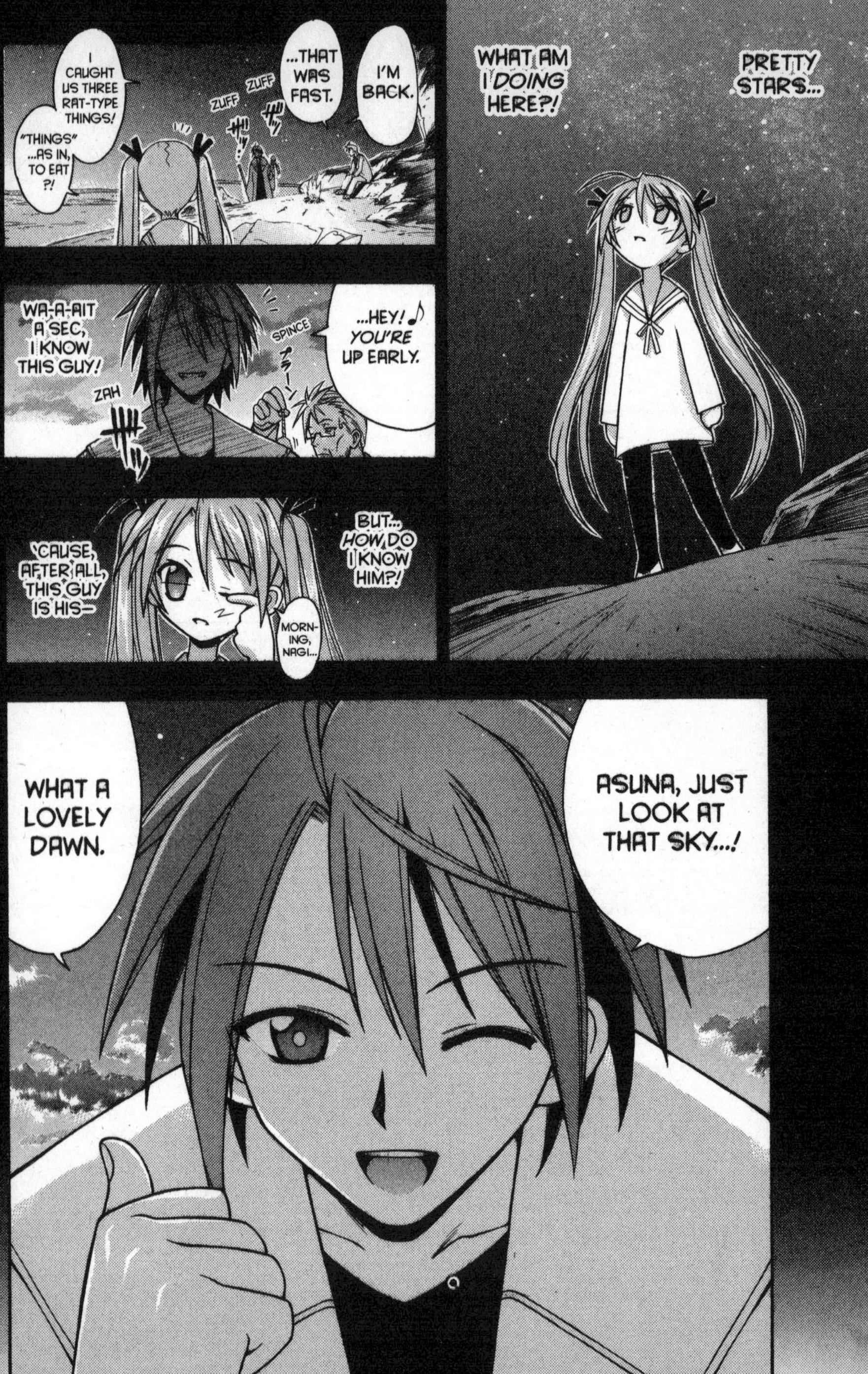
PRETTY STARS...
WHAT AM I DOING HERE?!
I'M BACK.
...THAT WAS FAST.
ZUFF ZUFF
I CAUGHT US THREE RAT-TYPE THINGS!
"THINGS" ...AS IN, TO EAT ?!
...HEY!♪ YOU'RE UP EARLY.
SPINCE
WA-A-AIT A SEC, I KNOW THIS GUY!
ZAH
BUT... HOW DO I KNOW HIM?!
MORNING, NAGI...
'CAUSE, AFTER ALL, THIS GUY IS HIS—
ASUNA, JUST LOOK AT THAT SKY...!
WHAT A LOVELY DAWN.

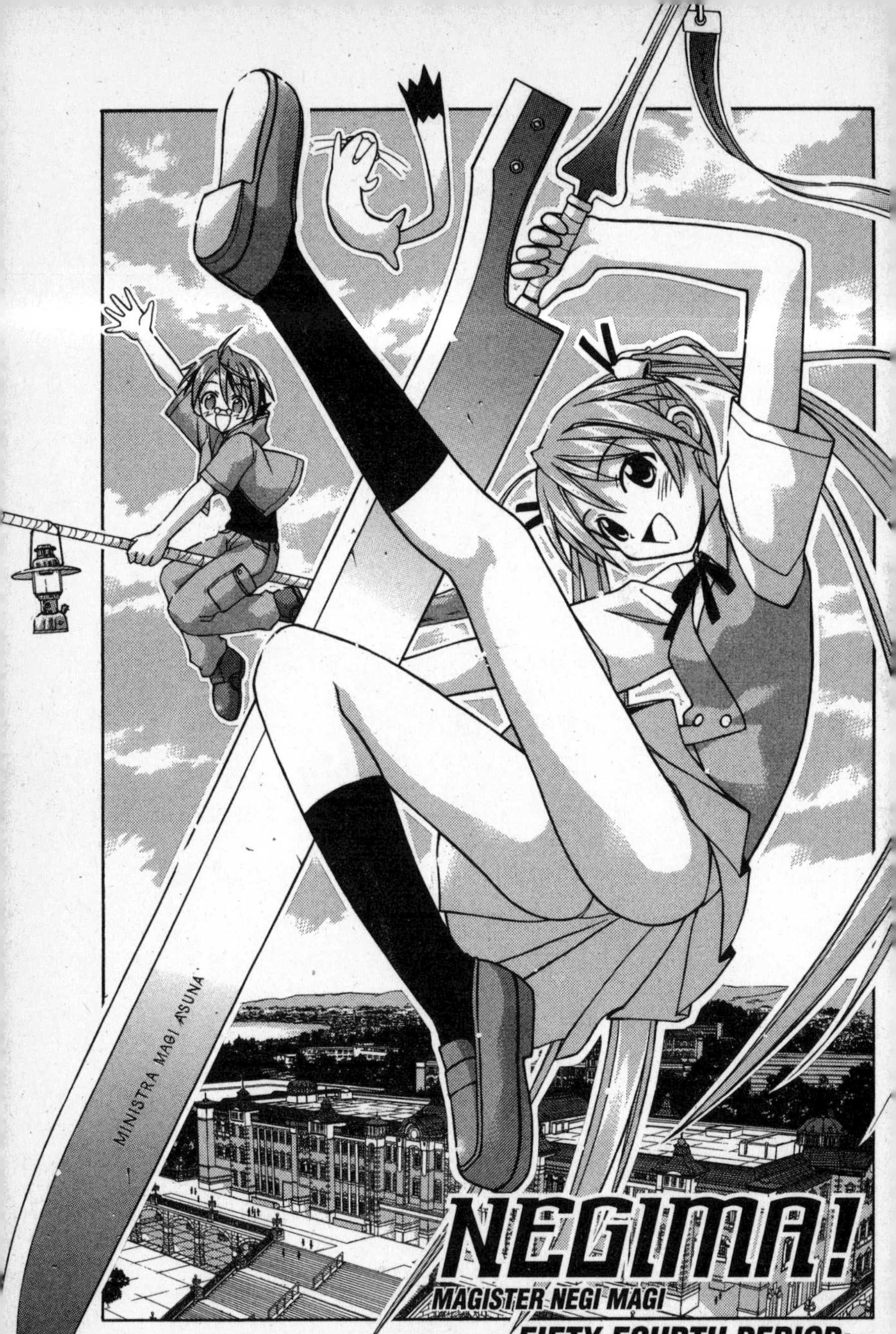
MINISTRA MAGI ASUNA
NEGIMA!
MAGISTER NEGI MAGI
FIFTY-FOURTH PERIOD:
LE MAP, L'AMOUR, LE CHOCOLAT♡

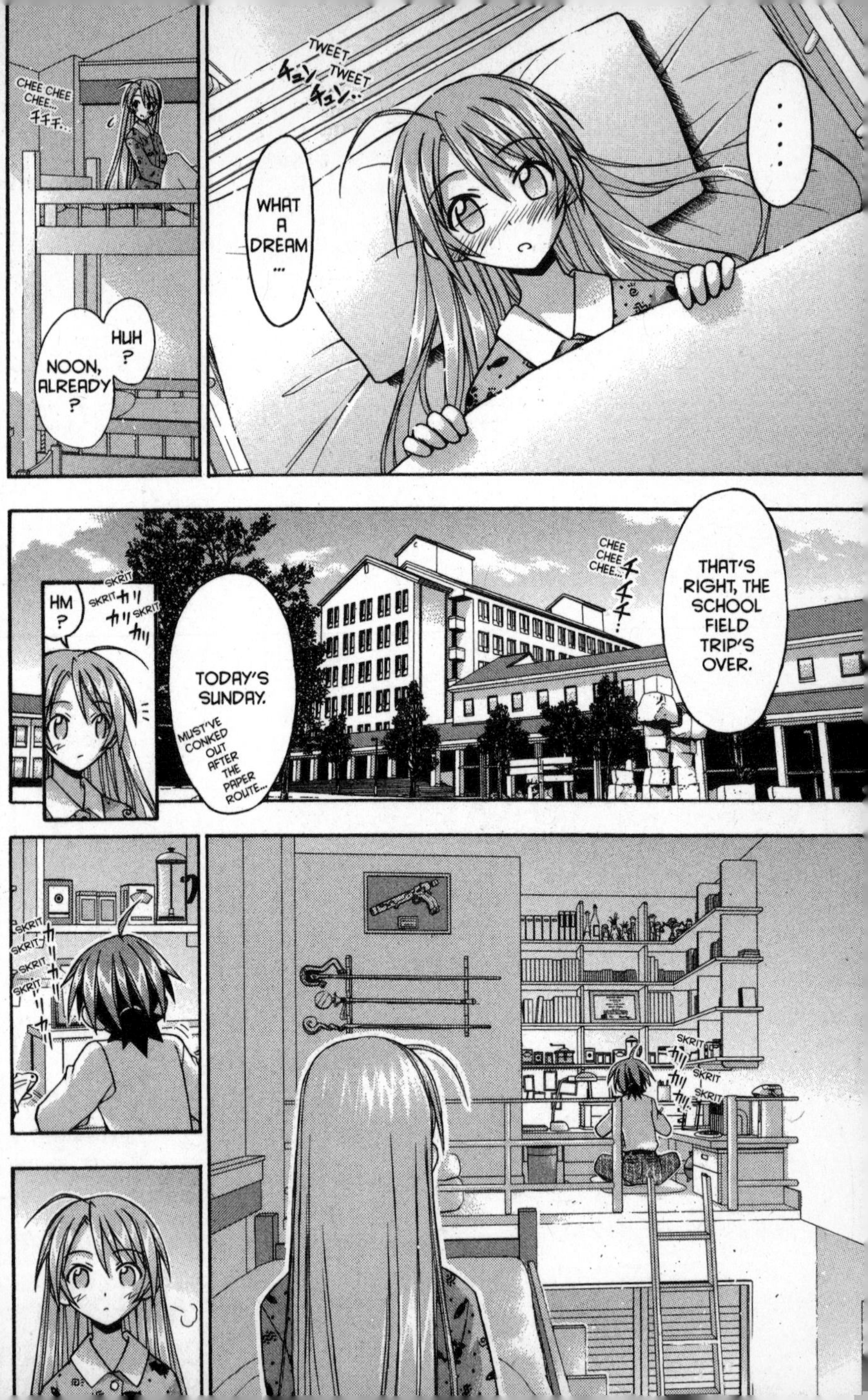
TWEET TWEET
チュン チュン…
…
WHAT A DREAM…
CHEE CHEE CHEE…
チチチ…
HUH?
NOON, ALREADY?
THAT'S RIGHT, THE SCHOOL FIELD TRIP'S OVER.
CHEE CHEE CHEE…
チチチ…
TODAY'S SUNDAY.
MUST'VE CONKED OUT AFTER THE PAPER ROUTE…
SKRIT SKRIT SKRIT
カリ カリ カリ
HM?
SKRIT SKRIT SKRIT
カリ カリ…
SKRIT SKRIT SKRIT SKRIT
カリ カリ カリ カリ

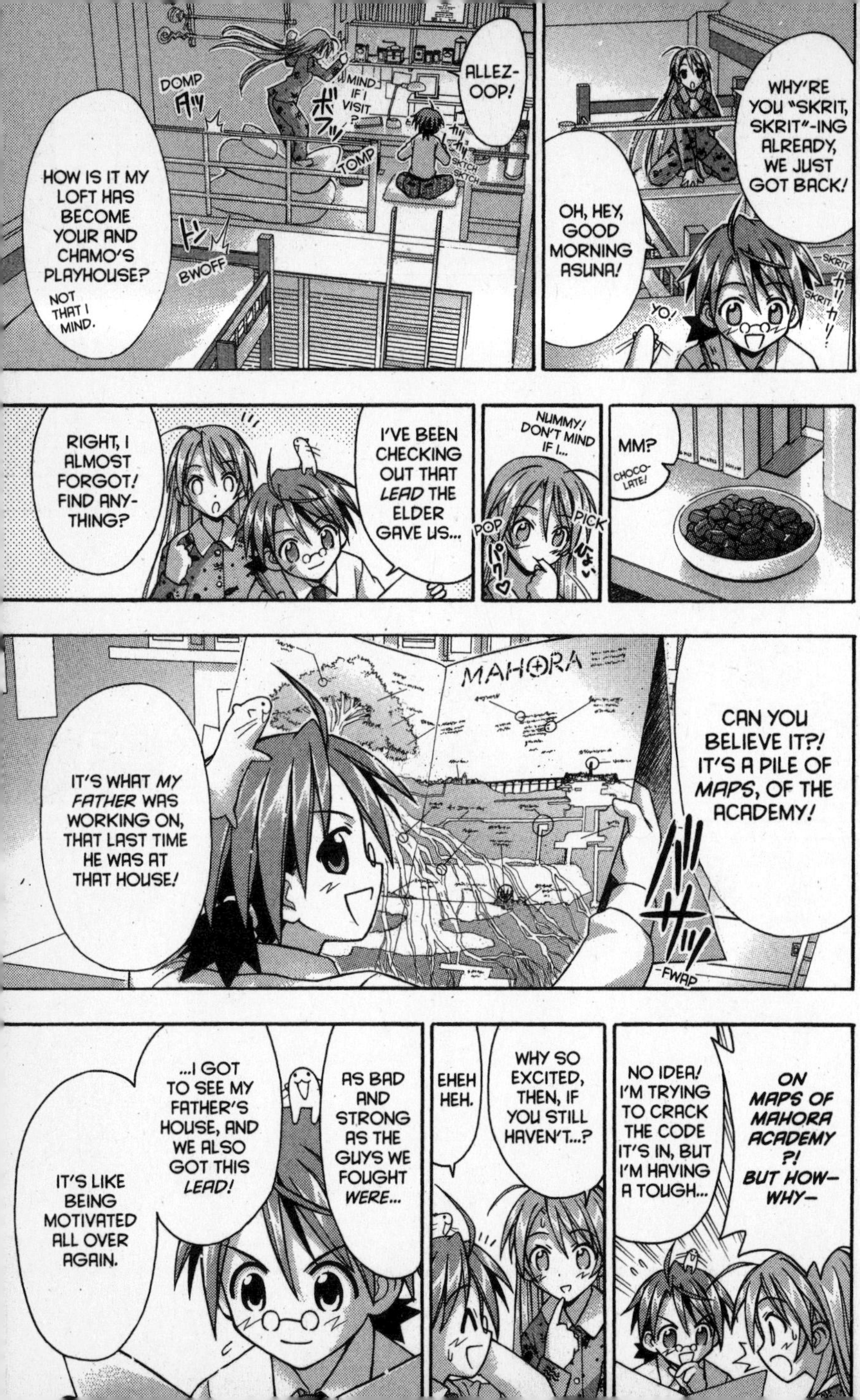
WHY'RE YOU "SKRIT, SKRIT"-ING ALREADY, WE JUST GOT BACK!
OH, HEY, GOOD MORNING ASUNA!
YO!
SKRIT
SKRIT
ALLEZ-OOP!
MIND IF I VISIT?
DOMP
TOMP
SKTCH SKTCH
HOW IS IT MY LOFT HAS BECOME YOUR AND CHAMO'S PLAYHOUSE?
NOT THAT I MIND.
BWOFF
MM?
CHOCOLATE!
NUMMY! DON'T MIND IF I...
PICK
POP
I'VE BEEN CHECKING OUT THAT *LEAD* THE ELDER GAVE US...
RIGHT, I ALMOST FORGOT! FIND ANYTHING?
CAN YOU BELIEVE IT?! IT'S A PILE OF *MAPS*, OF THE ACADEMY!
MAHORA
FWAP
IT'S WHAT *MY FATHER* WAS WORKING ON, THAT LAST TIME HE WAS AT THAT HOUSE!
ON MAPS OF MAHORA ACADEMY?! BUT HOW—WHY—
NO IDEA! I'M TRYING TO CRACK THE CODE IT'S IN, BUT I'M HAVING A TOUGH...
WHY SO EXCITED, THEN, IF YOU STILL HAVEN'T...?
EHEH HEH.
AS BAD AND STRONG AS THE GUYS WE FOUGHT *WERE*...
...I GOT TO SEE MY FATHER'S HOUSE, AND WE ALSO GOT THIS *LEAD*!
IT'S LIKE BEING MOTIVATED ALL OVER AGAIN.

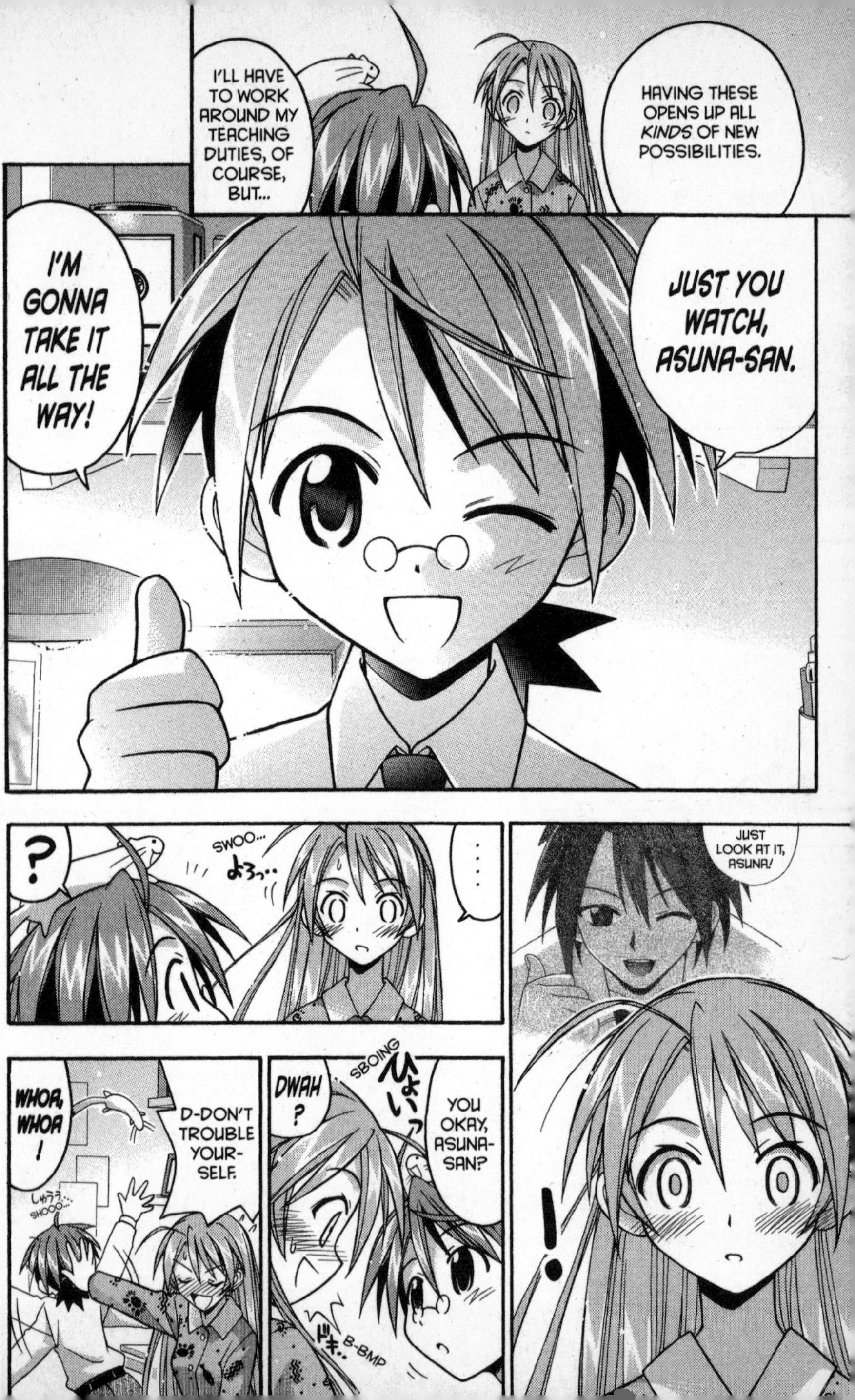
HAVING THESE OPENS UP ALL *KINDS* OF NEW POSSIBILITIES.
I'LL HAVE TO WORK AROUND MY TEACHING DUTIES, OF COURSE, BUT...
JUST YOU WATCH, ASUNA-SAN.
I'M GONNA TAKE IT ALL THE WAY!
JUST LOOK AT IT, ASUNA!
!
. . . .
SWOO...
よろっ…
?
YOU OKAY, ASUNA-SAN?
SBOING
ひょいっ
DWAH?
ドキ…
B-BMP
D-DON'T TROUBLE YOURSELF.
WHOA, WHOA!
しゅううう…
SHOOO...

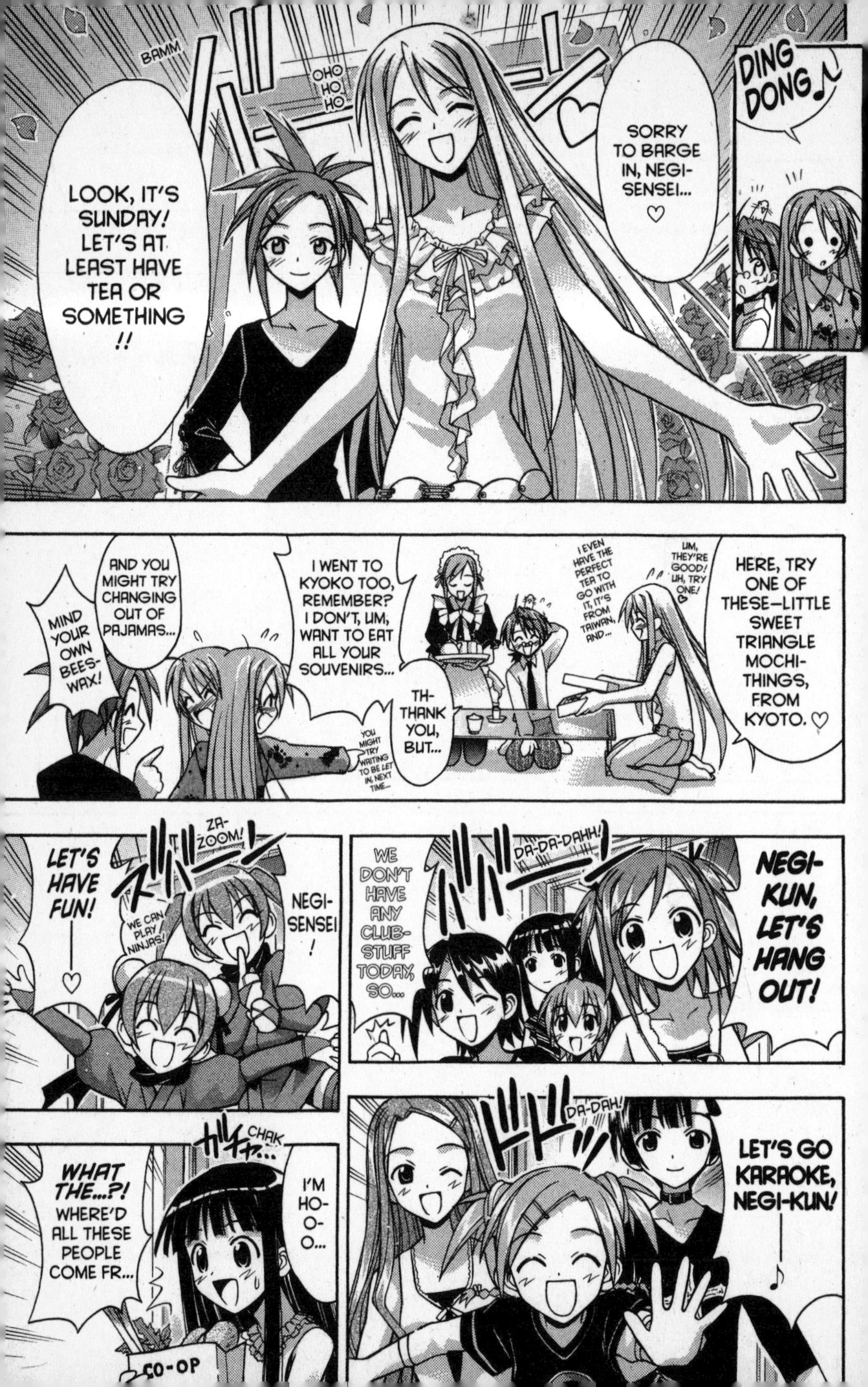
DING DONG♪
SORRY TO BARGE IN, NEGI-SENSEI... ♡
OHO HO HO
BAMM
LOOK, IT'S SUNDAY! LET'S AT LEAST HAVE TEA OR SOMETHING!!
HERE, TRY ONE OF THESE—LITTLE SWEET TRIANGLE MOCHI-THINGS, FROM KYOTO. ♡
UM, THEY'RE GOOD! UH, TRY ONE! ♡
I EVEN HAVE THE PERFECT TEA TO GO WITH IT, IT'S FROM TAIWAN, AND...
TH-THANK YOU, BUT...
I WENT TO KYOKO TOO, REMEMBER? I DON'T, UM, WANT TO EAT ALL YOUR SOUVENIRS...
YOU MIGHT TRY WAITING TO BE LET IN, NEXT TIME...
AND YOU MIGHT TRY CHANGING OUT OF PAJAMAS...
MIND YOUR OWN BEES-WAX!
NEGI-KUN, LET'S HANG OUT!
DA-DA-DAHH!
WE DON'T HAVE ANY CLUB-STUFF TODAY, SO...
NEGI-SENSEI!
ZA-ZOOM!
WE CAN PLAY NINJAS!
LET'S HAVE FUN! ♡
LET'S GO KARAOKE, NEGI-KUN! ♪
DA-DAH!
I'M HO-O-O...
CHAK
WHAT THE...?! WHERE'D ALL THESE PEOPLE COME FR...
CO-OP

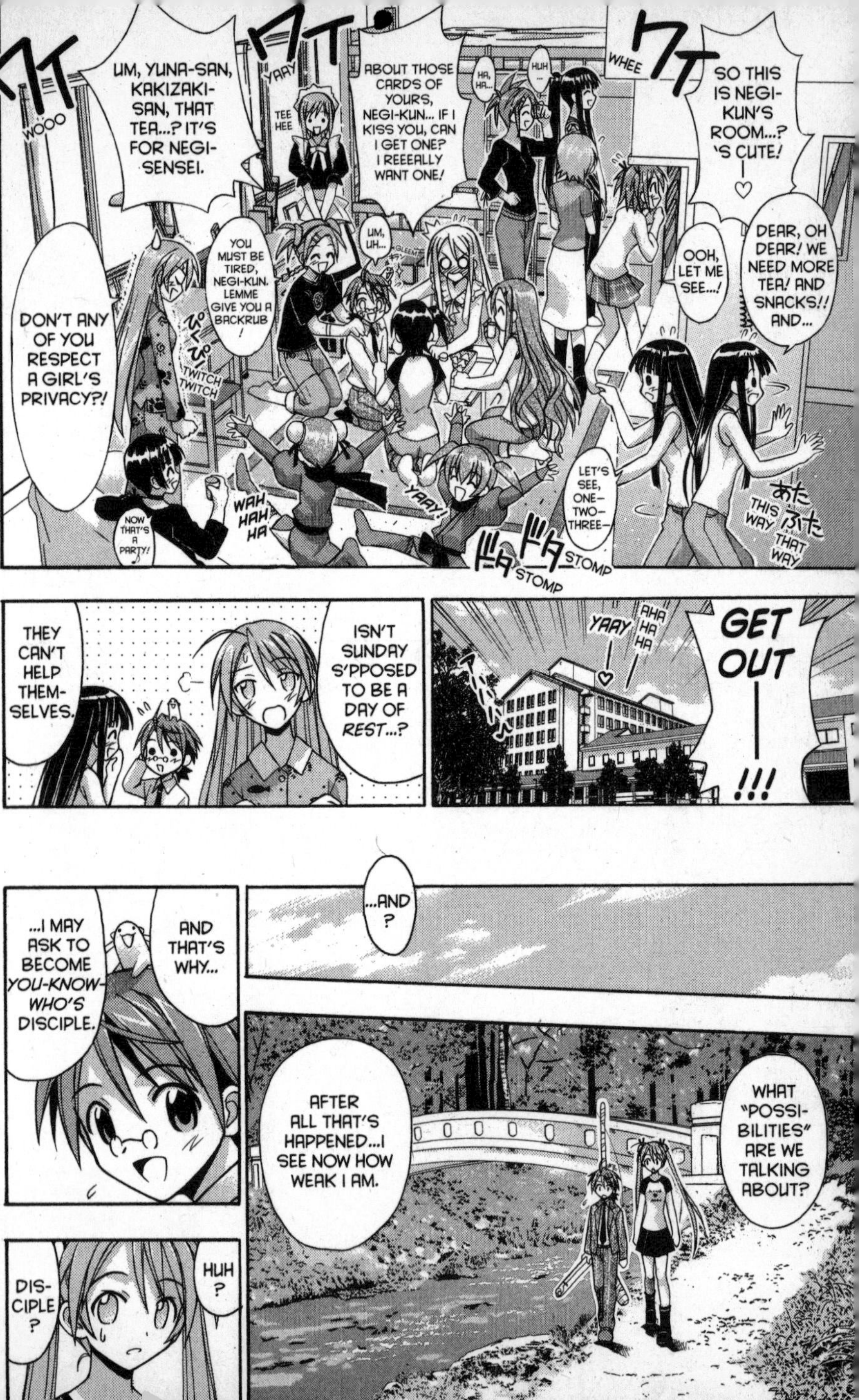
SO THIS IS NEGI-KUN'S ROOM...? 'S CUTE! ♡
WHEE
HUH...
HA, HA...
ABOUT THOSE CARDS OF YOURS, NEGI-KUN... IF I KISS YOU, CAN I GET ONE? I REEEALLY WANT ONE!
YAAY
TEE HEE
UM, YUNA-SAN, KAKIZAKI-SAN, THAT TEA...? IT'S FOR NEGI-SENSEI.
WOOO
DEAR, OH DEAR! WE NEED MORE TEA! AND SNACKS!! AND...
OOH, LET ME SEE...!
UM, UH...
GLEEM
YOU MUST BE TIRED, NEGI-KUN. LEMME GIVE YOU A BACKRUB!
TWITCH TWITCH
DON'T ANY OF YOU RESPECT A GIRL'S PRIVACY?!
THIS WAY THAT WAY
LET'S SEE, ONE—TWO—THREE—
YAAY!
WAH HAH HA
NOW THAT'S A PARTY! ♪
STOMP
STOMP
GET OUT—!!!
AHA HA HA
YAAY ♡
ISN'T SUNDAY S'PPOSED TO BE A DAY OF *REST*...?
THEY CAN'T HELP THEM-SELVES.
...AND?
WHAT "POSSI-BILITIES" ARE WE TALKING ABOUT?
AFTER ALL THAT'S HAPPENED...I SEE NOW HOW WEAK I AM.
AND THAT'S WHY...
...I MAY ASK TO BECOME *YOU-KNOW-WHO'S* DISCIPLE.
HUH?
DIS-CIPLE?

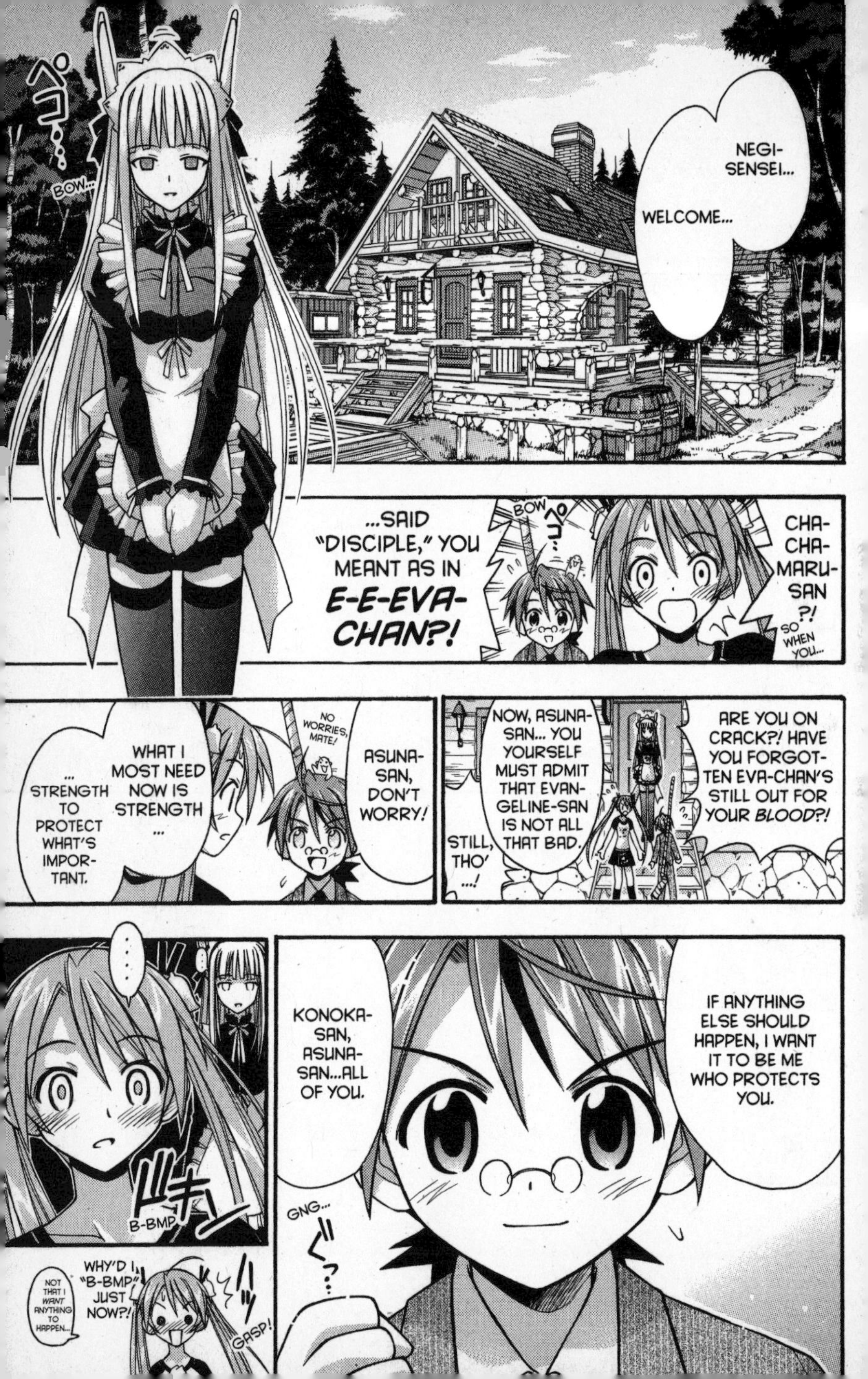
NEGI-SENSEI...
WELCOME...
CHA-CHA-MARU-SAN?!
SO WHEN YOU...
BOW
...SAID "DISCIPLE," YOU MEANT AS IN E-E-EVA-CHAN?!
ペコ…
BOW...
ARE YOU ON CRACK?! HAVE YOU FORGOTTEN EVA-CHAN'S STILL OUT FOR YOUR BLOOD?!
NOW, ASUNA-SAN... YOU YOURSELF MUST ADMIT THAT EVANGELINE-SAN IS NOT ALL THAT BAD.
STILL, THO' ...!
ASUNA-SAN, DON'T WORRY!
NO WORRIES, MATE!
WHAT I MOST NEED NOW IS STRENGTH ...
... STRENGTH TO PROTECT WHAT'S IMPORTANT.
IF ANYTHING ELSE SHOULD HAPPEN, I WANT IT TO BE ME WHO PROTECTS YOU.
KONOKA-SAN, ASUNA-SAN...ALL OF YOU.
GNG...
...
B-BMP
WHY'D I "B-BMP" JUST NOW?!
GASP!
NOT THAT I WANT ANYTHING TO HAPPEN...

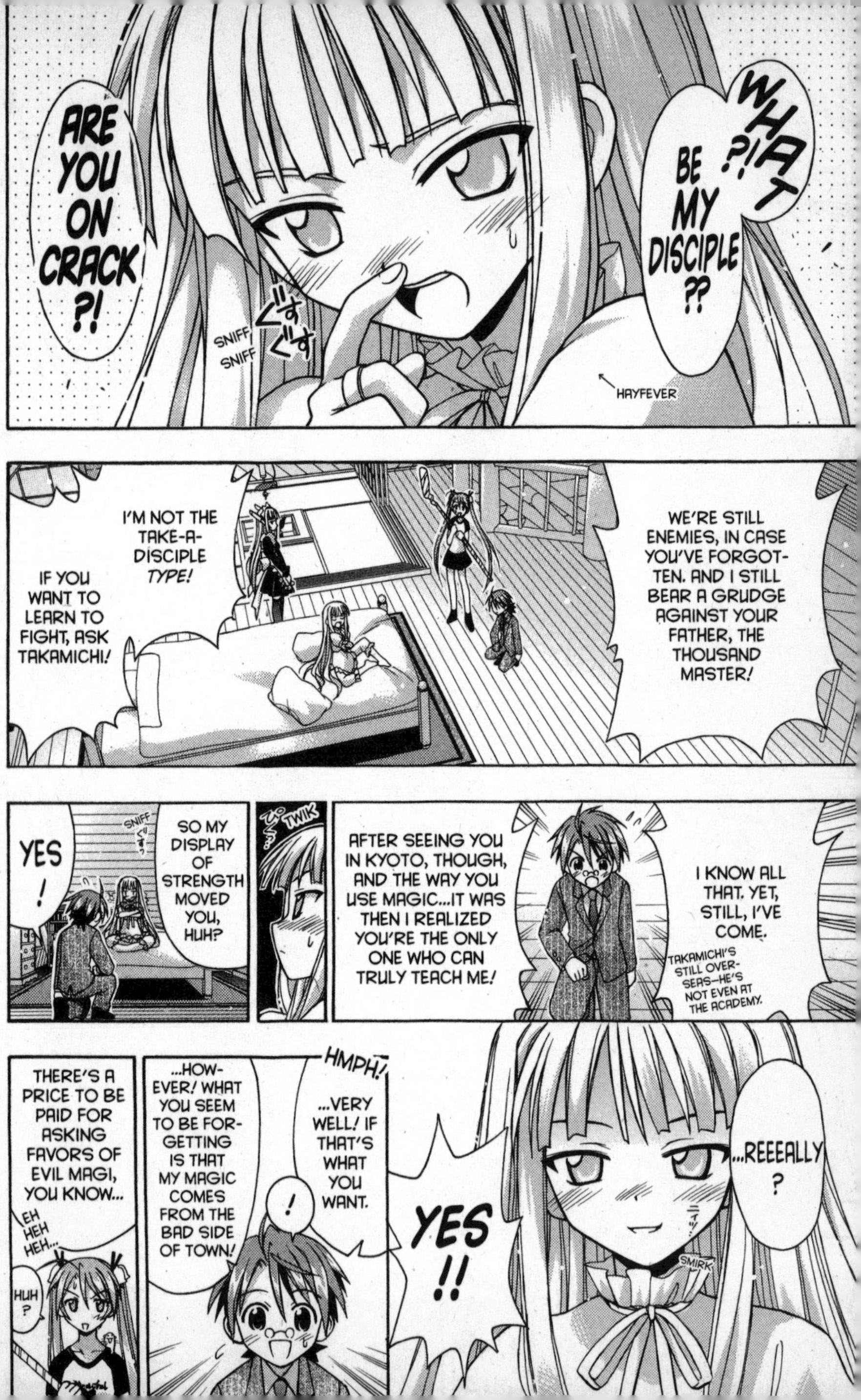
WHAT ?!! BE MY DISCIPLE ??
ARE YOU ON CRACK ?!
SNIFF SNIFF
HAYFEVER
WE'RE STILL ENEMIES, IN CASE YOU'VE FORGOTTEN. AND I STILL BEAR A GRUDGE AGAINST YOUR FATHER, THE THOUSAND MASTER!
I'M NOT THE TAKE-A-DISCIPLE TYPE!
IF YOU WANT TO LEARN TO FIGHT, ASK TAKAMICHI!
I KNOW ALL THAT. YET, STILL, I'VE COME.
TAKAMICHI'S STILL OVERSEAS—HE'S NOT EVEN AT THE ACADEMY.
AFTER SEEING YOU IN KYOTO, THOUGH, AND THE WAY YOU USE MAGIC...IT WAS THEN I REALIZED YOU'RE THE ONLY ONE WHO CAN TRULY TEACH ME!
TWIK
SO MY DISPLAY OF STRENGTH MOVED YOU, HUH?
SNIFF
YES !
...REEEALLY ?
SMIRK
YES !!
HMPH!
...VERY WELL! IF THAT'S WHAT YOU WANT.
!
...HOWEVER! WHAT YOU SEEM TO BE FORGETTING IS THAT MY MAGIC COMES FROM THE BAD SIDE OF TOWN!
THERE'S A PRICE TO BE PAID FOR ASKING FAVORS OF EVIL MAGI, YOU KNOW...
EH HEH HEH...
HUH ?

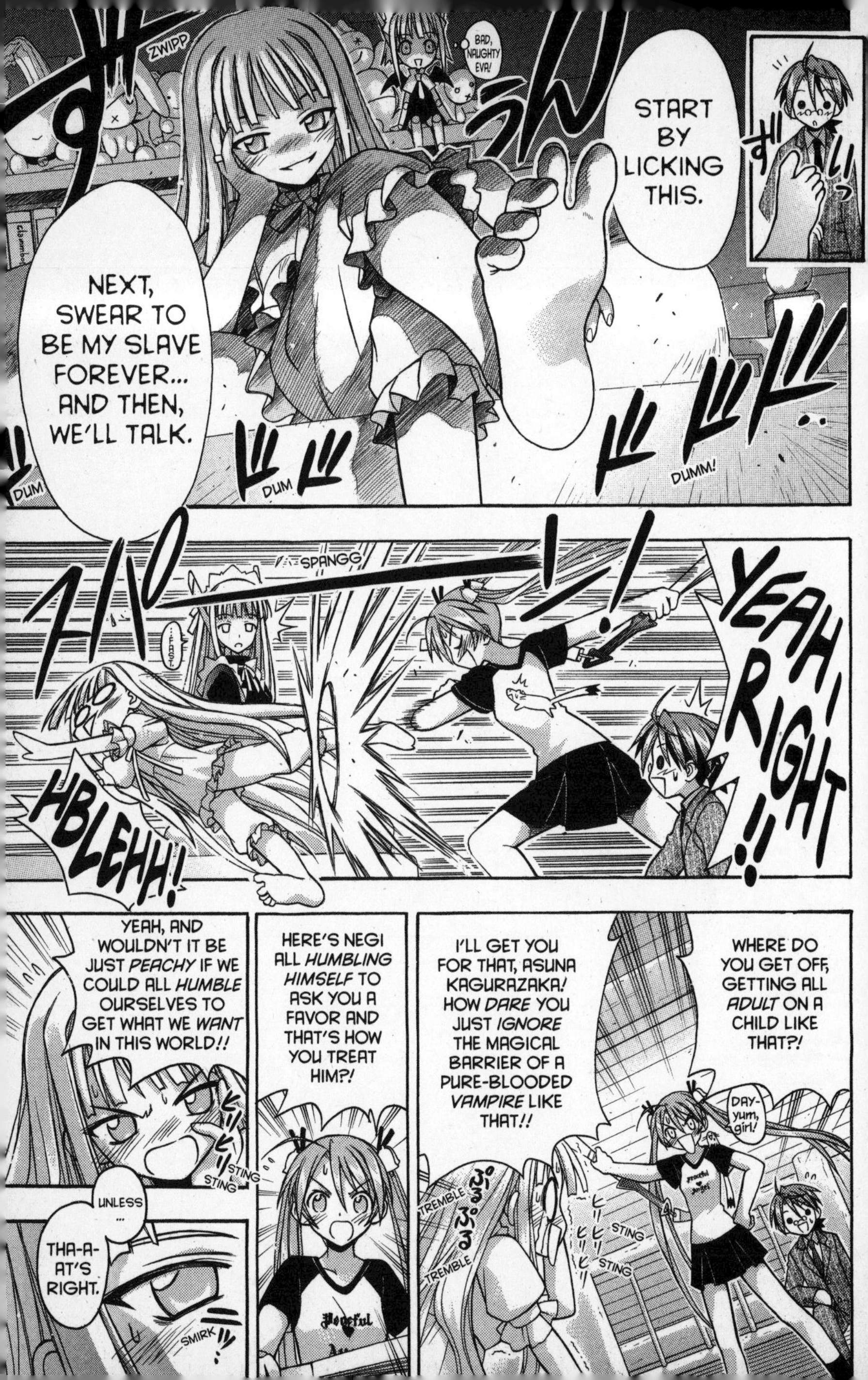
START BY LICKING THIS.
BAD, NAUGHTY EVA!
ZWIPP
NEXT, SWEAR TO BE MY SLAVE FOREVER... AND THEN, WE'LL TALK.
DUMM!
DUM
DUM
SPANGG
YEAH, RIGHT!!
...FAST.
HBLEHH!
WHERE DO YOU GET OFF, GETTING ALL *ADULT* ON A CHILD LIKE THAT?!
DAY-yum, girl!
I'LL GET YOU FOR THAT, ASUNA KAGURAZAKA! HOW *DARE* YOU JUST *IGNORE* THE MAGICAL BARRIER OF A PURE-BLOODED *VAMPIRE* LIKE THAT!!
STING
STING
TREMBLE
TREMBLE
HERE'S NEGI ALL *HUMBLING HIMSELF* TO ASK YOU A FAVOR AND THAT'S HOW YOU TREAT HIM?!
YEAH, AND WOULDN'T IT BE JUST *PEACHY* IF WE COULD ALL *HUMBLE* OURSELVES TO GET WHAT WE *WANT* IN THIS WORLD!!
STING
STING
UNLESS...
THA-A-AT'S RIGHT.
SMIRK

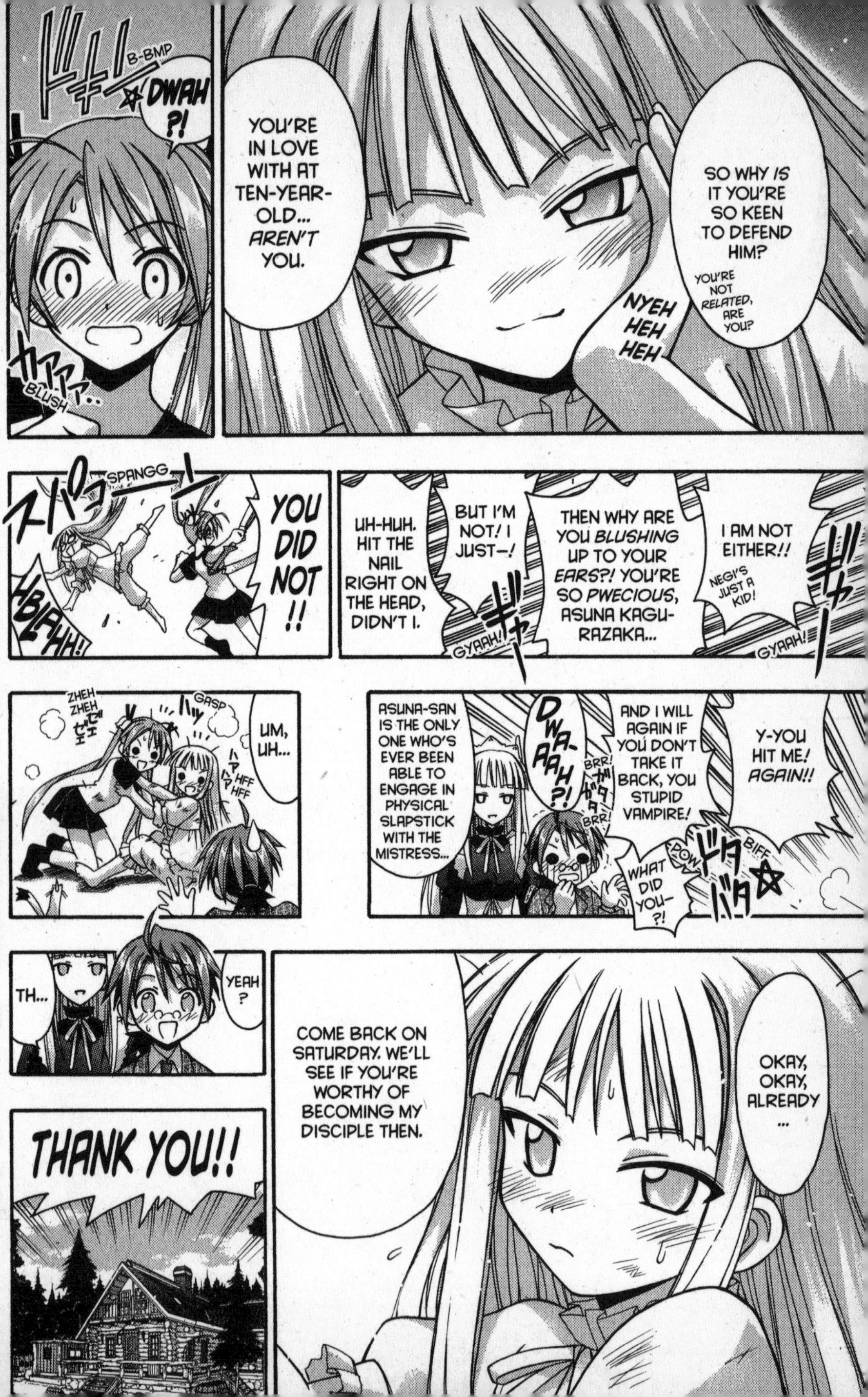
SO WHY IS IT YOU'RE SO KEEN TO DEFEND HIM?
YOU'RE NOT RELATED, ARE YOU?
NYEH HEH HEH
YOU'RE IN LOVE WITH AT TEN-YEAR-OLD... AREN'T YOU.
B-BMP
DWAH ?!
BLUSH
I AM NOT EITHER!!
NEGI'S JUST A KID!
GYAAH!
THEN WHY ARE YOU BLUSHING UP TO YOUR EARS?! YOU'RE SO PWECIOUS, ASUNA KAGURAZAKA...
BUT I'M NOT! I JUST—!
GYAAH!
UH-HUH. HIT THE NAIL RIGHT ON THE HEAD, DIDN'T I.
YOU DID NOT !!
SPANGG
HBLAHHH!!
Y-YOU HIT ME! AGAIN!!
AND I WILL AGAIN IF YOU DON'T TAKE IT BACK, YOU STUPID VAMPIRE!
BIFF
POW
WHAT DID YOU—?!
DWAAAH?!
BRR! BRR!
ASUNA-SAN IS THE ONLY ONE WHO'S EVER BEEN ABLE TO ENGAGE IN PHYSICAL SLAPSTICK WITH THE MISTRESS...
UM, UH...
GASP
HFF HFF
ZHEH ZHEH
OKAY, OKAY, ALREADY ...
COME BACK ON SATURDAY. WE'LL SEE IF YOU'RE WORTHY OF BECOMING MY DISCIPLE THEN.
YEAH ?
TH...
THANK YOU!!

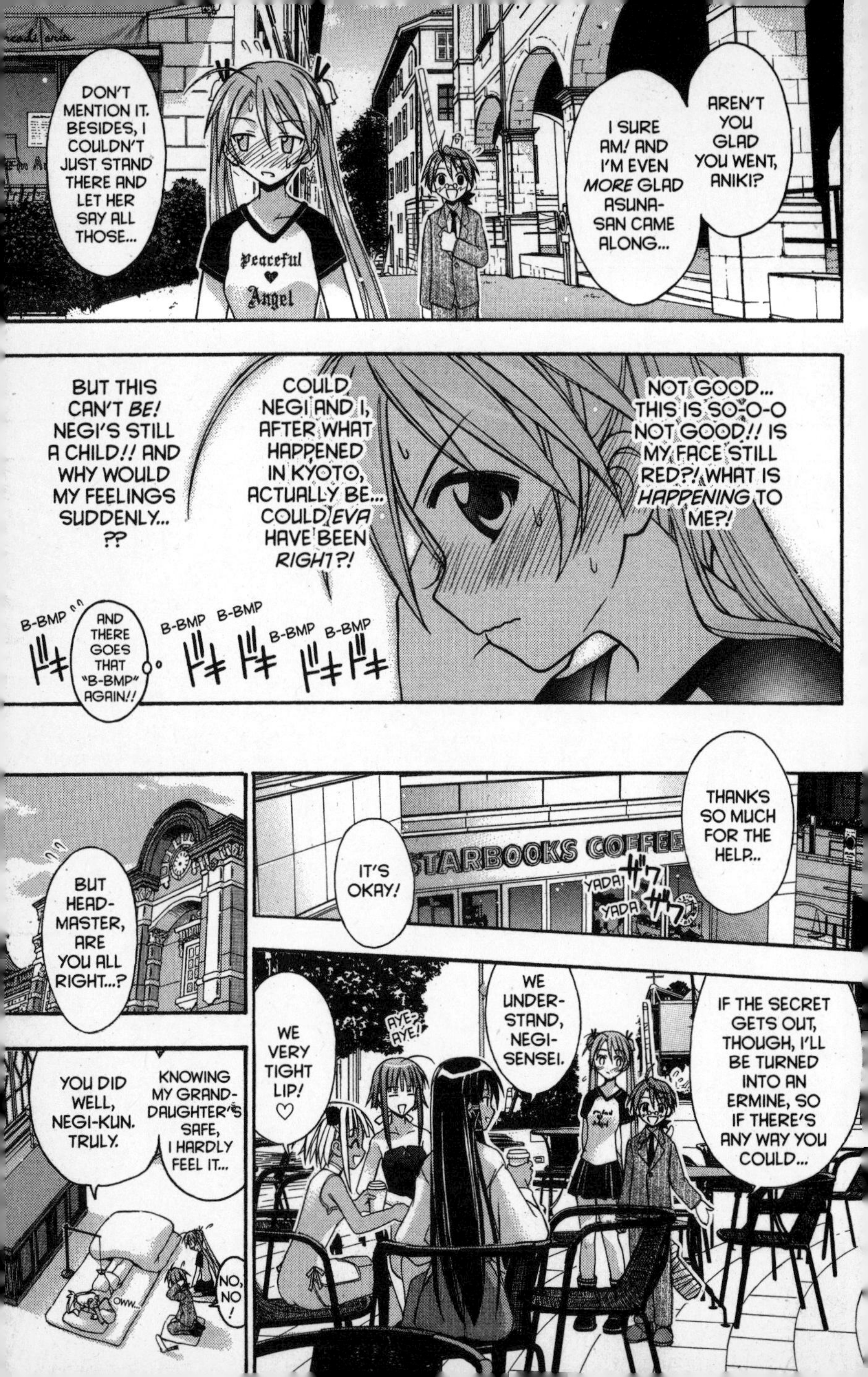
AREN'T YOU GLAD YOU WENT, ANIKI?
I SURE AM! AND I'M EVEN MORE GLAD ASUNA-SAN CAME ALONG...
DON'T MENTION IT. BESIDES, I COULDN'T JUST STAND THERE AND LET HER SAY ALL THOSE...
Peaceful Angel
NOT GOOD... THIS IS SO-O-O NOT GOOD!! IS MY FACE STILL RED?! WHAT IS HAPPENING TO ME?!
COULD NEGI AND I, AFTER WHAT HAPPENED IN KYOTO, ACTUALLY BE... COULD EVA HAVE BEEN RIGHT?!
BUT THIS CAN'T BE! NEGI'S STILL A CHILD!! AND WHY WOULD MY FEELINGS SUDDENLY... ??
B-BMP ドキ B-BMP ドキ B-BMP ドキ B-BMP ドキ B-BMP ドキ
AND THERE GOES THAT "B-BMP" AGAIN!!
THANKS SO MUCH FOR THE HELP...
STARBOOKS COFFEE
YADA ザワ YADA ザワ
IT'S OKAY!
IF THE SECRET GETS OUT, THOUGH, I'LL BE TURNED INTO AN ERMINE, SO IF THERE'S ANY WAY YOU COULD...
WE UNDERSTAND, NEGI-SENSEI.
AYE-AYE!
WE VERY TIGHT LIP! ♡
BUT HEAD-MASTER, ARE YOU ALL RIGHT...?
KNOWING MY GRAND-DAUGHTER'S SAFE, I HARDLY FEEL IT...
YOU DID WELL, NEGI-KUN. TRULY.
NO, NO!
OWW...

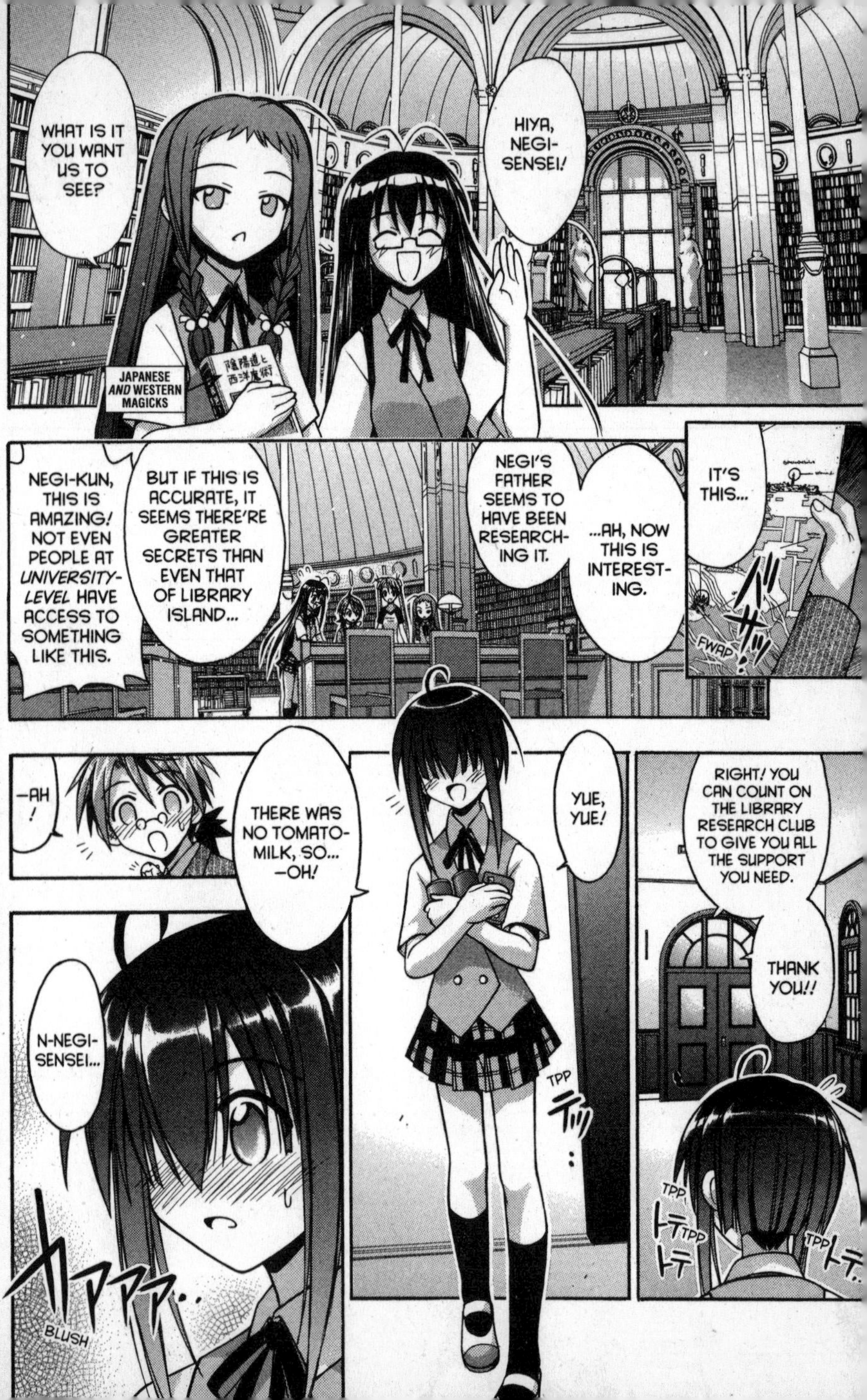
HIYA, NEGI-SENSEI!
WHAT IS IT YOU WANT US TO SEE?
陰陽道と西洋魔術
JAPANESE AND WESTERN MAGICKS
IT'S THIS...
FWAP
...AH, NOW THIS IS INTERESTING.
NEGI'S FATHER SEEMS TO HAVE BEEN RESEARCHING IT.
BUT IF THIS IS ACCURATE, IT SEEMS THERE'RE GREATER SECRETS THAN EVEN THAT OF LIBRARY ISLAND...
NEGI-KUN, THIS IS AMAZING! NOT EVEN PEOPLE AT UNIVERSITY-LEVEL HAVE ACCESS TO SOMETHING LIKE THIS.
RIGHT! YOU CAN COUNT ON THE LIBRARY RESEARCH CLUB TO GIVE YOU ALL THE SUPPORT YOU NEED.
THANK YOU!!
TPP
TPP
TPP
YUE, YUE!
TPP
THERE WAS NO TOMATO-MILK, SO... —OH!
—AH!
N-NEGI-SENSEI...
BLUSH

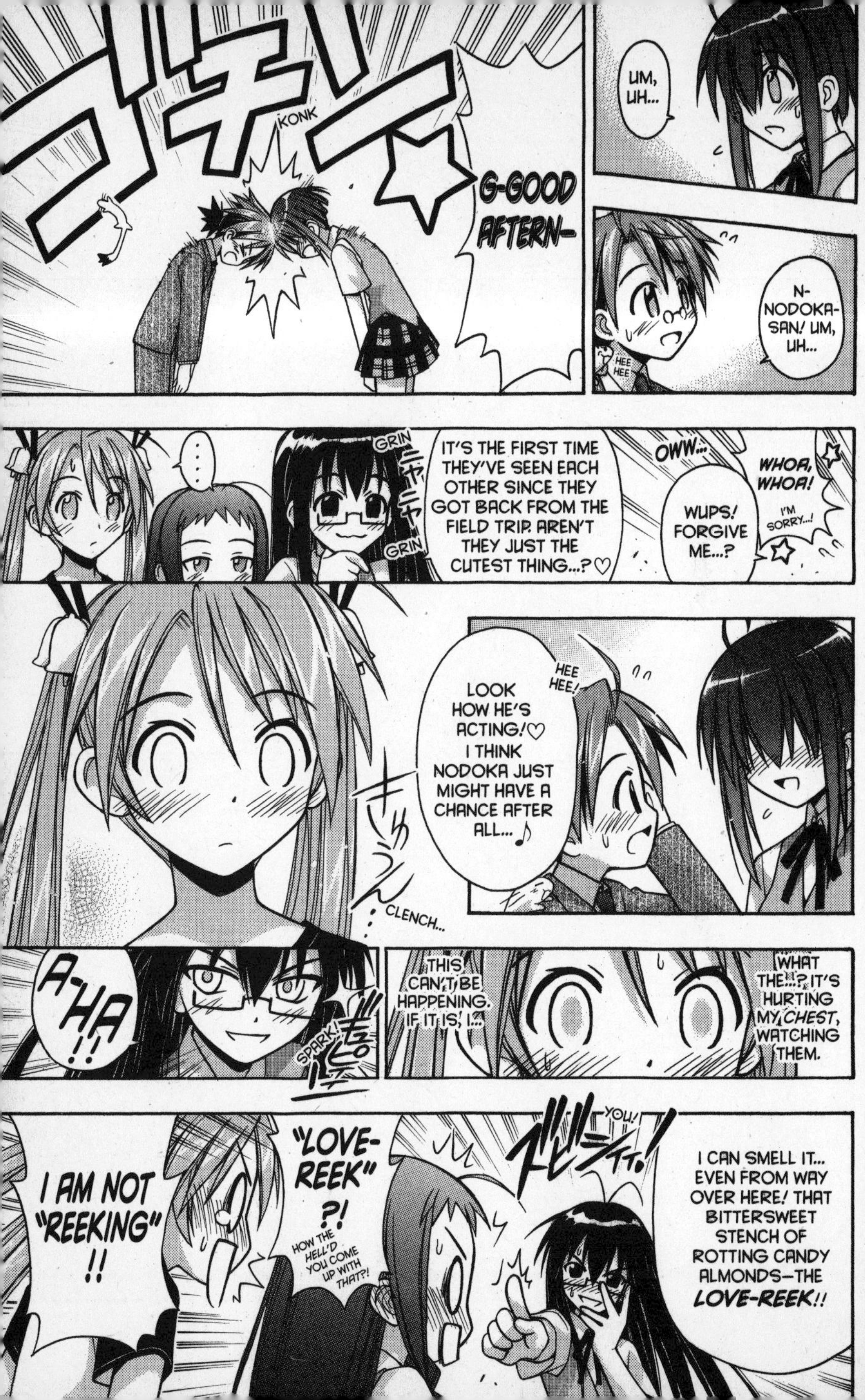
UM, UH...
N-NODOKA-SAN! UM, UH...
HEE HEE
KONK
G-GOOD AFTERN-
WHOA, WHOA!
I'M SORRY...!
OWW...
WUPS! FORGIVE ME...?
IT'S THE FIRST TIME THEY'VE SEEN EACH OTHER SINCE THEY GOT BACK FROM THE FIELD TRIP. AREN'T THEY JUST THE CUTEST THING...?♡
GRIN
GRIN
...
HEE HEE!
LOOK HOW HE'S ACTING!♡ I THINK NODOKA JUST MIGHT HAVE A CHANCE AFTER ALL...♪
CLENCH...
WHAT THE...? IT'S HURTING MY *CHEST*, WATCHING THEM.
THIS CAN'T BE HAPPENING. IF IT IS, I...
SPARK!
A-HA!!
I CAN SMELL IT... EVEN FROM WAY OVER HERE! THAT BITTERSWEET STENCH OF ROTTING CANDY ALMONDS—THE *LOVE-REEK*!!
YOU!
"LOVE-REEK"?!
HOW THE HELL'D YOU COME UP WITH THAT?!
I AM NOT "REEKING"!!

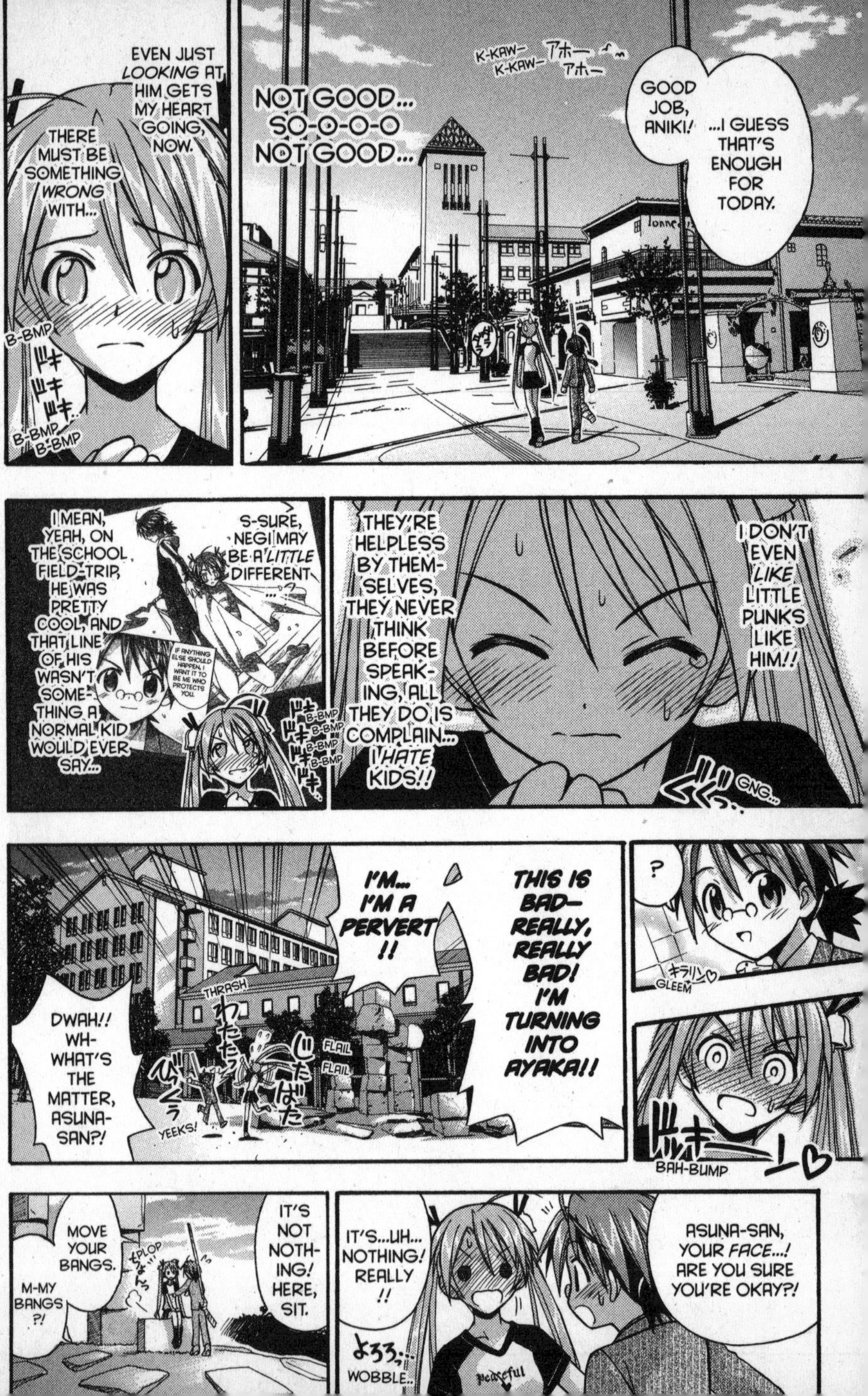
K-KAW アホー
K-KAW アホー
GOOD JOB, ANIKI!
...I GUESS THAT'S ENOUGH FOR TODAY.
NOT GOOD... SO-O-O-O NOT GOOD...
EVEN JUST *LOOKING* AT HIM GETS MY HEART GOING, NOW.
THERE MUST BE SOMETHING *WRONG* WITH...
B-BMP ドキ ドキ ドキ... B-BMP B-BMP
I DON'T EVEN *LIKE* LITTLE PUNKS LIKE HIM!!
THEY'RE HELPLESS BY THEMSELVES, THEY NEVER THINK BEFORE SPEAKING, ALL THEY DO IS COMPLAIN... I *HATE* KIDS!!
ぐぐっ... GNG...
S-SURE, NEGI MAY BE A *LITTLE* DIFFERENT...
I MEAN, YEAH, ON THE SCHOOL FIELD-TRIP, HE WAS PRETTY COOL, AND THAT LINE OF HIS WASN'T SOMETHING A NORMAL KID WOULD EVER SAY...
IF ANYTHING ELSE SHOULD HAPPEN, I WANT IT TO BE ME WHO PROTECTS YOU.
ドキ B-BMP ドキ B-BMP ドキ B-BMP ドキ... B-BMP
?
キラリン♡ GLEEM
ドッキーン♡ BAH-BUMP
THIS IS BAD—REALLY, REALLY BAD! I'M TURNING INTO AYAKA!!
I'M... I'M A PERVERT!!
DWAH!! WH-WHAT'S THE MATTER, ASUNA-SAN?!
わたた THRASH
じたばた FLAIL FLAIL
びくっ YEEKS!
ASUNA-SAN, YOUR *FACE*...! ARE YOU SURE YOU'RE OKAY?!
IT'S...UH... NOTHING! REALLY!!
よろろっ... WOBBLE...
IT'S NOT NOTHING! HERE, SIT.
MOVE YOUR BANGS.
M-MY BANGS?!
PLOP

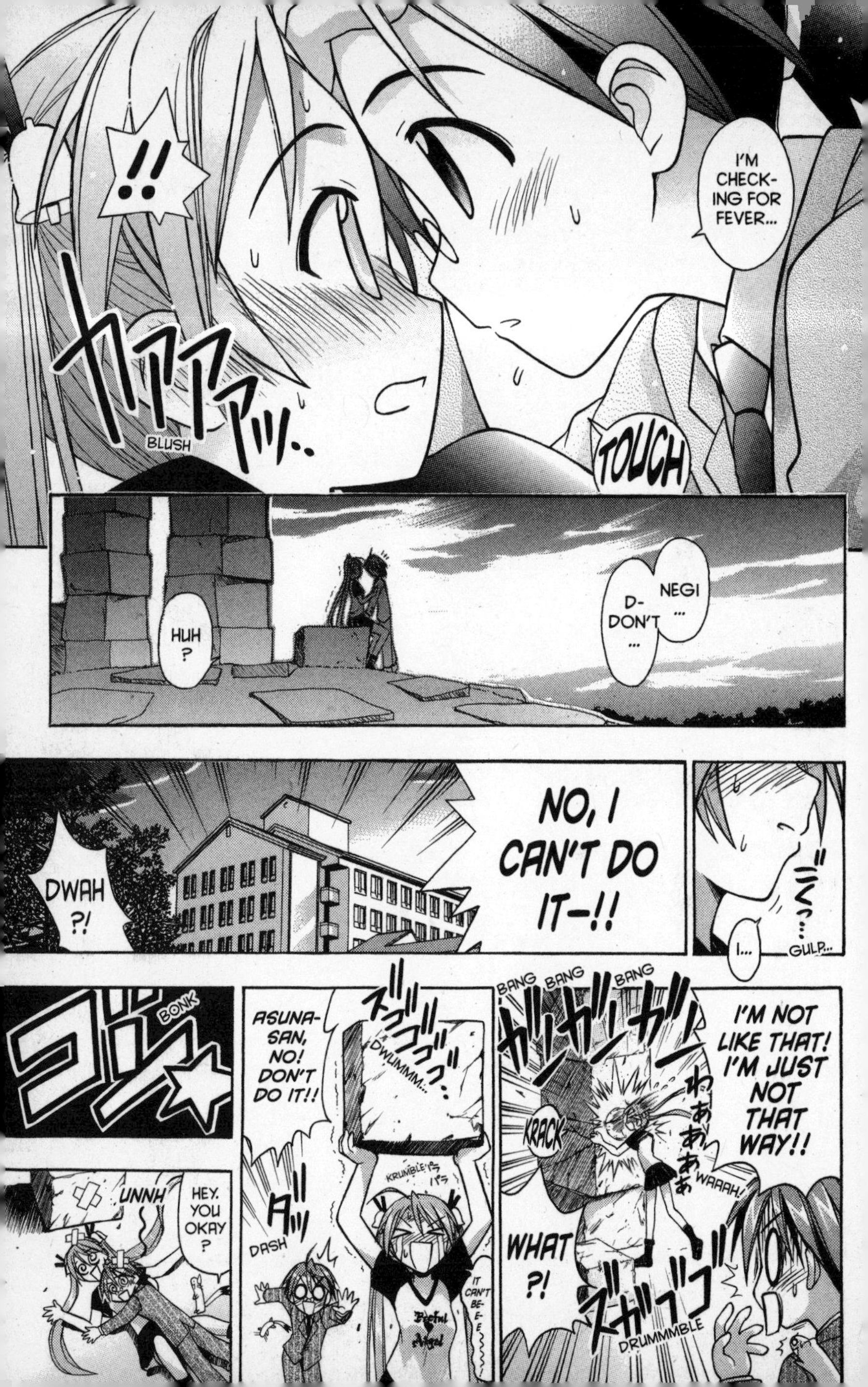

I'M CHECK-ING FOR FEVER...
TOUCH
!!
BLUSH
NEGI ...
D-DON'T ...
HUH ?
I...
GULP...
NO, I CAN'T DO IT-!!
DWAH ?!
I'M NOT LIKE THAT! I'M JUST NOT THAT WAY!!
BANG BANG BANG
KRACK
WAAAH!
WHAT ?!
DRUMMMBLE
ASUNA-SAN, NO! DON'T DO IT!!
DWUMMM...
KRUMBLE
DASH
IT CAN'T BE-E-E
BONK
UNNH
HEY. YOU OKAY ?

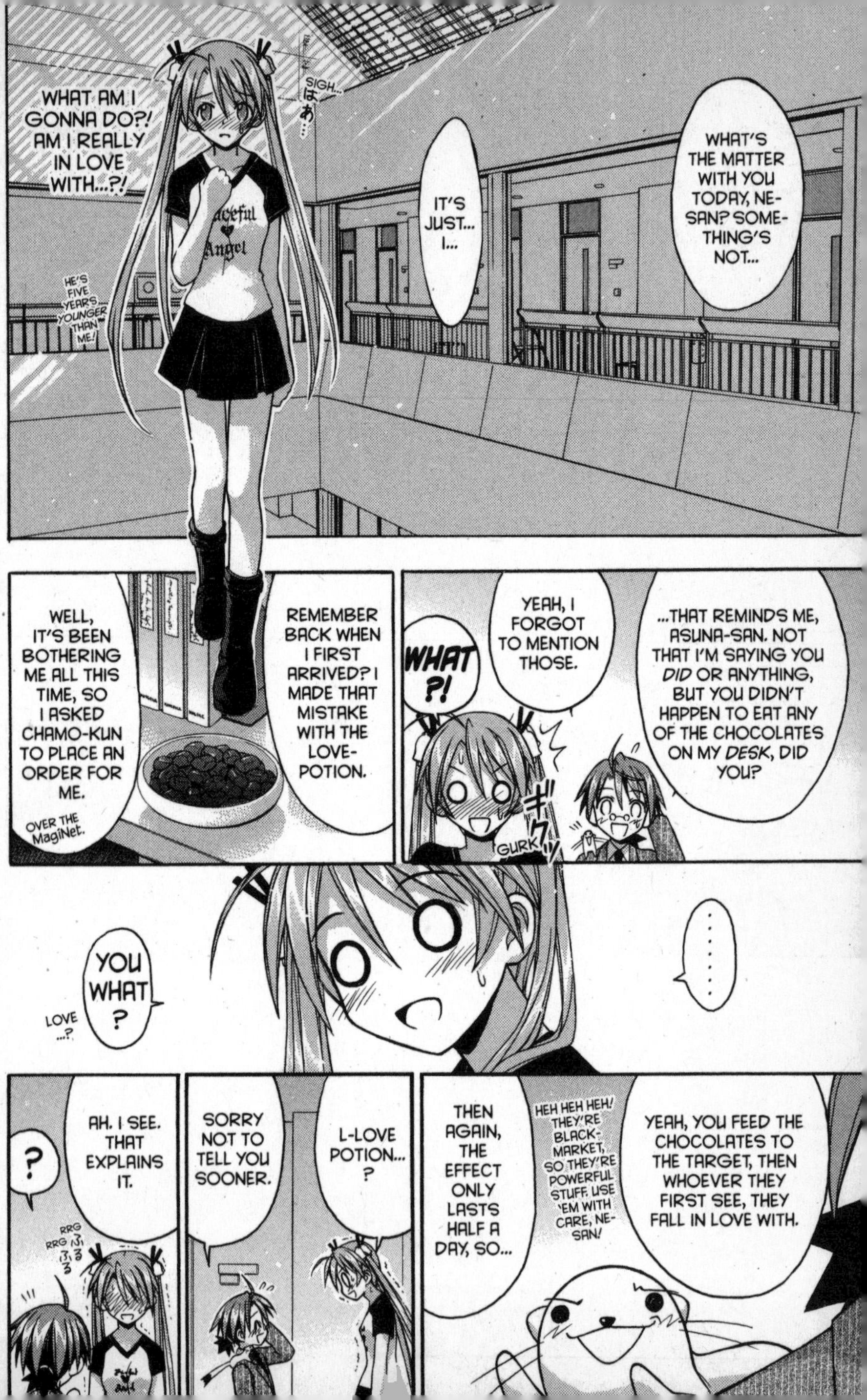
WHAT'S THE MATTER WITH YOU TODAY, NE-SAN? SOME-THING'S NOT...
IT'S JUST... I...
SIGH... はぁ…
WHAT AM I GONNA DO?! AM I REALLY IN LOVE WITH...?!
HE'S FIVE YEARS YOUNGER THAN ME!
...THAT REMINDS ME, ASUNA-SAN. NOT THAT I'M SAYING YOU *DID* OR ANYTHING, BUT YOU DIDN'T HAPPEN TO EAT ANY OF THE CHOCOLATES ON MY *DESK*, DID YOU?
YEAH, I FORGOT TO MENTION THOSE.
WHAT ?!
GURK ギクッ
REMEMBER BACK WHEN I FIRST ARRIVED? I MADE THAT MISTAKE WITH THE LOVE-POTION.
WELL, IT'S BEEN BOTHERING ME ALL THIS TIME, SO I ASKED CHAMO-KUN TO PLACE AN ORDER FOR ME.
OVER THE MagiNet.
......
YOU WHAT ?
LOVE ...?
YEAH, YOU FEED THE CHOCOLATES TO THE TARGET, THEN WHOEVER THEY FIRST SEE, THEY FALL IN LOVE WITH.
HEH HEH HEH! THEY'RE BLACK-MARKET, SO THEY'RE POWERFUL STUFF. USE 'EM WITH CARE, NE-SAN!
THEN AGAIN, THE EFFECT ONLY LASTS HALF A DAY, SO...
L-LOVE POTION... ?
SORRY NOT TO TELL YOU SOONER.
AH. I SEE. THAT EXPLAINS IT.
?
RRG RRG ふるふる

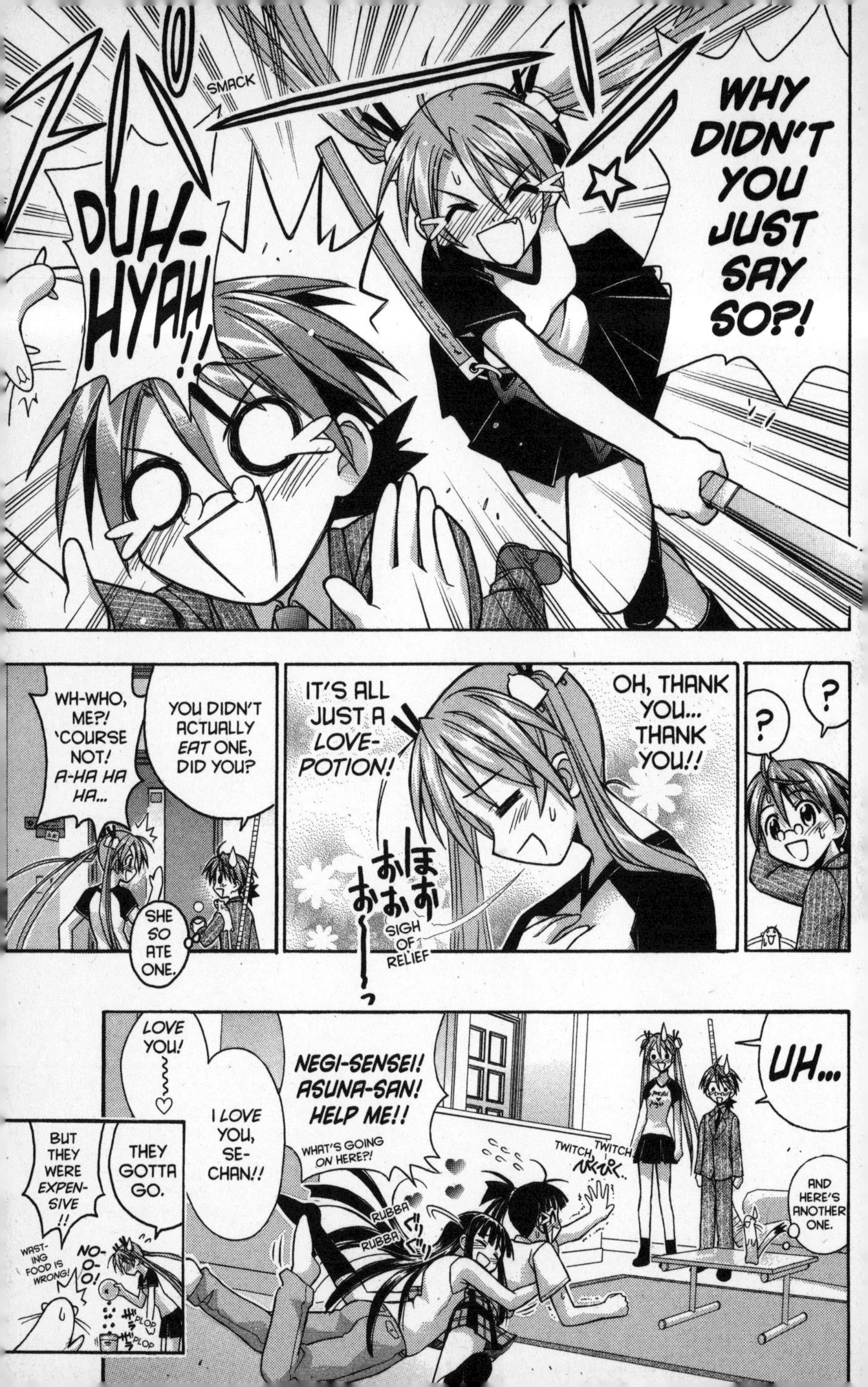
WHY DIDN'T YOU JUST SAY SO?!
SMACK
DUH-HYAH!!
?
?
OH, THANK YOU... THANK YOU!!
IT'S ALL JUST A *LOVE-POTION!*
ほおおお～っ
SIGH OF RELIEF
YOU DIDN'T ACTUALLY *EAT* ONE, DID YOU?
WH-WHO, ME?! 'COURSE NOT! *A-HA HA HA...*
SHE SO ATE ONE.
UH...
AND HERE'S ANOTHER ONE.
TWITCH, TWITCH
ぴくぴく
NEGI-SENSEI! ASUNA-SAN! HELP ME!!
WHAT'S GOING ON HERE?!
LOVE YOU! ～♡
I *LOVE* YOU, SE-CHAN!!
RUBBA RUBBA
THEY GOTTA GO.
BUT THEY WERE *EXPENSIVE!!*
NO-O-O!
WASTING FOOD IS WRONG!
PLOP PLOP

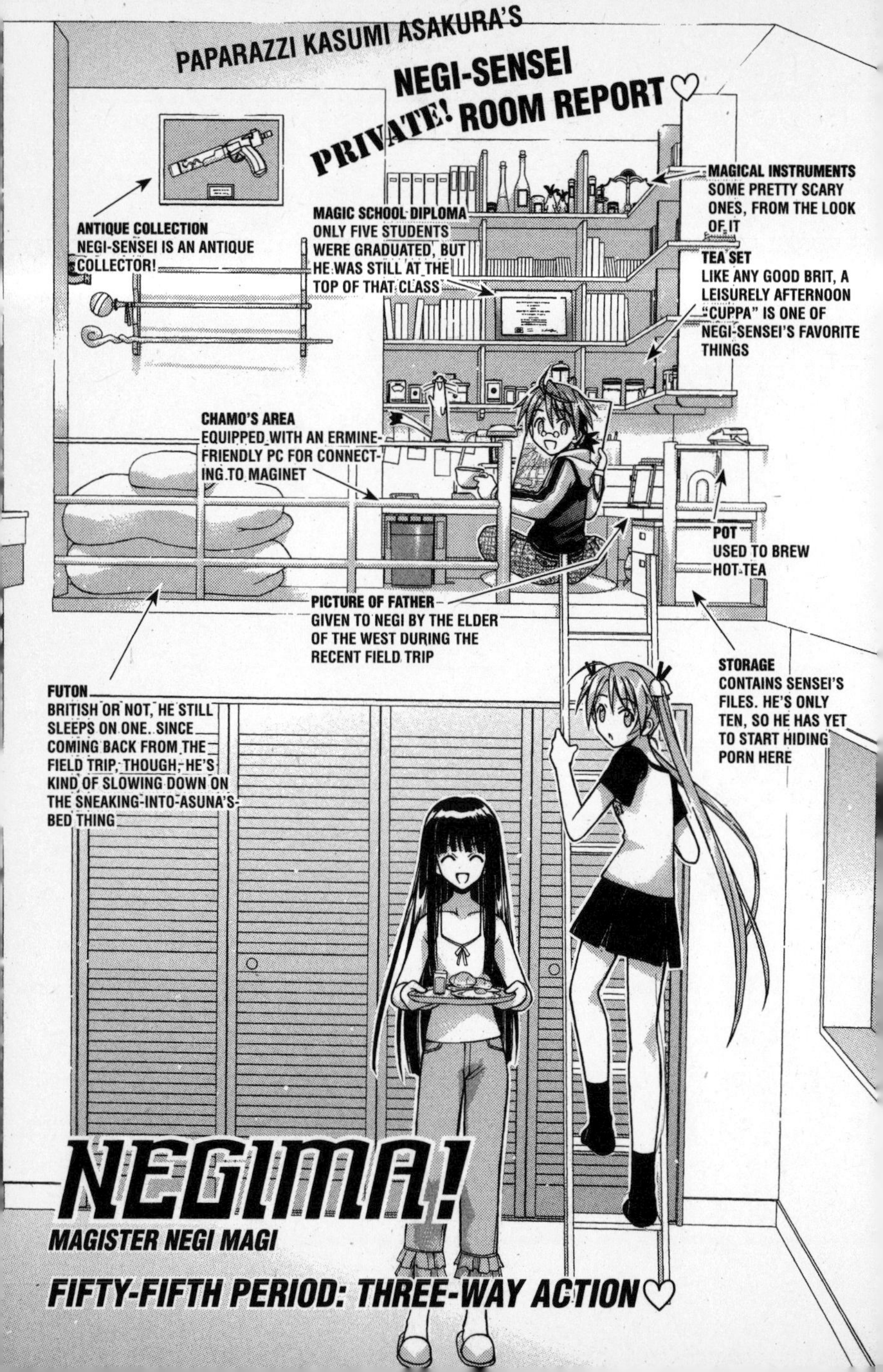
PAPARAZZI KASUMI ASAKURA'S
NEGI-SENSEI
PRIVATE! ROOM REPORT ♡
MAGICAL INSTRUMENTS
SOME PRETTY SCARY ONES, FROM THE LOOK OF IT
MAGIC SCHOOL DIPLOMA
ONLY FIVE STUDENTS WERE GRADUATED, BUT HE WAS STILL AT THE TOP OF THAT CLASS
ANTIQUE COLLECTION
NEGI-SENSEI IS AN ANTIQUE COLLECTOR!
TEA SET
LIKE ANY GOOD BRIT, A LEISURELY AFTERNOON "CUPPA" IS ONE OF NEGI-SENSEI'S FAVORITE THINGS
CHAMO'S AREA
EQUIPPED WITH AN ERMINE-FRIENDLY PC FOR CONNECTING TO MAGINET
POT
USED TO BREW HOT TEA
PICTURE OF FATHER
GIVEN TO NEGI BY THE ELDER OF THE WEST DURING THE RECENT FIELD TRIP
STORAGE
CONTAINS SENSEI'S FILES. HE'S ONLY TEN, SO HE HAS YET TO START HIDING PORN HERE
FUTON
BRITISH OR NOT, HE STILL SLEEPS ON ONE. SINCE COMING BACK FROM THE FIELD TRIP, THOUGH, HE'S KIND OF SLOWING DOWN ON THE SNEAKING-INTO-ASUNA'S-BED THING
NEGIMA!
MAGISTER NEGI MAGI
FIFTY-FIFTH PERIOD: THREE-WAY ACTION ♡

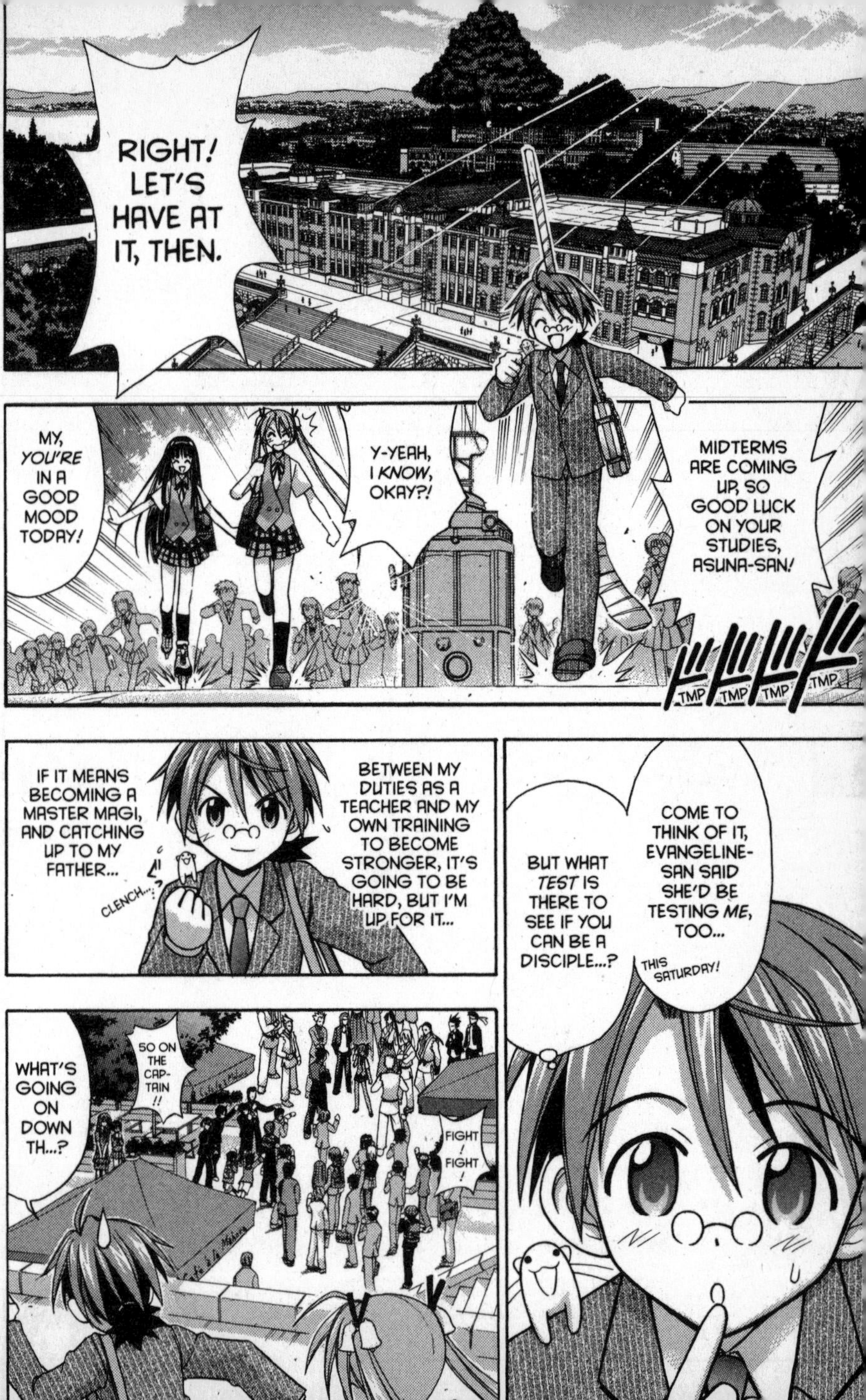
RIGHT! LET'S HAVE AT IT, THEN.
MIDTERMS ARE COMING UP, SO GOOD LUCK ON YOUR STUDIES, ASUNA-SAN!
Y-YEAH, I KNOW, OKAY?!
MY, YOU'RE IN A GOOD MOOD TODAY!
TMP TMP TMP TMP
COME TO THINK OF IT, EVANGELINE-SAN SAID SHE'D BE TESTING ME, TOO...
THIS SATURDAY!
BUT WHAT TEST IS THERE TO SEE IF YOU CAN BE A DISCIPLE...?
BETWEEN MY DUTIES AS A TEACHER AND MY OWN TRAINING TO BECOME STRONGER, IT'S GOING TO BE HARD, BUT I'M UP FOR IT...
IF IT MEANS BECOMING A MASTER MAGI, AND CATCHING UP TO MY FATHER...
CLENCH...
SO ON THE CAP-TAIN!!
FIGHT! FIGHT!
WHAT'S GOING ON DOWN TH...?

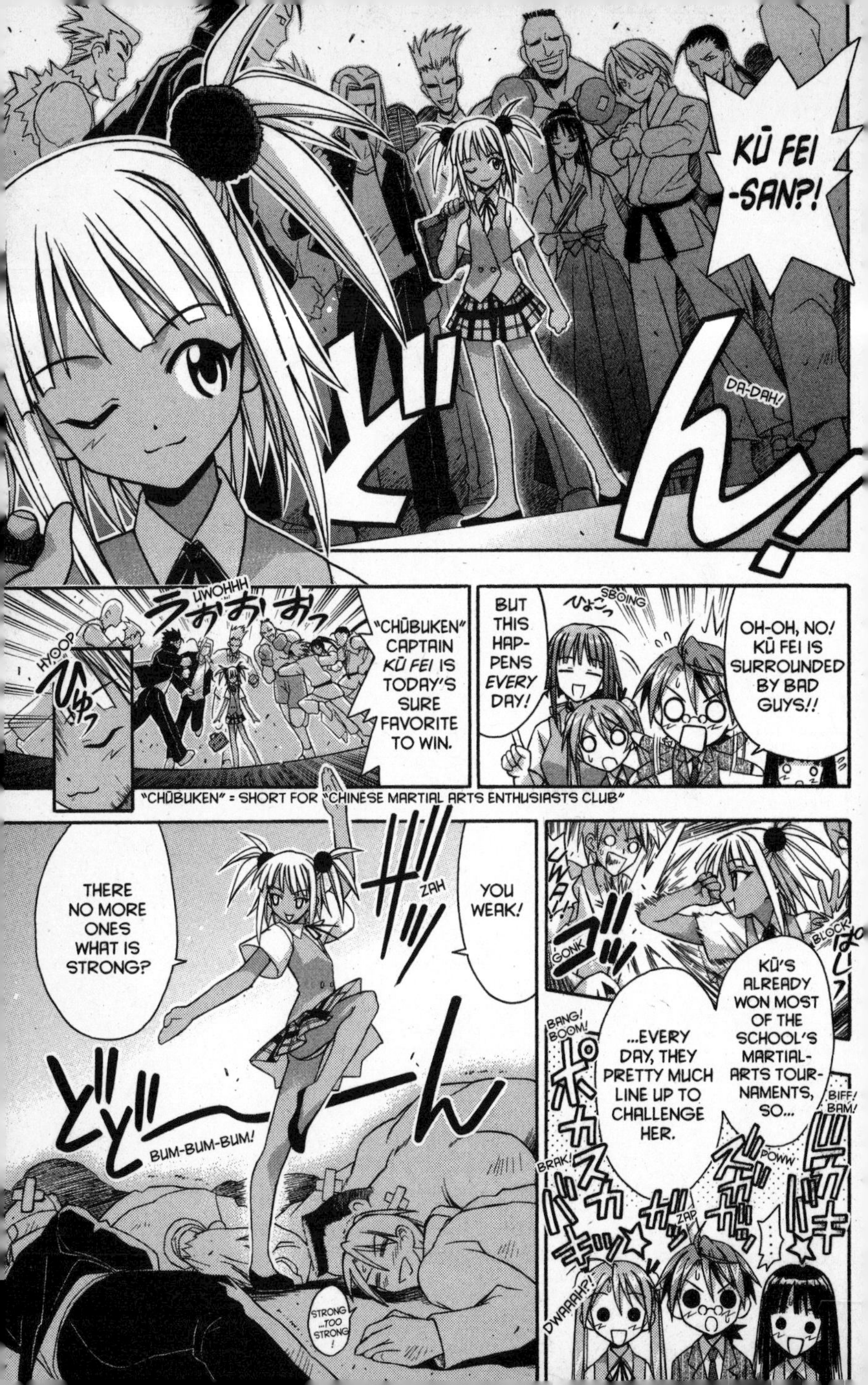

KŪ FEI -SAN?!
DA-DAH!
OH-OH, NO! KŪ FEI IS SURROUNDED BY BAD GUYS!!
SBOING
BUT THIS HAPPENS EVERY DAY!
"CHŪBUKEN" CAPTAIN KŪ FEI IS TODAY'S SURE FAVORITE TO WIN.
UWOHHH
HYOOP
"CHŪBUKEN" = SHORT FOR "CHINESE MARTIAL ARTS ENTHUSIASTS CLUB"
BLOCK
GONK
KŪ'S ALREADY WON MOST OF THE SCHOOL'S MARTIAL-ARTS TOURNAMENTS, SO...
...EVERY DAY, THEY PRETTY MUCH LINE UP TO CHALLENGE HER.
BIFF! BAM!
BANG! BOOM!
POWW
BRAK!
ZAP
DWAAAH?!
YOU WEAK!
ZAH
THERE NO MORE ONES WHAT IS STRONG?
BUM-BUM-BUM!
STRONG ...TOO STRONG!

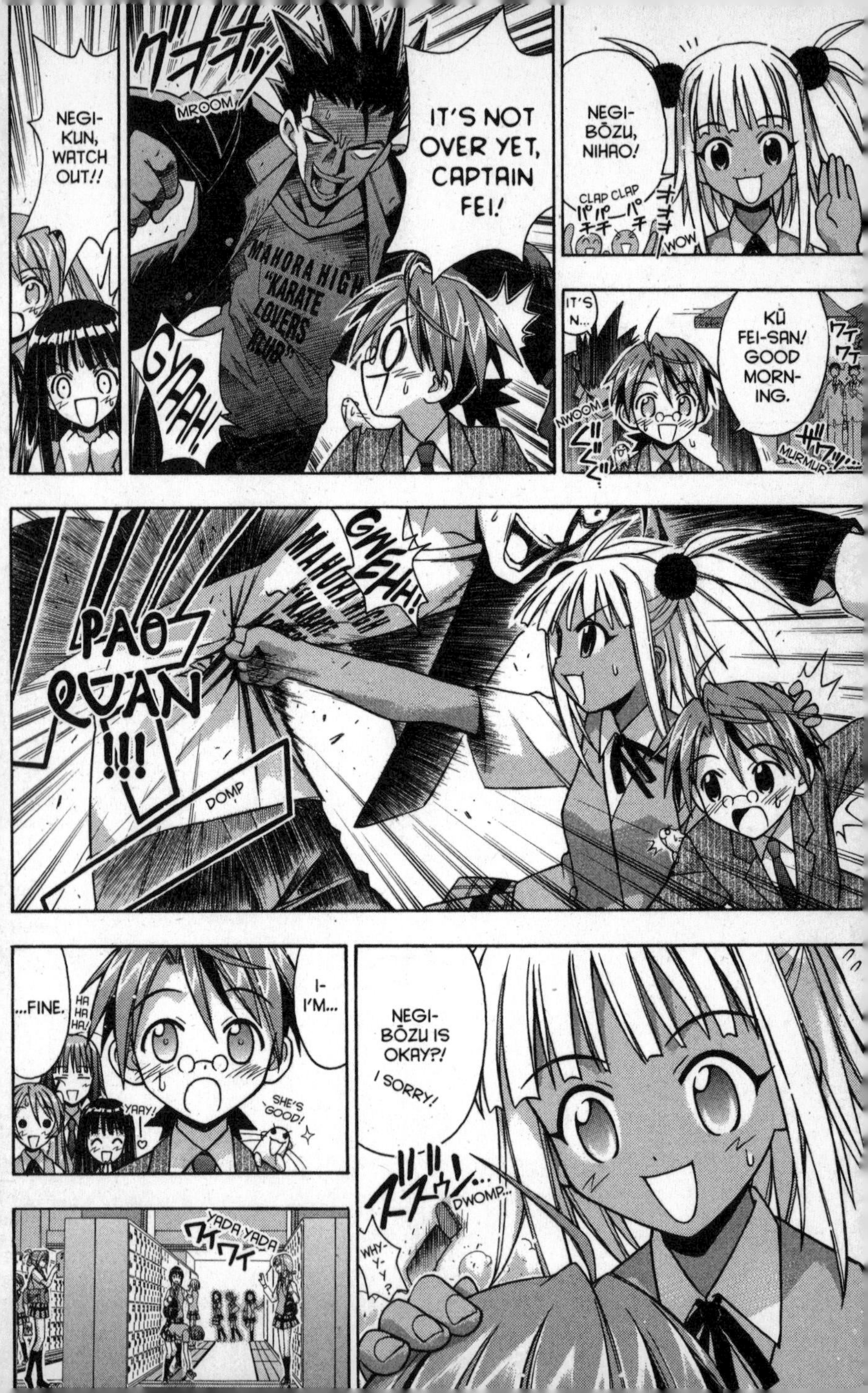
NEGI-BŌZU, NIHAO!
CLAP CLAP
WOW
KŪ FEI-SAN! GOOD MORNING.
IT'S N...
NWOOM
MURMUR
MROOM
IT'S NOT OVER YET, CAPTAIN FEI!
MAHORA HIGH "KARATE LOVERS CLUB"
GYAAH!
NEGI-KUN, WATCH OUT!!
GWEHH!
PAO QUAN!!!
DOMP
NEGI-BŌZU IS OKAY?!
I SORRY!
DWOMP...
WHY-Y-Y?
I- I'M...
...FINE.
HA HA HA!
YAAY!
SHE'S GOOD!
YADA YADA
ワイワイ

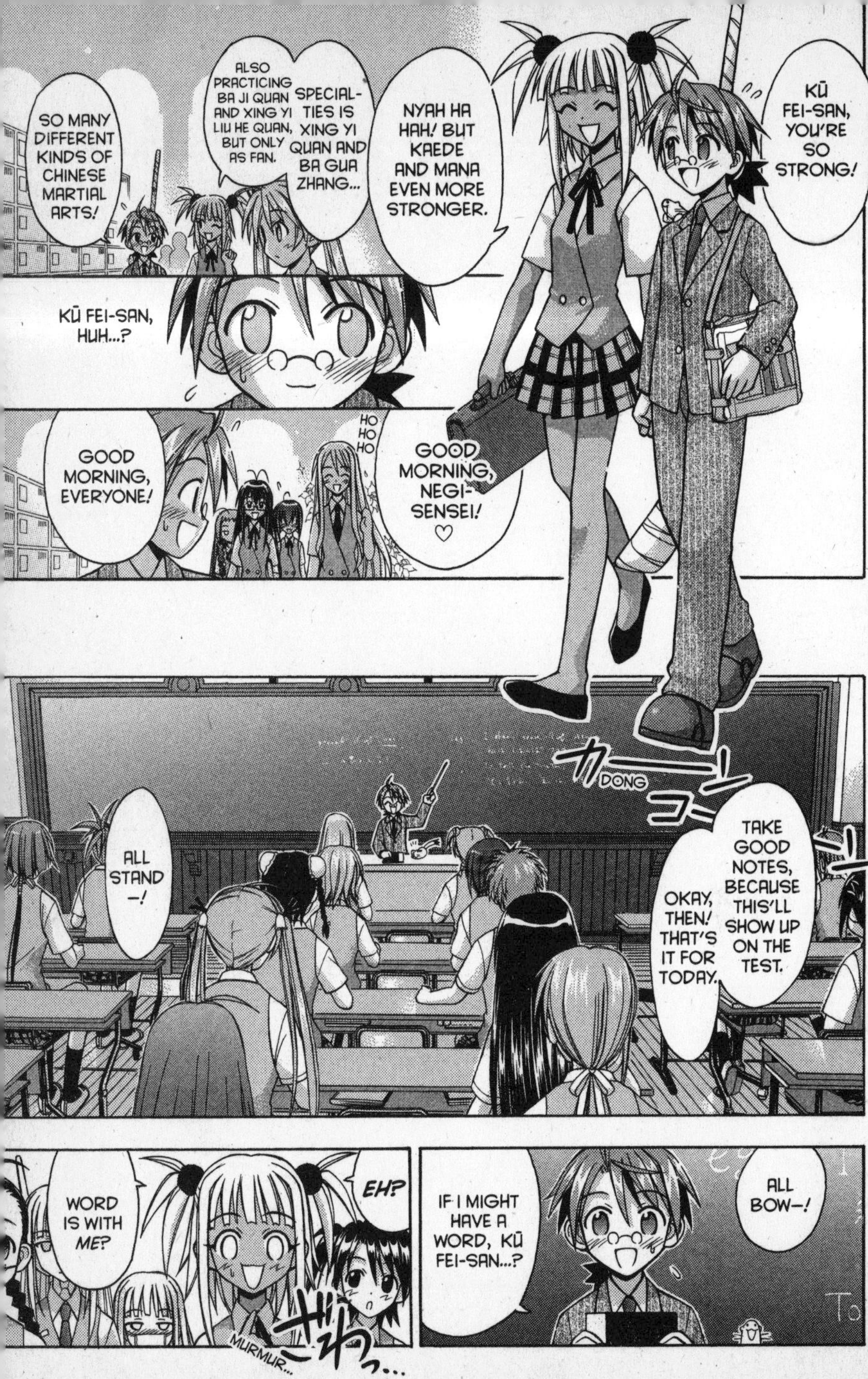
KŪ FEI-SAN, YOU'RE SO STRONG!
NYAH HA HAH! BUT KAEDE AND MANA EVEN MORE STRONGER.
SPECIAL-TIES IS XING YI QUAN AND BA GUA ZHANG...
ALSO PRACTICING BA JI QUAN AND XING YI LIU HE QUAN, BUT ONLY AS FAN.
SO MANY DIFFERENT KINDS OF CHINESE MARTIAL ARTS!
KŪ FEI-SAN, HUH...?
GOOD MORNING, NEGI-SENSEI! ♡
HO HO HO
GOOD MORNING, EVERYONE!
DONG
TAKE GOOD NOTES, BECAUSE THIS'LL SHOW UP ON THE TEST.
OKAY, THEN! THAT'S IT FOR TODAY.
ALL STAND—!
ALL BOW—!
IF I MIGHT HAVE A WORD, KŪ FEI-SAN...?
EH?
WORD IS WITH ME?
MURMUR...

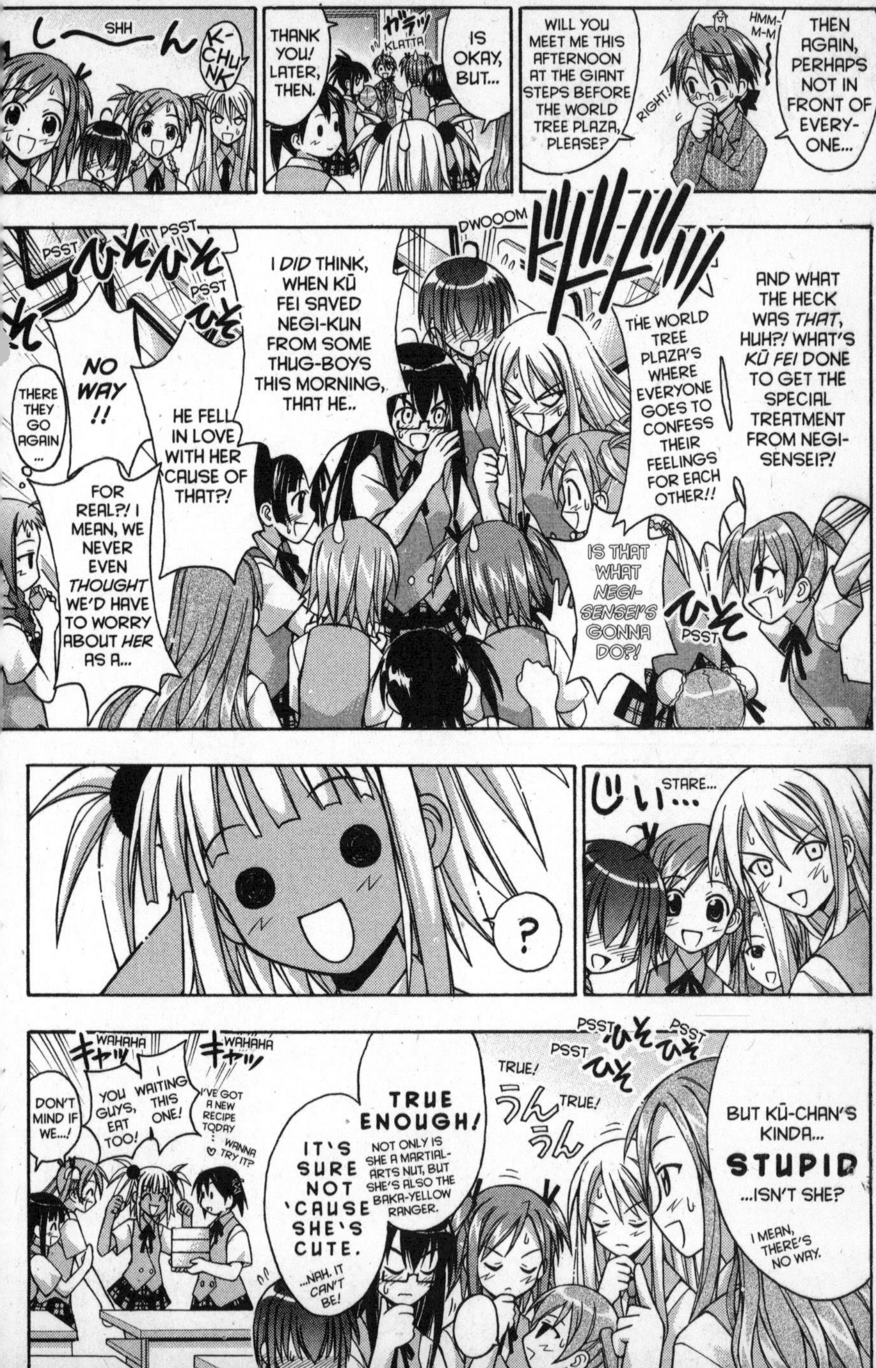
THEN AGAIN, PERHAPS NOT IN FRONT OF EVERY-ONE...
HMM-M-M
WILL YOU MEET ME THIS AFTERNOON AT THE GIANT STEPS BEFORE THE WORLD TREE PLAZA, PLEASE?
RIGHT!
IS OKAY, BUT...
KLATTA
THANK YOU! LATER, THEN.
K-CHUNK
SHH
AND WHAT THE HECK WAS *THAT*, HUH?! WHAT'S *KŪ FEI* DONE TO GET THE SPECIAL TREATMENT FROM NEGI-SENSEI?!
DWOOOM
THE WORLD TREE PLAZA'S WHERE EVERYONE GOES TO CONFESS THEIR FEELINGS FOR EACH OTHER!!
IS THAT WHAT NEGI-SENSEI'S GONNA DO?!
PSST
I *DID* THINK, WHEN KŪ FEI SAVED NEGI-KUN FROM SOME THUG-BOYS THIS MORNING, THAT HE..
HE FELL IN LOVE WITH HER CAUSE OF THAT?!
PSST
PSST
PSST
NO WAY!!
FOR REAL?! I MEAN, WE NEVER EVEN *THOUGHT* WE'D HAVE TO WORRY ABOUT *HER* AS A...
THERE THEY GO AGAIN...
STARE...
?
BUT KŪ-CHAN'S KINDA... STUPID ...ISN'T SHE?
I MEAN, THERE'S NO WAY.
PSST
PSST
PSST
TRUE!
TRUE!
TRUE ENOUGH!
NOT ONLY IS SHE A MARTIAL-ARTS NUT, BUT SHE'S ALSO THE BAKA-YELLOW RANGER.
IT'S SURE NOT 'CAUSE SHE'S CUTE.
...NAH. IT CAN'T BE!
WAHAHA
I'VE GOT A NEW RECIPE TODAY
WANNA TRY IT?
I WAITING THIS ONE!
YOU GUYS, EAT TOO!
DON'T MIND IF WE...!
WAHAHA

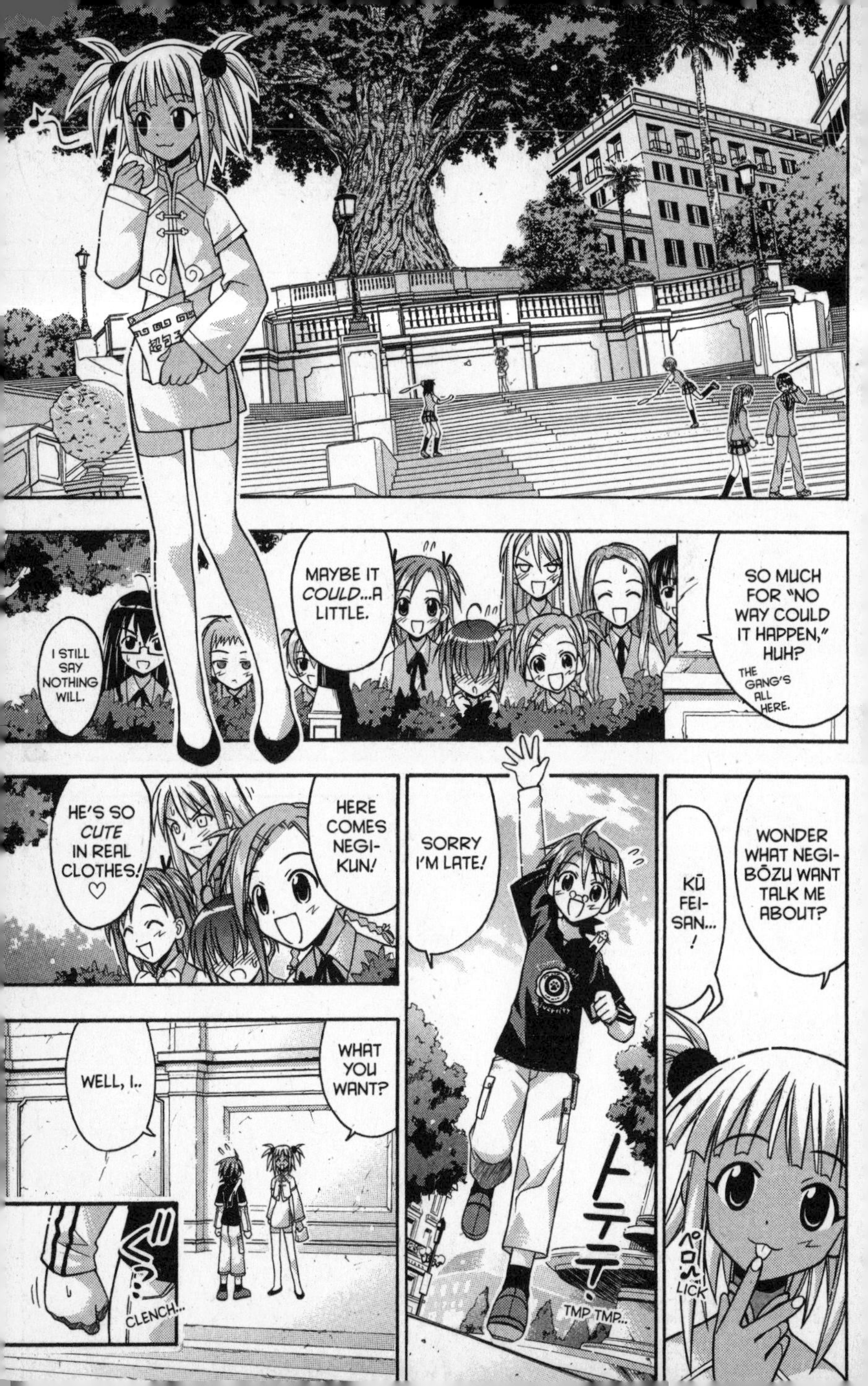
超包子
SO MUCH FOR "NO WAY COULD IT HAPPEN," HUH?
THE GANG'S ALL HERE.
MAYBE IT *COULD*...A LITTLE.
I STILL SAY NOTHING WILL.
WONDER WHAT NEGI-BŌZU WANT TALK ME ABOUT?
KŪ FEI-SAN...!
ペロッ
LICK
SORRY I'M LATE!
トテテ
TMP TMP...
HERE COMES NEGI-KUN!
HE'S SO *CUTE* IN REAL CLOTHES! ♡
WHAT YOU WANT?
WELL, I..
ぐっ
CLENCH...

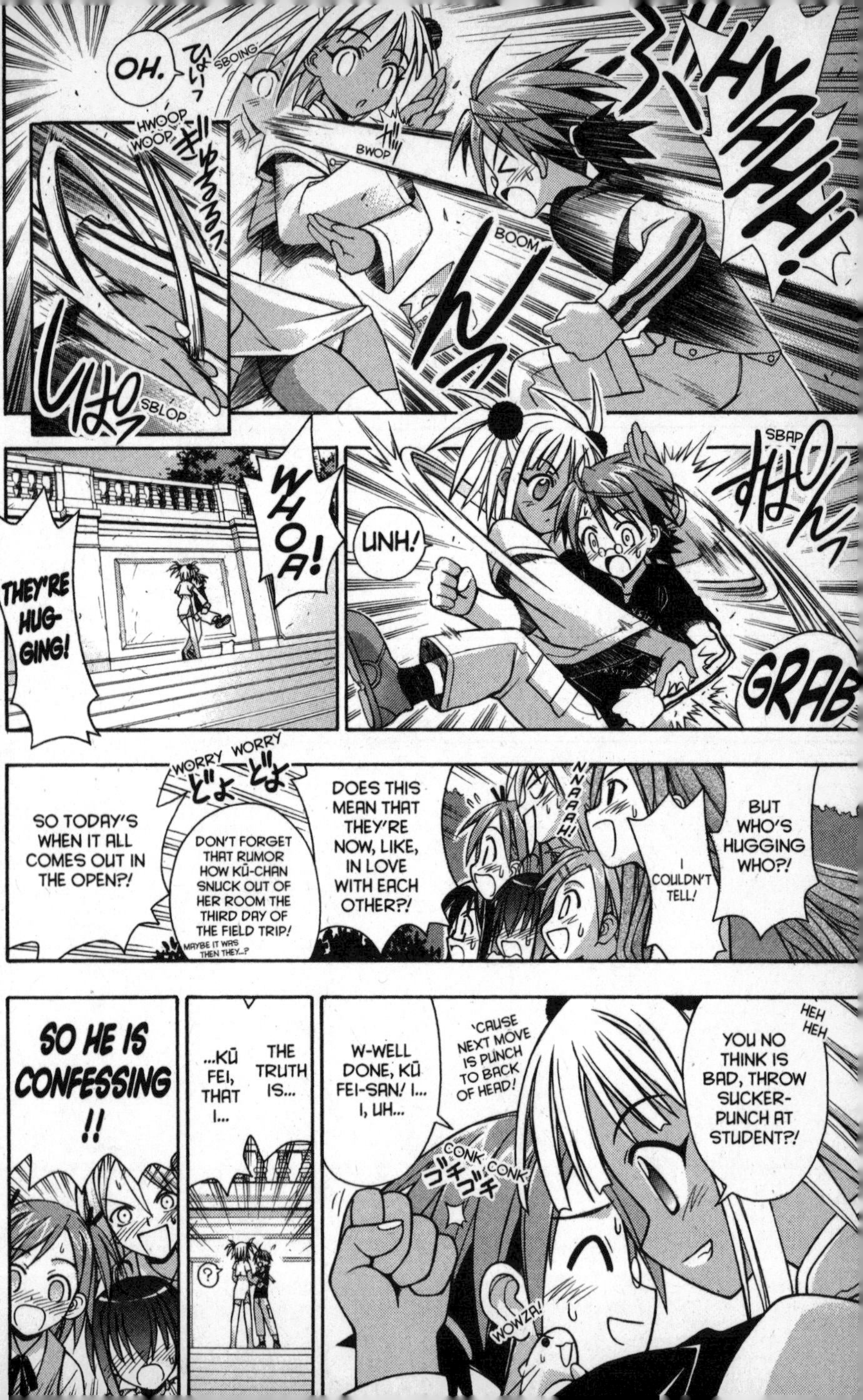
HYAAAH!!
BOOM
BWOP
OH.
SBOING
HWOOP WOOP
SBLOP
SBAP
UNH!
GRAB
WHOA!
THEY'RE HUG-GING!
BUT WHO'S HUGGING WHO?!
I COULDN'T TELL!
NNAAAAH!
DOES THIS MEAN THAT THEY'RE NOW, LIKE, IN LOVE WITH EACH OTHER?!
WORRY WORRY
DON'T FORGET THAT RUMOR HOW KŪ-CHAN SNUCK OUT OF HER ROOM THE THIRD DAY OF THE FIELD TRIP!
MAYBE IT WAS THEN THEY...?
SO TODAY'S WHEN IT ALL COMES OUT IN THE OPEN?!
HEH HEH
YOU NO THINK IS BAD, THROW SUCKER-PUNCH AT STUDENT?!
'CAUSE NEXT MOVE IS PUNCH TO BACK OF HEAD!
CONK CONK
W-WELL DONE, KŪ FEI-SAN! I... I, UH...
WOWZA!
THE TRUTH IS...
...KŪ FEI, THAT I...
?
SO HE IS CONFESSING!!

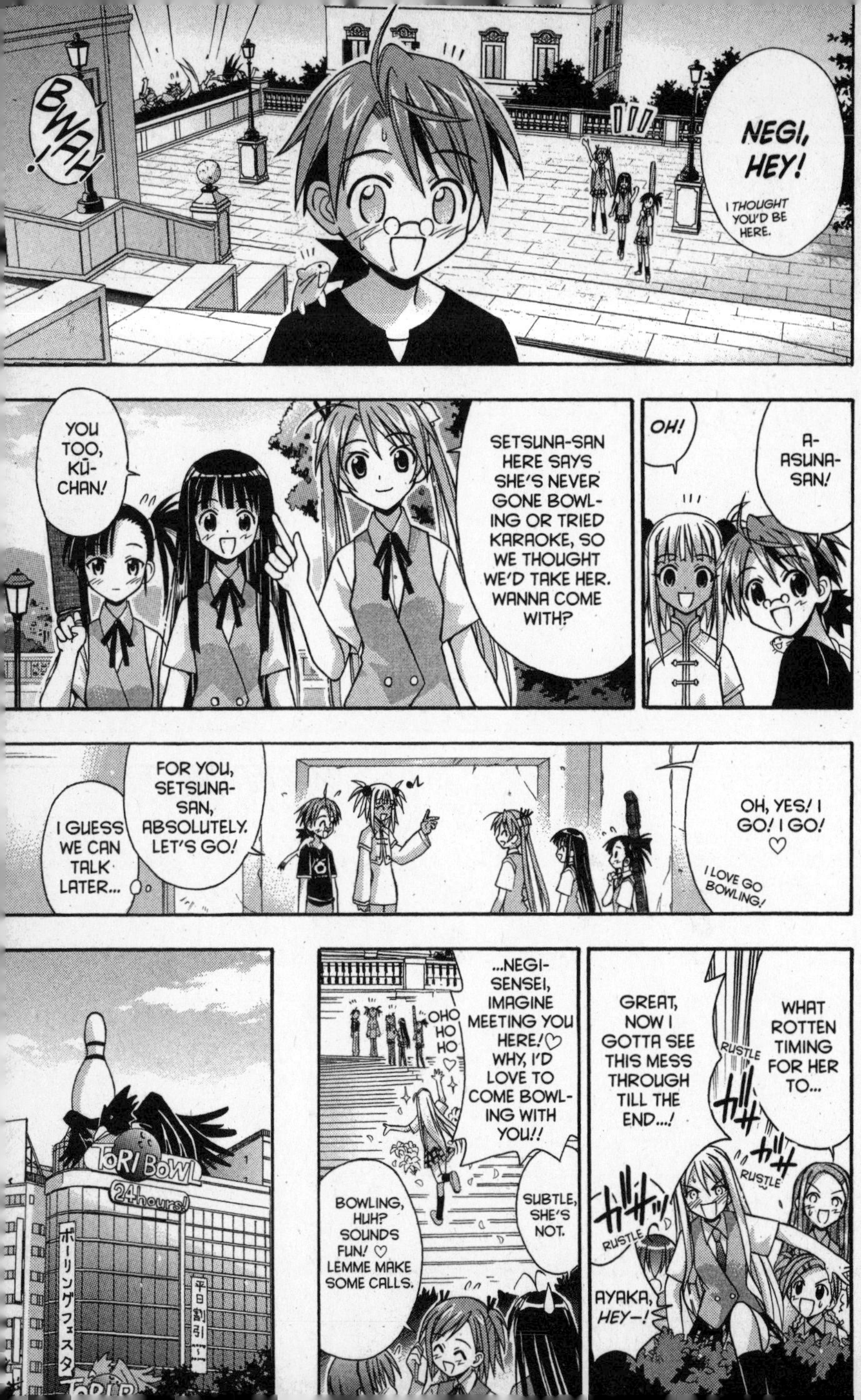
NEGI, HEY!
I THOUGHT YOU'D BE HERE.
BWAH!
A-ASUNA-SAN!
OH!
SETSUNA-SAN HERE SAYS SHE'S NEVER GONE BOWLING OR TRIED KARAOKE, SO WE THOUGHT WE'D TAKE HER. WANNA COME WITH?
YOU TOO, KŪ-CHAN!
OH, YES! I GO! I GO! ♡
I LOVE GO BOWLING!
FOR YOU, SETSUNA-SAN, ABSOLUTELY. LET'S GO!
I GUESS WE CAN TALK LATER...
WHAT ROTTEN TIMING FOR HER TO...
RUSTLE
GREAT, NOW I GOTTA SEE THIS MESS THROUGH TILL THE END...!
RUSTLE
RUSTLE
AYAKA, HEY-!
...NEGI-SENSEI, IMAGINE MEETING YOU HERE! ♡ WHY, I'D LOVE TO COME BOWLING WITH YOU!!
OHO HO HO ♡
SUBTLE, SHE'S NOT.
BOWLING, HUH? SOUNDS FUN! ♡ LEMME MAKE SOME CALLS.
TORI BOWL
24hours!
ボーリングフェスタ
平日割引

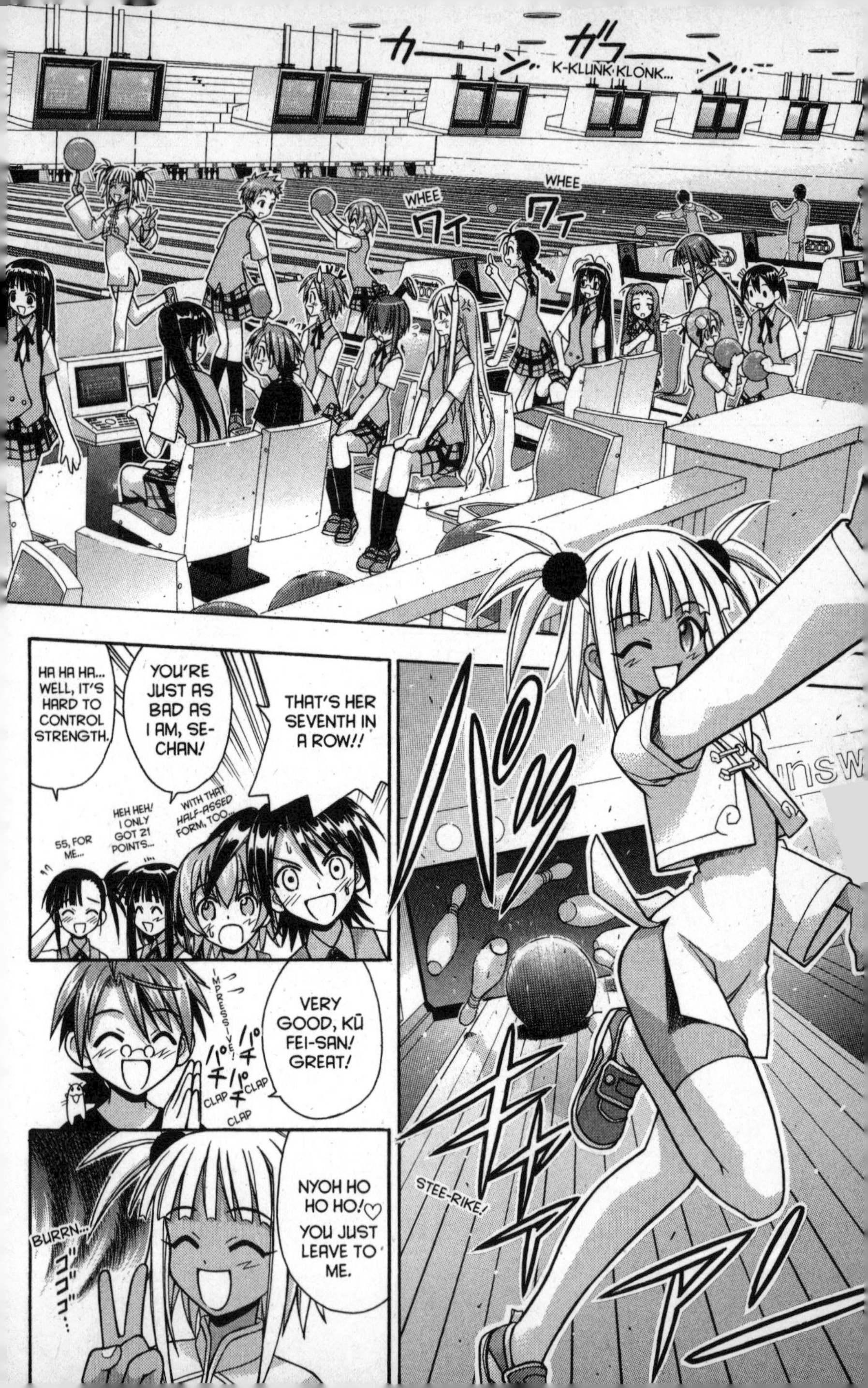
カーーン ガラーーン…
K-KLUNK KLONK...
WHEE
ワイ
WHEE
ワイ
パッ
STEE-RIKE!
THAT'S HER SEVENTH IN A ROW!!
YOU'RE JUST AS BAD AS I AM, SE-CHAN!
HA HA HA... WELL, IT'S HARD TO CONTROL STRENGTH.
WITH THAT HALF-ASSED FORM, TOO...
HEH HEH! I ONLY GOT 21 POINTS...
55, FOR ME...
VERY GOOD, KŪ FEI-SAN! GREAT!
IMPRESSIVE!
パチ パチ パチ
CLAP CLAP CLAP
NYOH HO HO HO!♡ YOU JUST LEAVE TO ME.
BURRN...
ゴゴゴ…

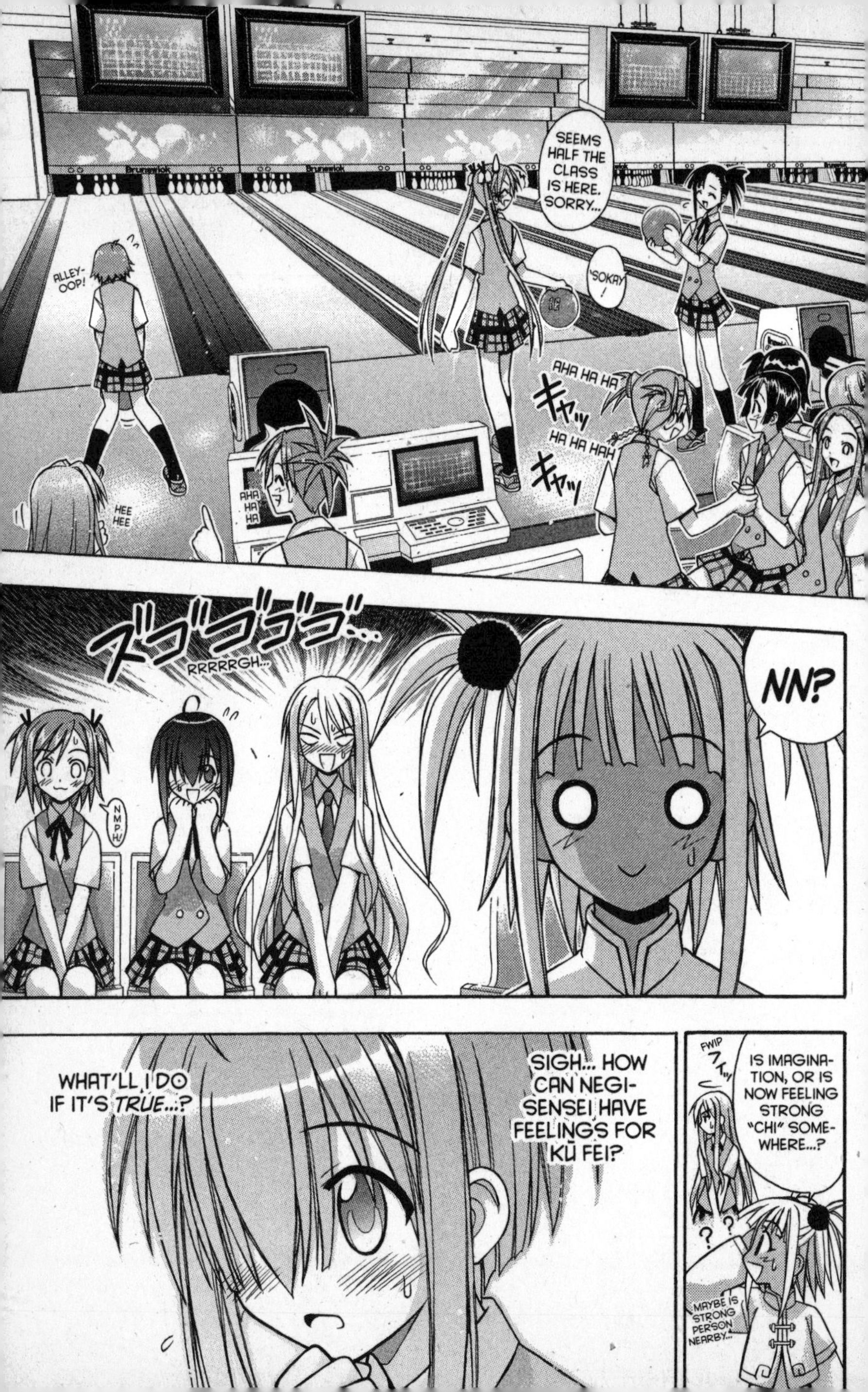
SEEMS HALF THE CLASS IS HERE. SORRY...
'SOKAY!
AHA HA HA
キャッ
HA HA HAH
キャッ
AHA HA HA
ALLEY-OOP!
HEE HEE
NN?
ズゴゴゴゴ…
RRRRRGH...
NMPH!
IS IMAGINATION, OR IS NOW FEELING STRONG "CHI" SOMEWHERE...?
FWIP
フイッ
MAYBE IS STRONG PERSON NEARBY...
SIGH... HOW CAN NEGI-SENSEI HAVE FEELINGS FOR KŪ FEI?
WHAT'LL I DO IF IT'S *TRUE*...?

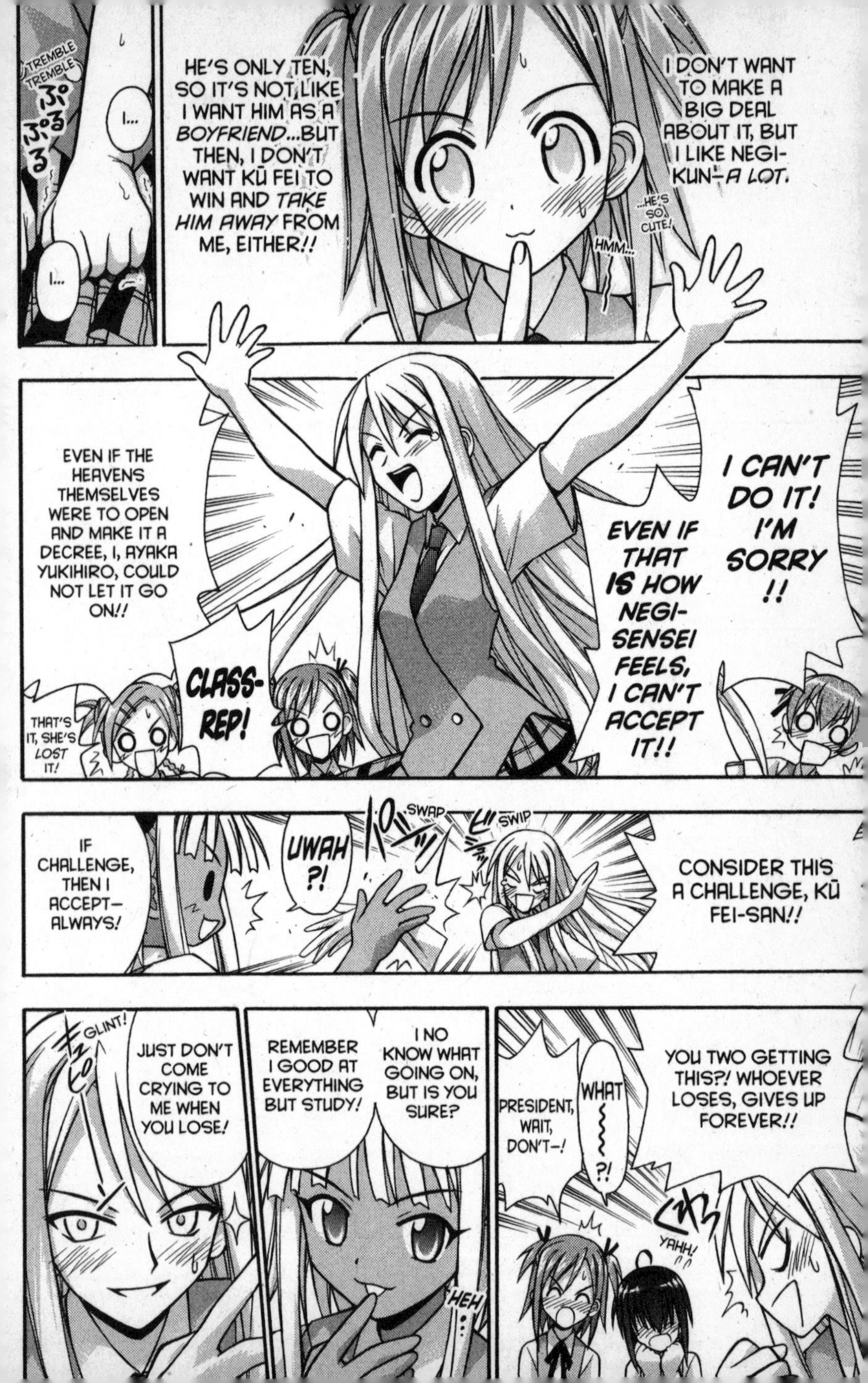

I DON'T WANT TO MAKE A BIG DEAL ABOUT IT, BUT I LIKE NEGI-KUN—A LOT.
...HE'S SO CUTE!
HMM...
HE'S ONLY TEN, SO IT'S NOT LIKE I WANT HIM AS A BOYFRIEND...BUT THEN, I DON'T WANT KŪ FEI TO WIN AND TAKE HIM AWAY FROM ME, EITHER!!
TREMBLE TREMBLE
ぷるぷる
I...
I...
I CAN'T DO IT! I'M SORRY!!
EVEN IF THAT IS HOW NEGI-SENSEI FEELS, I CAN'T ACCEPT IT!!
EVEN IF THE HEAVENS THEMSELVES WERE TO OPEN AND MAKE IT A DECREE, I, AYAKA YUKIHIRO, COULD NOT LET IT GO ON!!
CLASS-REP!
THAT'S IT, SHE'S LOST IT!
CONSIDER THIS A CHALLENGE, KŪ FEI-SAN!!
SWIP
SWAP
UWAH ?!
IF CHALLENGE, THEN I ACCEPT—ALWAYS!
YOU TWO GETTING THIS?! WHOEVER LOSES, GIVES UP FOREVER!!
WHAT~~~?!
PRESIDENT, WAIT, DON'T—!
YAHH!
I NO KNOW WHAT GOING ON, BUT IS YOU SURE?
REMEMBER I GOOD AT EVERYTHING BUT STUDY!
HEH
GLINT!
JUST DON'T COME CRYING TO ME WHEN YOU LOSE!

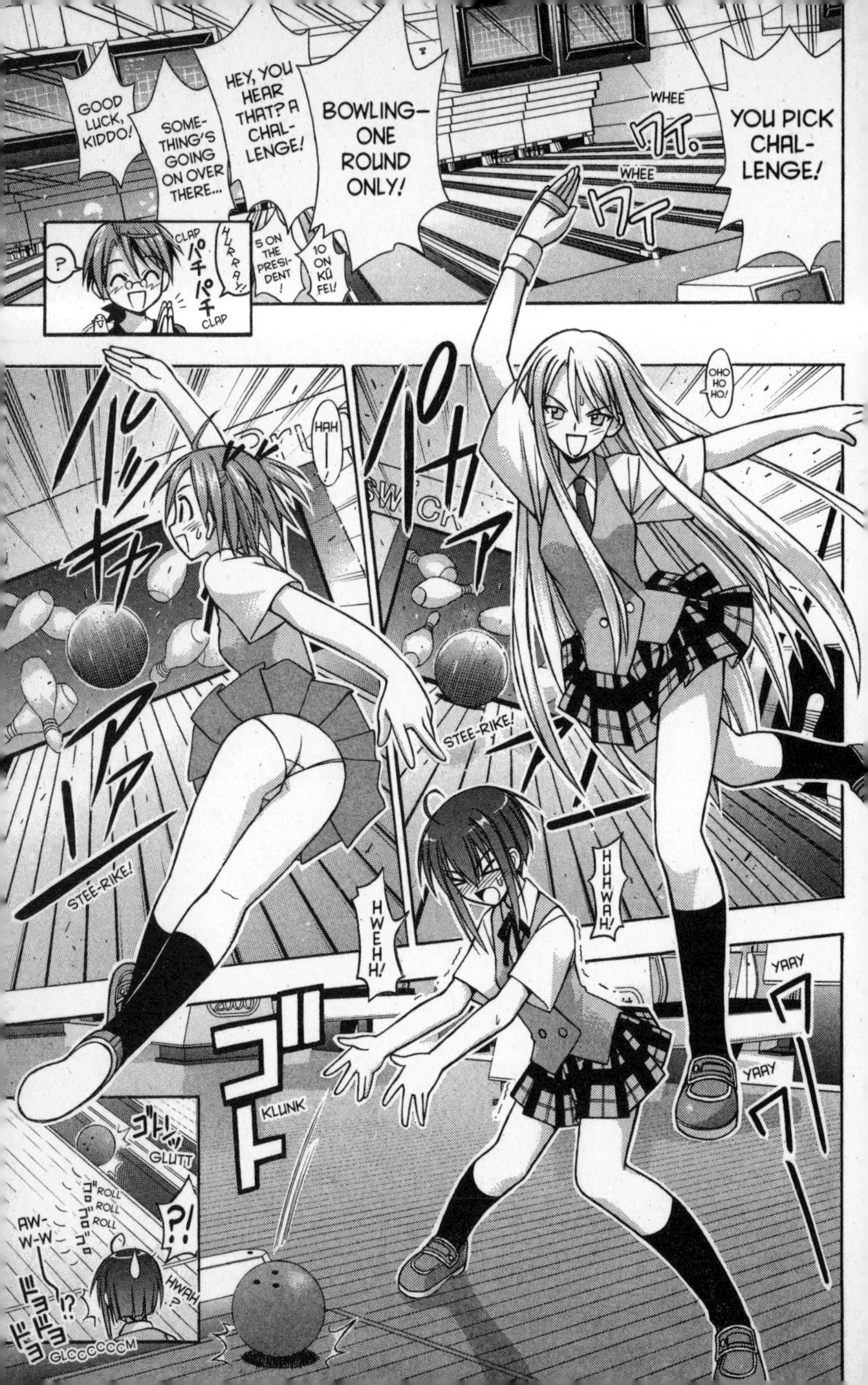
YOU PICK CHALLENGE!
WHEE
ワイ。
WHEE
ワイ
BOWLING—ONE ROUND ONLY!
HEY, YOU HEAR THAT? A CHALLENGE!
SOMETHING'S GOING ON OVER THERE...
GOOD LUCK, KIDDO!
10 ON KŪ FEI!
5 ON THE PRESIDENT!
HURRAY!
CLAP
パチパチ
CLAP
?
OHO HO HO!
パカァ
STEE-RIKE!
HAH!
STEE-RIKE!
HUHWAH!
HWEEH!
ゴト
KLUNK
YAAY
YAAY
ゴトッ
GLUTT
ROLL ROLL ROLL
?!
AW-W-W
HWAH?
!?
GLOOOOOOM

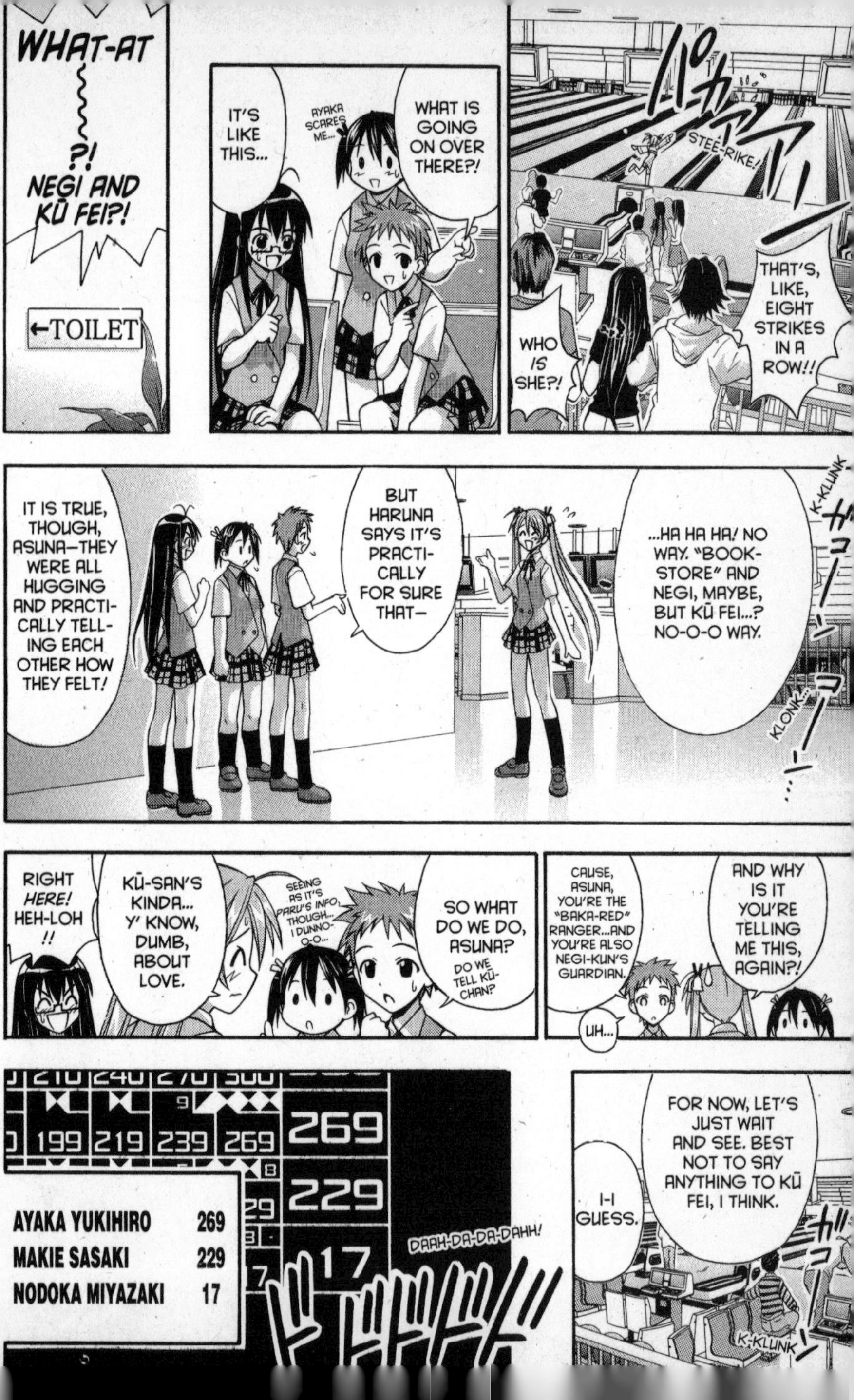

STEE-RIKE!
THAT'S, LIKE, EIGHT STRIKES IN A ROW!!
WHO IS SHE?!
WHAT IS GOING ON OVER THERE?!
AYAKA SCARES ME...
IT'S LIKE THIS...
WHAT-AT ~~~ ?! NEGI AND KŪ FEI?!
←TOILET
K-KLUNK
...HA HA HA! NO WAY. "BOOK-STORE" AND NEGI, MAYBE, BUT KŪ FEI...? NO-O-O WAY.
KLONK...
BUT HARUNA SAYS IT'S PRACTI-CALLY FOR SURE THAT—
IT IS TRUE, THOUGH, ASUNA—THEY WERE ALL HUGGING AND PRACTI-CALLY TELL-ING EACH OTHER HOW THEY FELT!
AND WHY IS IT YOU'RE TELLING ME THIS, AGAIN?!
CAUSE, ASUNA, YOU'RE THE "BAKA-RED" RANGER...AND YOU'RE ALSO NEGI-KUN'S GUARDIAN.
UH...
SO WHAT DO WE DO, ASUNA?
DO WE TELL KŪ-CHAN?
SEEING AS IT'S PARU'S INFO, THOUGH... I DUNNO-O-O...
KŪ-SAN'S KINDA... Y' KNOW, DUMB, ABOUT LOVE.
RIGHT HERE! HEH-LOH !!
FOR NOW, LET'S JUST WAIT AND SEE. BEST NOT TO SAY ANYTHING TO KŪ FEI, I THINK.
I-I GUESS.
K-KLUNK
210 240 270 300
199 219 239 269
269
229
17
AYAKA YUKIHIRO 269
MAKIE SASAKI 229
NODOKA MIYAZAKI 17
DAAH-DA-DA-DAHH!

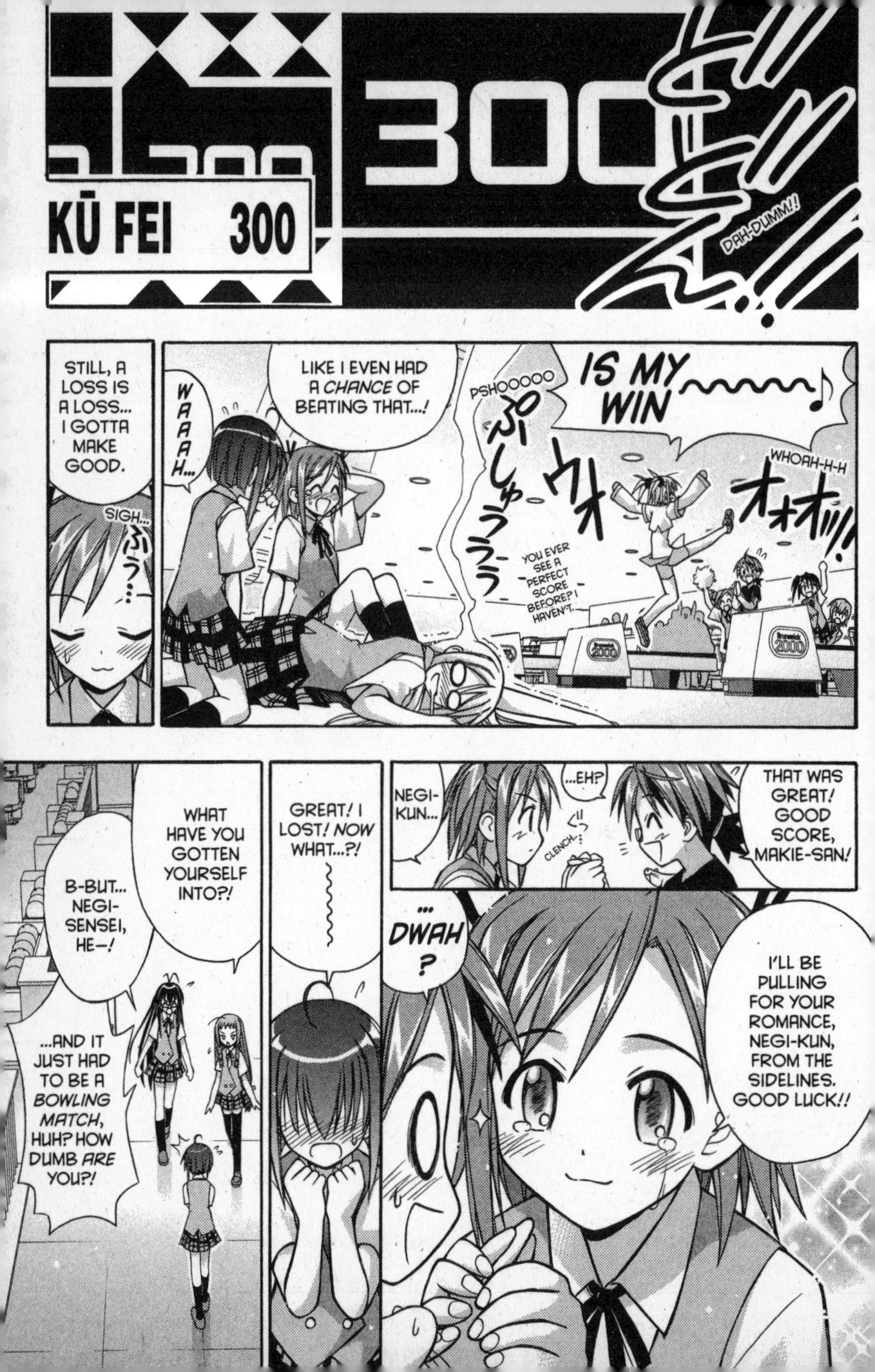

300
KŪ FEI 300
DAH-DUMM!!
IS MY WIN ~~~♪
WHOAH-H-H
オオオッ!!
ウオ
PSHOOOOO
ぷしゅラララ
YOU EVER SEE A PERFECT SCORE BEFORE? I HAVEN'T.
LIKE I EVEN HAD A CHANCE OF BEATING THAT...!
WAAAAH...
STILL, A LOSS IS A LOSS... I GOTTA MAKE GOOD.
SIGH...
ふぅ...
THAT WAS GREAT! GOOD SCORE, MAKIE-SAN!
...EH?
CLENCH
ぐっ
NEGI-KUN...
I'LL BE PULLING FOR YOUR ROMANCE, NEGI-KUN, FROM THE SIDELINES. GOOD LUCK!!
...DWAH?
GREAT! I LOST! NOW WHAT...?!
WHAT HAVE YOU GOTTEN YOURSELF INTO?!
B-BUT... NEGI-SENSEI, HE—!
...AND IT JUST HAD TO BE A BOWLING MATCH, HUH? HOW DUMB ARE YOU?!

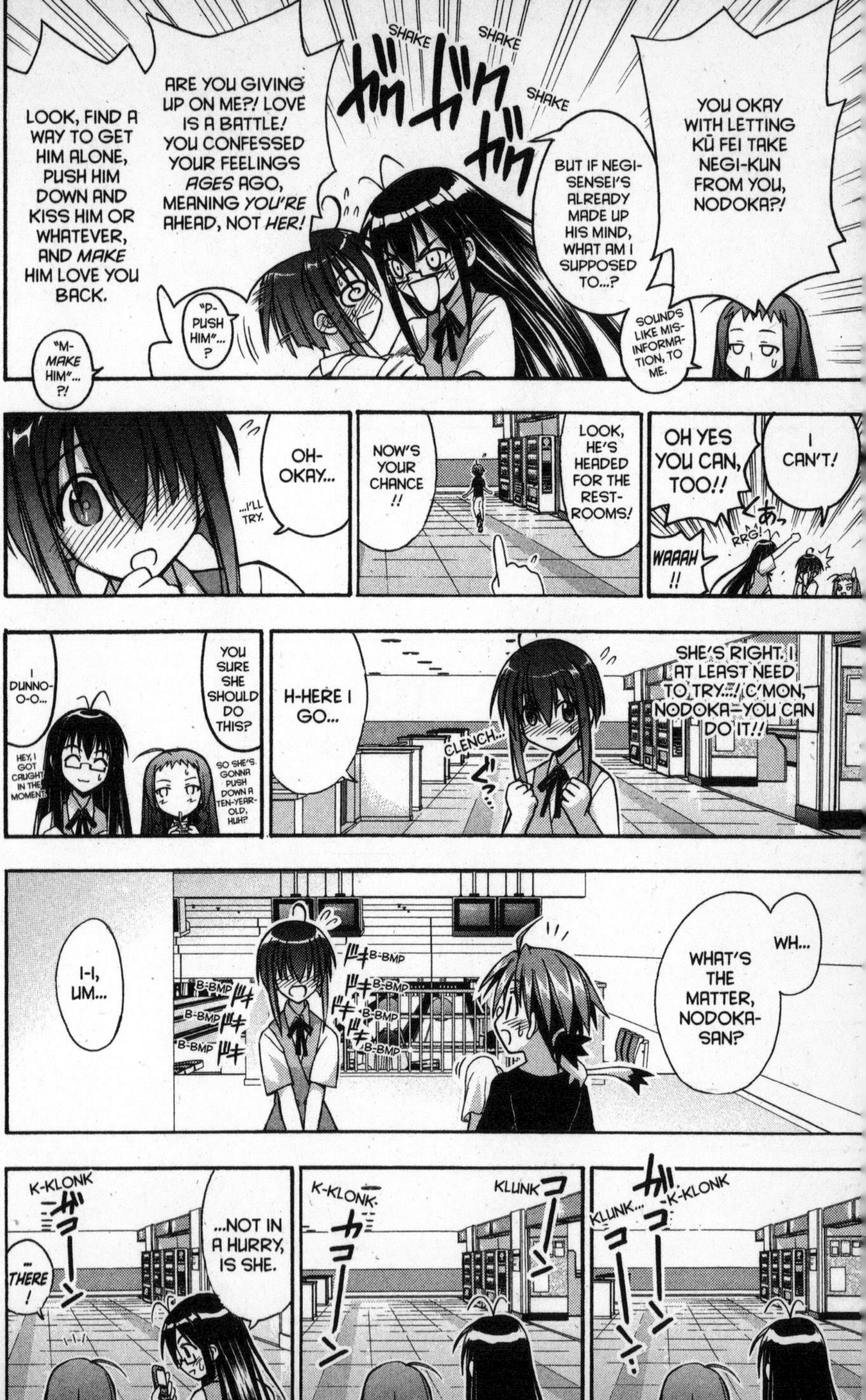
YOU OKAY WITH LETTING KŪ FEI TAKE NEGI-KUN FROM YOU, NODOKA?!
SHAKE
SHAKE
SHAKE
BUT IF NEGI-SENSEI'S ALREADY MADE UP HIS MIND, WHAT AM I SUPPOSED TO...?
ARE YOU GIVING UP ON ME?! LOVE IS A BATTLE! YOU CONFESSED YOUR FEELINGS AGES AGO, MEANING YOU'RE AHEAD, NOT HER!
LOOK, FIND A WAY TO GET HIM ALONE, PUSH HIM DOWN AND KISS HIM OR WHATEVER, AND MAKE HIM LOVE YOU BACK.
SOUNDS LIKE MISINFORMATION, TO ME.
"P-PUSH HIM"...?
"M-MAKE HIM"...?!
I CAN'T!
OH YES YOU CAN, TOO!!
RRG!
WAAAH!!
LOOK, HE'S HEADED FOR THE RESTROOMS!
NOW'S YOUR CHANCE!!
OH-OKAY...
...I'LL TRY.
SHE'S RIGHT. I AT LEAST NEED TO TRY...! C'MON, NODOKA—YOU CAN DO IT!!
CLENCH...
H-HERE I GO...
YOU SURE SHE SHOULD DO THIS?
I DUNNO-O-O...
SO SHE'S GONNA PUSH DOWN A TEN-YEAR-OLD, HUH?
HEY, I GOT CAUGHT IN THE MOMENT.
WH...
WHAT'S THE MATTER, NODOKA-SAN?
B-BMP
B-BMP
B-BMP
B-BMP
B-BMP
B-BMP
I-I, UM...
K-KLONK
KLUNK...
KLUNK
K-KLONK
K-KLONK
...NOT IN A HURRY, IS SHE.
...THERE!

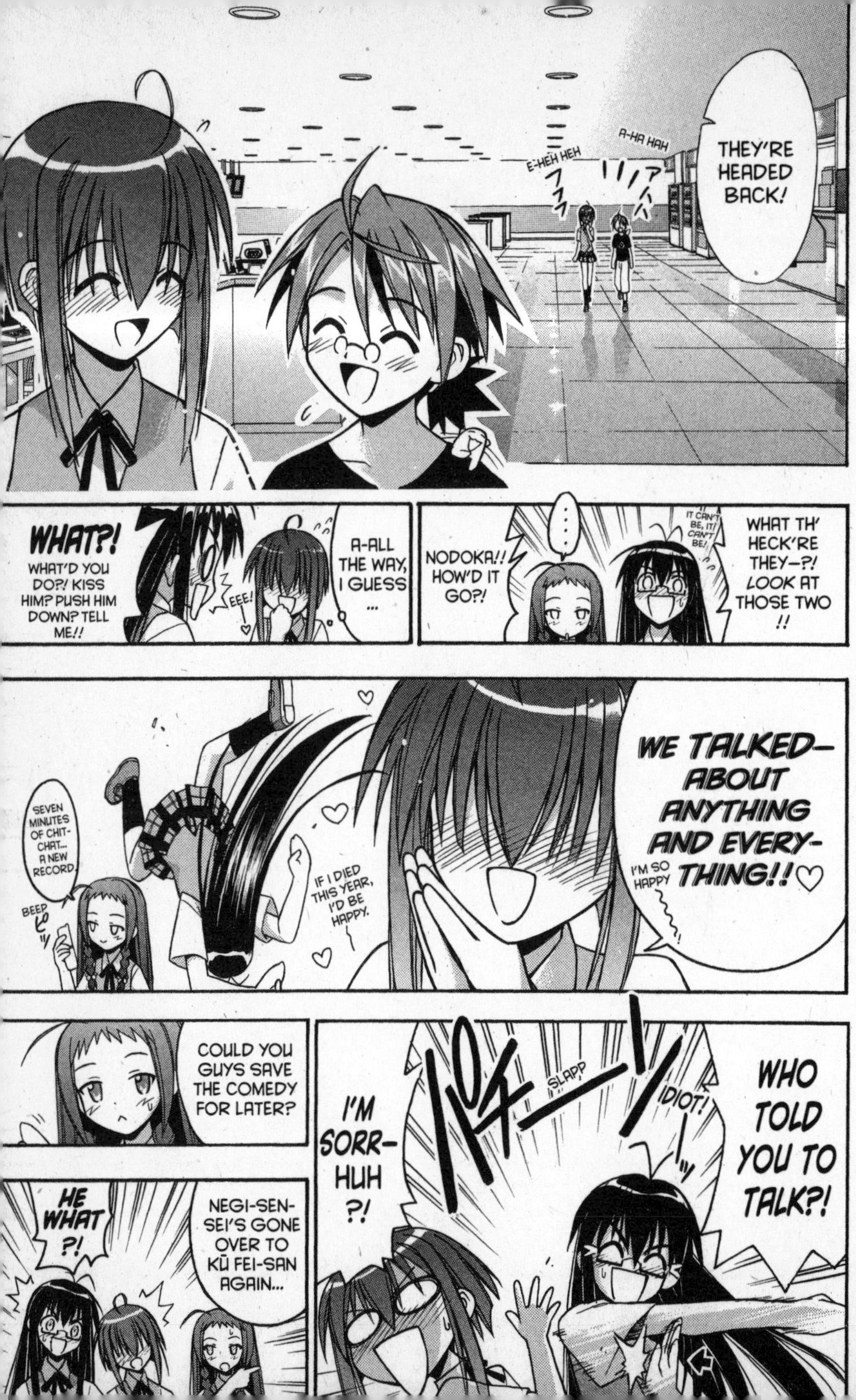
THEY'RE HEADED BACK!
A-HA HAH
E-HEH HEH
WHAT TH' HECK'RE THEY—?! LOOK AT THOSE TWO !!
IT CAN'T BE, IT CAN'T BE!
...
NODOKA!! HOW'D IT GO?!
A-ALL THE WAY, I GUESS ...
EEE!
WHAT?!
WHAT'D YOU DO?! KISS HIM? PUSH HIM DOWN? TELL ME!!
WE TALKED— ABOUT ANYTHING AND EVERY-THING!!
I'M SO HAPPY
IF I DIED THIS YEAR, I'D BE HAPPY.
SEVEN MINUTES OF CHIT-CHAT... A NEW RECORD.
BEEP
WHO TOLD YOU TO TALK?!
IDIOT!
SLAPP
I'M SORR- HUH ?!
COULD YOU GUYS SAVE THE COMEDY FOR LATER?
NEGI-SEN-SEI'S GONE OVER TO KŪ FEI-SAN AGAIN...
HE WHAT ?!

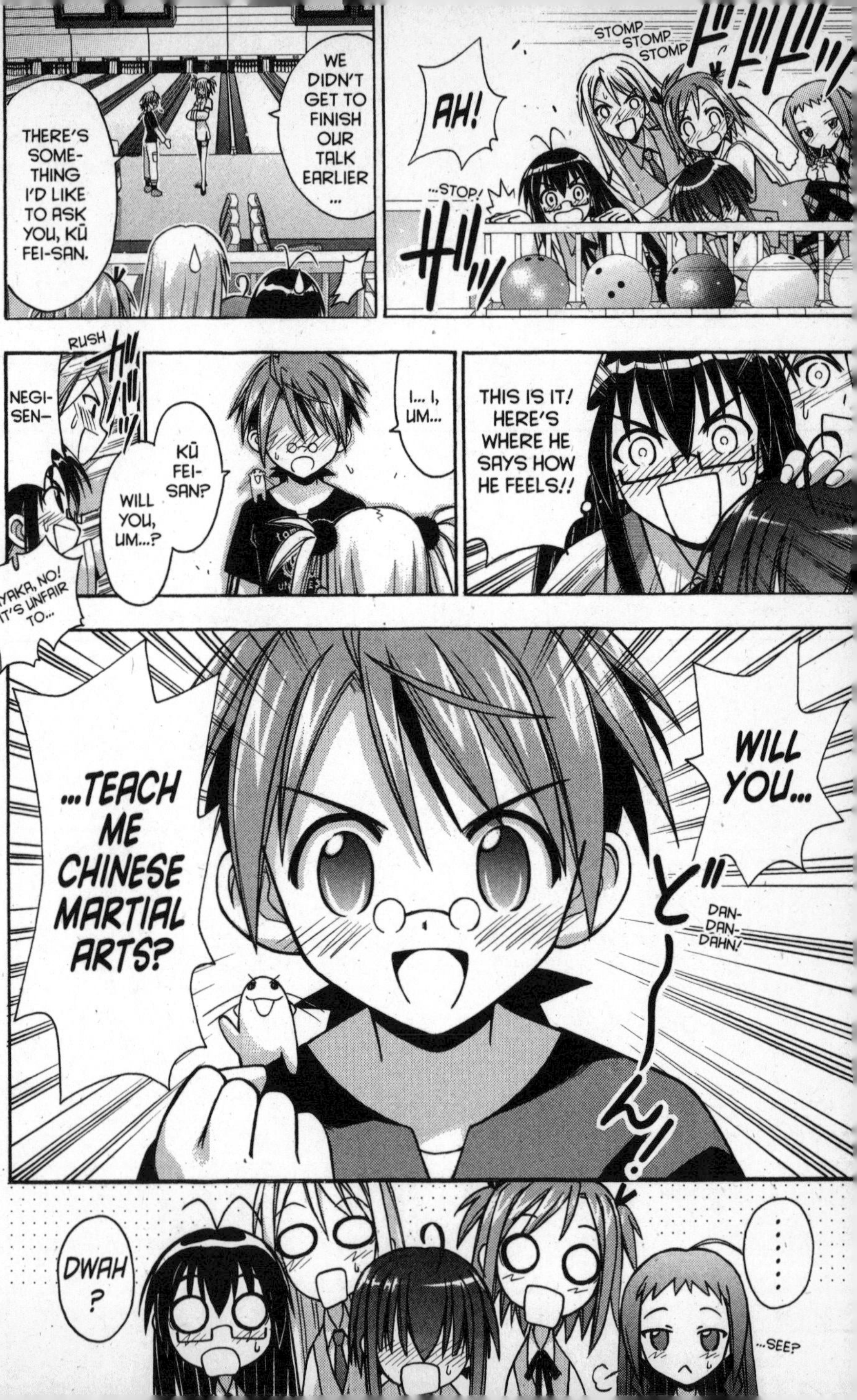

STOMP STOMP STOMP
AH!
...STOP!
WE DIDN'T GET TO FINISH OUR TALK EARLIER ...
THERE'S SOME-THING I'D LIKE TO ASK YOU, KŪ FEI-SAN.
THIS IS IT! HERE'S WHERE HE SAYS HOW HE FEELS!!
I... I, UM...
KŪ FEI-SAN?
WILL YOU, UM...?
RUSH
NEGI-SEN-
AYAKA, NO! IT'S UNFAIR TO...
WILL YOU...
...TEACH ME CHINESE MARTIAL ARTS?
DAN-DAN-DAHN!
......
DWAH?
...SEE?

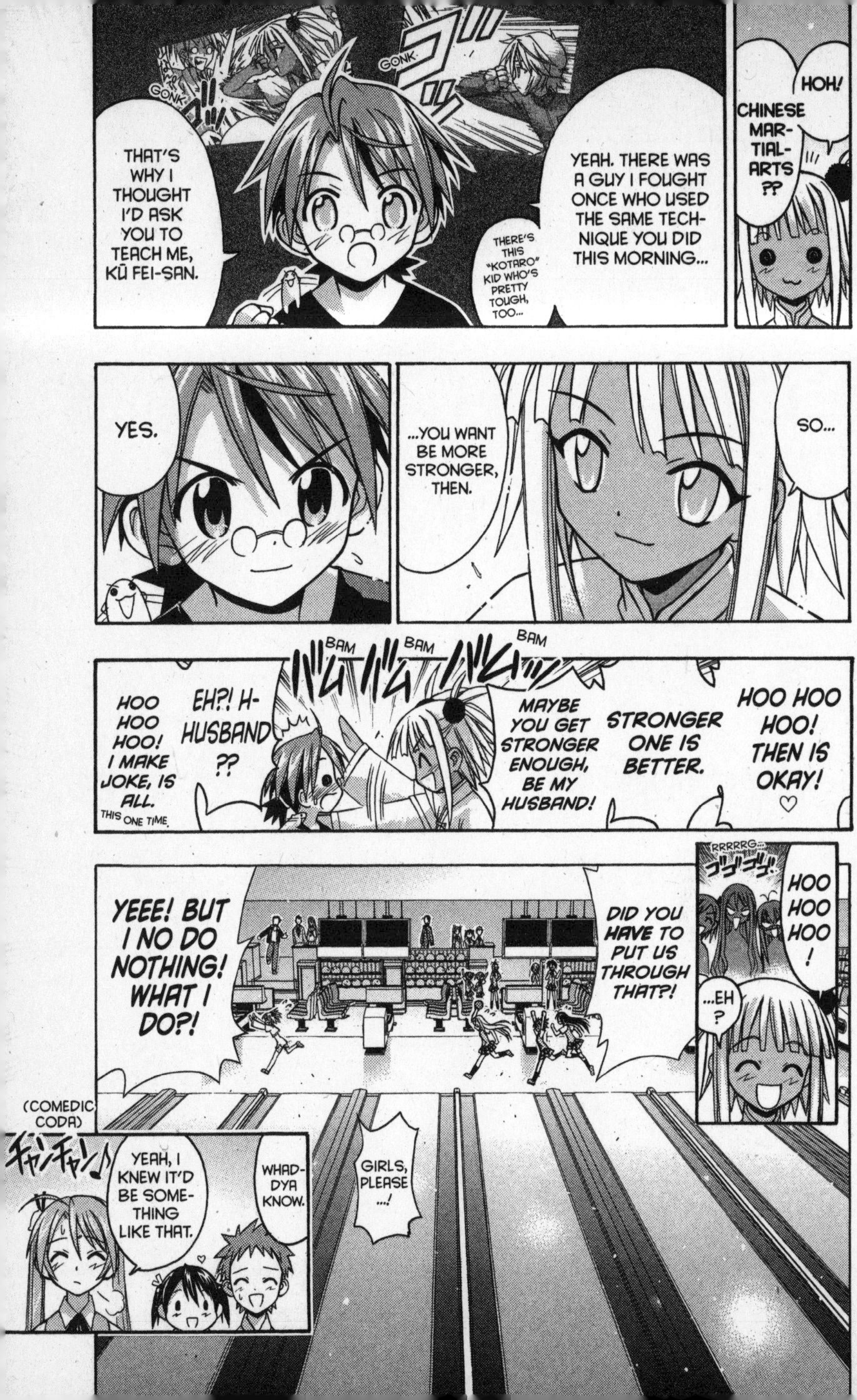
HOH!
CHINESE MARTIAL-ARTS ??
GONK
GONK
YEAH. THERE WAS A GUY I FOUGHT ONCE WHO USED THE SAME TECHNIQUE YOU DID THIS MORNING...
THERE'S THIS "KOTARO" KID WHO'S PRETTY TOUGH, TOO...
THAT'S WHY I THOUGHT I'D ASK YOU TO TEACH ME, KŪ FEI-SAN.
SO...
...YOU WANT BE MORE STRONGER, THEN.
YES.
HOO HOO HOO! THEN IS OKAY! ♡
STRONGER ONE IS BETTER.
MAYBE YOU GET STRONGER ENOUGH, BE MY HUSBAND!
BAM
BAM
BAM
EH?! H-HUSBAND ??
HOO HOO HOO! I MAKE JOKE, IS ALL.
THIS ONE TIME.
RRRRRG...
HOO HOO HOO!
...EH?
DID YOU HAVE TO PUT US THROUGH THAT?!
YEEE! BUT I NO DO NOTHING! WHAT I DO?!
GIRLS, PLEASE ...!
WHADDYA KNOW.
YEAH, I KNEW IT'D BE SOMETHING LIKE THAT.
(COMEDIC CODA)

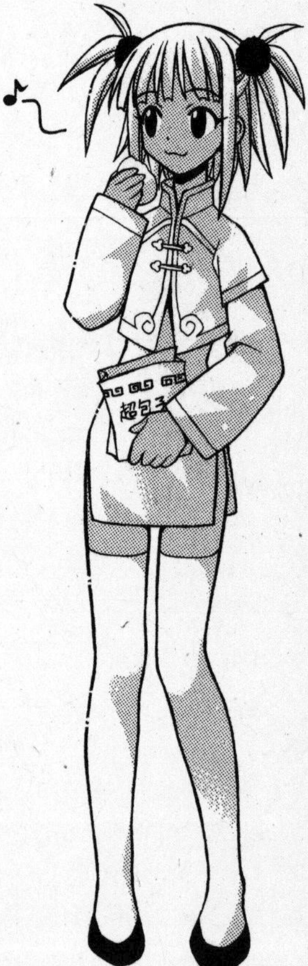
超包子

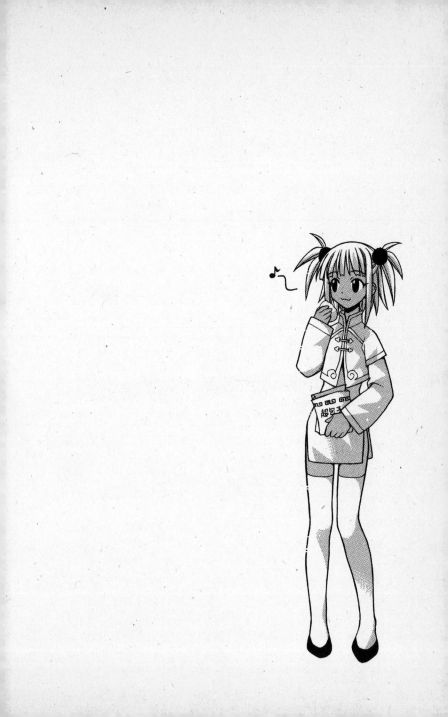

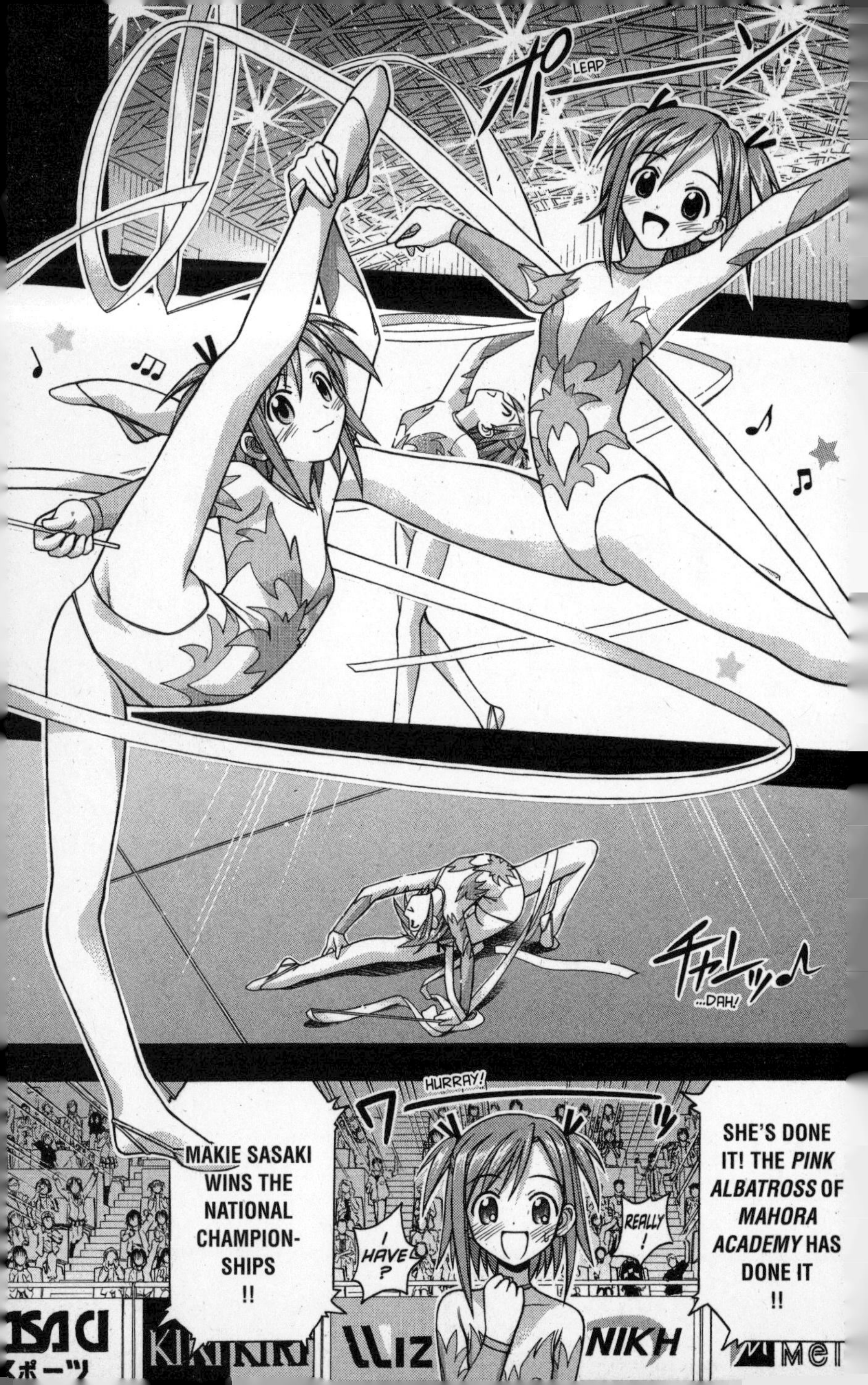
ポ
LEAP
ーン
チャレッ♪
...DAH!
SHE'S DONE IT! THE *PINK ALBATROSS* OF *MAHORA ACADEMY* HAS DONE IT !!
ワーッ
HURRAY!
REALLY!
I HAVE?
MAKIE SASAKI WINS THE NATIONAL CHAMPION-SHIPS !!
NIKH
IIIZ
KIKIKIKI
スポーツ

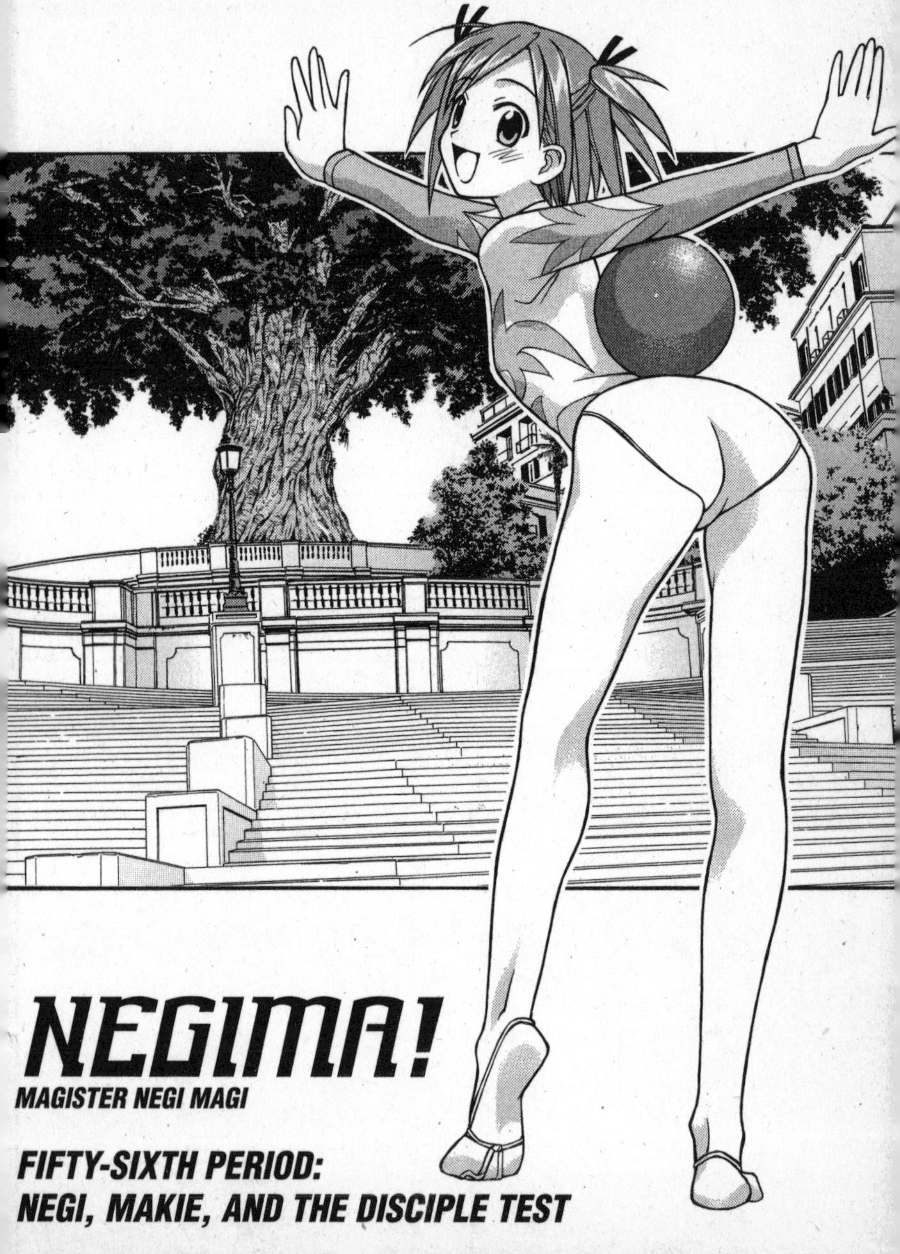

NEGIMA!

MAGISTER NEGI MAGI

FIFTY-SIXTH PERIOD:
NEGI, MAKIE, AND THE DISCIPLE TEST

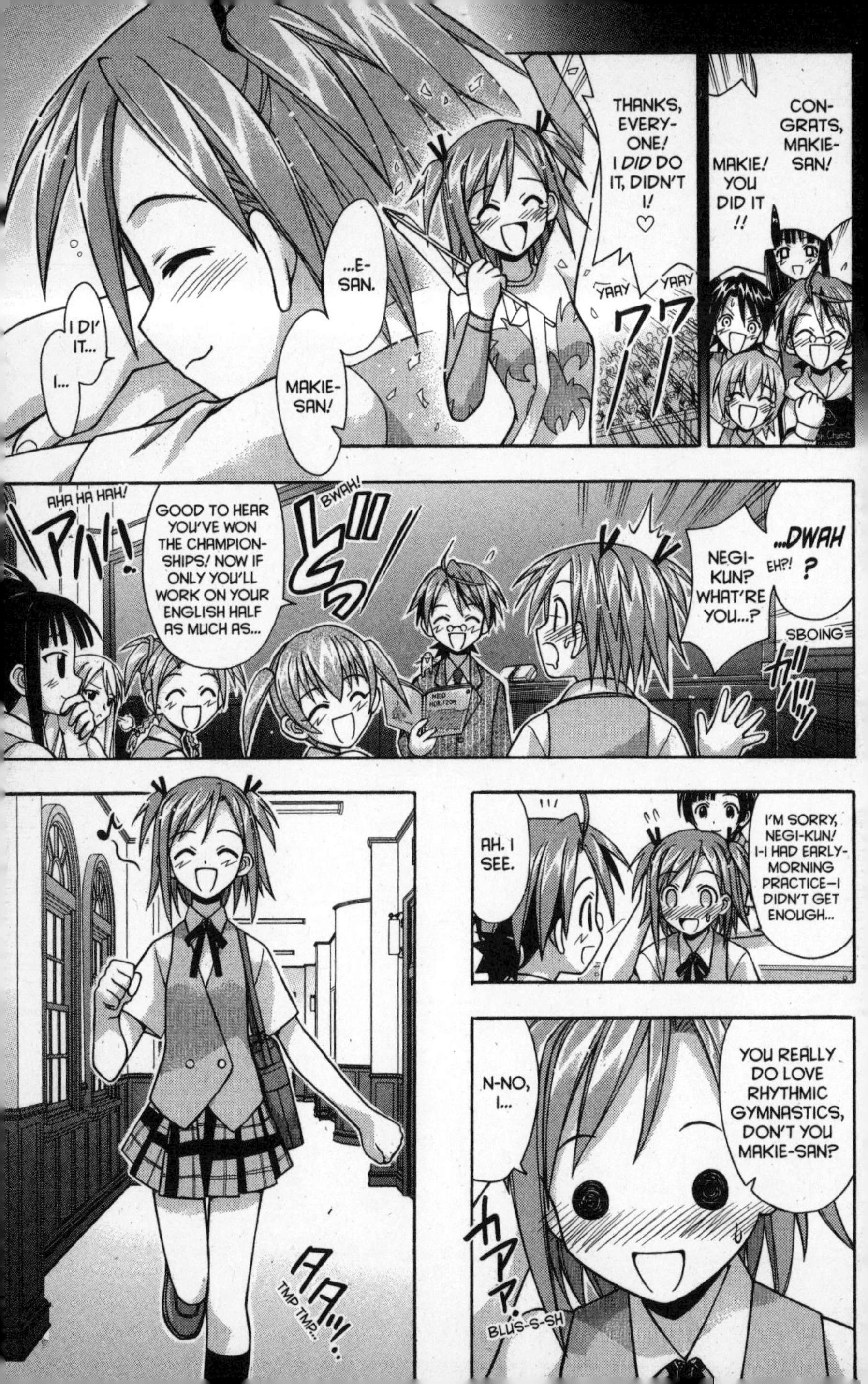
CON-GRATS, MAKIE-SAN!
MAKIE! YOU DID IT !!
THANKS, EVERY-ONE! I *DID* DO IT, DIDN'T I! ♡
YAAY
YAAY
...E-SAN.
MAKIE-SAN!
I DI' IT... I...
...DWAH ?
EH?!
NEGI-KUN? WHAT'RE YOU...?
SBOING
BWAH!
GOOD TO HEAR YOU'VE WON THE CHAMPION-SHIPS! NOW IF ONLY YOU'LL WORK ON YOUR ENGLISH HALF AS MUCH AS...
AHA HA HAH!
I'M SORRY, NEGI-KUN! I-I HAD EARLY-MORNING PRACTICE—I DIDN'T GET ENOUGH...
AH. I SEE.
YOU REALLY DO LOVE RHYTHMIC GYMNASTICS, DON'T YOU MAKIE-SAN?
N-NO, I...
BLUS-S-SH
TMP TMP...

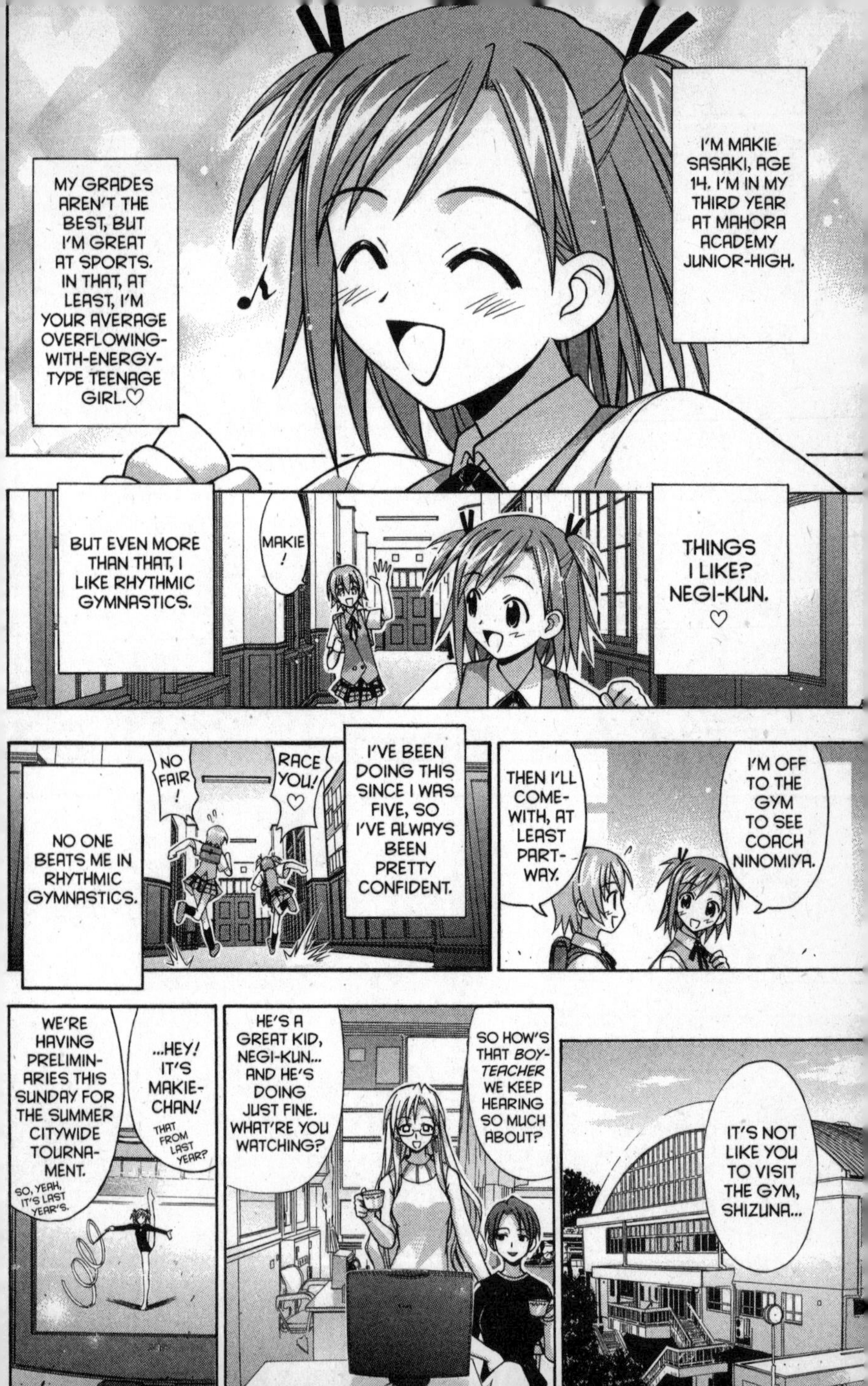
I'M MAKIE SASAKI, AGE 14. I'M IN MY THIRD YEAR AT MAHORA ACADEMY JUNIOR-HIGH.
MY GRADES AREN'T THE BEST, BUT I'M GREAT AT SPORTS. IN THAT, AT LEAST, I'M YOUR AVERAGE OVERFLOWING-WITH-ENERGY-TYPE TEENAGE GIRL.♡
THINGS I LIKE? NEGI-KUN. ♡
MAKIE!
BUT EVEN MORE THAN THAT, I LIKE RHYTHMIC GYMNASTICS.
I'M OFF TO THE GYM TO SEE COACH NINOMIYA.
THEN I'LL COME-WITH, AT LEAST PART-WAY.
I'VE BEEN DOING THIS SINCE I WAS FIVE, SO I'VE ALWAYS BEEN PRETTY CONFIDENT.
RACE YOU! ♡
NO FAIR!
NO ONE BEATS ME IN RHYTHMIC GYMNASTICS.
IT'S NOT LIKE YOU TO VISIT THE GYM, SHIZUNA...
SO HOW'S THAT *BOY-TEACHER* WE KEEP HEARING SO MUCH ABOUT?
HE'S A GREAT KID, NEGI-KUN... AND HE'S DOING JUST FINE. WHAT'RE YOU WATCHING?
...HEY! IT'S MAKIE-CHAN!
THAT FROM LAST YEAR?
WE'RE HAVING PRELIMINARIES THIS SUNDAY FOR THE SUMMER CITYWIDE TOURNAMENT.
SO, YEAH, IT'S LAST YEAR'S.

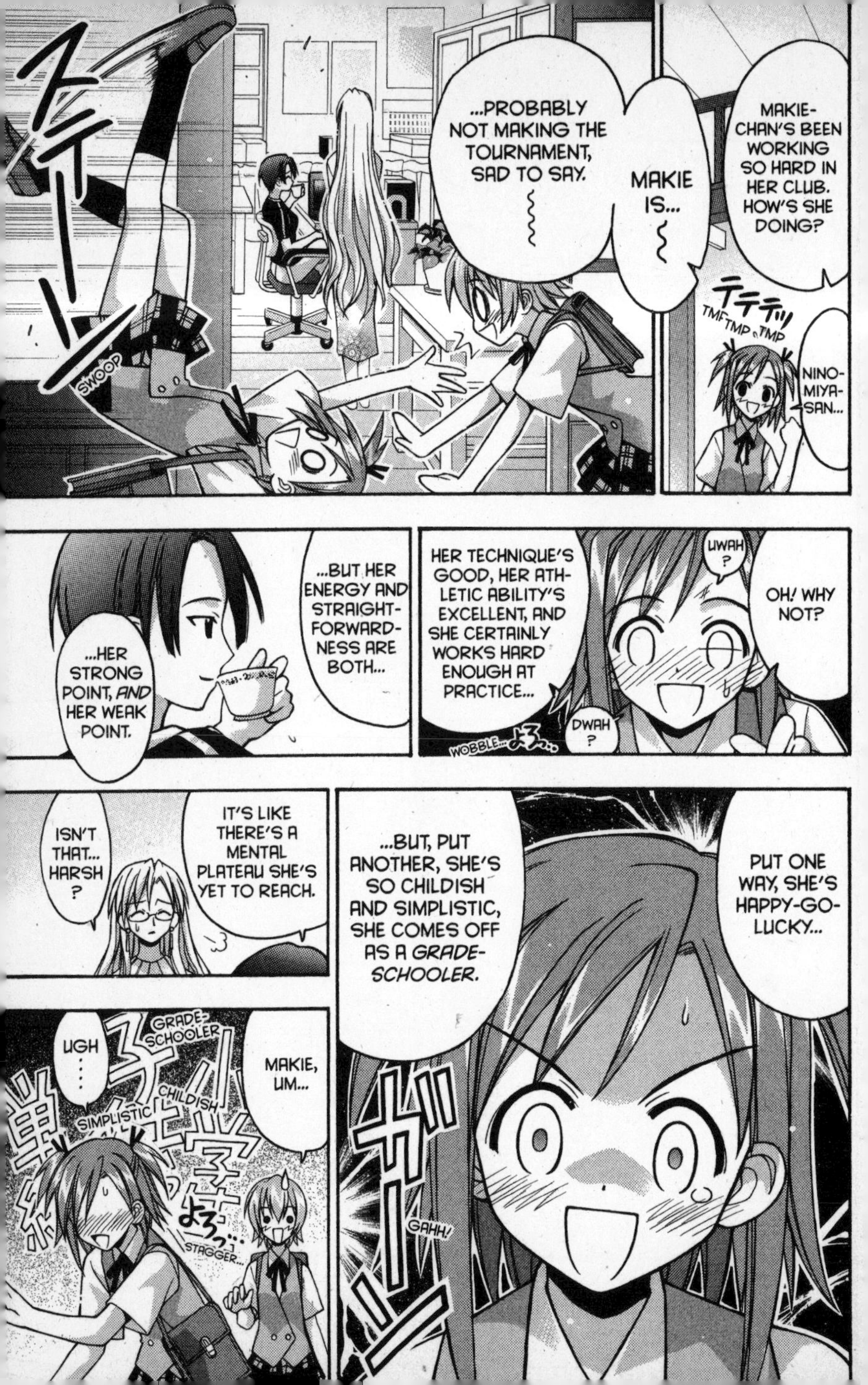
MAKIE-CHAN'S BEEN WORKING SO HARD IN HER CLUB. HOW'S SHE DOING?
テテテッ
TMP TMP TMP
NINO-MIYA-SAN...
MAKIE IS...
...PROBABLY NOT MAKING THE TOURNAMENT, SAD TO SAY.
SWOOP
OH! WHY NOT?
UWAH ?
HER TECHNIQUE'S GOOD, HER ATH-LETIC ABILITY'S EXCELLENT, AND SHE CERTAINLY WORKS HARD ENOUGH AT PRACTICE...
DWAH ?
WOBBLE... よろっ...
...BUT HER ENERGY AND STRAIGHT-FORWARD-NESS ARE BOTH...
...HER STRONG POINT, *AND* HER WEAK POINT.
PUT ONE WAY, SHE'S HAPPY-GO-LUCKY...
...BUT, PUT ANOTHER, SHE'S SO CHILDISH AND SIMPLISTIC, SHE COMES OFF AS A *GRADE-SCHOOLER*.
GAHH!
IT'S LIKE THERE'S A MENTAL PLATEAU SHE'S YET TO REACH.
ISN'T THAT... HARSH ?
MAKIE, UM...
UGH.....
GRADE-SCHOOLER
CHILDISH
SIMPLISTIC
よろっ
STAGGER...

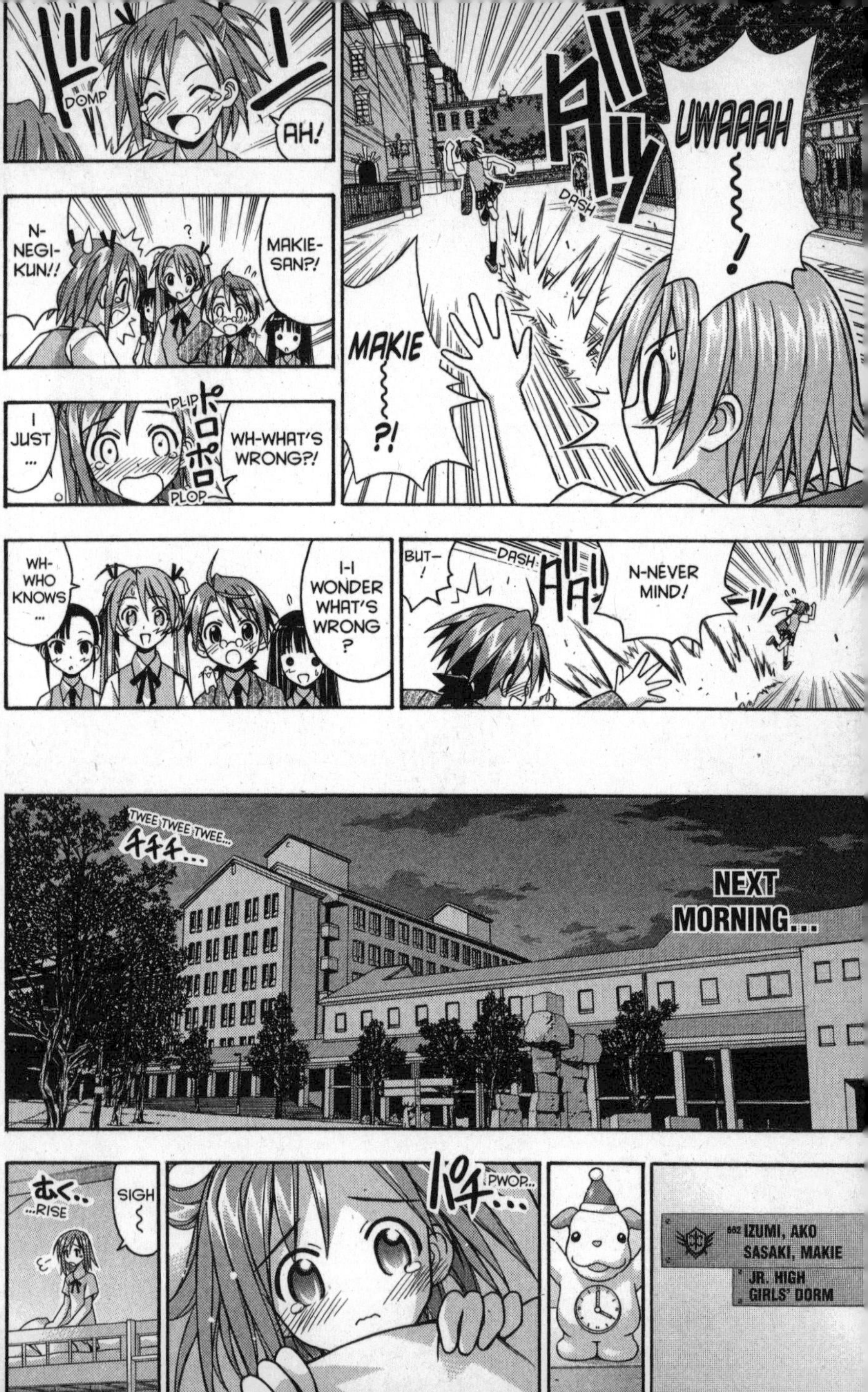
UWAAAH ~!
DASH
MAKIE ~?!
AH!
DOMP
MAKIE-SAN?!
?
N-NEGI-KUN!!
WH-WHAT'S WRONG?!
PLIP
ポロポロ
PLOP
I JUST ...
N-NEVER MIND!
DASH
BUT-!
I-I WONDER WHAT'S WRONG?
WH-WHO KNOWS ...
NEXT MORNING...
TWEE TWEE TWEE...
チチチ...
662 IZUMI, AKO
SASAKI, MAKIE
JR. HIGH GIRLS' DORM
PWOP...
パチ...
SIGH ~
むく..
...RISE

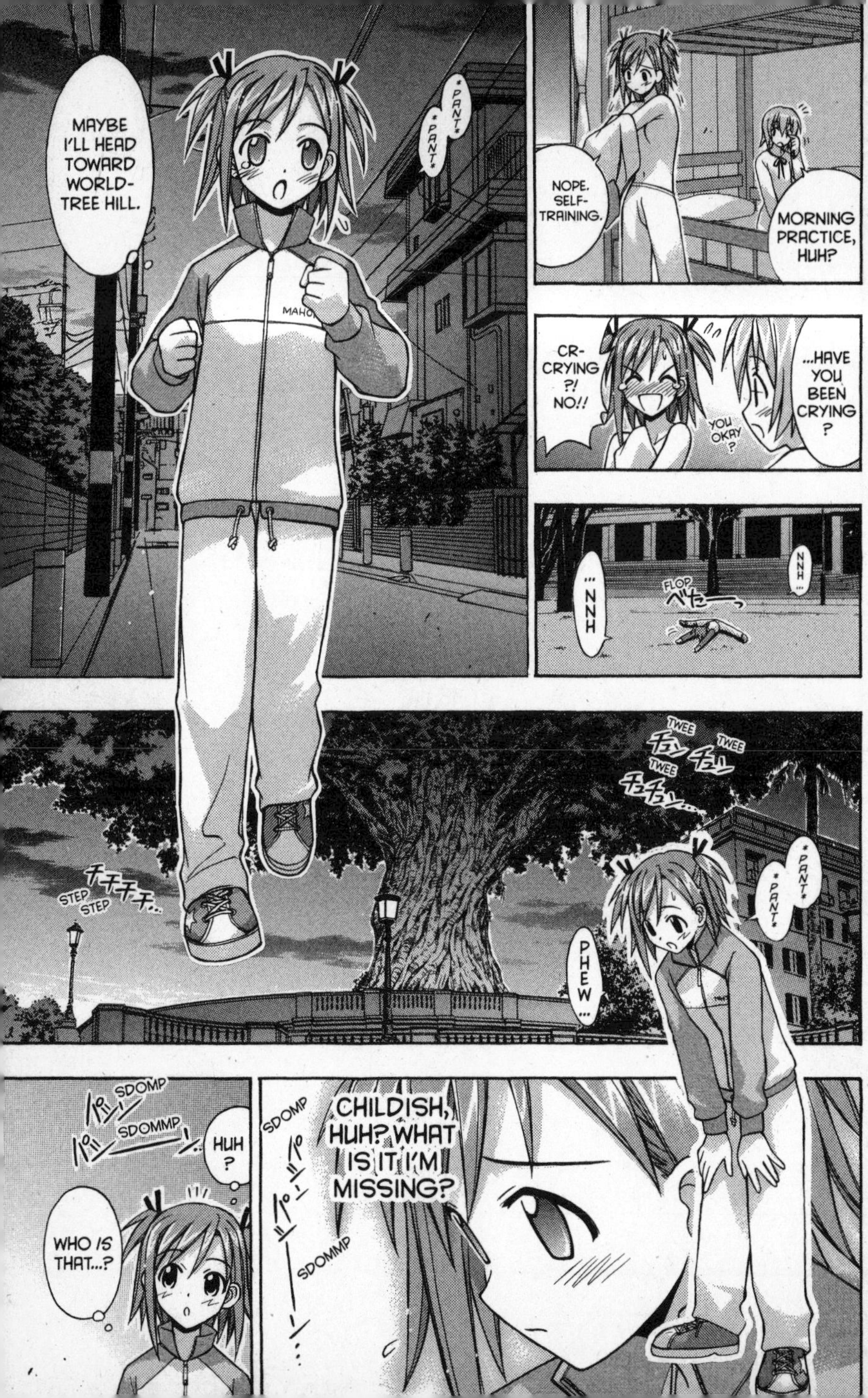
MORNING PRACTICE, HUH?
NOPE. SELF-TRAINING.
...HAVE YOU BEEN CRYING?
YOU OKAY?
CR-CRYING?! NO!!
NNH...
FLOP
...NNH
PANT *PANT*
MAYBE I'LL HEAD TOWARD WORLD-TREE HILL.
MAHO
TWEE TWEE TWEE
PANT *PANT*
PHEW...
STEP STEP
CHILDISH, HUH? WHAT IS IT I'M MISSING?
SDOMP
SDOMMP
SDOMP
SDOMMP
HUH?
WHO IS THAT...?

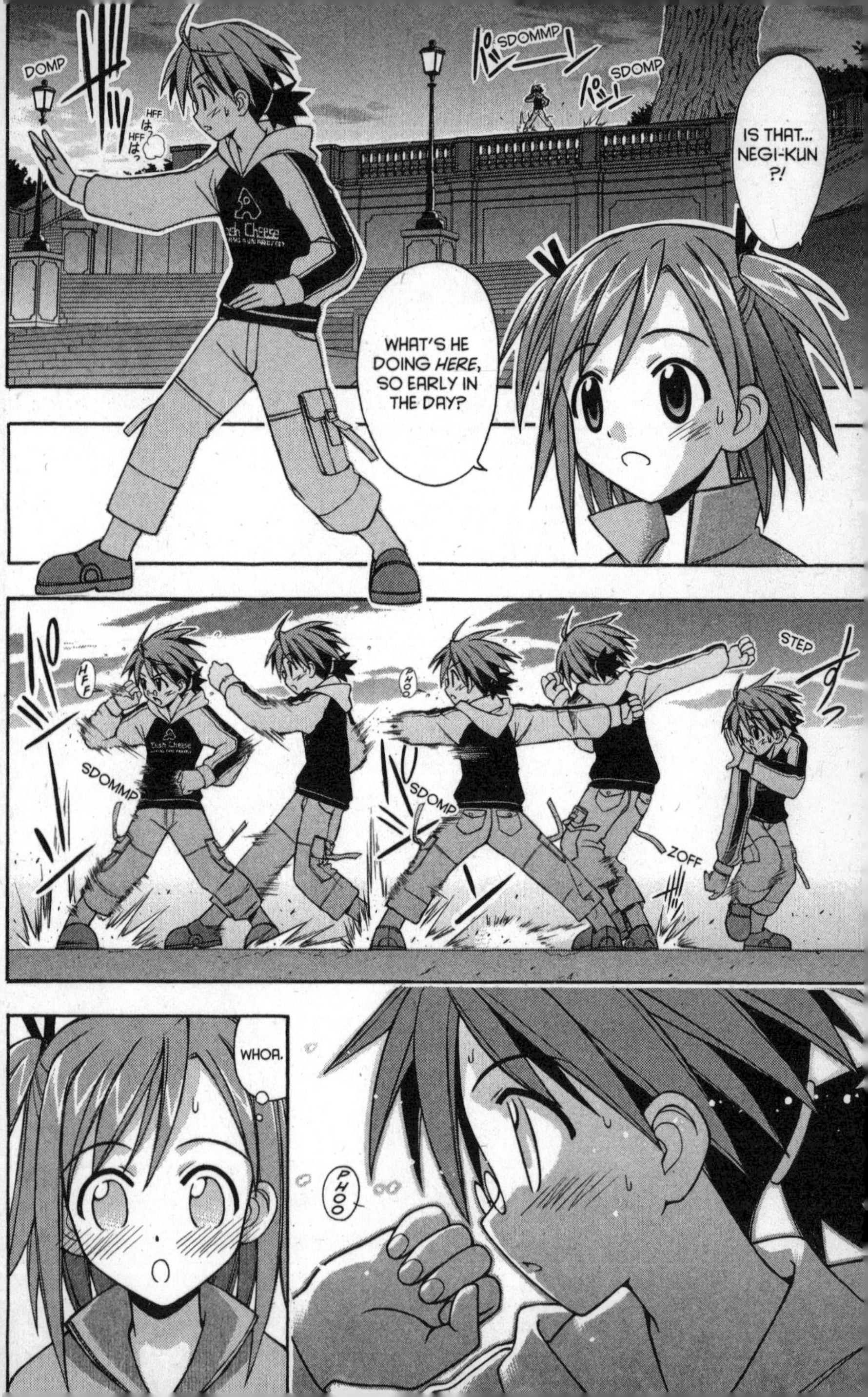
SDOMP
SDOMMP
IS THAT... NEGI-KUN ?!
WHAT'S HE DOING HERE, SO EARLY IN THE DAY?
HFF
HFF
DOMP
STEP
ZOFF
SDOMP
PHOO
SDOMMP
HFF
PHOO
WHOA.

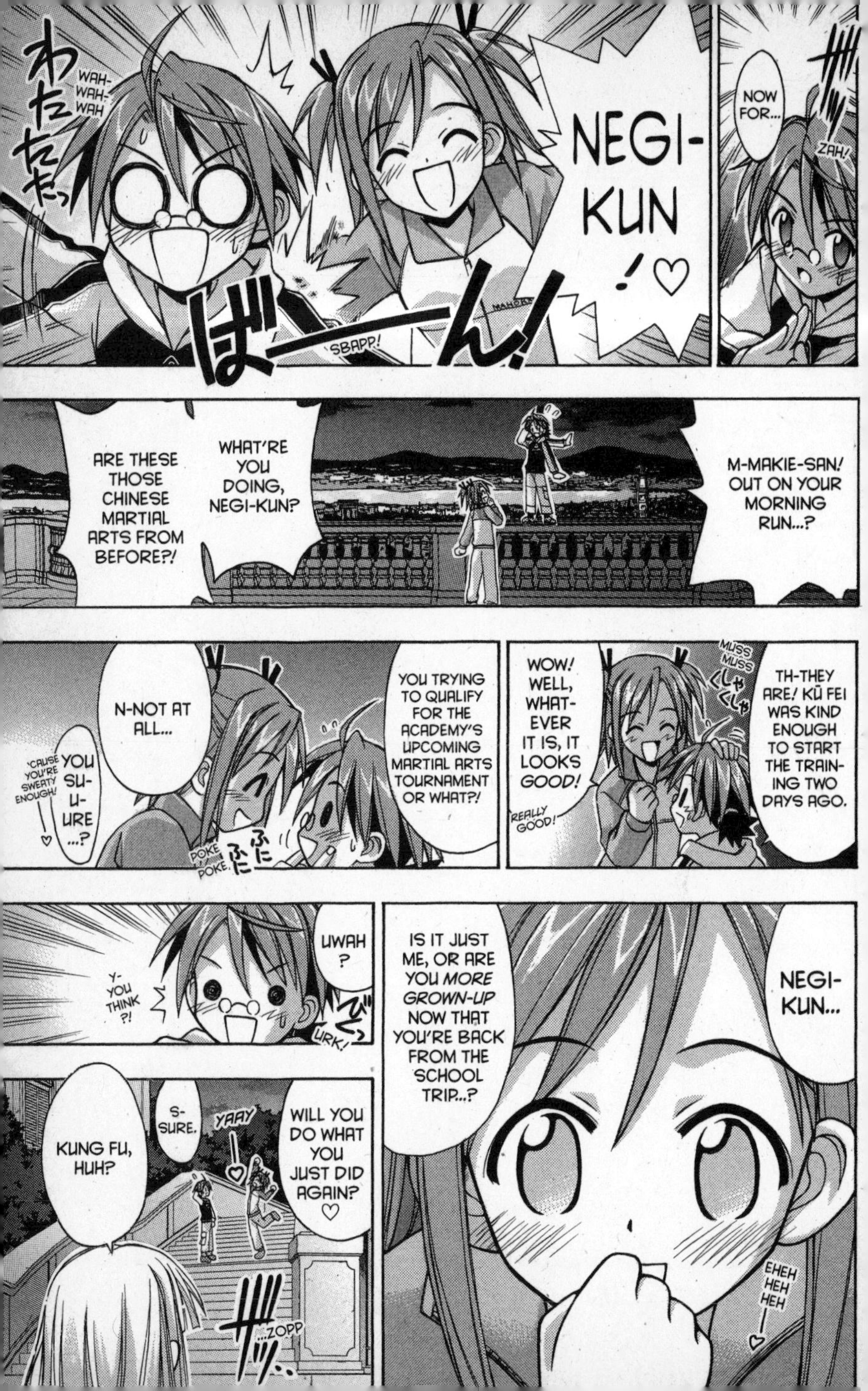
NOW FOR...
ZAH!
NEGI-KUN!♡
WAH-WAH-WAH
わたたたっ
ばーん!
SBAPP!
M-MAKIE-SAN! OUT ON YOUR MORNING RUN...?
WHAT'RE YOU DOING, NEGI-KUN?
ARE THESE THOSE CHINESE MARTIAL ARTS FROM BEFORE?!
TH-THEY ARE! KŪ FEI WAS KIND ENOUGH TO START THE TRAINING TWO DAYS AGO.
MUSS MUSS
くしゃくしゃ
WOW! WELL, WHATEVER IT IS, IT LOOKS *GOOD!*
REALLY GOOD!
YOU TRYING TO QUALIFY FOR THE ACADEMY'S UPCOMING MARTIAL ARTS TOURNAMENT OR WHAT?!
N-NOT AT ALL...
ふにふに
POKE POKE
YOU SU-U-URE...?
'CAUSE YOU'RE SWEATY ENOUGH! ♡
NEGI-KUN...
IS IT JUST ME, OR ARE YOU *MORE GROWN-UP* NOW THAT YOU'RE BACK FROM THE SCHOOL TRIP...?
EHEH HEH HEH ♡
UWAH?
びくっ
URK!
Y-YOU THINK?!
WILL YOU DO WHAT YOU JUST DID AGAIN? ♡
YAAY ♡
S-SURE.
KUNG FU, HUH?
ザッ
...ZOPP

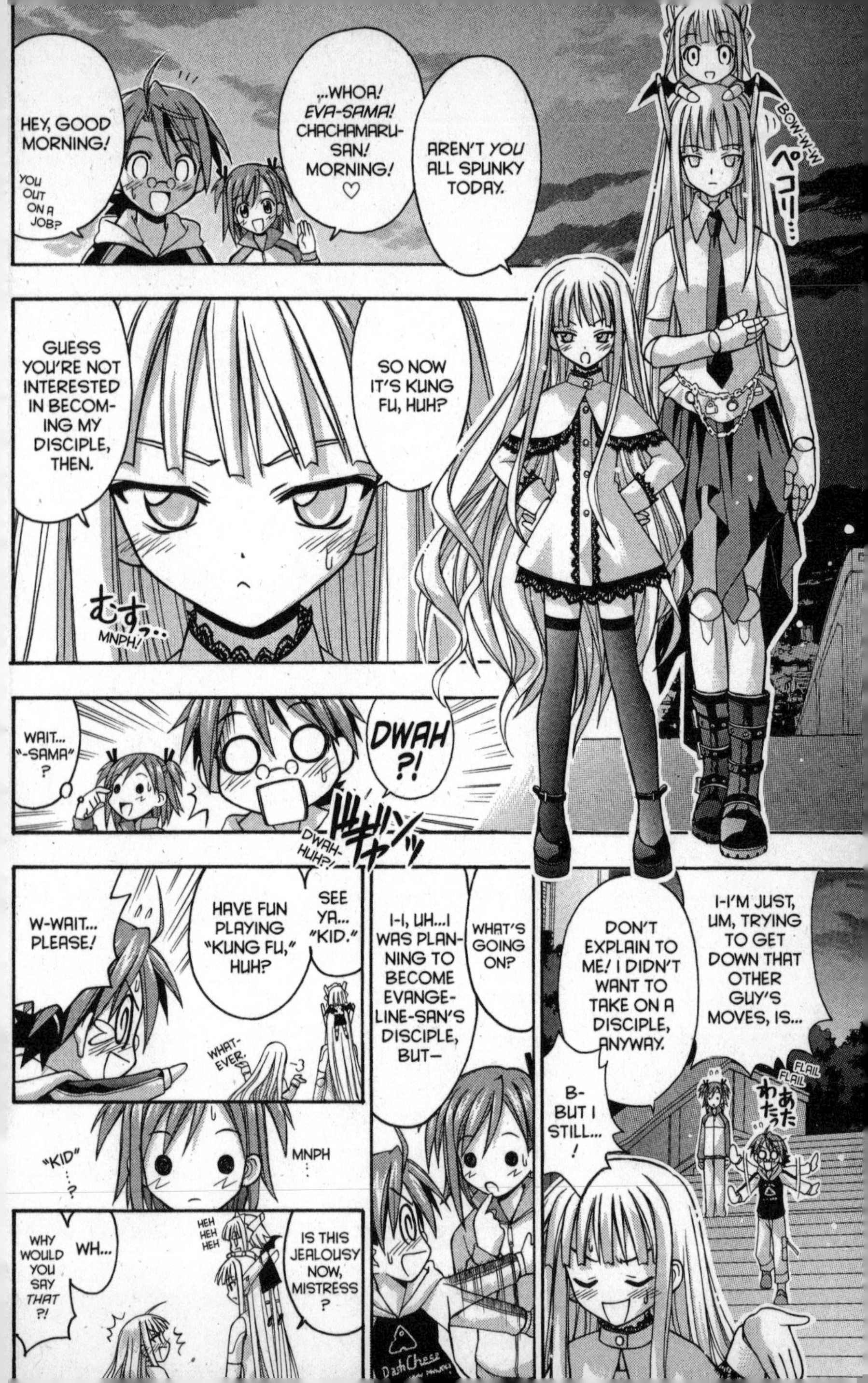

HEY, GOOD MORNING!
YOU OUT ON A JOB?
...WHOA! EVA-SAMA! CHACHAMARU-SAN! MORNING! ♡
AREN'T YOU ALL SPUNKY TODAY.
BOW-W-W
ペコリ!!…
SO NOW IT'S KUNG FU, HUH?
GUESS YOU'RE NOT INTERESTED IN BECOMING MY DISCIPLE, THEN.
むすっ…
MNPH!
DWAH ?!
DWAH-HUH?!
WAIT... "-SAMA" ?
I-I'M JUST, UM, TRYING TO GET DOWN THAT OTHER GUY'S MOVES, IS...
DON'T EXPLAIN TO ME! I DIDN'T WANT TO TAKE ON A DISCIPLE, ANYWAY.
B- BUT I STILL... !
FLAIL FLAIL
WHAT'S GOING ON?
I-I, UH...I WAS PLANNING TO BECOME EVANGELINE-SAN'S DISCIPLE, BUT—
SEE YA... "KID."
HAVE FUN PLAYING "KUNG FU," HUH?
W-WAIT... PLEASE!
WHAT-EVER.
MNPH ...
"KID" ...?
IS THIS JEALOUSY NOW, MISTRESS ?
HEH HEH HEH
WH...
WHY WOULD YOU SAY THAT ?!

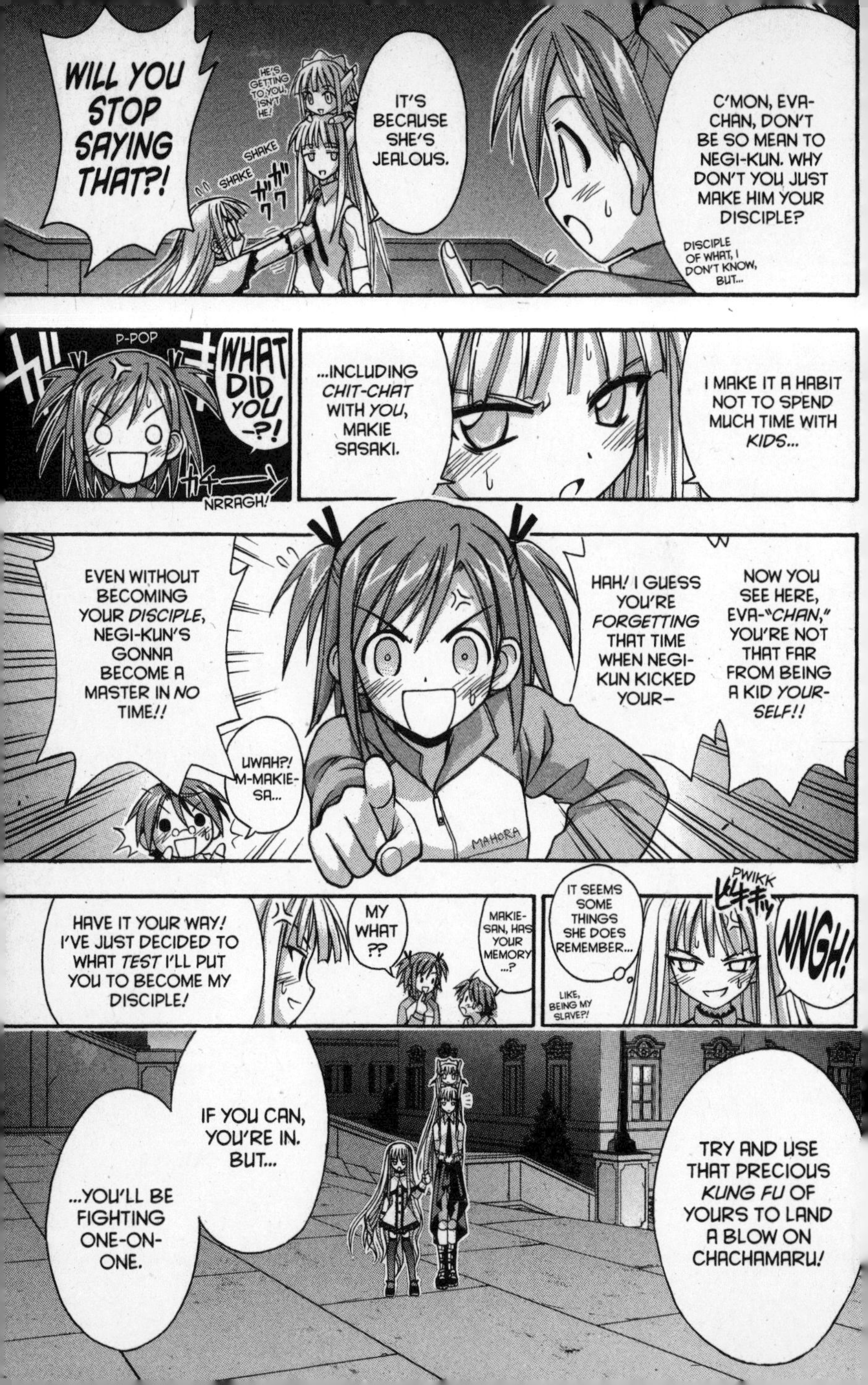
C'MON, EVA-CHAN, DON'T BE SO MEAN TO NEGI-KUN. WHY DON'T YOU JUST MAKE HIM YOUR DISCIPLE?
DISCIPLE OF WHAT, I DON'T KNOW, BUT...
IT'S BECAUSE SHE'S JEALOUS.
HE'S GETTING TO YOU, ISN'T HE!
SHAKE
SHAKE
WILL YOU STOP SAYING THAT?!
I MAKE IT A HABIT NOT TO SPEND MUCH TIME WITH *KIDS*...
...INCLUDING *CHIT-CHAT* WITH *YOU*, MAKIE SASAKI.
P-POP
WHAT DID YOU—?!
NRRAGH!
NOW YOU SEE HERE, EVA-"*CHAN*," YOU'RE NOT THAT FAR FROM BEING A KID *YOURSELF*!!
HAH! I GUESS YOU'RE *FORGETTING* THAT TIME WHEN NEGI-KUN KICKED YOUR—
EVEN WITHOUT BECOMING YOUR *DISCIPLE*, NEGI-KUN'S GONNA BECOME A MASTER IN *NO* TIME!!
UWAH?! M-MAKIE-SA...
MAHORA
PWIKK
NNGH!
IT SEEMS SOME THINGS SHE DOES REMEMBER...
LIKE, BEING MY SLAVE?!
MAKIE-SAN, HAS YOUR MEMORY ...?
MY WHAT ??
HAVE IT YOUR WAY! I'VE JUST DECIDED TO WHAT *TEST* I'LL PUT YOU TO BECOME MY DISCIPLE!
TRY AND USE THAT PRECIOUS *KUNG FU* OF YOURS TO LAND A BLOW ON CHACHAMARU!
IF YOU CAN, YOU'RE IN. BUT...
...YOU'LL BE FIGHTING ONE-ON-ONE.

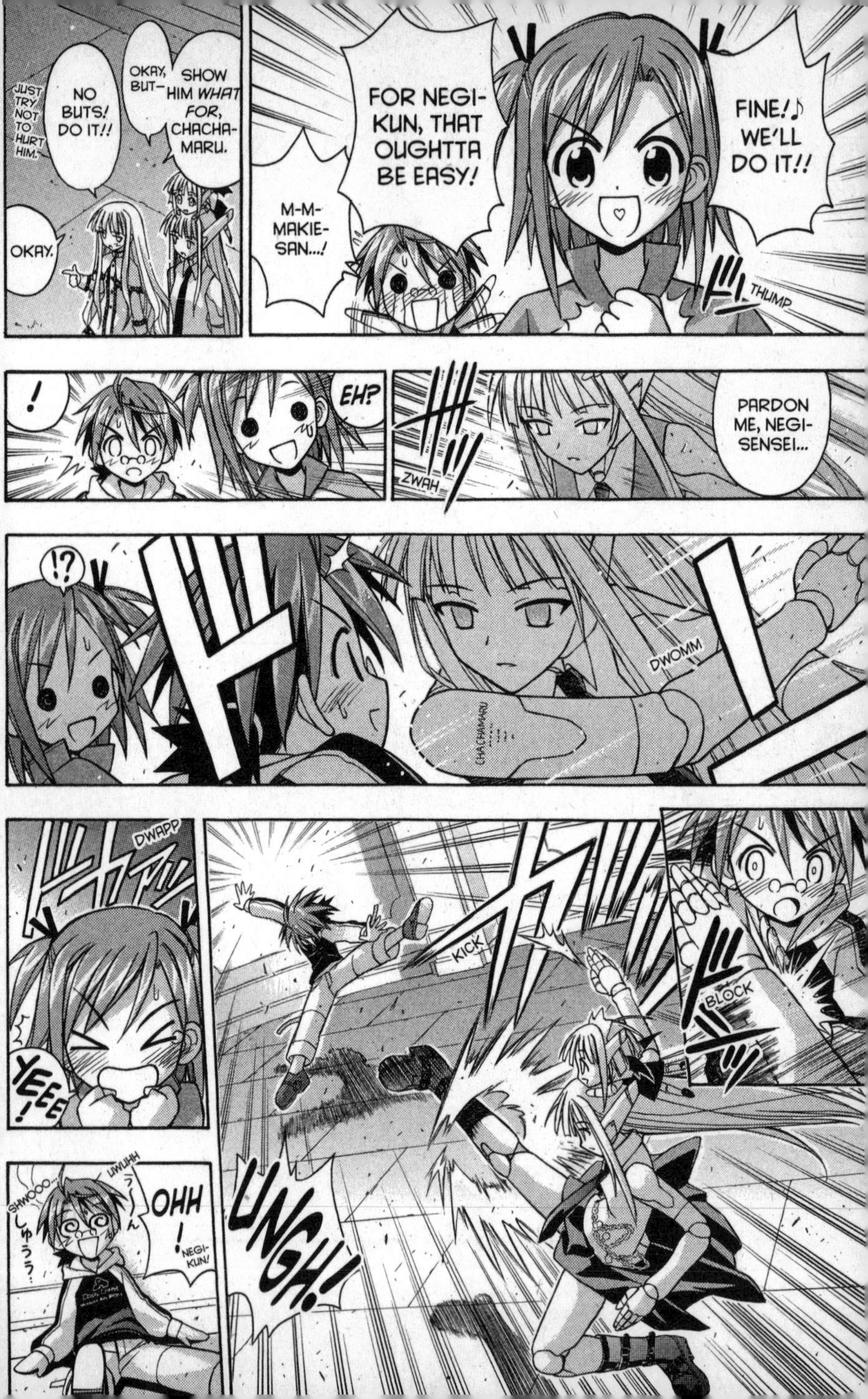
FINE!♪ WE'LL DO IT!!
FOR NEGI-KUN, THAT OUGHTTA BE EASY!
M-M-MAKIE-SAN...!
THUMP
SHOW HIM WHAT FOR, CHACHAMARU.
OKAY, BUT—
NO BUTS! DO IT!!
JUST TRY NOT TO HURT HIM.
OKAY.
PARDON ME, NEGI-SENSEI...
ZWAH
EH?
!
DWOMM
CHACHAMARU
!?
BLOCK
KICK
UNGH!
DWAPP
YEEE!
OHH! NEGI-KUN!
UWUHH
SHWOOO...

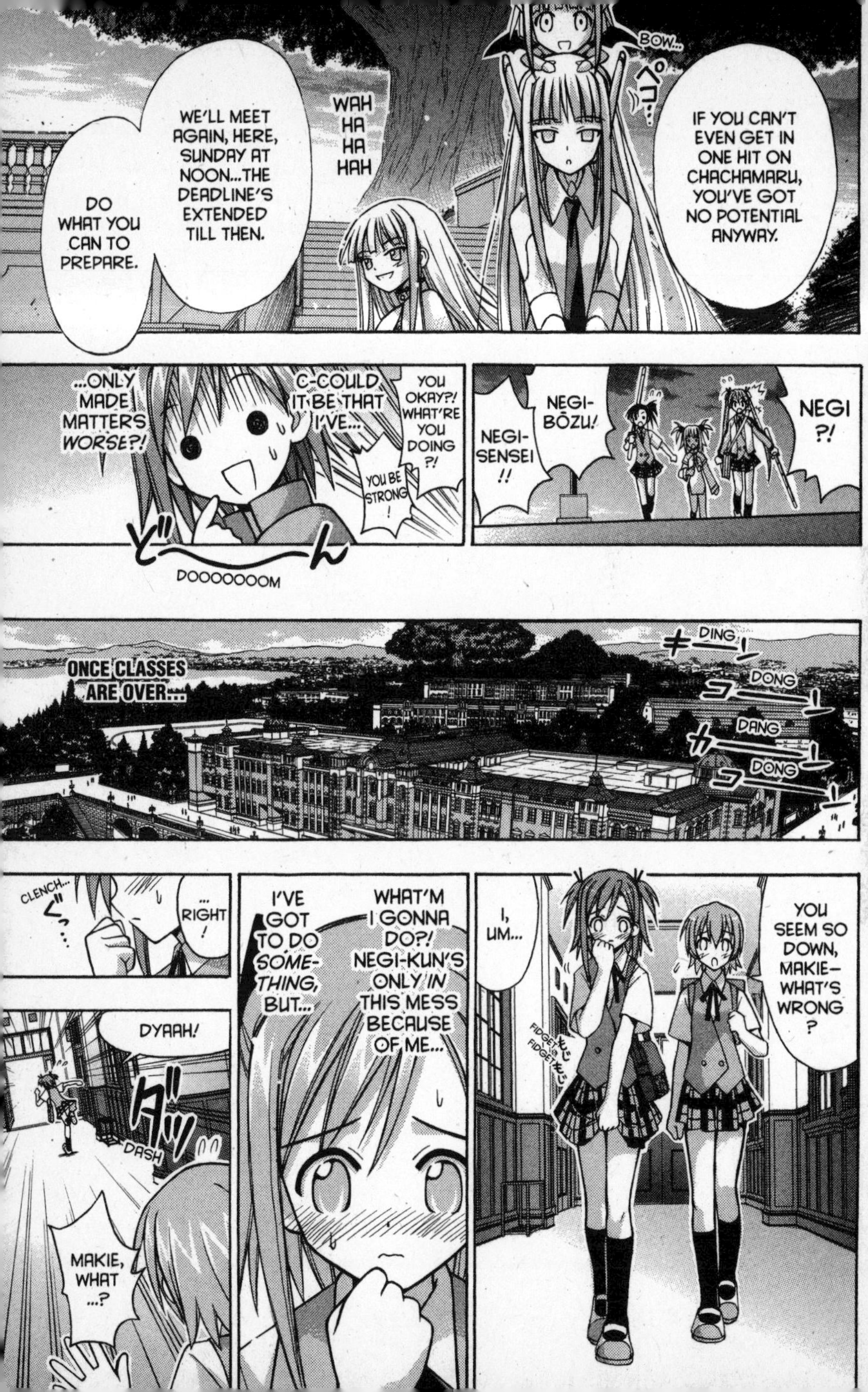
BOW...
IF YOU CAN'T EVEN GET IN ONE HIT ON CHACHAMARU, YOU'VE GOT NO POTENTIAL ANYWAY.
WAH HA HA HAH
WE'LL MEET AGAIN, HERE, SUNDAY AT NOON...THE DEADLINE'S EXTENDED TILL THEN.
DO WHAT YOU CAN TO PREPARE.
NEGI ?!
NEGI-BŌZU!
NEGI-SENSEI !!
YOU OKAY?! WHAT'RE YOU DOING ?!
YOU BE STRONG !
C-COULD IT BE THAT I'VE...
...ONLY MADE MATTERS *WORSE*?!
DOOOOOOOM
DING
DONG
DANG
DONG
ONCE CLASSES ARE OVER...
YOU SEEM SO DOWN, MAKIE—WHAT'S WRONG ?
I, UM...
FIDGET FIDGET
WHAT'M I GONNA DO?! NEGI-KUN'S ONLY *IN* THIS MESS BECAUSE OF ME...
I'VE GOT TO DO *SOME-THING*, BUT...
... RIGHT !
CLENCH...
DYAAH!
DASH
MAKIE, WHAT ...?

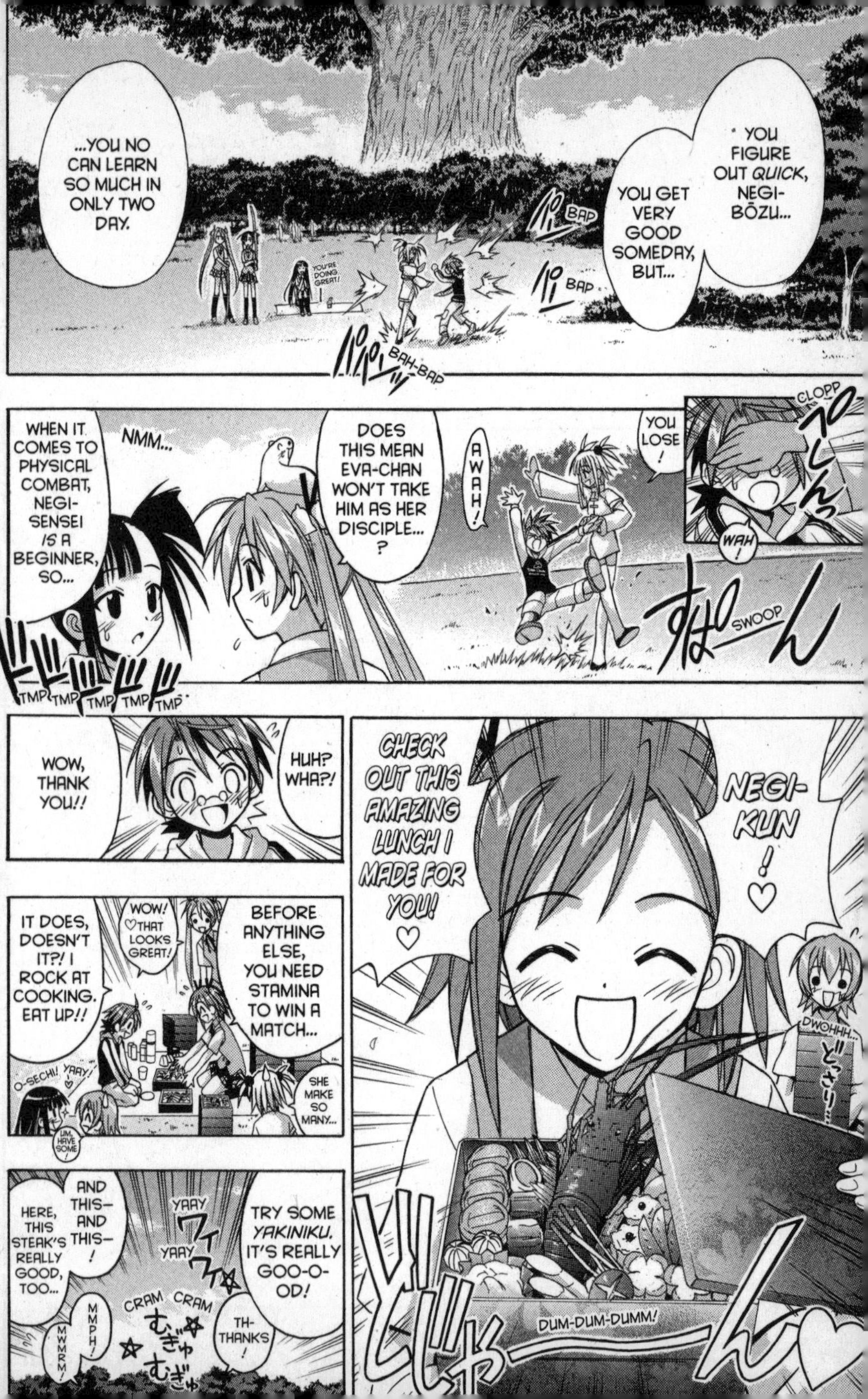
YOU FIGURE OUT *QUICK*, NEGI-BŌZU...
YOU GET VERY GOOD SOMEDAY, BUT...
BAP
BAP
YOU'RE DOING GREAT!
BAH-BAP
...YOU NO CAN LEARN SO MUCH IN ONLY TWO DAY.
CLOPP
YOU LOSE!
WAH!
AWAH!
SWOOP
DOES THIS MEAN EVA-CHAN WON'T TAKE HIM AS HER DISCIPLE...?
NMM...
WHEN IT COMES TO PHYSICAL COMBAT, NEGI-SENSEI *IS* A BEGINNER, SO...
TMP TMP TMP TMP TMP
NEGI-KUN! ♡
CHECK OUT THIS AMAZING LUNCH I MADE FOR YOU! ♡
DWOHHH...
DUM-DUM-DUMM!
HUH? WHA?!
WOW, THANK YOU!!
BEFORE ANYTHING ELSE, YOU NEED STAMINA TO WIN A MATCH...
WOW! ♡THAT LOOKS GREAT!
IT DOES, DOESN'T IT?! I ROCK AT COOKING. EAT UP!!
SHE MAKE SO MANY...
O-SECHI! YAAY! ♡
UM, HAVE SOME!
TRY SOME *YAKINIKU*. IT'S REALLY GOO-O-OD!
YAAY
YAAY
AND THIS— AND THIS—!
HERE, THIS STEAK'S REALLY GOOD, TOO...
TH-THANKS!
CRAM CRAM
MMPH!
MWMRM!

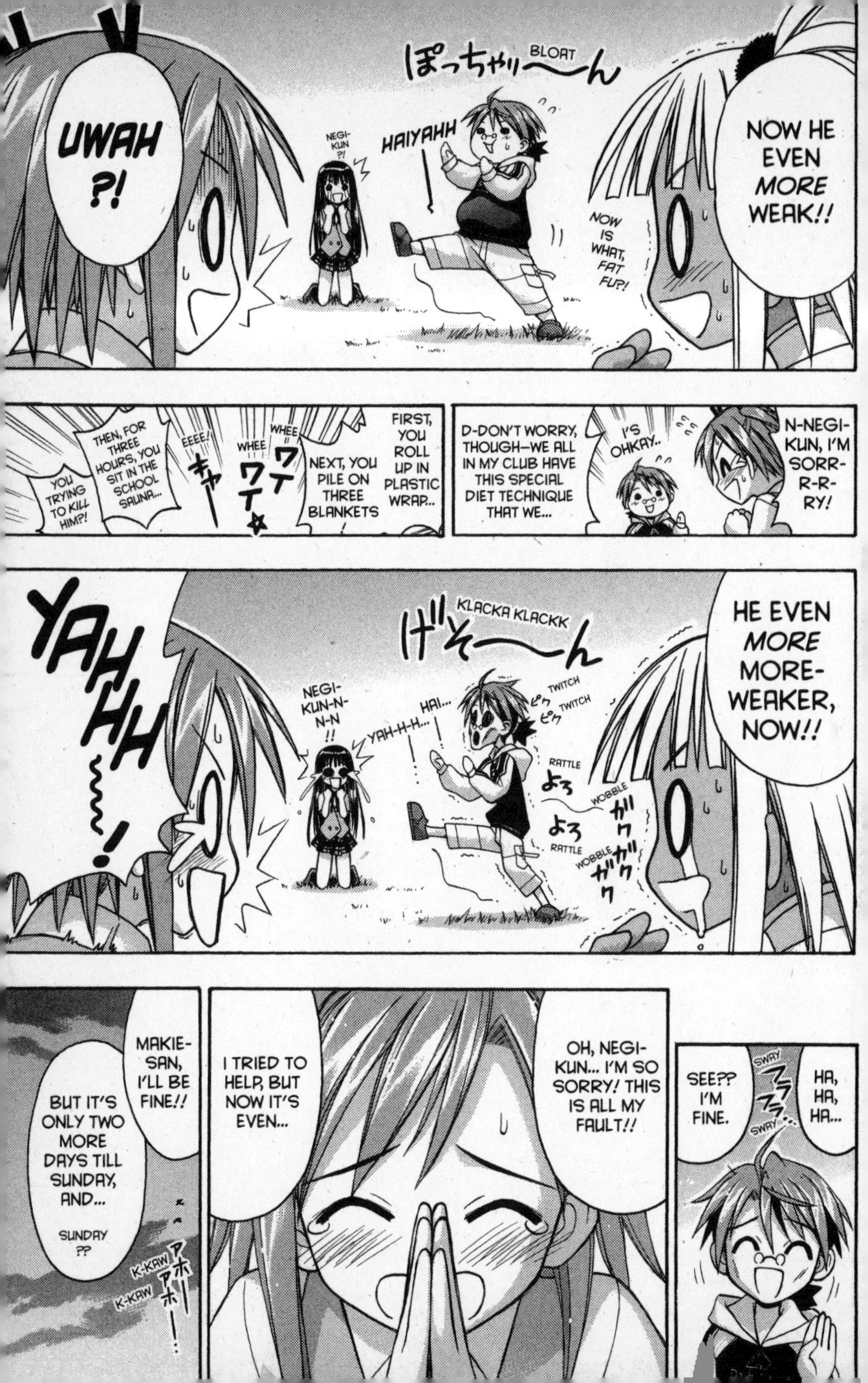
NOW HE EVEN MORE WEAK!!
NOW IS WHAT, FAT FU?!
ぽっちゃり～ん BLOAT
HAIYAHH
NEGI-KUN ?!
UWAH ?!
N-NEGI-KUN, I'M SORR-R-R-RY!
I'S OHKAY..
D-DON'T WORRY, THOUGH—WE ALL IN MY CLUB HAVE THIS SPECIAL DIET TECHNIQUE THAT WE...
FIRST, YOU ROLL UP IN PLASTIC WRAP...
NEXT, YOU PILE ON THREE BLANKETS
ワイワイ WHEE WHEE
キャー EEEE!
THEN, FOR THREE HOURS, YOU SIT IN THE SCHOOL SAUNA...
YOU TRYING TO KILL HIM?!
HE EVEN MORE MORE-WEAKER, NOW!!
げそ～ん KLACKA KLACKK
ピク TWITCH ピク TWITCH
よろ RATTLE よろ RATTLE
ガクガクガク WOBBLE WOBBLE
HAI...
YAH-H-H...
NEGI-KUN-N-N !!
YAHHH～!
HA, HA, HA...
フラフラ SWAY SWAY
SEE?? I'M FINE.
OH, NEGI-KUN... I'M SO SORRY! THIS IS ALL MY FAULT!!
I TRIED TO HELP, BUT NOW IT'S EVEN...
MAKIE-SAN, I'LL BE FINE!!
BUT IT'S ONLY TWO MORE DAYS TILL SUNDAY, AND...
SUNDAY ??
アホー K-KAW アホー K-KAW

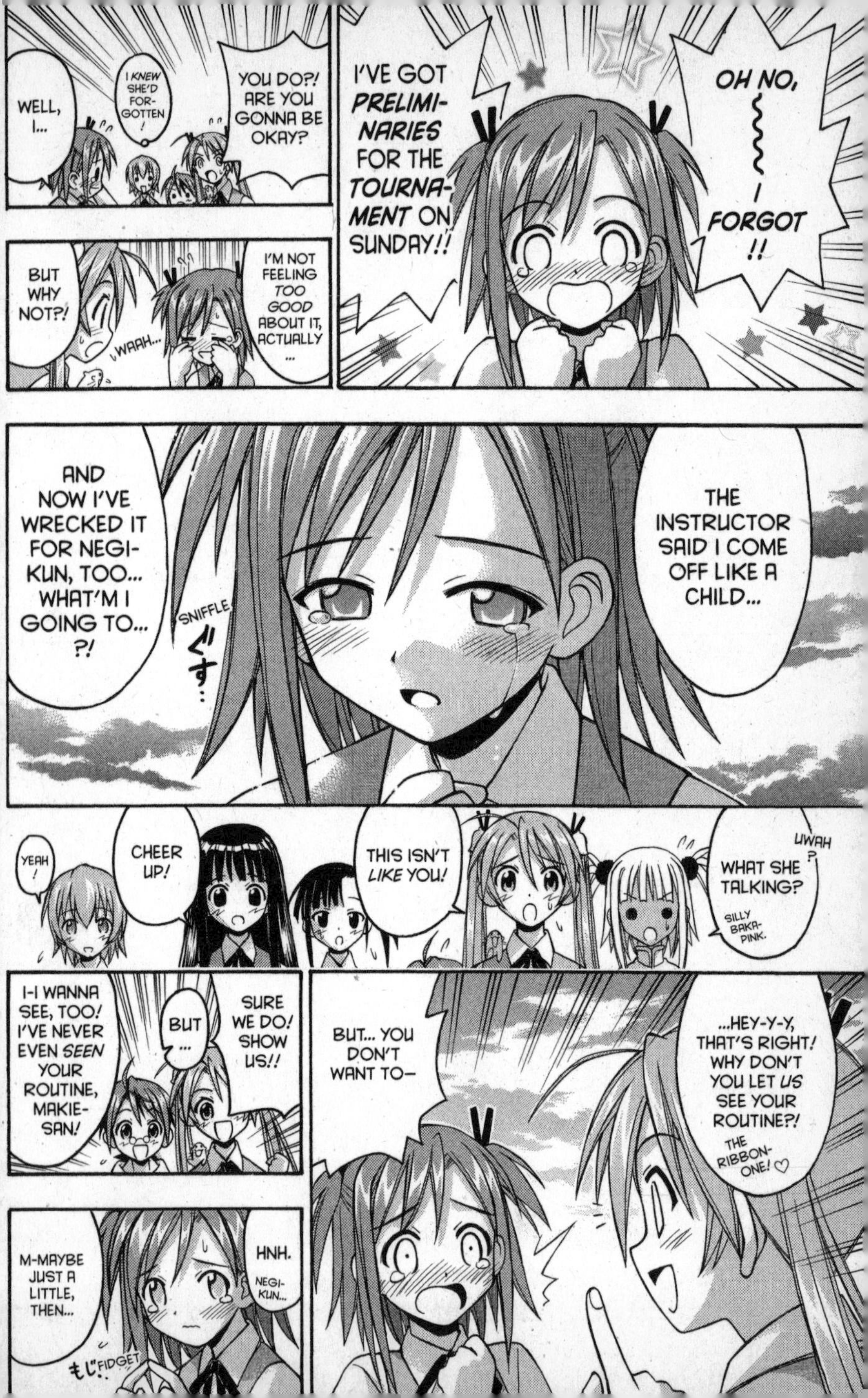
OH NO, ~~~ I FORGOT !!
I'VE GOT *PRELIMINARIES* FOR THE *TOURNAMENT* ON SUNDAY!!
YOU DO?! ARE YOU GONNA BE OKAY?
I *KNEW* SHE'D FORGOTTEN!
WELL, I...
I'M NOT FEELING *TOO GOOD* ABOUT IT, ACTUALLY...
WAAAH...
BUT WHY NOT?!
THE INSTRUCTOR SAID I COME OFF LIKE A CHILD...
SNIFFLE
ぐす
AND NOW I'VE WRECKED IT FOR NEGI-KUN, TOO... WHAT'M I GOING TO...?!
UWAH?
WHAT SHE TALKING?
SILLY BAKA-PINK.
THIS ISN'T *LIKE* YOU!
CHEER UP!
YEAH!
...HEY-Y-Y, THAT'S RIGHT! WHY DON'T YOU LET *US* SEE YOUR ROUTINE?!
THE RIBBON-ONE! ♡
BUT... YOU DON'T WANT TO—
SURE WE DO! SHOW US!!
BUT...
I-I WANNA SEE, TOO! I'VE NEVER EVEN *SEEN* YOUR ROUTINE, MAKIE-SAN!
HNH.
NEGI-KUN...
M-MAYBE JUST A LITTLE, THEN...
もじ FIDGET

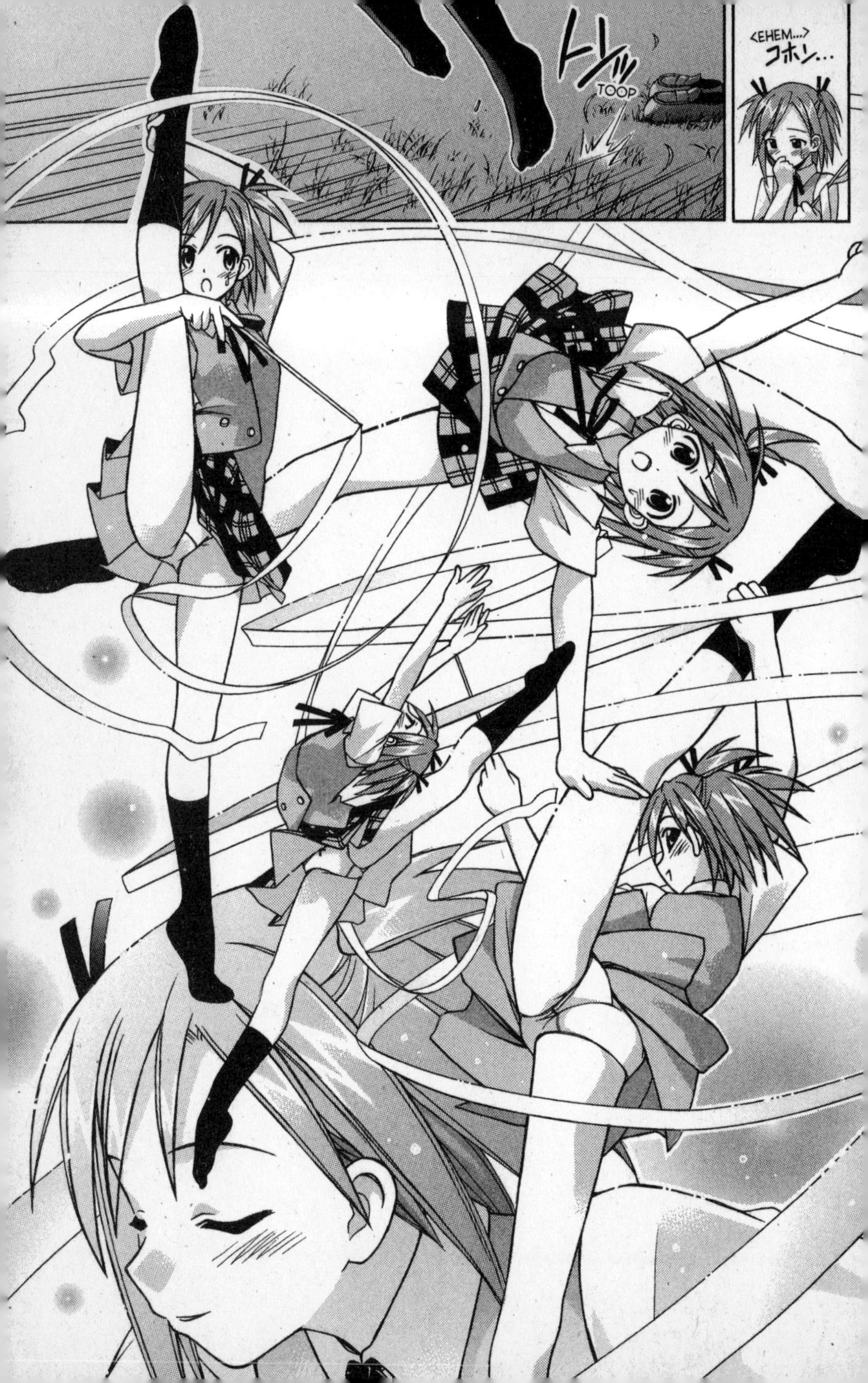
<EHEM...>
コホン…
トンッ
TOOP

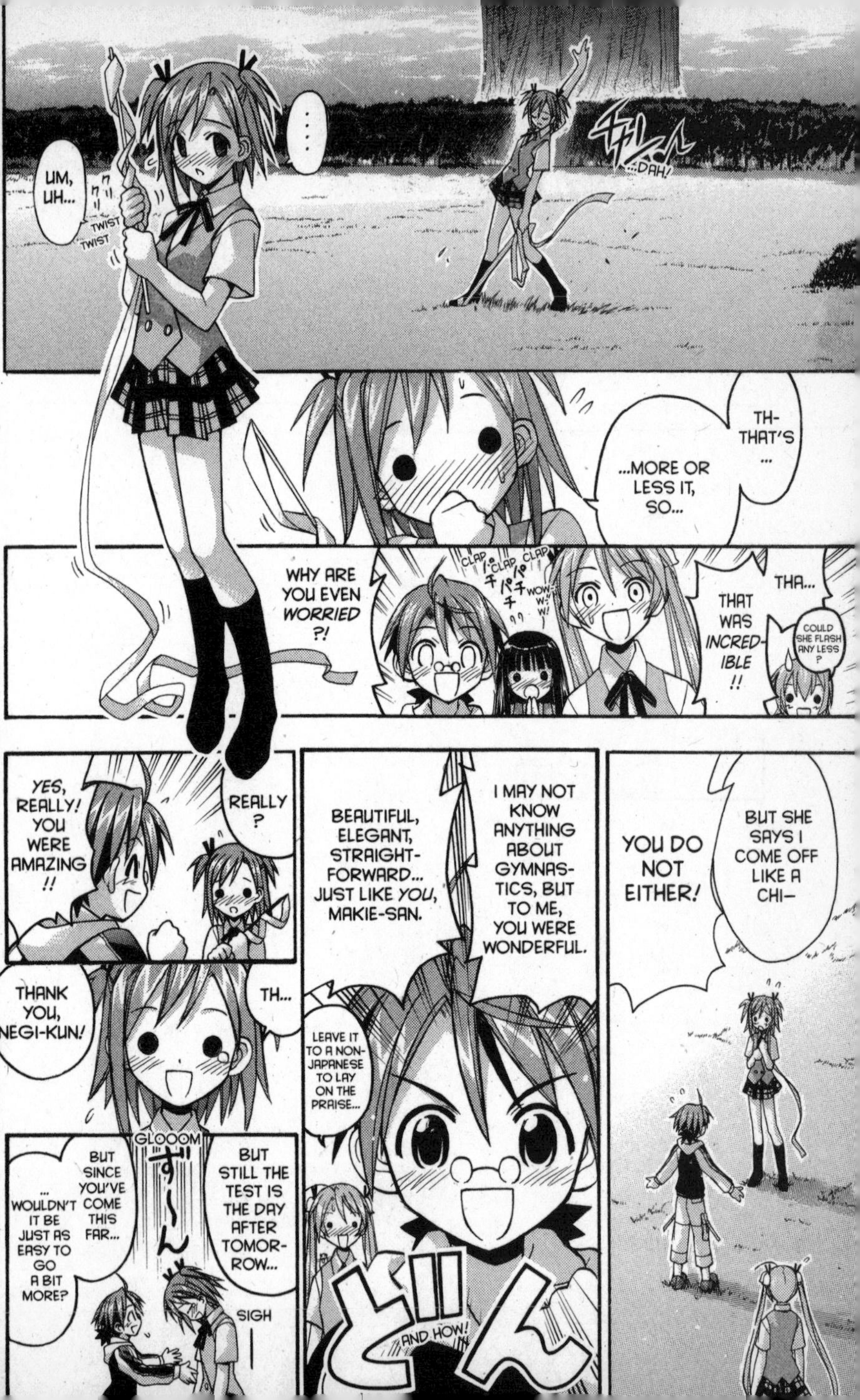

...DAH!
...
UM, UH...
TWIST TWIST
TH- THAT'S ...
...MORE OR LESS IT, SO...
THA...
THAT WAS INCREDIBLE!!
COULD SHE FLASH ANY LESS?
CLAP CLAP CLAP
WOW-W!
WHY ARE YOU EVEN WORRIED?!
BUT SHE SAYS I COME OFF LIKE A CHI—
YOU DO NOT EITHER!
I MAY NOT KNOW ANYTHING ABOUT GYMNASTICS, BUT TO ME, YOU WERE WONDERFUL.
BEAUTIFUL, ELEGANT, STRAIGHT-FORWARD... JUST LIKE YOU, MAKIE-SAN.
LEAVE IT TO A NON-JAPANESE TO LAY ON THE PRAISE...
AND HOW!
REALLY?
YES, REALLY! YOU WERE AMAZING!!
TH...
THANK YOU, NEGI-KUN!
BUT STILL THE TEST IS THE DAY AFTER TOMORROW...
GLOOOM
BUT SINCE YOU'VE COME THIS FAR...
...WOULDN'T IT BE JUST AS EASY TO GO A BIT MORE?
SIGH

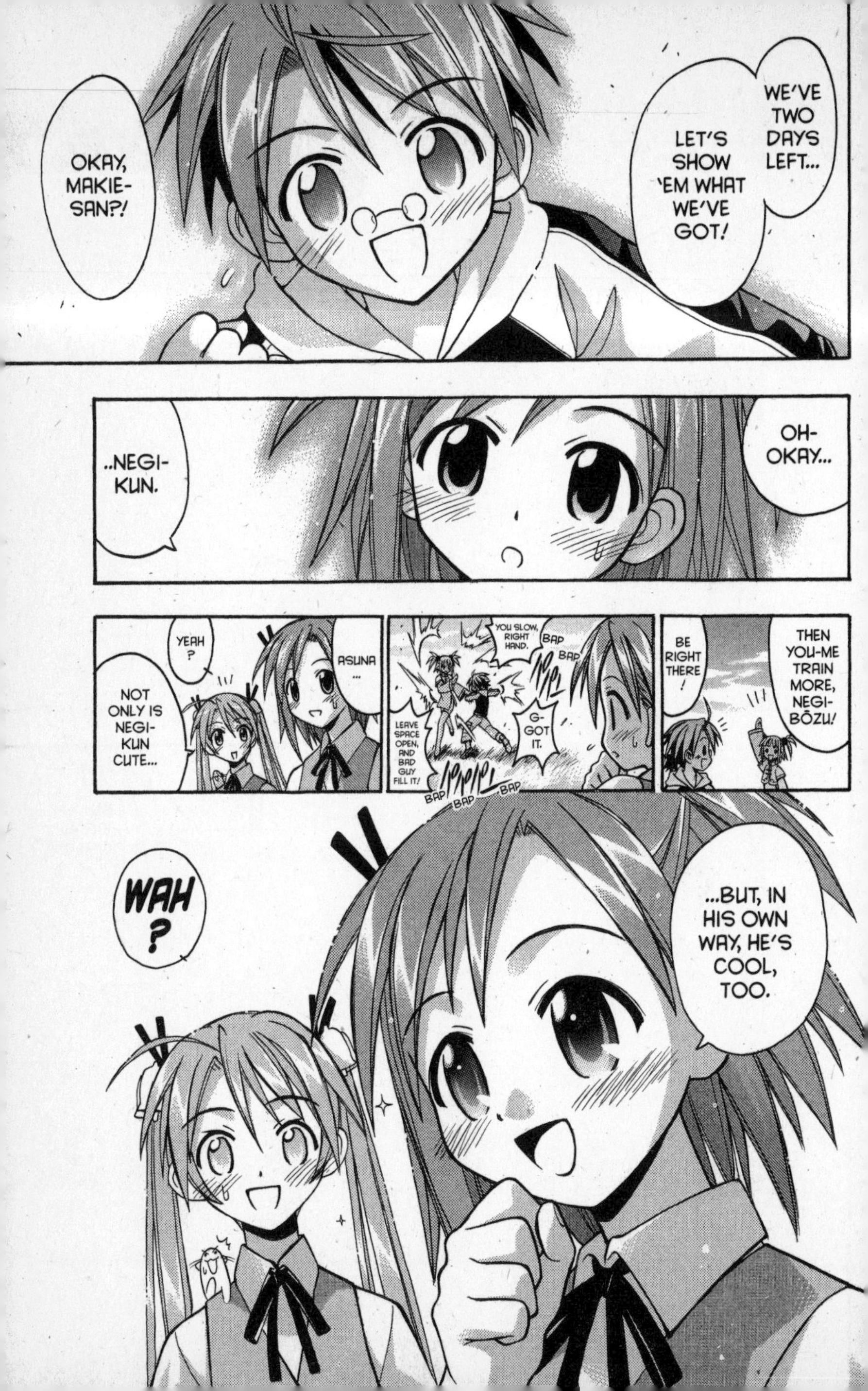
WE'VE TWO DAYS LEFT...
LET'S SHOW 'EM WHAT WE'VE GOT!
OKAY, MAKIE-SAN?!
OH-OKAY...
...NEGI-KUN.
THEN YOU-ME TRAIN MORE, NEGI-BŌZU!
BE RIGHT THERE!
YOU SLOW, RIGHT HAND.
BAP BAP
G-GOT IT.
LEAVE SPACE OPEN, AND BAD GUY FILL IT!
BAP BAP BAP
ASUNA...
YEAH?
NOT ONLY IS NEGI-KUN CUTE...
...BUT, IN HIS OWN WAY, HE'S COOL, TOO.
WAH?

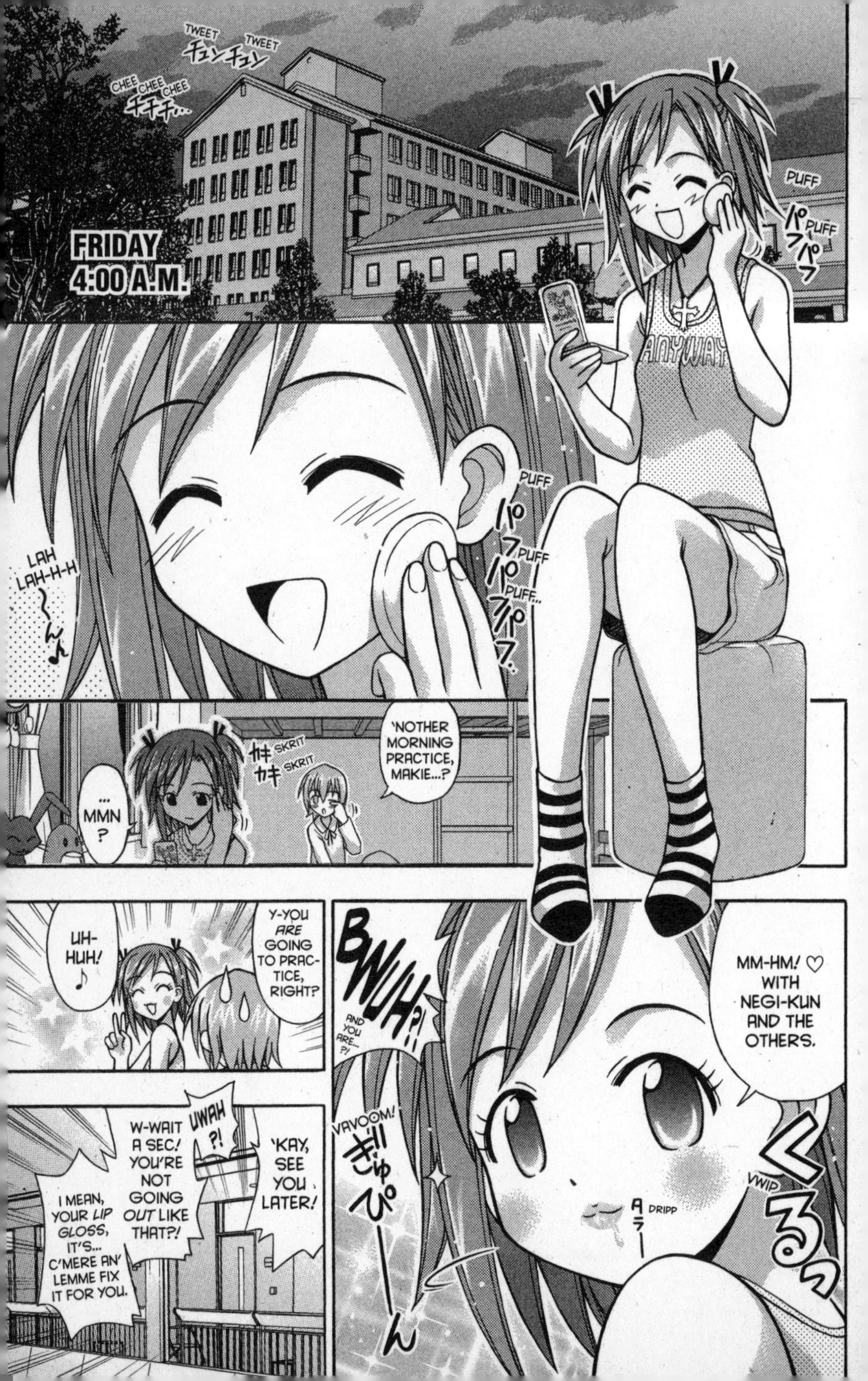
TWEET TWEET
チュンチュン
CHEE CHEE CHEE
チチチ…
FRIDAY 4:00 A.M.
PUFF PUFF
パフパフ
PUFF PUFF PUFF...
パフパフパフパフ…
LAH LAH-H-H ~ん♪
'NOTHER MORNING PRACTICE, MAKIE...?
SKRIT SKRIT
カキカキ
... MMN ?
MM-HM! ♡ WITH NEGI-KUN AND THE OTHERS.
VWIP
くるっ
DRIPP
タラー
BWUH?!
AND YOU ARE...?!
VAVOOM!
Y-YOU ARE GOING TO PRACTICE, RIGHT?
UH-HUH! ♪
'KAY, SEE YOU LATER!
UWAH ?!
W-WAIT A SEC! YOU'RE NOT GOING OUT LIKE THAT?!
I MEAN, YOUR LIP GLOSS, IT'S... C'MERE AN' LEMME FIX IT FOR YOU.

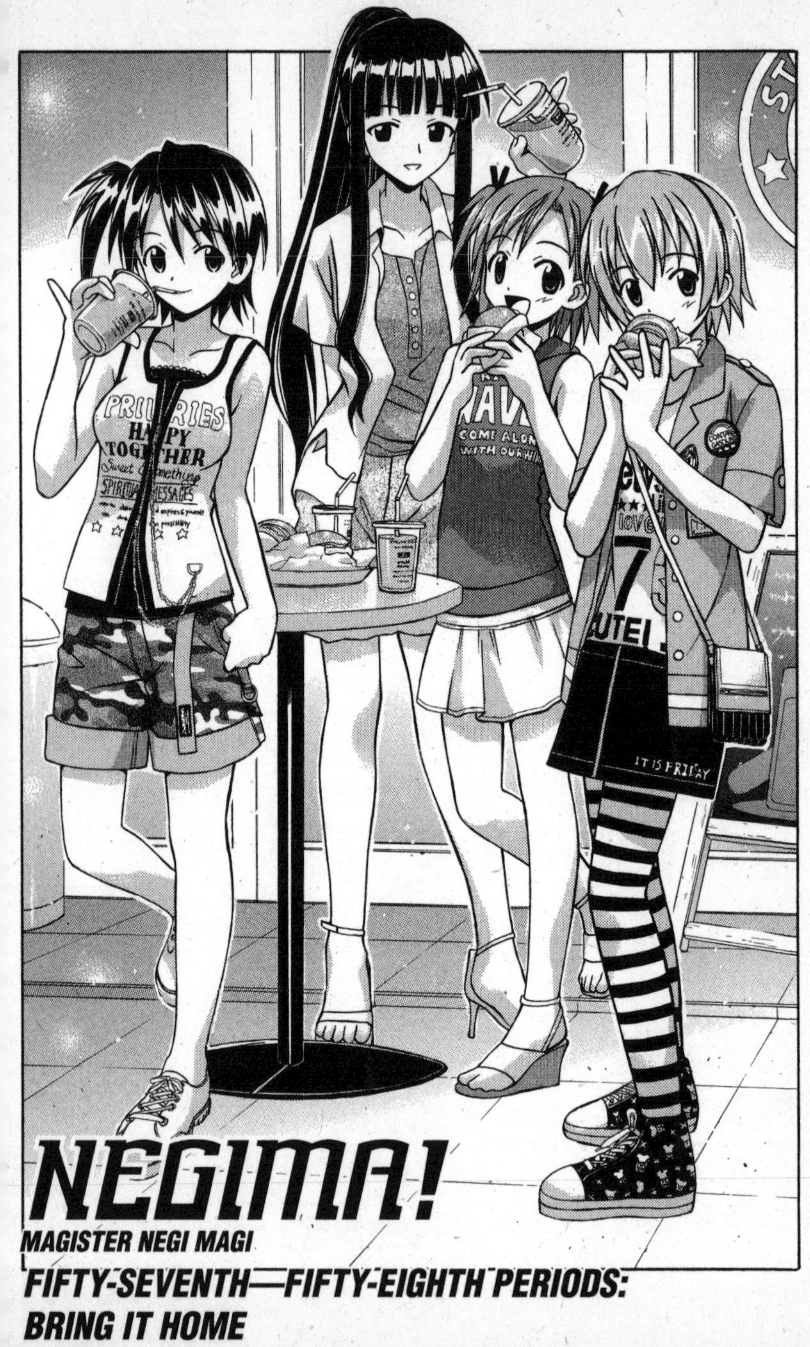
HAPPY TOGETHER
IT IS FRIDAY

NEGIMA!

MAGISTER NEGI MAGI

FIFTY-SEVENTH—FIFTY-EIGHTH PERIODS: BRING IT HOME

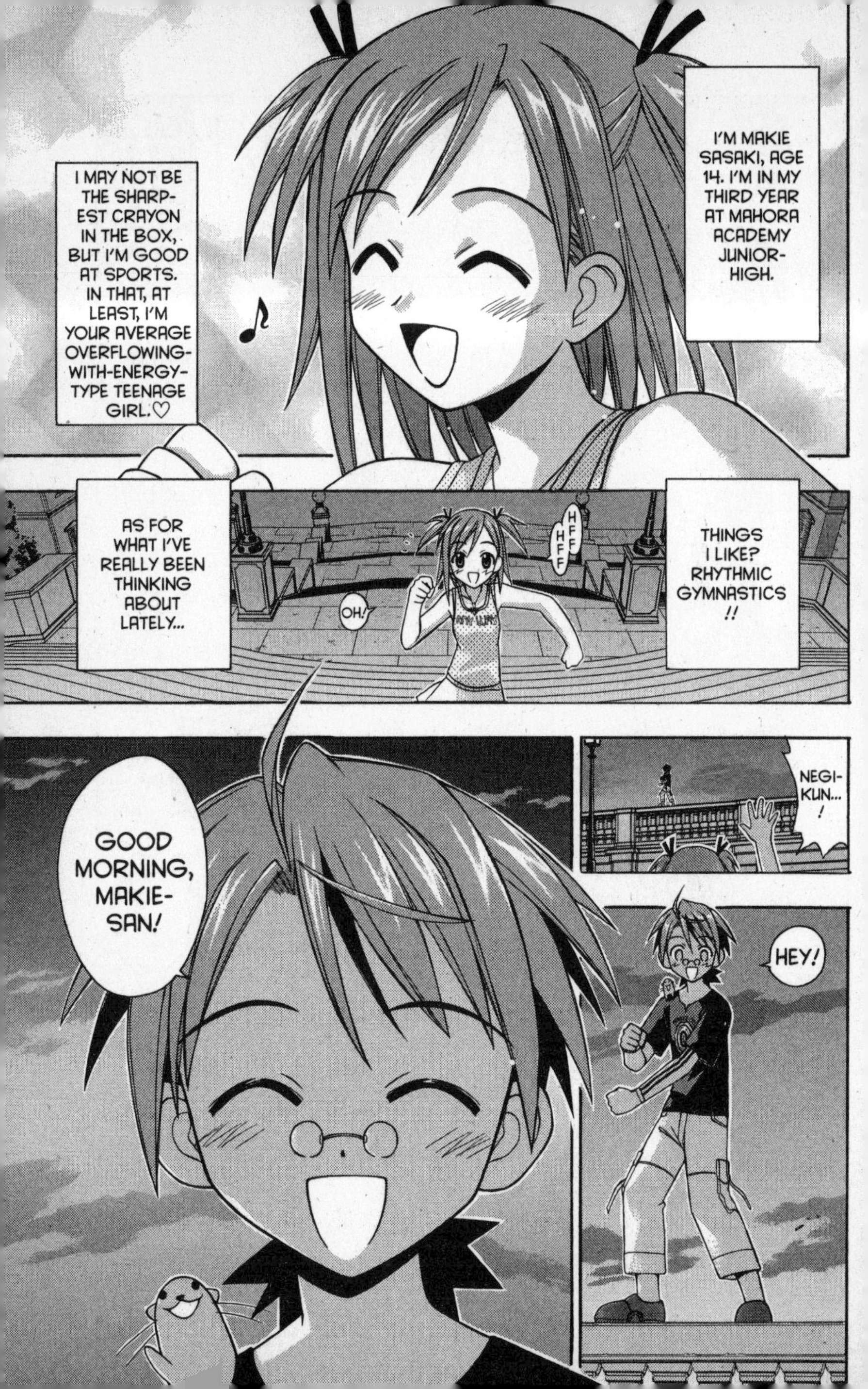
I'M MAKIE SASAKI, AGE 14. I'M IN MY THIRD YEAR AT MAHORA ACADEMY JUNIOR-HIGH.
I MAY NOT BE THE SHARPEST CRAYON IN THE BOX, BUT I'M GOOD AT SPORTS. IN THAT, AT LEAST, I'M YOUR AVERAGE OVERFLOWING-WITH-ENERGY-TYPE TEENAGE GIRL.♡
THINGS I LIKE? RHYTHMIC GYMNASTICS !!
HFF HFF
OH!
AS FOR WHAT I'VE REALLY BEEN THINKING ABOUT LATELY...
NEGI-KUN...!
HEY!
GOOD MORNING, MAKIE-SAN!

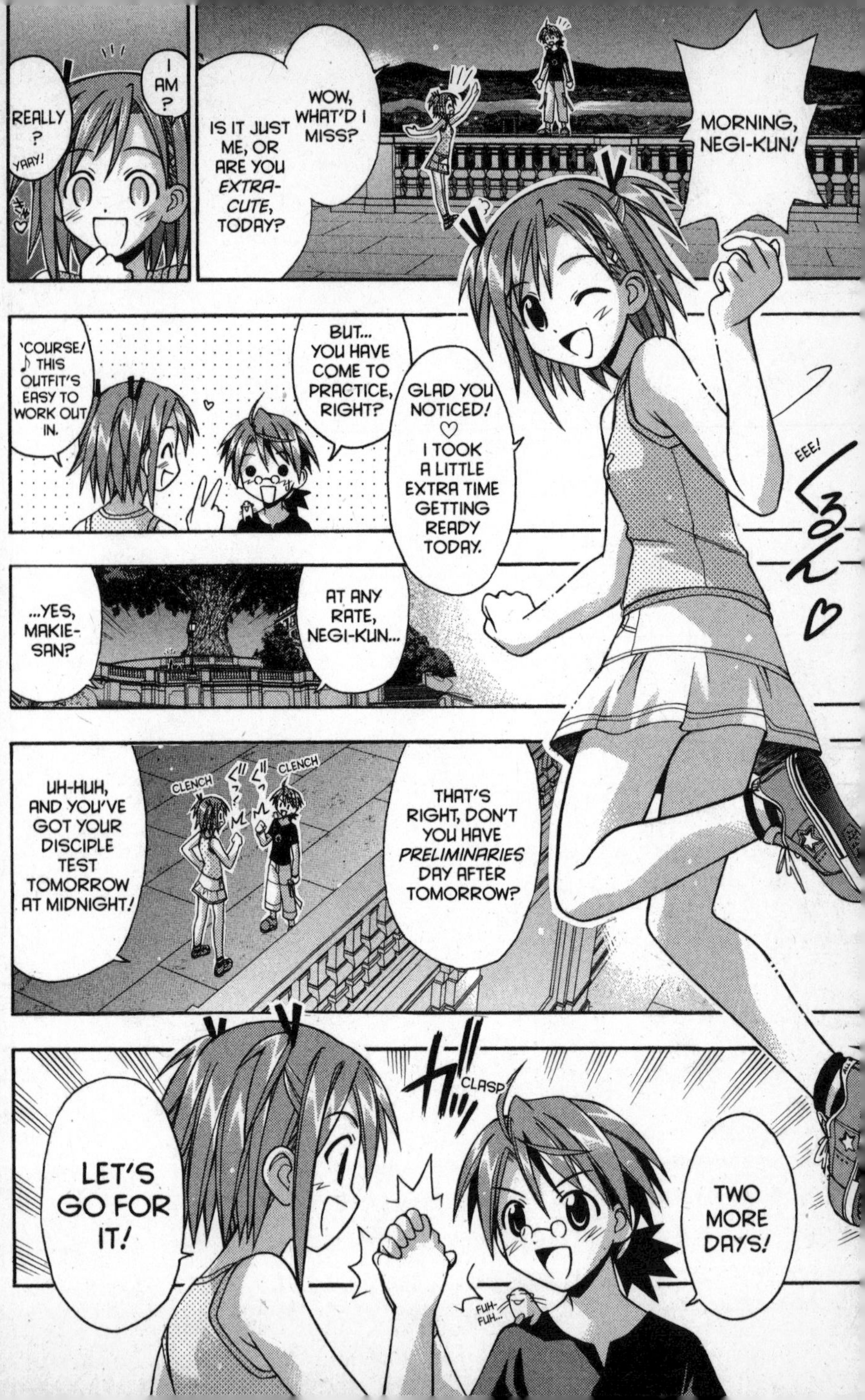
MORNING, NEGI-KUN!
EEE!
くるん
WOW, WHAT'D I MISS?
IS IT JUST ME, OR ARE YOU *EXTRA-CUTE*, TODAY?
I AM?
REALLY?
YAAY!
GLAD YOU NOTICED! ♡ I TOOK A LITTLE EXTRA TIME GETTING READY TODAY.
BUT... YOU HAVE COME TO PRACTICE, RIGHT?
'COURSE! ♪ THIS OUTFIT'S EASY TO WORK OUT IN.
AT ANY RATE, NEGI-KUN...
...YES, MAKIE-SAN?
THAT'S RIGHT, DON'T YOU HAVE *PRELIMINARIES* DAY AFTER TOMORROW?
UH-HUH, AND YOU'VE GOT YOUR DISCIPLE TEST TOMORROW AT MIDNIGHT!
CLENCH
CLENCH
TWO MORE DAYS!
CLASP
LET'S GO FOR IT!
FUH-FUH...

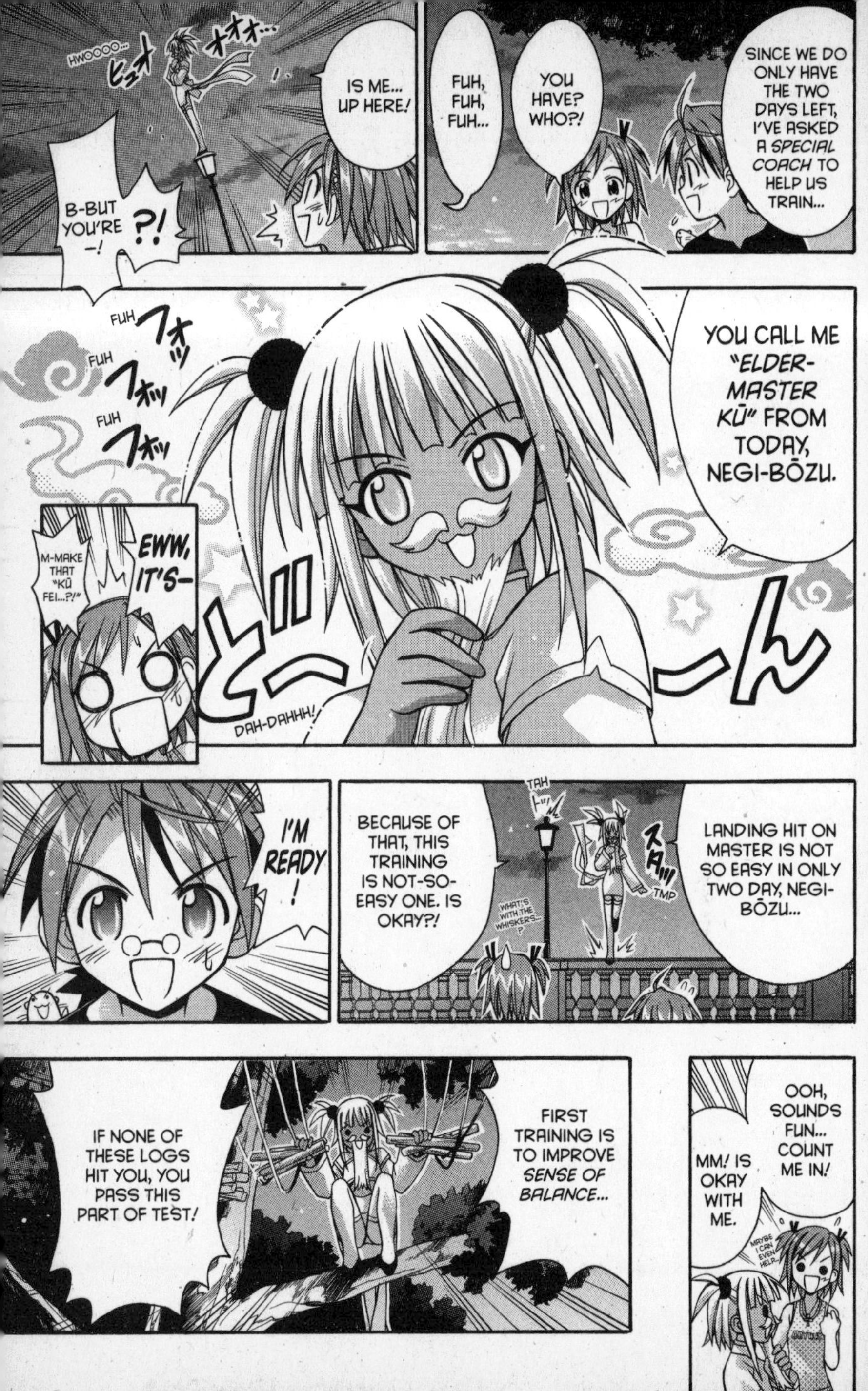
SINCE WE DO ONLY HAVE THE TWO DAYS LEFT, I'VE ASKED A *SPECIAL COACH* TO HELP US TRAIN...
YOU HAVE? WHO?!
FUH, FUH, FUH...
IS ME... UP HERE!
HWOOOO...
B-BUT YOU'RE —!
?!
YOU CALL ME "*ELDER-MASTER KŪ*" FROM TODAY, NEGI-BŌZU.
FUH
FUH
FUH
DAH-DAHHH!
EWW, IT'S—
M-MAKE THAT "KŪ FEI...?!"
LANDING HIT ON MASTER IS NOT SO EASY IN ONLY TWO DAY, NEGI-BŌZU...
TAH
TMP
WHAT'S WITH THE WHISKERS...?
BECAUSE OF THAT, THIS TRAINING IS NOT-SO-EASY ONE. IS OKAY?!
I'M READY!
OOH, SOUNDS FUN... COUNT ME IN!
MM! IS OKAY WITH ME.
MAYBE I CAN EVEN HELP...
FIRST TRAINING IS TO IMPROVE *SENSE OF BALANCE*...
IF NONE OF THESE LOGS HIT YOU, YOU PASS THIS PART OF TEST!

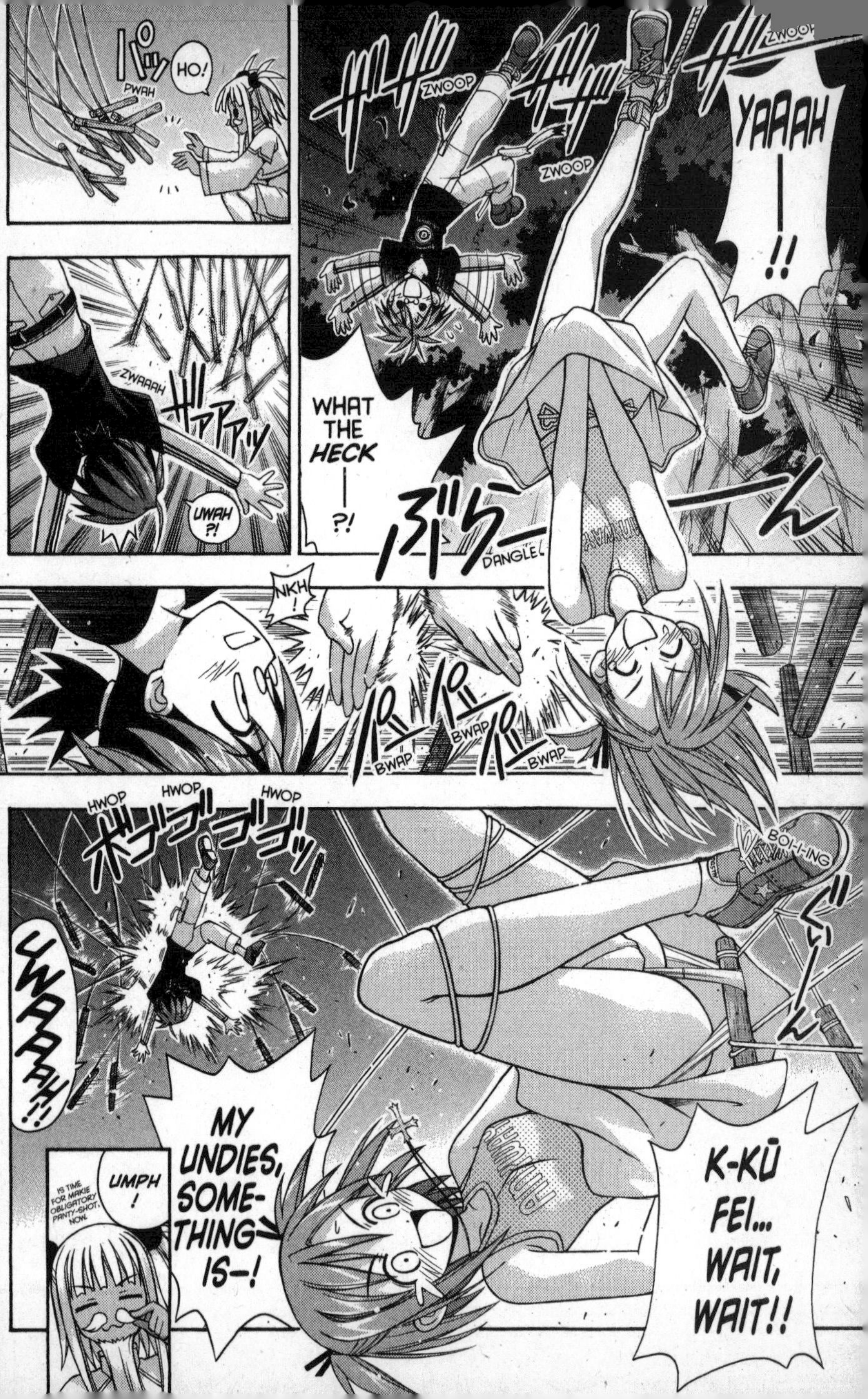

ZWOOP
ZWOOP
ZWOOP
YAAAH—!!
WHAT THE HECK—?!
ぶらーん
DANGLE
パッ
PWAH
HO!
ザァアァッ
ZWAAAH
UWAH?!
NKH!
パ パ パ
BWAP BWAP BWAP
HWOP HWOP HWOP
ボゴゴッ
K-KŪ FEI... WAIT, WAIT!!
BOI-I-ING
MY UNDIES, SOME-THING IS—!
UWAAAAH!!
UMPH!
IS TIME FOR MAKIE OBLIGATORY PANTY-SHOT, NOW.

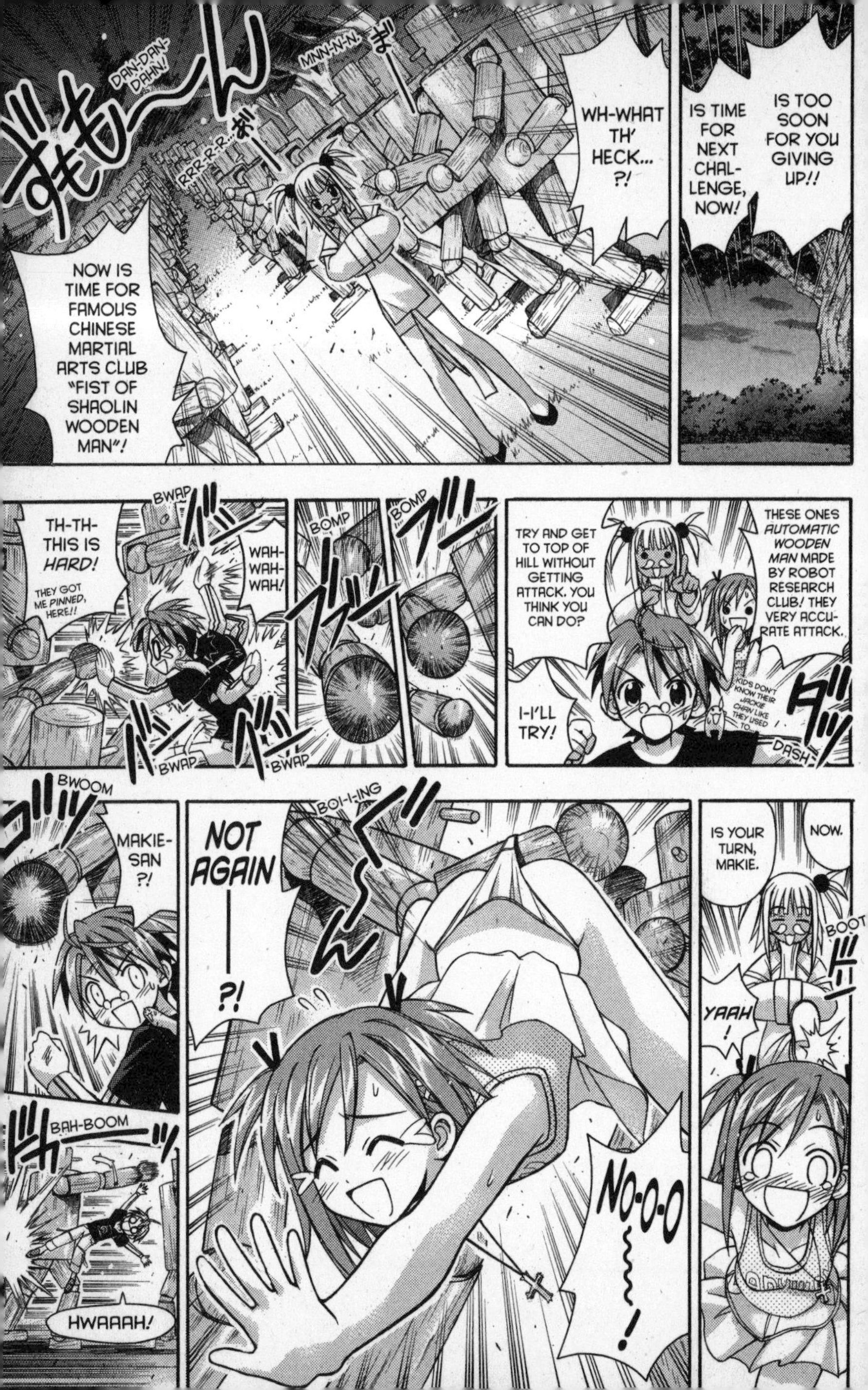
IS TOO SOON FOR YOU GIVING UP!!
IS TIME FOR NEXT CHAL-LENGE, NOW!
WH-WHAT TH' HECK...?!
MNN-N-N.
DAN-DAN-DAHN!
RRR-R-R...
NOW IS TIME FOR FAMOUS CHINESE MARTIAL ARTS CLUB "FIST OF SHAOLIN WOODEN MAN"!
THESE ONES *AUTOMATIC WOODEN MAN* MADE BY ROBOT RESEARCH CLUB! THEY VERY ACCU-RATE ATTACK.
TRY AND GET TO TOP OF HILL WITHOUT GETTING ATTACK. YOU THINK YOU CAN DO?
I-I'LL TRY!
KIDS DON'T KNOW THEIR JACKIE CHAN LIKE THEY USED TO...
DASH
BOMP
BOMP
BWAP
WAH-WAH-WAH!
TH-TH-THIS IS *HARD!*
THEY GOT ME *PINNED,* HERE!!
BWAP
BWAP
NOW.
IS YOUR TURN, MAKIE.
BOOT
YAAH!
BOI-I-ING
NOT AGAIN—?!
NO-O-O~!
BWOOM
MAKIE-SAN?!
BAH-BOOM
HWAAAH!

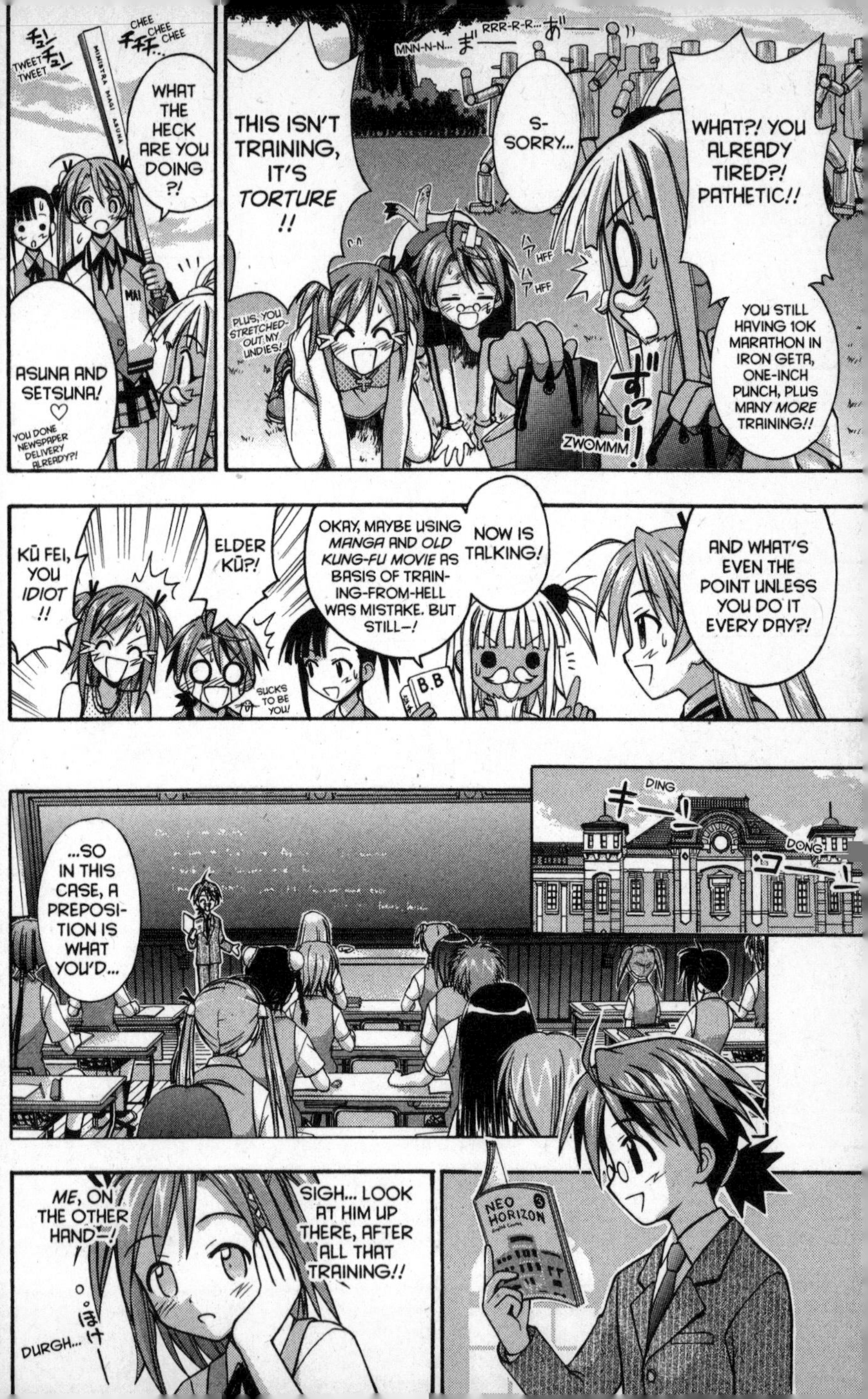
MNN-N-N... まー
RRR-R-R... あー
WHAT?! YOU ALREADY TIRED?! PATHETIC!!
S-SORRY...
THIS ISN'T TRAINING, IT'S *TORTURE*!!
HFF HFF
YOU STILL HAVING 10K MARATHON IN IRON GETA, ONE-INCH PUNCH, PLUS MANY *MORE* TRAINING!!
ずっしー ZWOMMM
PLUS, YOU STRETCHED-OUT MY UNDIES!
TWEET TWEET
CHEE CHEE CHEE
MINISTRA MAGI ASUNA
WHAT THE HECK ARE YOU DOING?!
ASUNA AND SETSUNA! ♡
YOU DONE NEWSPAPER DELIVERY ALREADY?!
AND WHAT'S EVEN THE POINT UNLESS YOU DO IT EVERY DAY?!
NOW IS TALKING!
OKAY, MAYBE USING *MANGA* AND *OLD KUNG-FU MOVIE* AS BASIS OF TRAINING-FROM-HELL WAS MISTAKE. BUT STILL—!
B.B
ELDER KŪ?!
KŪ FEI, YOU *IDIOT*!!
SUCKS TO BE YOU!
DING
DONG
...SO IN THIS CASE, A PREPOSITION IS WHAT YOU'D...
NEO HORIZON
SIGH... LOOK AT HIM UP THERE, AFTER ALL THAT TRAINING!!
ME, ON THE OTHER HAND—!
DURGH... ほけー

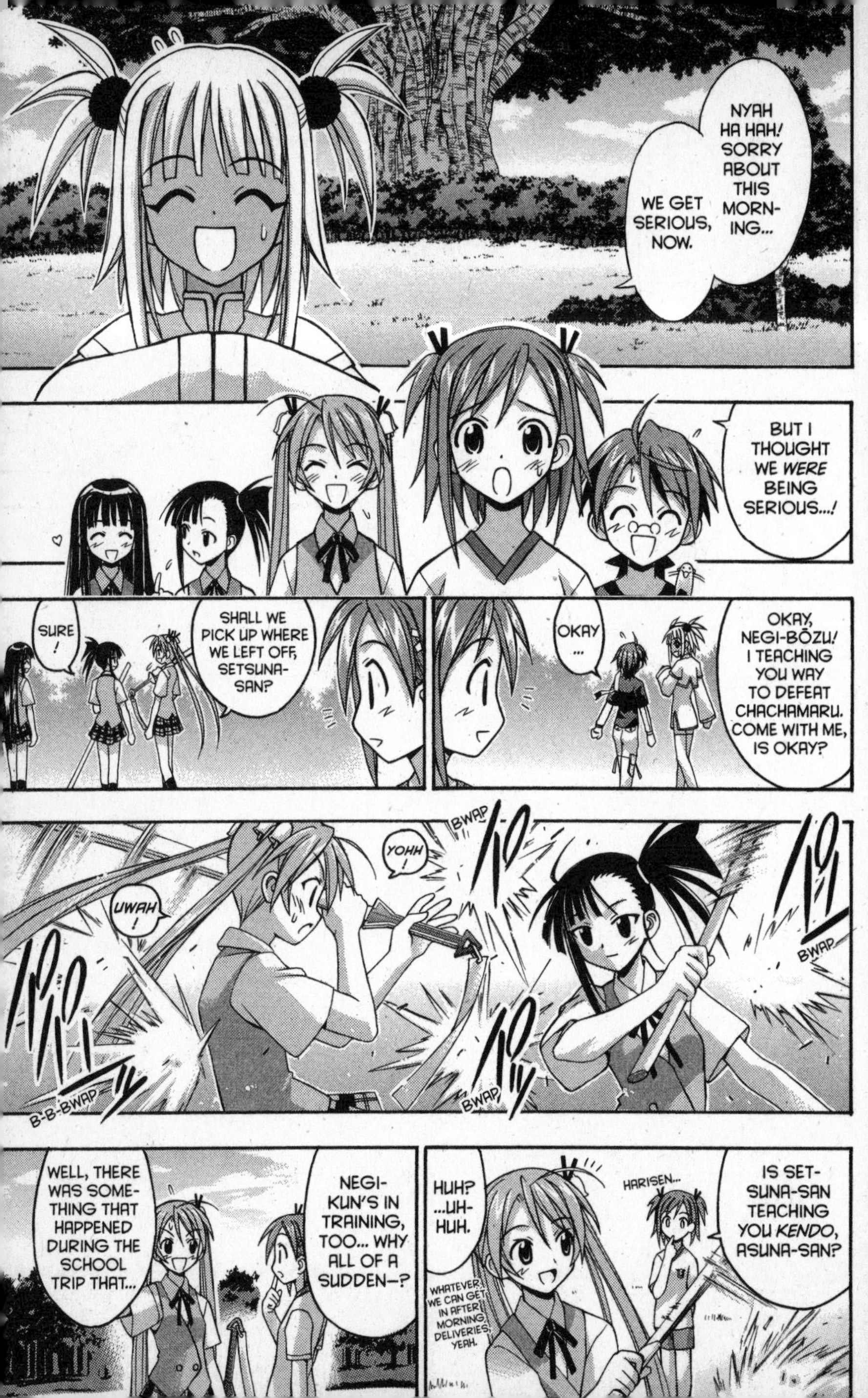
NYAH HA HAH! SORRY ABOUT THIS MORNING...
WE GET SERIOUS, NOW.
BUT I THOUGHT WE *WERE* BEING SERIOUS...!
OKAY, NEGI-BŌZU! I TEACHING YOU WAY TO DEFEAT CHACHAMARU. COME WITH ME, IS OKAY?
OKAY...
SHALL WE PICK UP WHERE WE LEFT OFF, SETSUNA-SAN?
SURE!
BWAP
YOHH!
BWAP
UWAH!
BWAP
B-B-BWAP
IS SET-SUNA-SAN TEACHING YOU *KENDO*, ASUNA-SAN?
HARISEN...
HUH? ...UH-HUH.
WHATEVER WE CAN GET IN AFTER MORNING DELIVERIES, YEAH.
NEGI-KUN'S IN TRAINING, TOO... WHY ALL OF A SUDDEN—?
WELL, THERE WAS SOMETHING THAT HAPPENED DURING THE SCHOOL TRIP THAT...

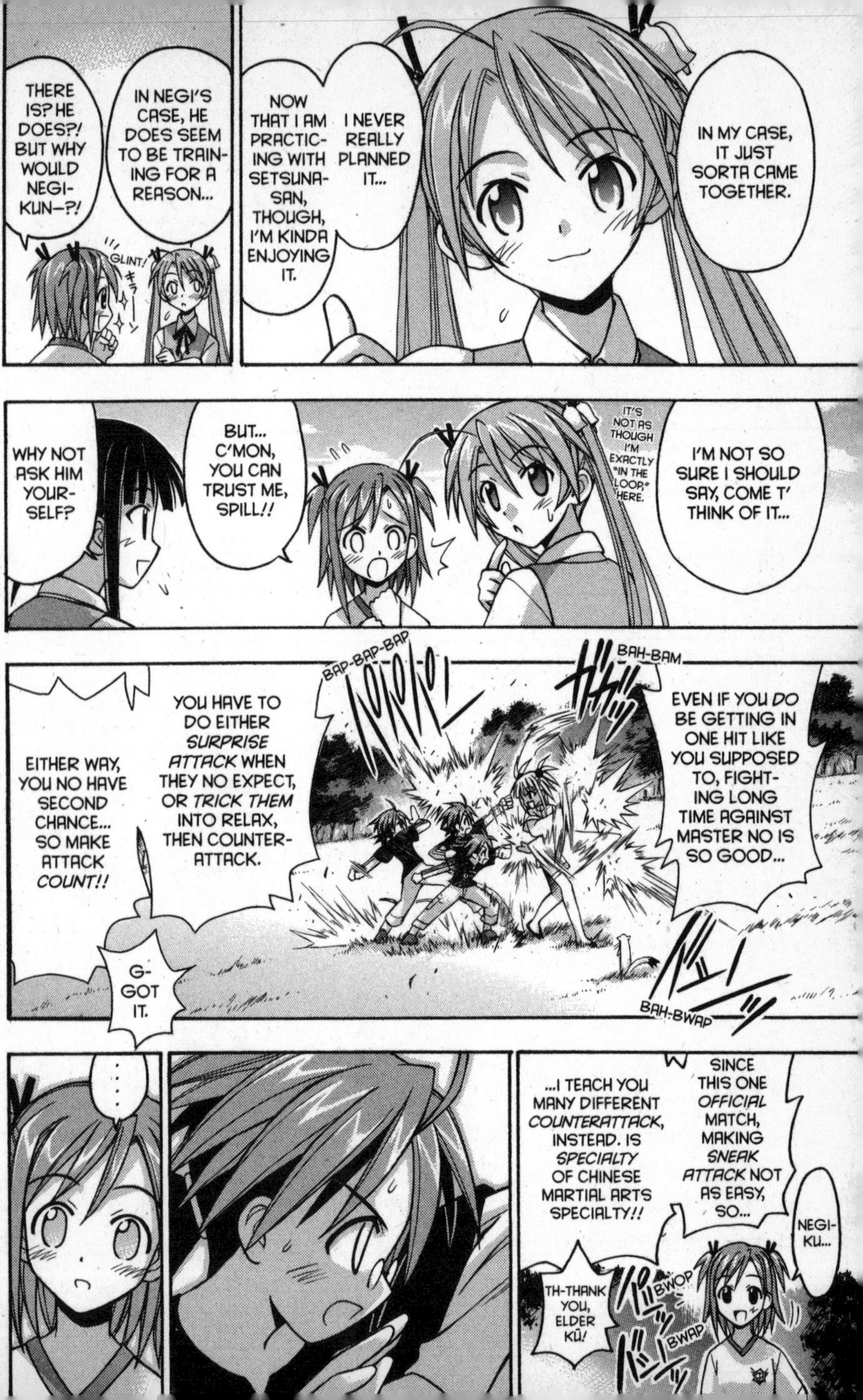
IN MY CASE, IT JUST SORTA CAME TOGETHER.
I NEVER REALLY PLANNED IT...
NOW THAT I AM PRACTICING WITH SETSUNA-SAN, THOUGH, I'M KINDA ENJOYING IT.
IN NEGI'S CASE, HE DOES SEEM TO BE TRAINING FOR A REASON...
THERE IS? HE DOES?! BUT WHY WOULD NEGI-KUN—?!
GLINT!
I'M NOT SO SURE I SHOULD SAY, COME T' THINK OF IT...
IT'S NOT AS THOUGH I'M EXACTLY "IN THE LOOP," HERE.
BUT... C'MON, YOU CAN TRUST ME, SPILL!!
WHY NOT ASK HIM YOURSELF?
BAH-BAM
EVEN IF YOU *DO* BE GETTING IN ONE HIT LIKE YOU SUPPOSED TO, FIGHTING LONG TIME AGAINST MASTER NO IS SO GOOD...
BAP-BAP-BAP
YOU HAVE TO DO EITHER *SURPRISE ATTACK* WHEN THEY NO EXPECT, OR *TRICK THEM* INTO RELAX, THEN COUNTERATTACK.
EITHER WAY, YOU NO HAVE SECOND CHANCE... SO MAKE ATTACK *COUNT!!*
G-GOT IT.
BAH-BWAP
SINCE THIS ONE *OFFICIAL* MATCH, MAKING *SNEAK ATTACK* NOT AS EASY, SO...
...I TEACH YOU MANY DIFFERENT *COUNTERATTACK*, INSTEAD. IS *SPECIALTY* OF CHINESE MARTIAL ARTS SPECIALTY!!
NEGI-KU...
BWOP
BWAP
TH-THANK YOU, ELDER KŪ!
......

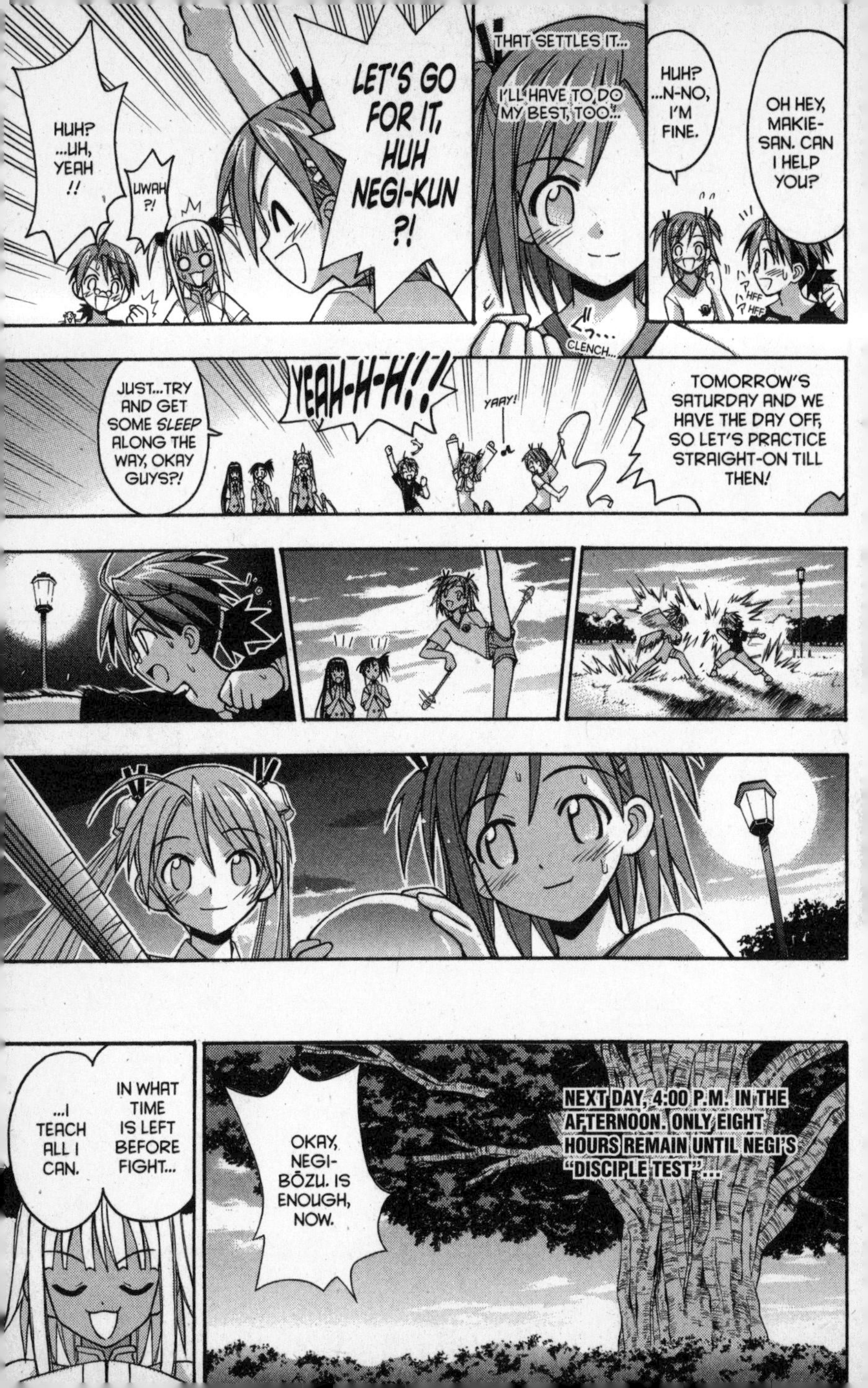

OH HEY, MAKIE-SAN. CAN I HELP YOU?
HUH? ...N-NO, I'M FINE.
HFF HFF
THAT SETTLES IT...
I'LL HAVE TO DO MY BEST, TOO...
CLENCH...
LET'S GO FOR IT, HUH NEGI-KUN?!
UWAH?!
HUH? ...UH, YEAH!!
TOMORROW'S SATURDAY AND WE HAVE THE DAY OFF, SO LET'S PRACTICE STRAIGHT-ON TILL THEN!
YAAY!
YEAH-H-H!!
JUST...TRY AND GET SOME *SLEEP* ALONG THE WAY, OKAY GUYS?!
NEXT DAY, 4:00 P.M. IN THE AFTERNOON. ONLY EIGHT HOURS REMAIN UNTIL NEGI'S "DISCIPLE TEST"...
OKAY, NEGI-BŌZU. IS ENOUGH, NOW.
IN WHAT TIME IS LEFT BEFORE FIGHT...
...I TEACH ALL I CAN.

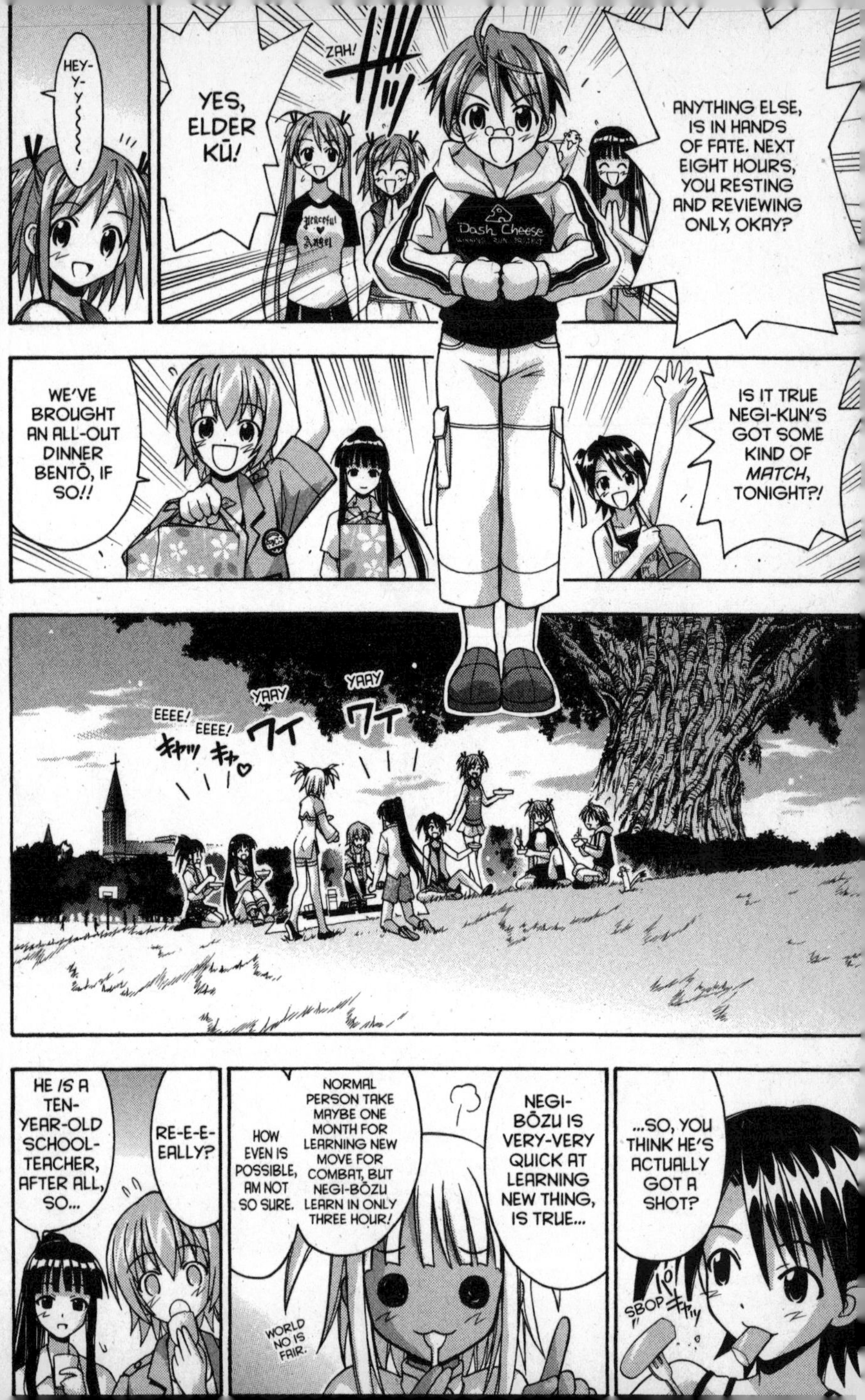
ANYTHING ELSE, IS IN HANDS OF FATE. NEXT EIGHT HOURS, YOU RESTING AND REVIEWING ONLY, OKAY?
ZAH!
YES, ELDER KŪ!
HEY-Y-Y~~~!
IS IT TRUE NEGI-KUN'S GOT SOME KIND OF *MATCH*, TONIGHT?!
WE'VE BROUGHT AN ALL-OUT DINNER BENTŌ, IF SO!!
YAAY
YAAY
EEEE!
EEEE!
...SO, YOU THINK HE'S ACTUALLY GOT A SHOT?
SBOP
NEGI-BŌZU IS VERY-VERY QUICK AT LEARNING NEW THING, IS TRUE...
NORMAL PERSON TAKE MAYBE ONE MONTH FOR LEARNING NEW MOVE FOR COMBAT, BUT NEGI-BŌZU LEARN IN ONLY THREE HOUR!
HOW EVEN IS POSSIBLE, AM NOT SO SURE.
WORLD NO IS FAIR.
RE-E-E-EALLY?
HE *IS* A TEN-YEAR-OLD SCHOOL-TEACHER, AFTER ALL, SO...

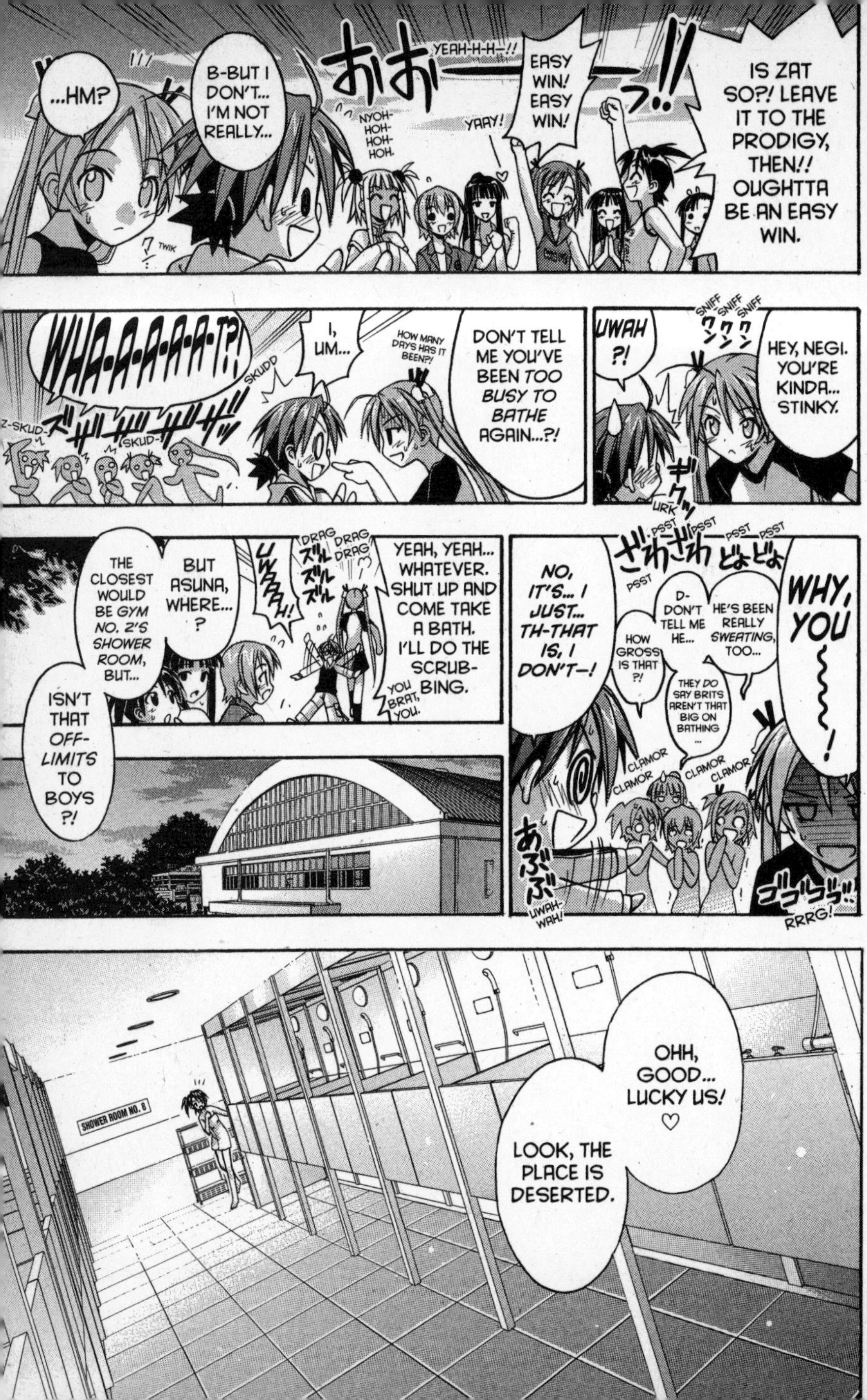
IS ZAT SO?! LEAVE IT TO THE PRODIGY, THEN!! OUGHTTA BE AN EASY WIN.
おおーーっ!!
YEAH-H-H—!!
EASY WIN! EASY WIN!
YAAY!
NYOH-HOH-HOH-HOH.
B-BUT I DON'T... I'M NOT REALLY...
TWIK
...HM?
HEY, NEGI. YOU'RE KINDA... STINKY.
SNIFF SNIFF SNIFF
UWAH?!
URK
DON'T TELL ME YOU'VE BEEN TOO BUSY TO BATHE AGAIN...?!
HOW MANY DAYS HAS IT BEEN?!
I, UM...
WHA-A-A-A-A-T?!
SKUDD
Z-SKUD
SKUD
ざわざわ どよどよ
PSST PSST PSST PSST PSST
WHY, YOU~~~!
HE'S BEEN REALLY SWEATING, TOO...
D-DON'T TELL ME HE...
HOW GROSS IS THAT?!
THEY DO SAY BRITS AREN'T THAT BIG ON BATHING...
NO, IT'S... I JUST... TH-THAT IS, I DON'T—!
CLAMOR CLAMOR CLAMOR CLAMOR
RRRG!
UWAH-WAH!
YEAH, YEAH... WHATEVER. SHUT UP AND COME TAKE A BATH. I'LL DO THE SCRUB-BING.
DRAG DRAG DRAG
YOU BRAT, YOU.
BUT ASUNA, WHERE...?
THE CLOSEST WOULD BE GYM NO. 2'S SHOWER ROOM, BUT...
ISN'T THAT OFF-LIMITS TO BOYS?!
SHOWER ROOM NO. 8
OHH, GOOD... LUCKY US! ♡
LOOK, THE PLACE IS DESERTED.

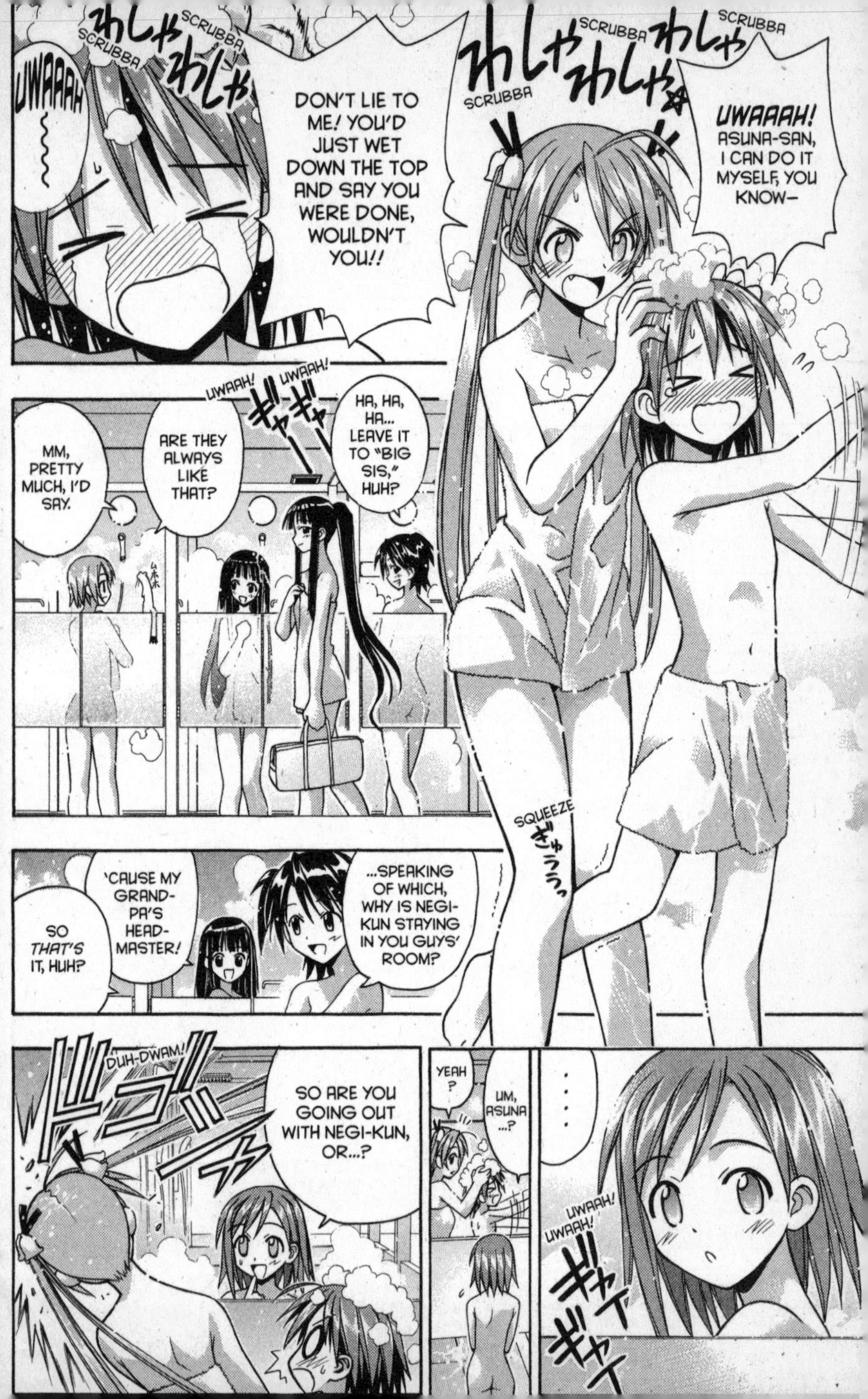
SCRUBBA SCRUBBA
SCRUBBA
UWAAAH! ASUNA-SAN, I CAN DO IT MYSELF, YOU KNOW–
DON'T LIE TO ME! YOU'D JUST WET DOWN THE TOP AND SAY YOU WERE DONE, WOULDN'T YOU!!
SQUEEZE
SCRUBBA
SCRUBBA
UWAAAH
UWAAH! UWAAH!
HA, HA, HA... LEAVE IT TO "BIG SIS," HUH?
ARE THEY ALWAYS LIKE THAT?
MM, PRETTY MUCH, I'D SAY.
...SPEAKING OF WHICH, WHY IS NEGI-KUN STAYING IN YOU GUYS' ROOM?
'CAUSE MY GRAND-PA'S HEAD-MASTER!
SO *THAT'S* IT, HUH?
UWAAH! UWAAH!
....
UM, ASUNA ...?
YEAH ?
SO ARE YOU GOING OUT WITH NEGI-KUN, OR...?
DUH-DWAM!!

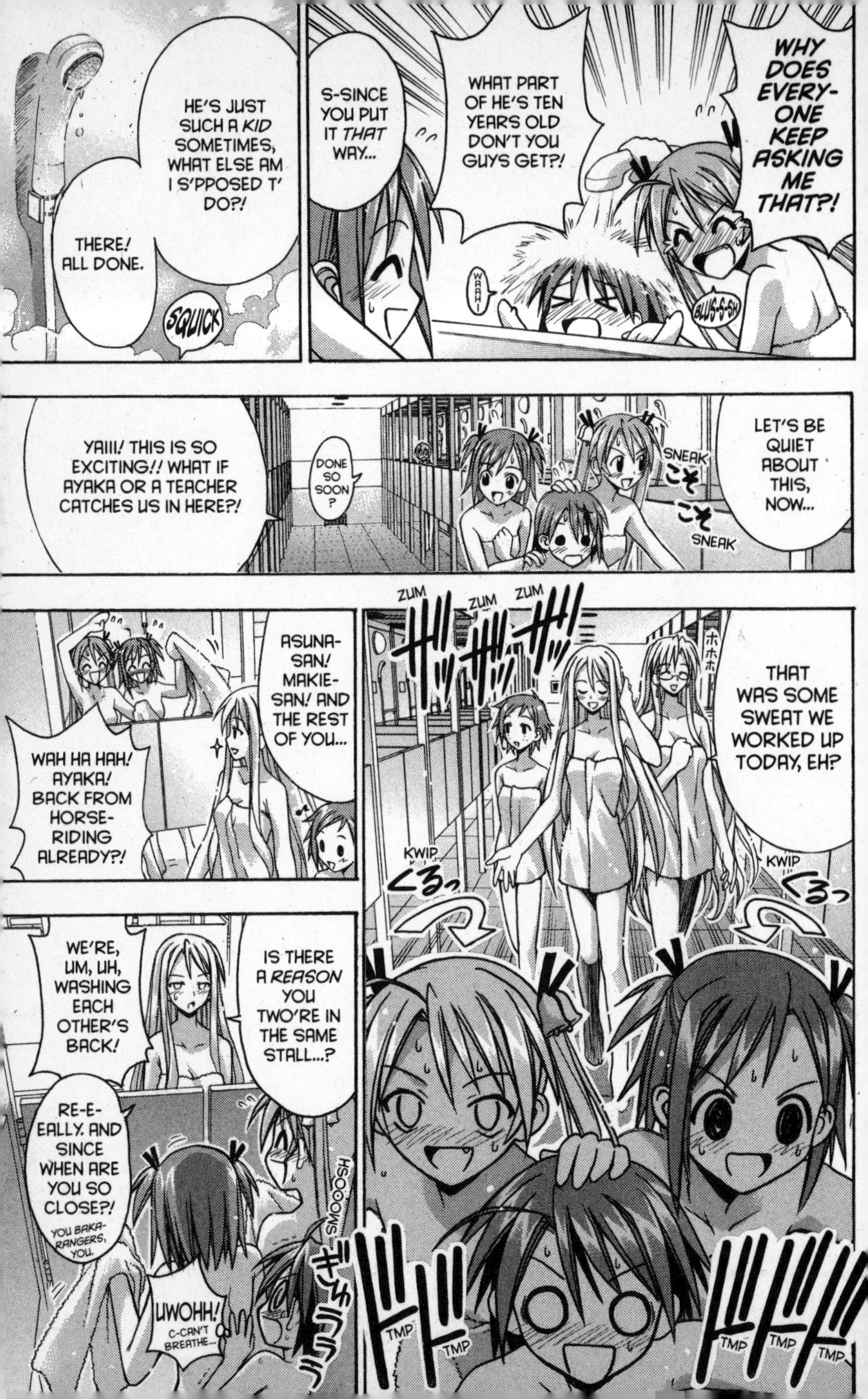
WHY DOES EVERY-ONE KEEP ASKING ME THAT?!
WHAT PART OF HE'S TEN YEARS OLD DON'T YOU GUYS GET?!
S-SINCE YOU PUT IT *THAT* WAY...
WAAH!
BLUS-S-SH
HE'S JUST SUCH A *KID* SOMETIMES, WHAT ELSE AM I S'PPOSED T' DO?!
THERE! ALL DONE.
SQUICK
LET'S BE QUIET ABOUT THIS, NOW...
SNEAK
こそ
こそ
SNEAK
DONE SO SOON?
YAIII! THIS IS SO EXCITING!! WHAT IF AYAKA OR A TEACHER CATCHES US IN HERE?!
THAT WAS SOME SWEAT WE WORKED UP TODAY, EH?
ホホホ
ZUM
ZUM
ZUM
KWIP
くるっ
KWIP
くるっ
TMP
TMP
TMP
TMP
TMP
ASUNA-SAN! MAKIE-SAN! AND THE REST OF YOU...
WAH HA HAH! AYAKA! BACK FROM HORSE-RIDING ALREADY?!
IS THERE A *REASON* YOU TWO'RE IN THE SAME STALL...?
WE'RE, UM, UH, WASHING EACH OTHER'S BACK!
RE-E-EALLY. AND SINCE WHEN ARE YOU SO CLOSE?!
YOU BAKA-RANGERS, YOU.
SMOOOSH
UWOHH!
C-CAN'T BREATHE...

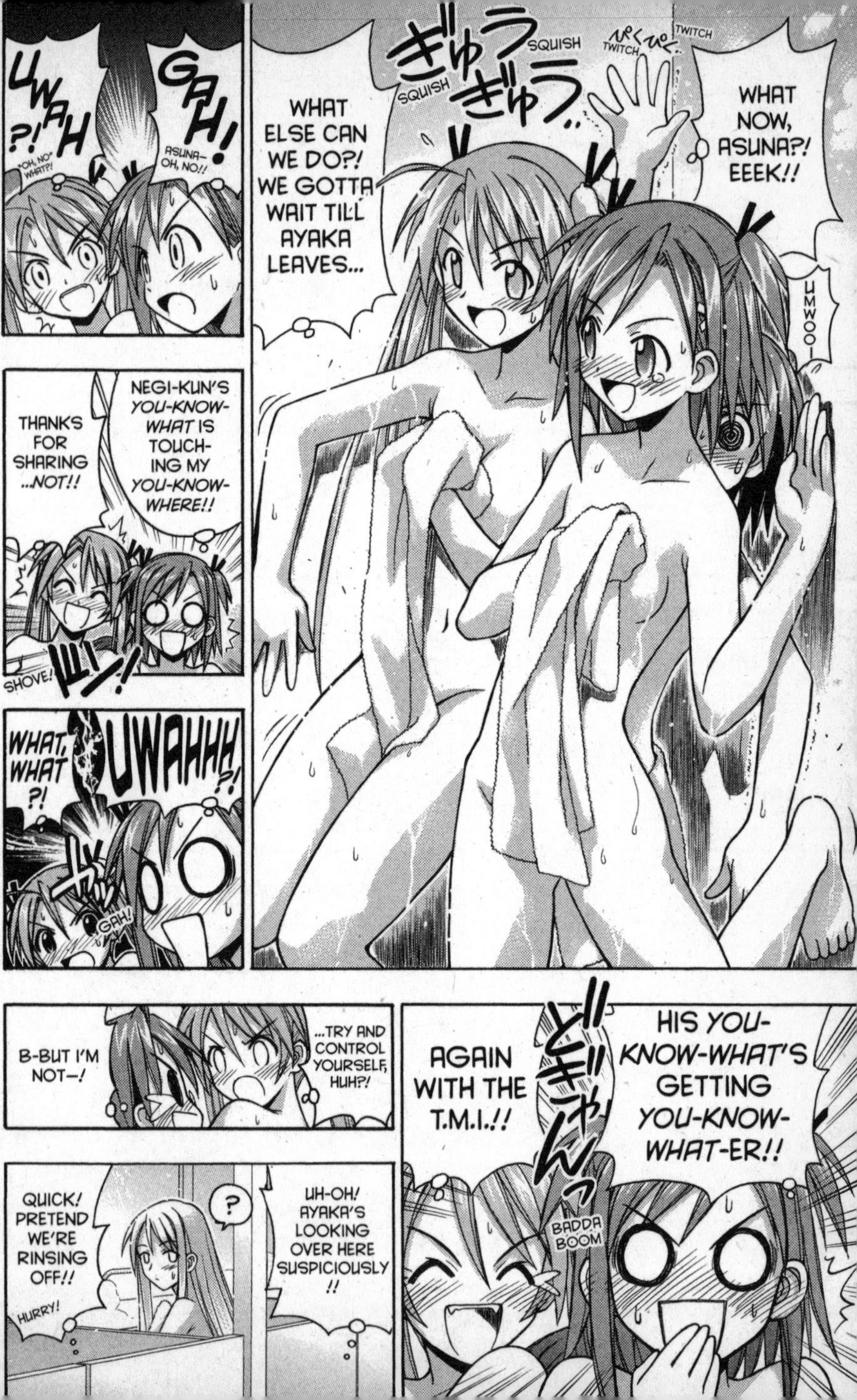

ぴくぴく
TWITCH
TWITCH
WHAT NOW, ASUNA?! EEEK!!
ぎゅうぎゅう
SQUISH
SQUISH
WHAT ELSE CAN WE DO?! WE GOTTA WAIT TILL AYAKA LEAVES...
UMWOO!
GAH!
ASUNA— OH, NO!!
UWAH ?!
"OH, NO" WHAT?!
NEGI-KUN'S *YOU-KNOW-WHAT* IS TOUCHING MY *YOU-KNOW-WHERE!!*
THANKS FOR SHARING ...*NOT!!*
SHOVE!
UWAHH ?!
WHAT, WHAT ?!
GAH!
HIS *YOU-KNOW-WHAT'S* GETTING *YOU-KNOW-WHAT-ER!!*
AGAIN WITH THE T.M.I.!!
BADDA BOOM
...TRY AND CONTROL YOURSELF, HUH?!
B-BUT I'M NOT—!
UH-OH! AYAKA'S LOOKING OVER HERE SUSPICIOUSLY !!
?
QUICK! PRETEND WE'RE RINSING OFF!!
HURRY!

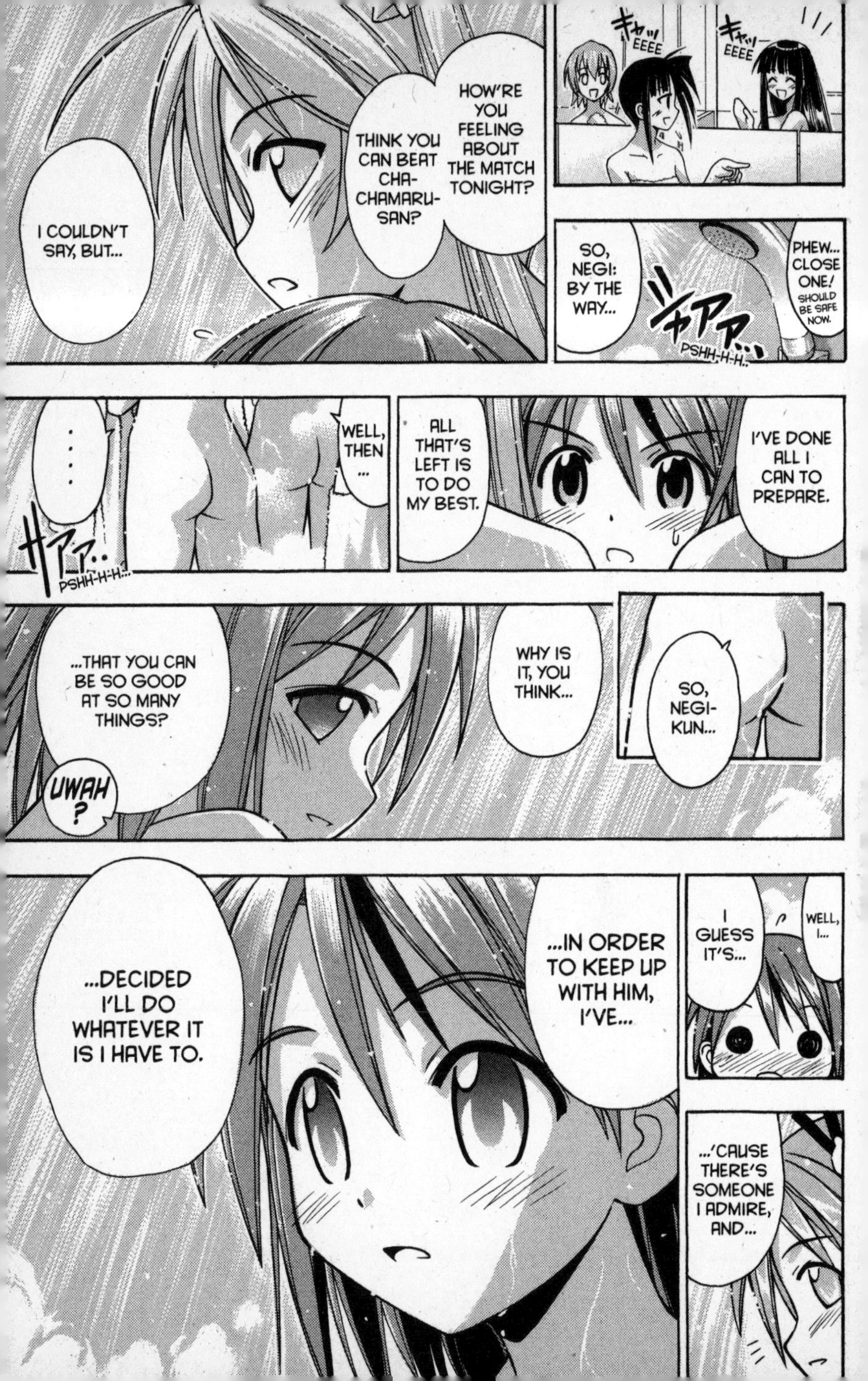

キャッ
EEEE
キャッ
EEEE
PHEW... CLOSE ONE!
SHOULD BE SAFE NOW.
PSHH-H-H...
SO, NEGI: BY THE WAY...
HOW'RE YOU FEELING ABOUT THE MATCH TONIGHT?
THINK YOU CAN BEAT CHA-CHAMARU-SAN?
I COULDN'T SAY, BUT...
I'VE DONE ALL I CAN TO PREPARE.
ALL THAT'S LEFT IS TO DO MY BEST.
WELL, THEN...
....
PSHH-H-H...
SO, NEGI-KUN...
WHY IS IT, YOU THINK...
...THAT YOU CAN BE SO GOOD AT SO MANY THINGS?
UWAH?
WELL, I...
I GUESS IT'S...
...'CAUSE THERE'S SOMEONE I ADMIRE, AND...
...IN ORDER TO KEEP UP WITH HIM, I'VE...
...DECIDED I'LL DO WHATEVER IT IS I HAVE TO.

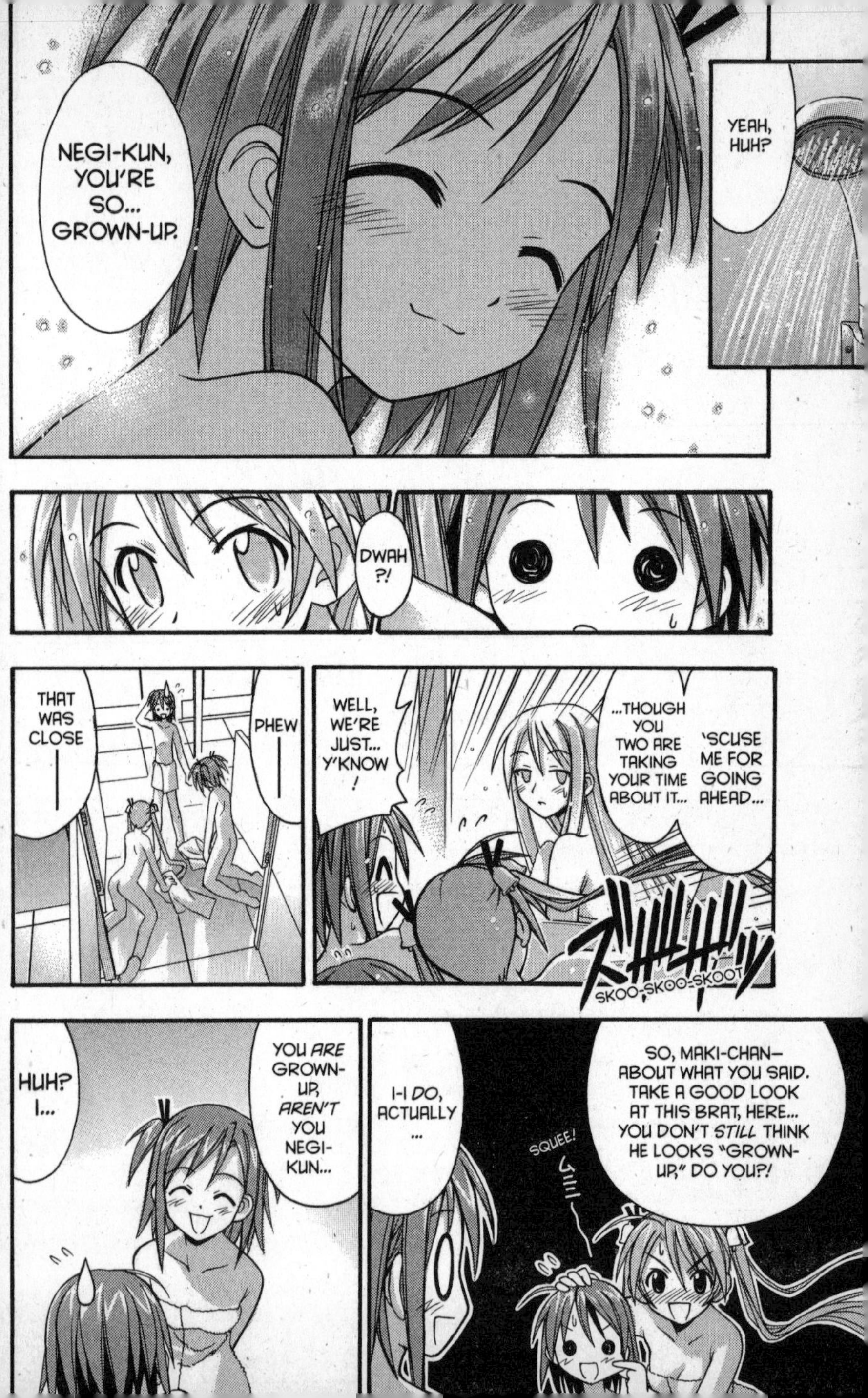
YEAH, HUH?
NEGI-KUN, YOU'RE SO... GROWN-UP.
DWAH?!
'SCUSE ME FOR GOING AHEAD...
...THOUGH YOU TWO ARE TAKING YOUR TIME ABOUT IT...
WELL, WE'RE JUST... Y'KNOW!
SKOO-SKOO-SKOOT
PHEW
THAT WAS CLOSE
SO, MAKI-CHAN— ABOUT WHAT YOU SAID. TAKE A GOOD LOOK AT THIS BRAT, HERE... YOU DON'T *STILL* THINK HE LOOKS "GROWN-UP," DO YOU?!
SQUEE!
I-I *DO*, ACTUALLY...
YOU *ARE* GROWN-UP, *AREN'T* YOU NEGI-KUN...
HUH? I...

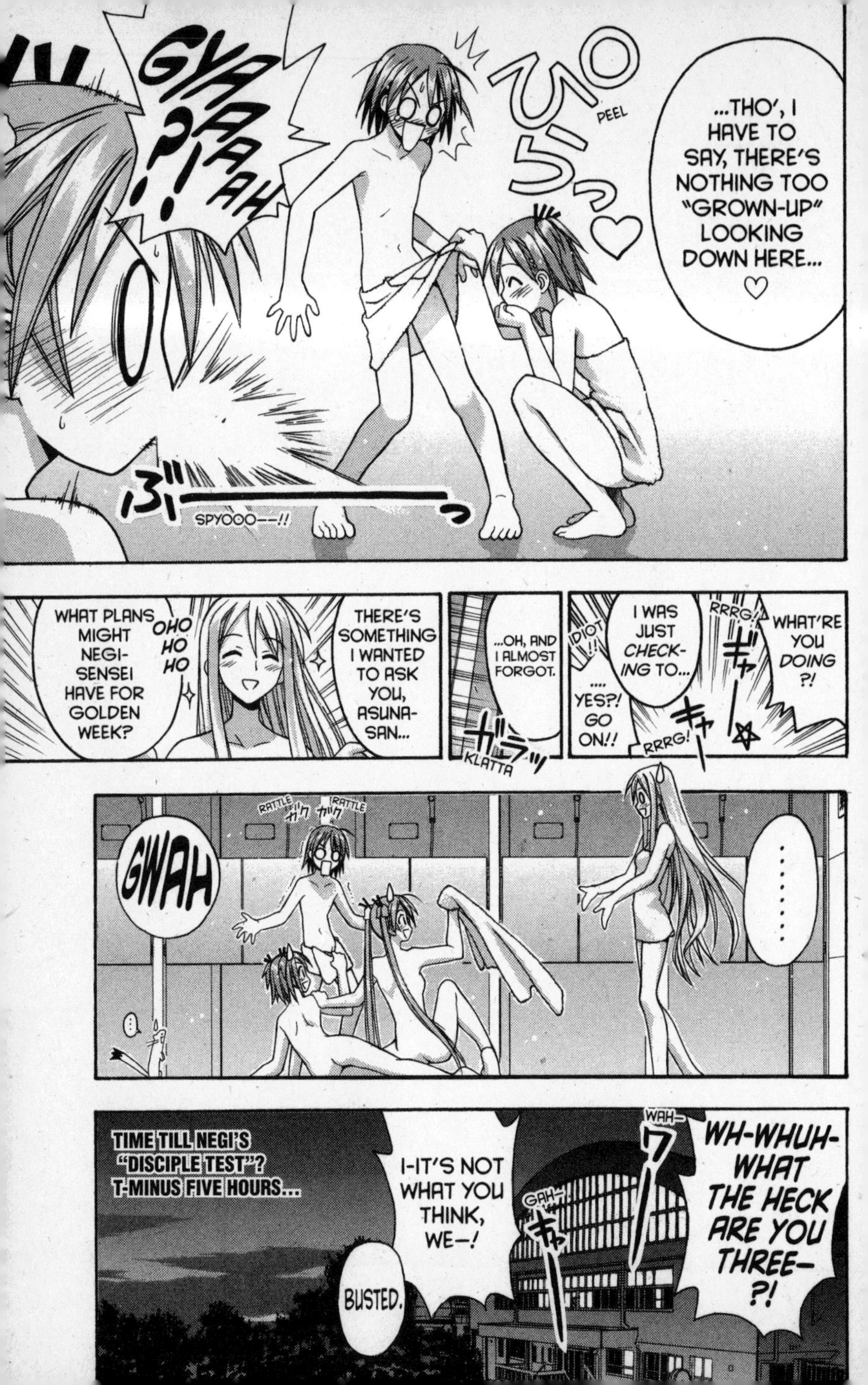
...THO', I HAVE TO SAY, THERE'S NOTHING TOO "GROWN-UP" LOOKING DOWN HERE... ♡
PEEL
GYAAAAH?!!
SPYOOO--!!
WHAT'RE YOU DOING?!
RRRG!
I WAS JUST CHECKING TO...
IDIOT!!
....YES?! GO ON!!
RRRG!
...OH, AND I ALMOST FORGOT.
KLATTA
THERE'S SOMETHING I WANTED TO ASK YOU, ASUNA-SAN...
OHO HO HO
WHAT PLANS MIGHT NEGI-SENSEI HAVE FOR GOLDEN WEEK?
......
RATTLE RATTLE
GWAH
...
WH-WHUH-WHAT THE HECK ARE YOU THREE-?!
WAH-
GAH-
I-IT'S NOT WHAT YOU THINK, WE-!
BUSTED.
TIME TILL NEGI'S "DISCIPLE TEST"? T-MINUS FIVE HOURS...

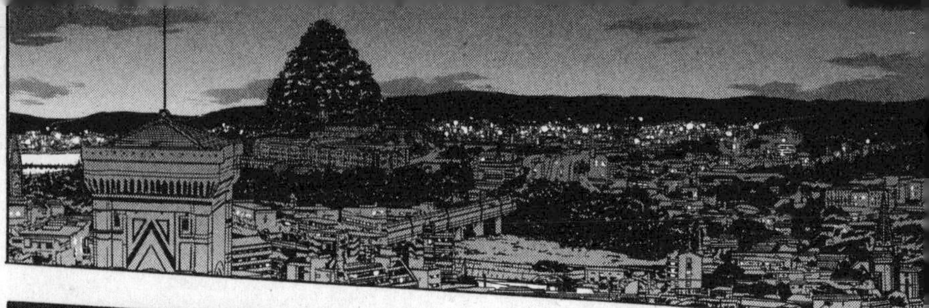
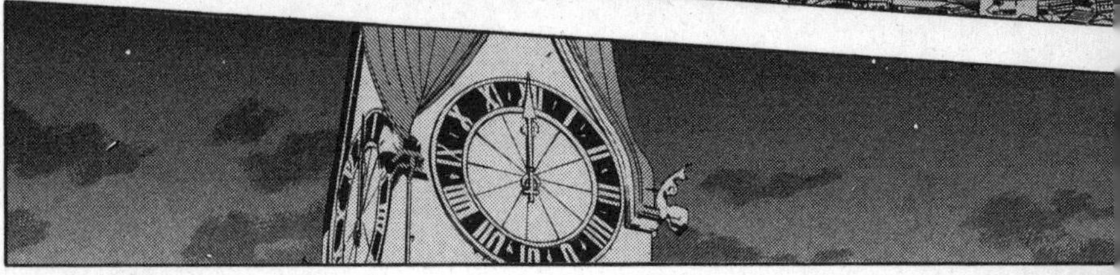
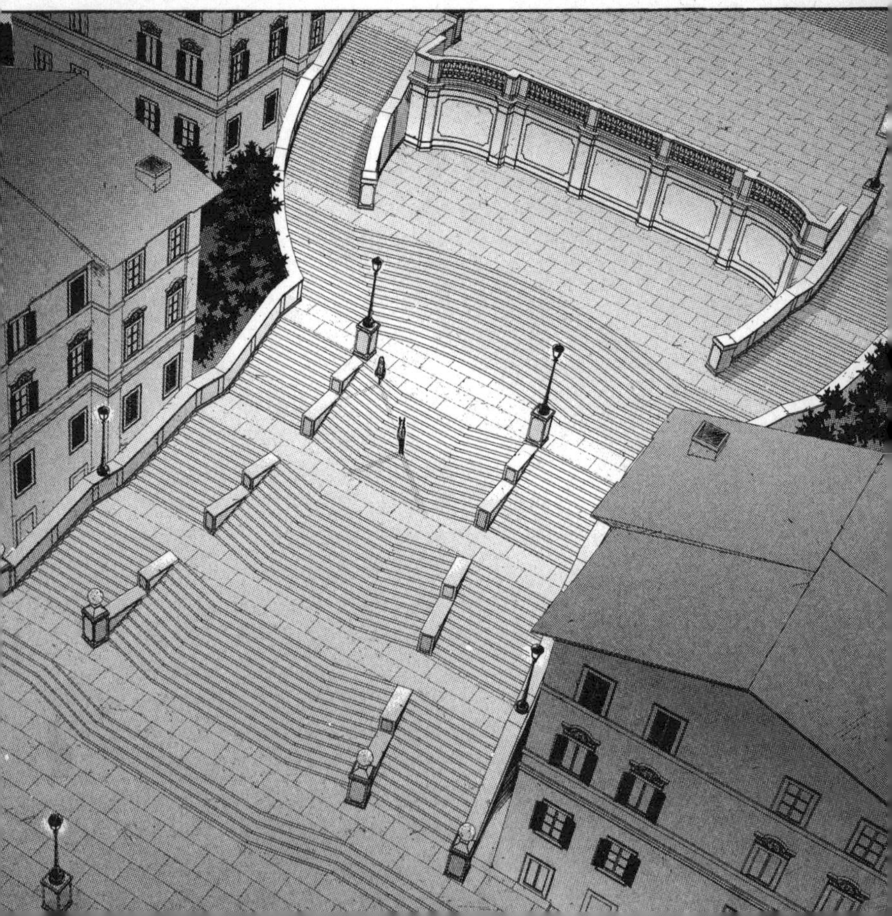

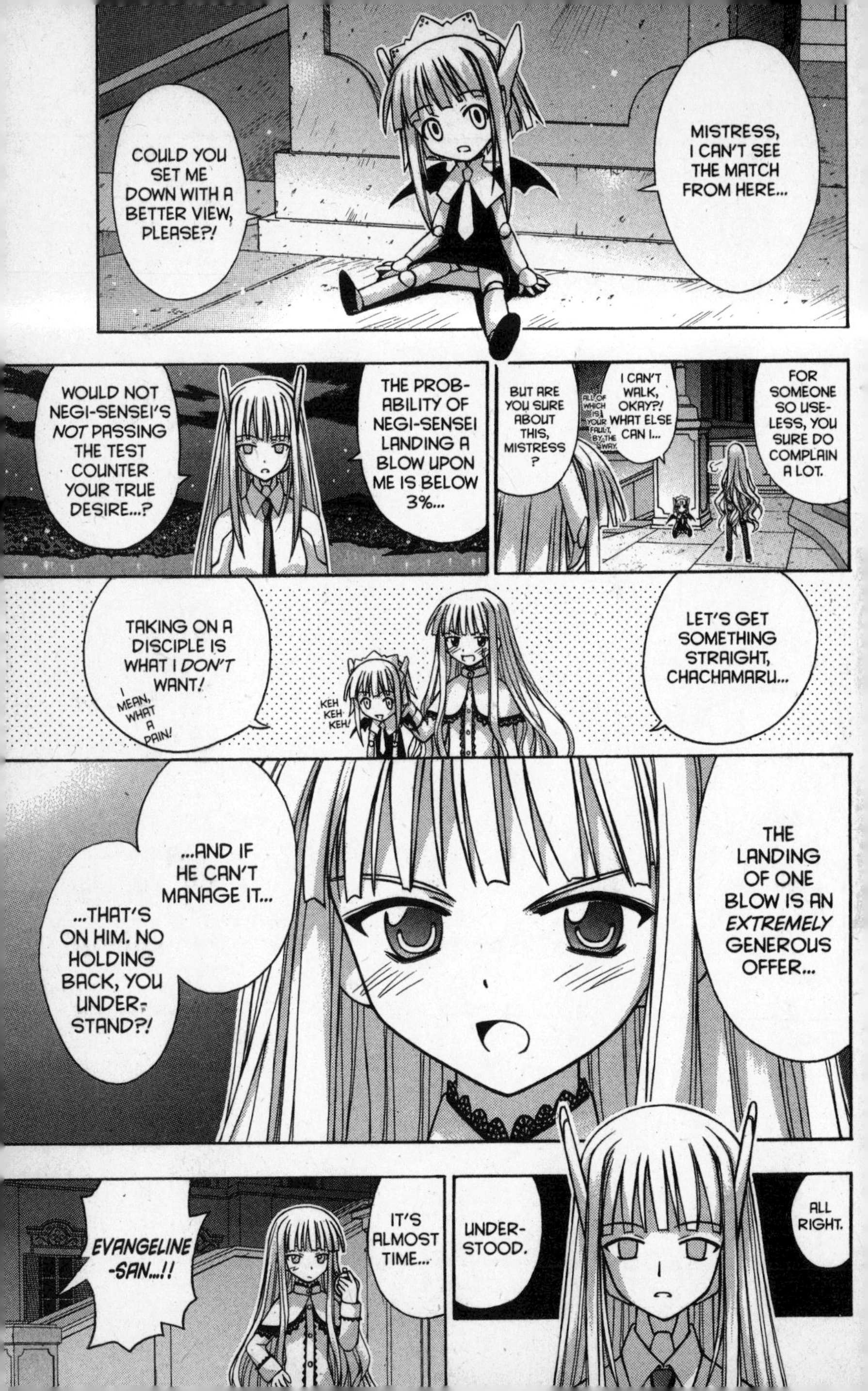
MISTRESS, I CAN'T SEE THE MATCH FROM HERE...
COULD YOU SET ME DOWN WITH A BETTER VIEW, PLEASE?!
FOR SOMEONE SO USE-LESS, YOU SURE DO COMPLAIN A LOT.
I CAN'T WALK, OKAY?! WHAT ELSE CAN I...
ALL OF WHICH IS YOUR FAULT, BY THE WAY.
BUT ARE YOU SURE ABOUT THIS, MISTRESS?
THE PROB-ABILITY OF NEGI-SENSEI LANDING A BLOW UPON ME IS BELOW 3%...
WOULD NOT NEGI-SENSEI'S *NOT* PASSING THE TEST COUNTER YOUR TRUE DESIRE...?
LET'S GET SOMETHING STRAIGHT, CHACHAMARU...
KEH KEH KEH!
TAKING ON A DISCIPLE IS WHAT I *DON'T* WANT!
I MEAN, WHAT A PAIN!
THE LANDING OF ONE BLOW IS AN *EXTREMELY* GENEROUS OFFER...
...AND IF HE CAN'T MANAGE IT...
...THAT'S ON HIM. NO HOLDING BACK, YOU UNDER-STAND?!
ALL RIGHT.
UNDER-STOOD.
IT'S ALMOST TIME...
EVANGELINE-SAN...!!

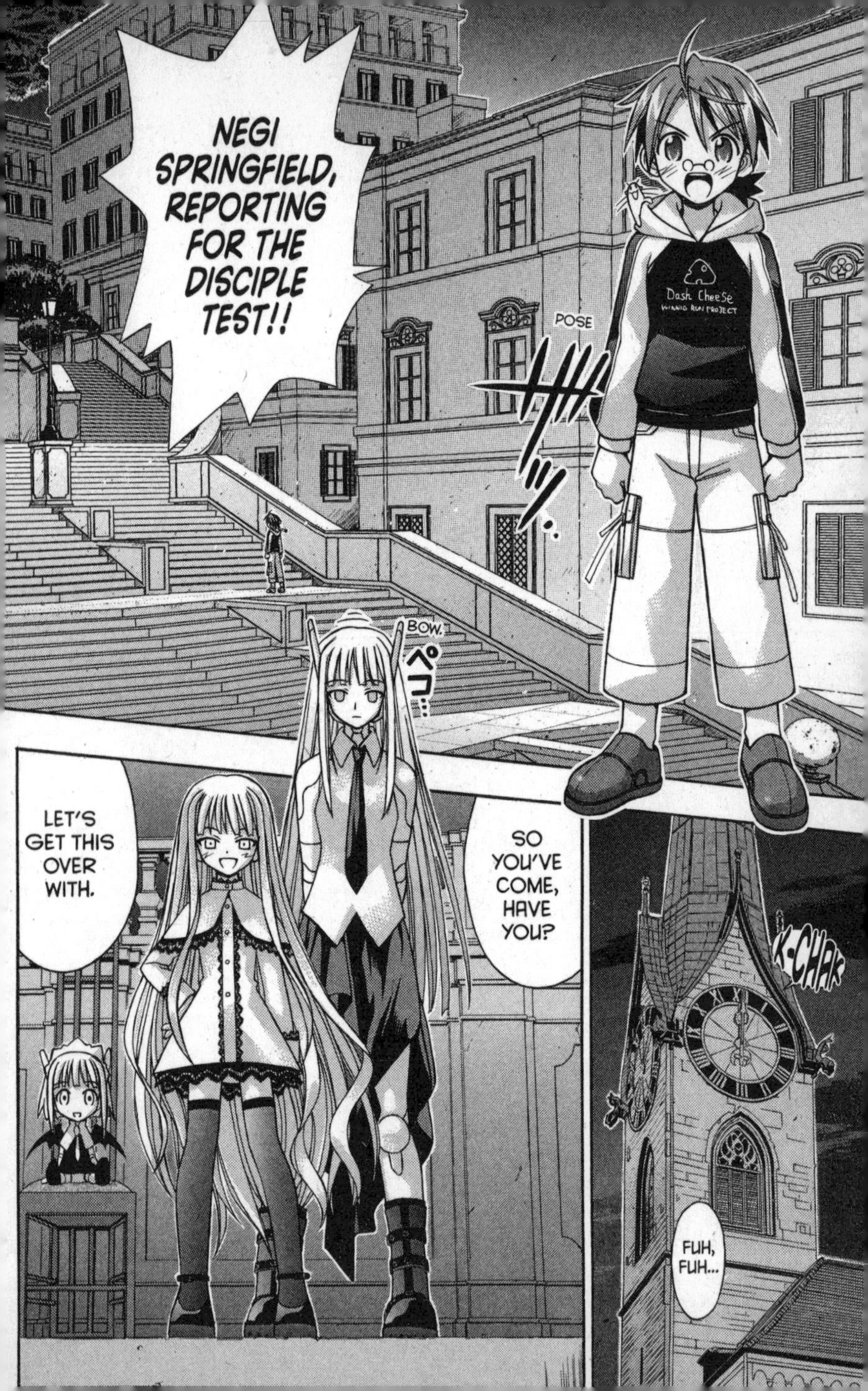
NEGI SPRINGFIELD, REPORTING FOR THE DISCIPLE TEST!!
POSE
K-CHAK
FUH, FUH...
BOW.
ペコ…
SO YOU'VE COME, HAVE YOU?
LET'S GET THIS OVER WITH.

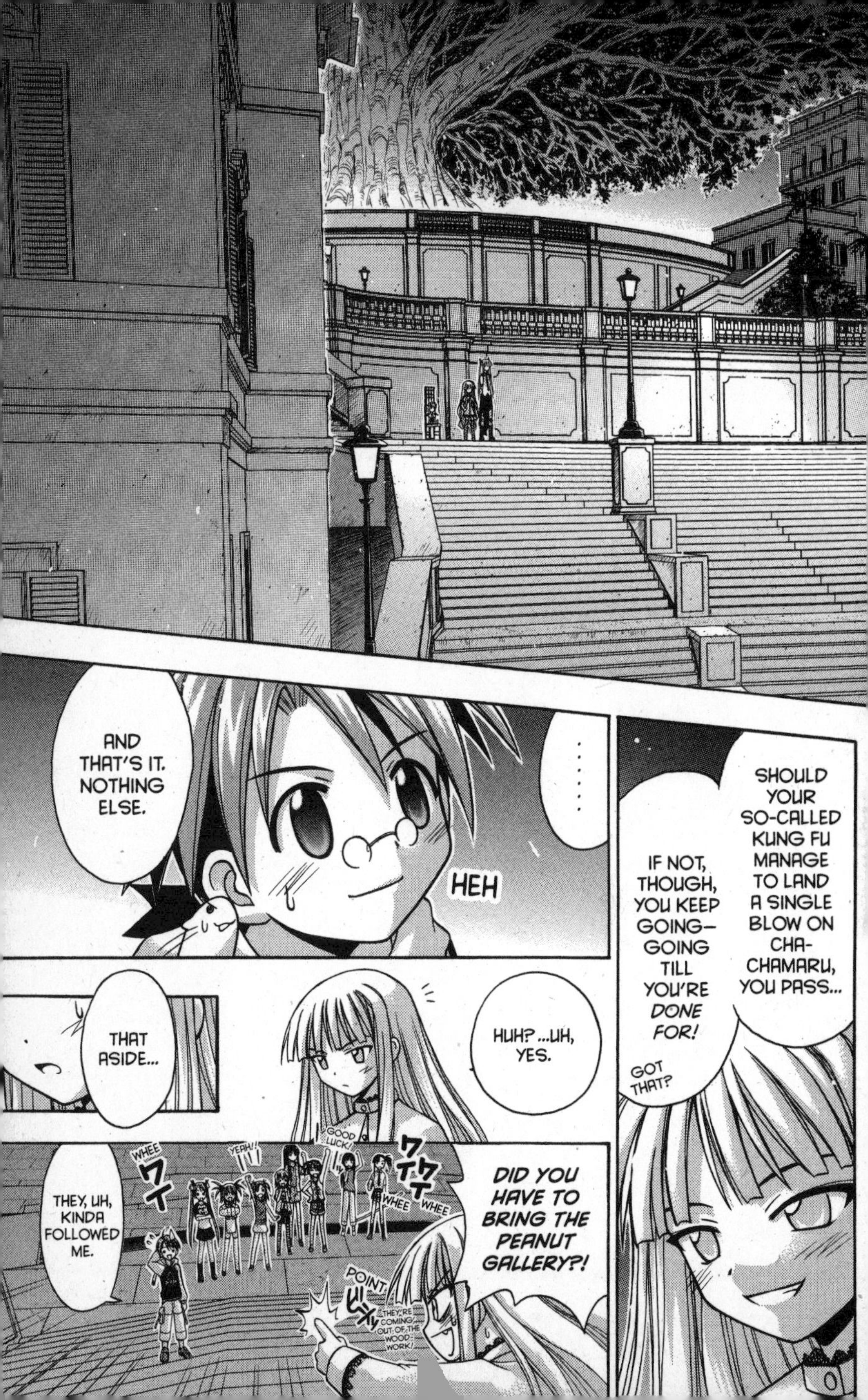
SHOULD YOUR SO-CALLED KUNG FU MANAGE TO LAND A SINGLE BLOW ON CHA-CHAMARU, YOU PASS...
IF NOT, THOUGH, YOU KEEP GOING—GOING TILL YOU'RE *DONE FOR!*
GOT THAT?
......
AND THAT'S IT. NOTHING ELSE.
HEH
HUH? ...UH, YES.
THAT ASIDE...
DID YOU HAVE TO BRING THE PEANUT GALLERY?!
WHEE
WHEE
GOOD LUCK!
YEAH!!
WHEE
THEY, UH, KINDA FOLLOWED ME.
POINT
THEY'RE COMING OUT OF THE WOODWORK!

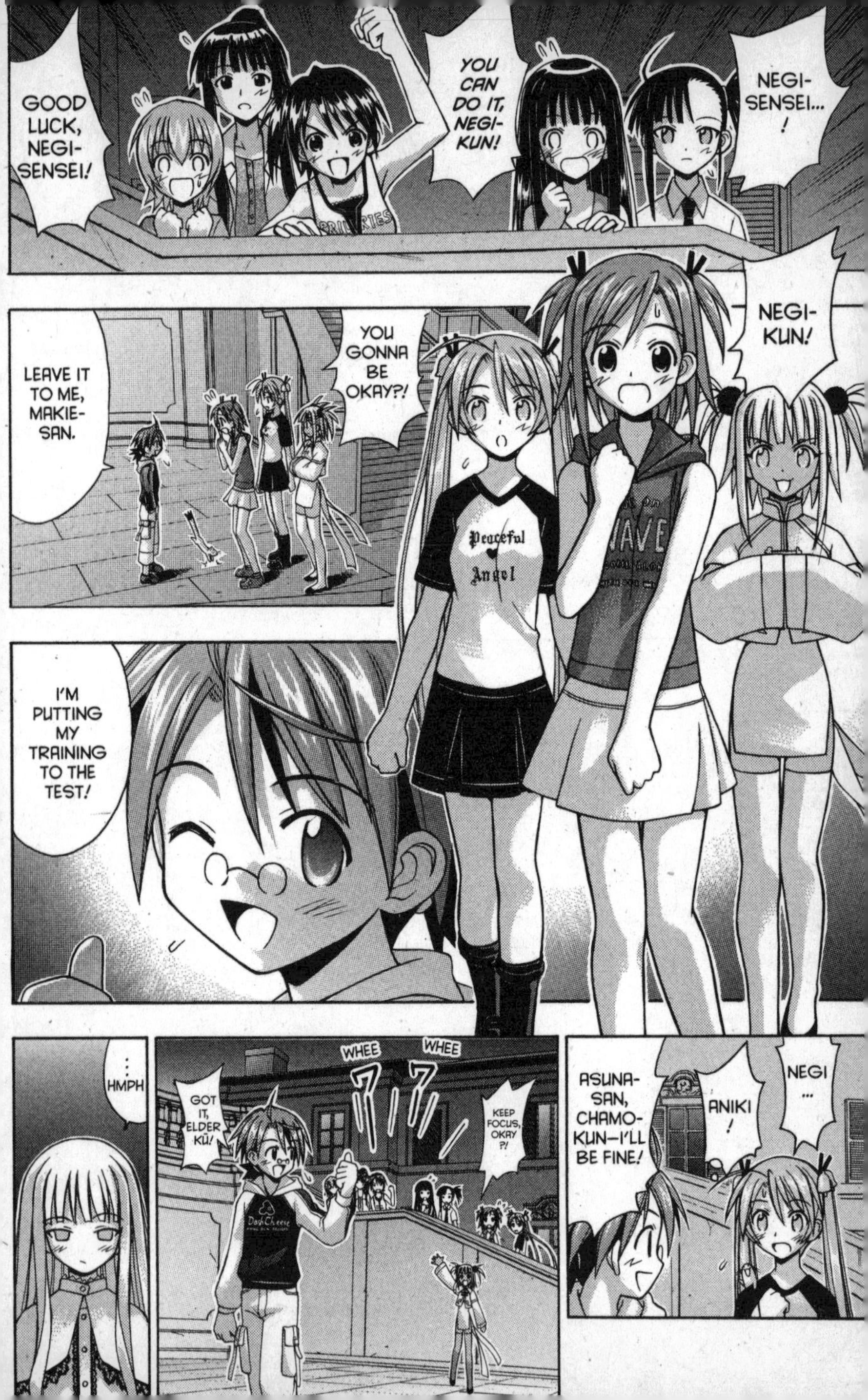
NEGI-SENSEI... !
YOU CAN DO IT, NEGI-KUN!
GOOD LUCK, NEGI-SENSEI!
NEGI-KUN!
YOU GONNA BE OKAY?!
LEAVE IT TO ME, MAKIE-SAN.
I'M PUTTING MY TRAINING TO THE TEST!
NEGI ...
ANIKI !
ASUNA-SAN, CHAMO-KUN—I'LL BE FINE!
WHEE
WHEE
KEEP FOCUS, OKAY ?!
GOT IT, ELDER KŪ!
... HMPH

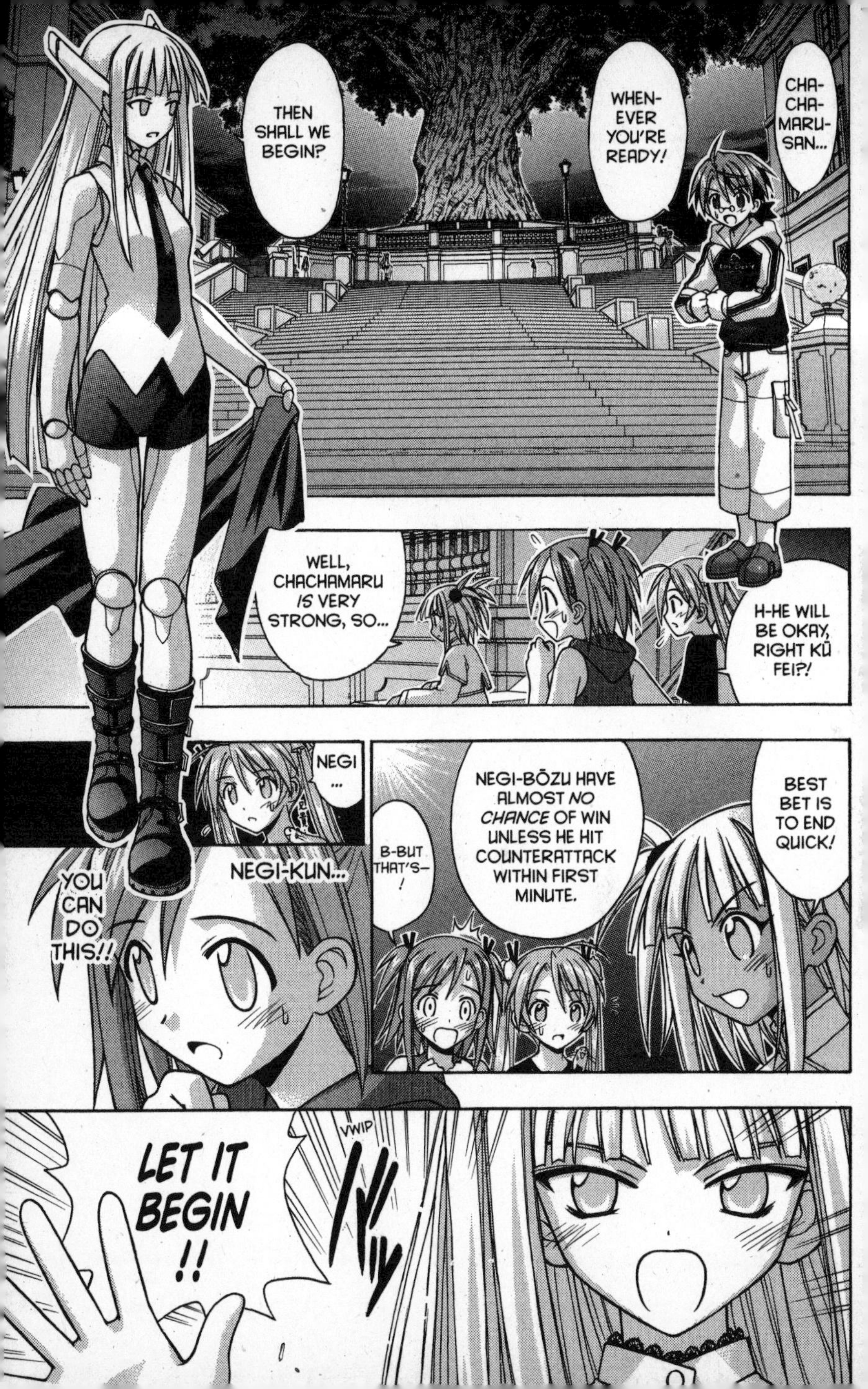
CHA-CHA-MARU-SAN...
WHEN-EVER YOU'RE READY!
THEN SHALL WE BEGIN?
H-HE WILL BE OKAY, RIGHT KŪ FEI?!
WELL, CHACHAMARU *IS* VERY STRONG, SO...
BEST BET IS TO END QUICK!
NEGI-BŌZU HAVE ALMOST *NO CHANCE* OF WIN UNLESS HE HIT COUNTERATTACK WITHIN FIRST MINUTE.
B-BUT THAT'S—!
NEGI ...
NEGI-KUN...
YOU CAN DO THIS!!
VWIP
LET IT BEGIN!!

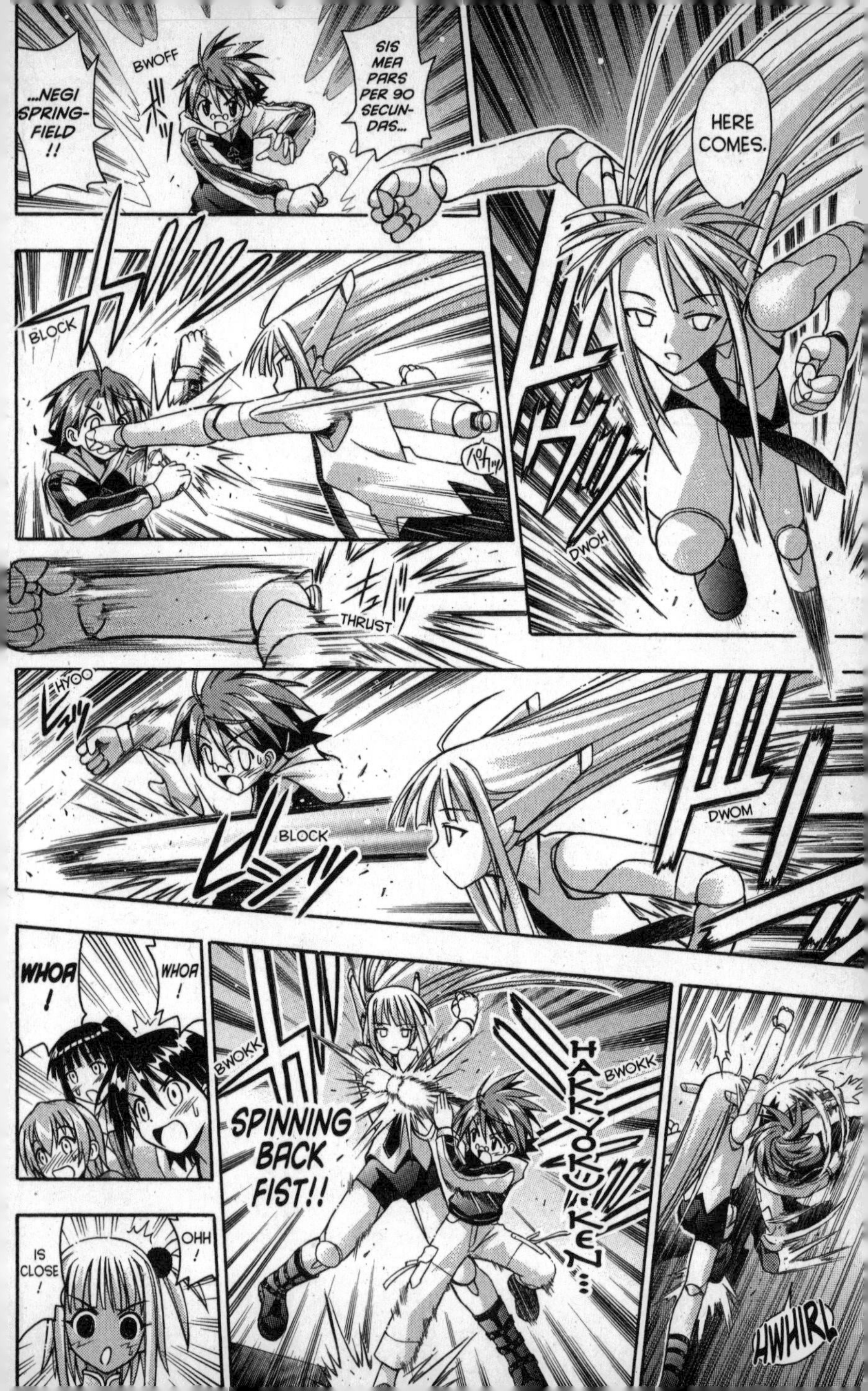
HERE COMES.
DWOH
SIS MEA PARS PER 90 SECUNDAS...
BWOFF
...NEGI SPRINGFIELD!!
BLOCK
THRUST
DWOM
BLOCK
HYOO
HWHIRL
BWOKK
HAKKYOKU-KEN...
BWOKK
SPINNING BACK FIST!!
WHOA!
WHOA!
OHH!
IS CLOSE!

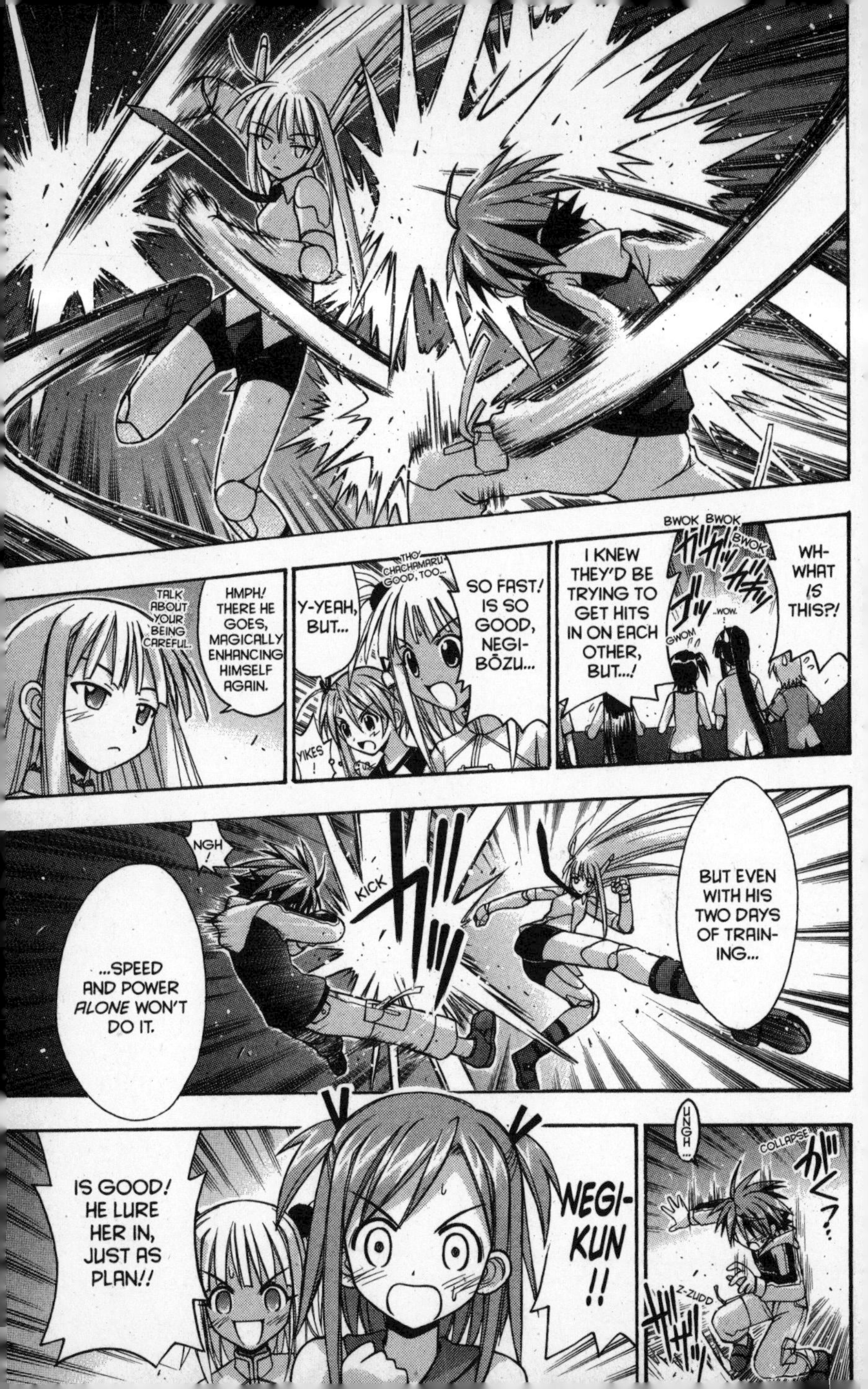
BWOK BWOK BWOK
WH- WHAT *IS* THIS?!
...WOW.
GWOM
I KNEW THEY'D BE TRYING TO GET HITS IN ON EACH OTHER, BUT...!
SO FAST! IS SO GOOD, NEGI-BŌZU...
THO' CHACHAMARU GOOD, TOO...
Y-YEAH, BUT...
YIKES!
HMPH! THERE HE GOES, MAGICALLY ENHANCING HIMSELF AGAIN.
TALK ABOUT YOUR BEING CAREFUL.
BUT EVEN WITH HIS TWO DAYS OF TRAIN-ING...
KICK
NGH!
...SPEED AND POWER *ALONE* WON'T DO IT.
UNGH...
COLLAPSE
Z-ZUDD
NEGI-KUN!!
IS GOOD! HE LURE HER IN, JUST AS PLAN!!

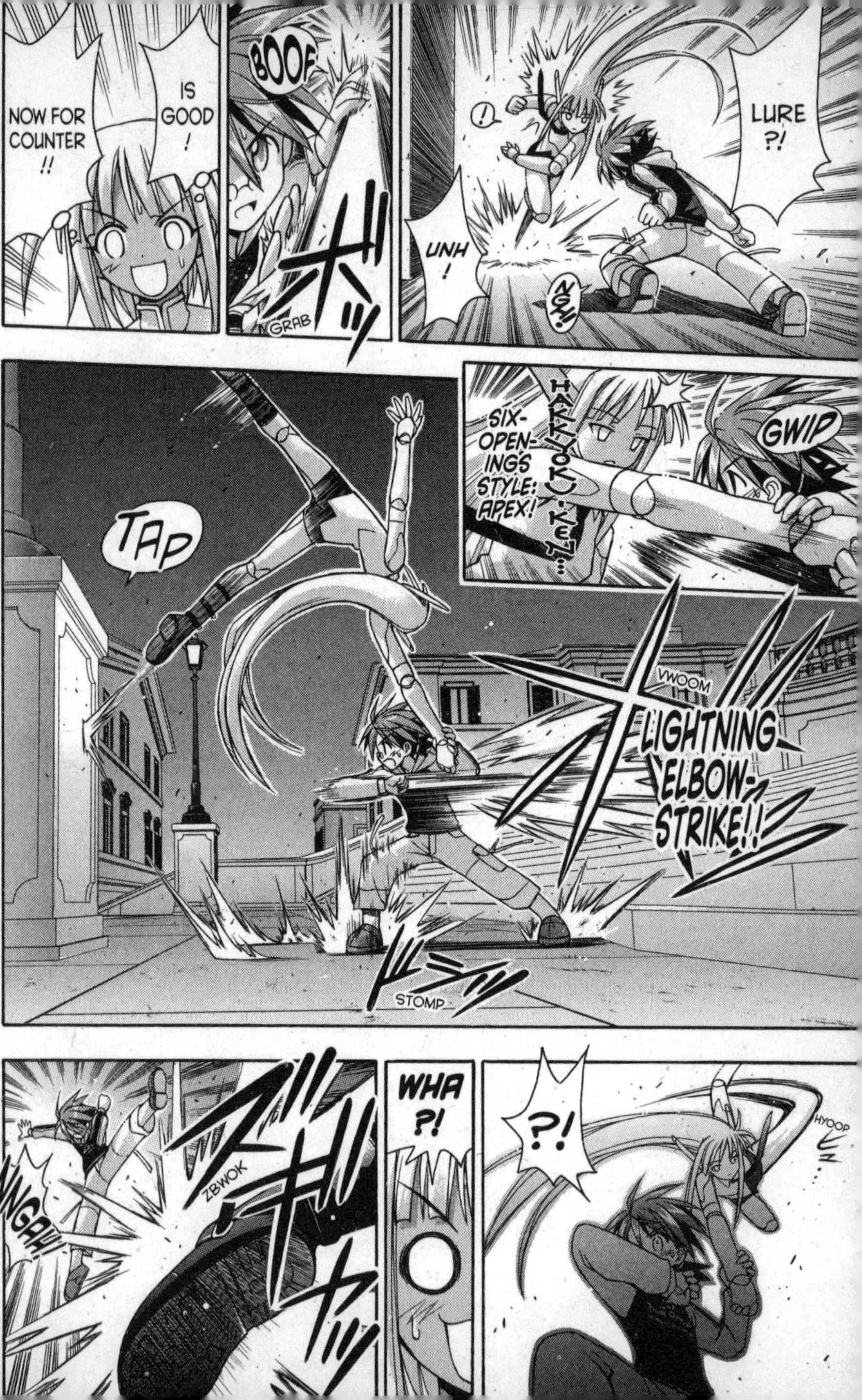
LURE ?!
!
UNH !
NGH!!
BOOF
GRAB
IS GOOD !
NOW FOR COUNTER !!
GWIP
HAKKYOKU-KEN...
SIX-OPENINGS STYLE: APEX!
TAP
VWOOM
LIGHTNING ELBOW-STRIKE!!
STOMP
HYOOP
?!
WHA ?!
ZBWOK
NNGAH!!

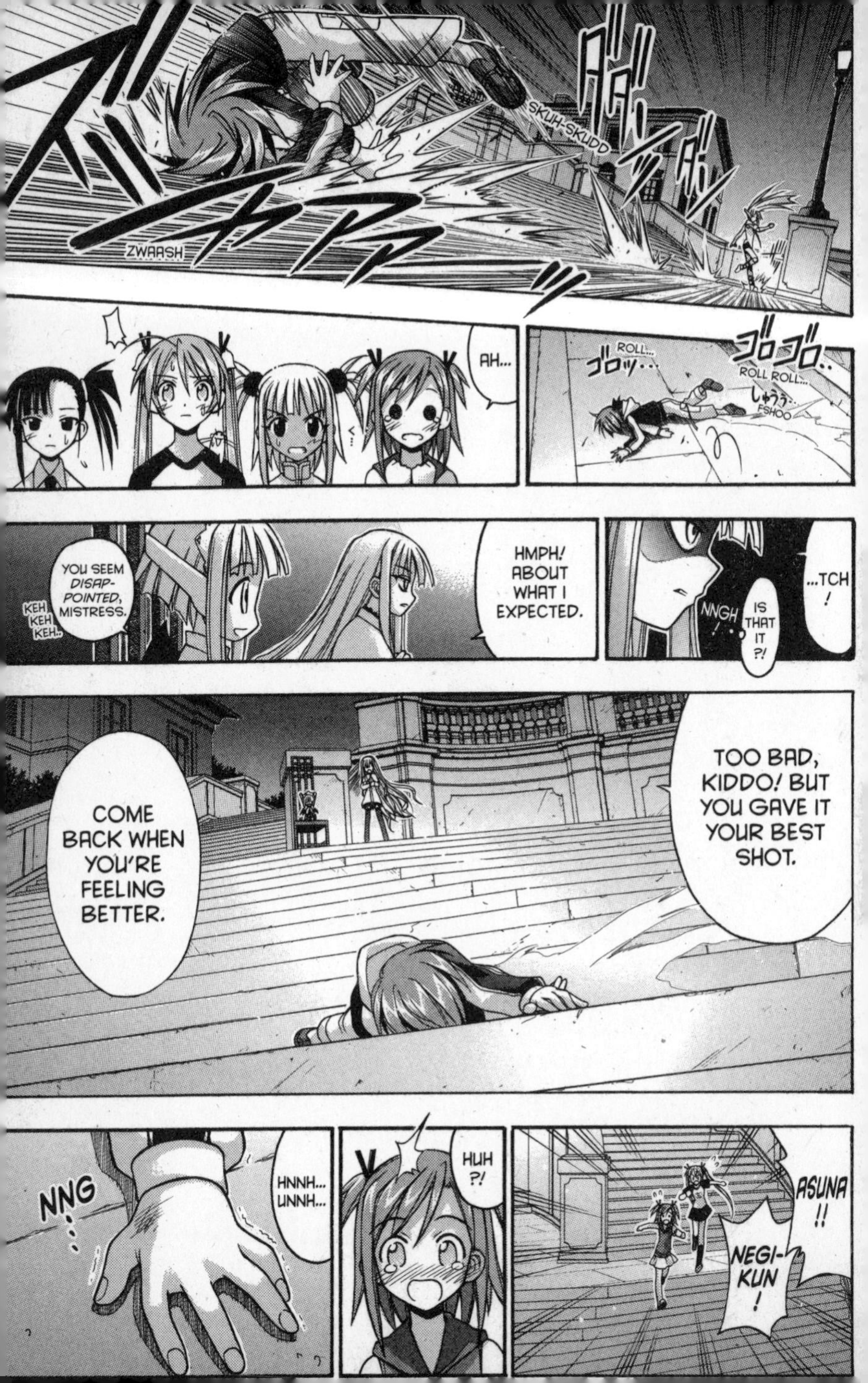
SKUH-SKUDD
ZWAASH
ゴロゴロ..
ROLL ROLL...
ゴロッ...
ROLL...
しゅうう..
FSHOO
AH...
...TCH!
IS THAT IT?!
NNGH!...
HMPH! ABOUT WHAT I EXPECTED.
YOU SEEM *DISAP-POINTED*, MISTRESS.
KEH KEH KEH..
TOO BAD, KIDDO! BUT YOU GAVE IT YOUR BEST SHOT.
COME BACK WHEN YOU'RE FEELING BETTER.
ASUNA!!
NEGI-KUN!
HUH?!
HNNH... UNNH...
NNG...

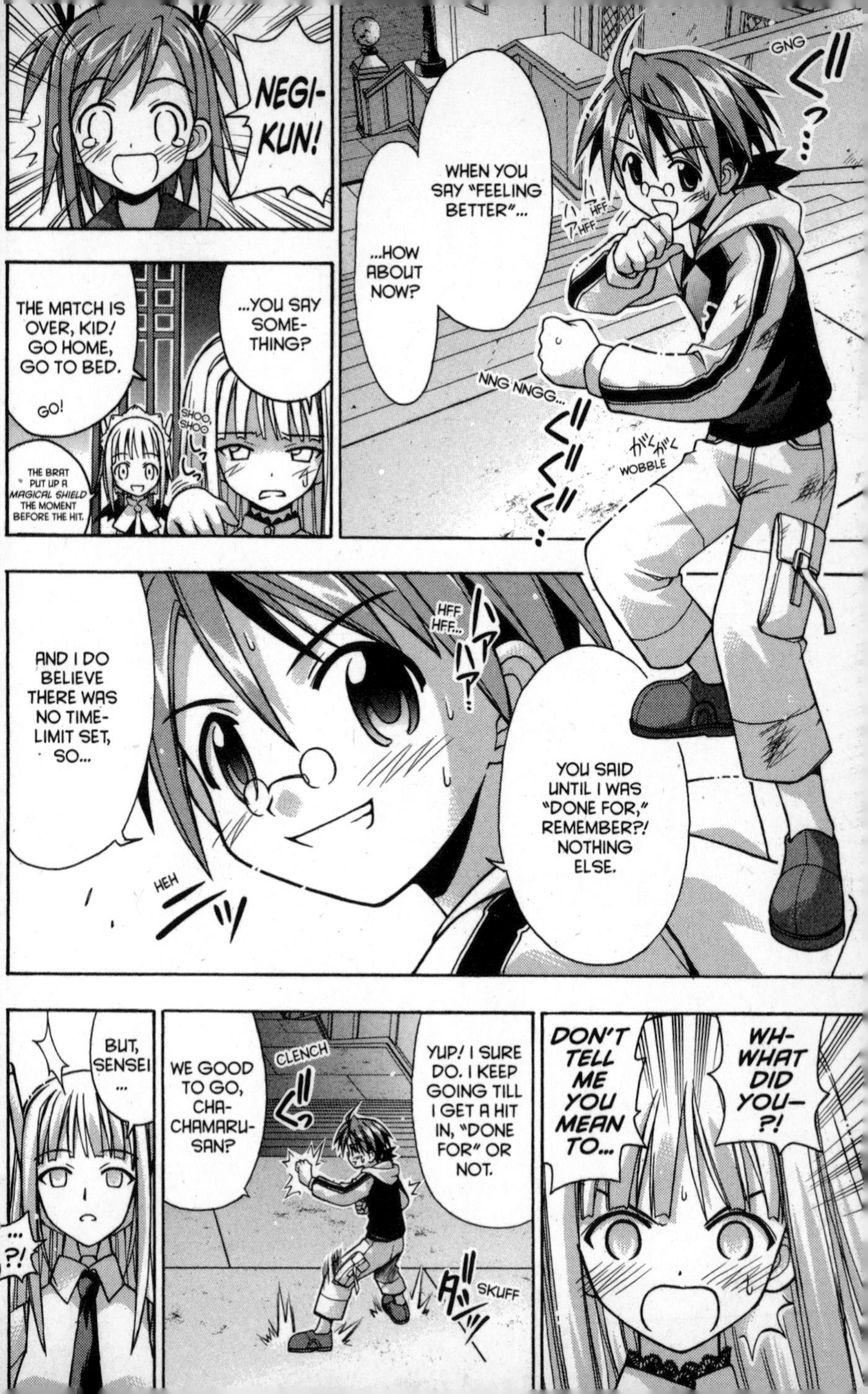
GNG
WHEN YOU SAY "FEELING BETTER"...
...HOW ABOUT NOW?
HFF HFF
NNG NNGG...
WOBBLE
NEGI-KUN!
...YOU SAY SOME-THING?
THE MATCH IS OVER, KID! GO HOME, GO TO BED.
GO!
SHOO, SHOO
THE BRAT PUT UP A MAGICAL SHIELD THE MOMENT BEFORE THE HIT.
YOU SAID UNTIL I WAS "DONE FOR," REMEMBER?! NOTHING ELSE.
HFF HFF...
AND I DO BELIEVE THERE WAS NO TIME-LIMIT SET, SO...
HEH
WH-WHAT DID YOU-?!
DON'T TELL ME YOU MEAN TO...
YUP! I SURE DO. I KEEP GOING TILL I GET A HIT IN, "DONE FOR" OR NOT.
WE GOOD TO GO, CHA-CHAMARU-SAN?
CLENCH
SKUFF
BUT, SENSEI ...
...?!

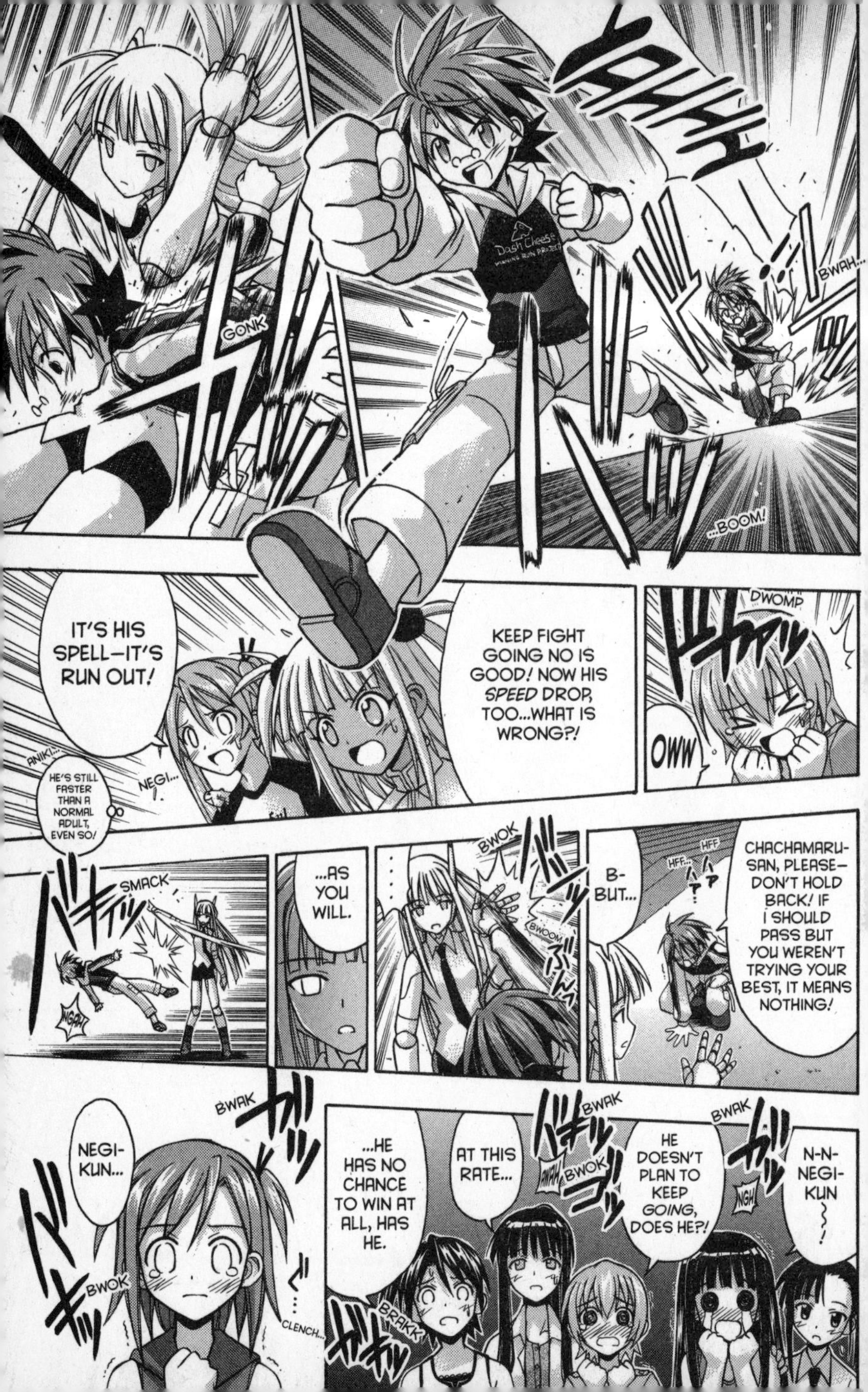
BWAH...
GONK
...BOOM!
DWOMP
OWW
KEEP FIGHT GOING NO IS GOOD! NOW HIS *SPEED* DROP, TOO...WHAT IS WRONG?!
IT'S HIS SPELL—IT'S RUN OUT!
ANIKI...
NEGI...
HE'S STILL FASTER THAN A NORMAL ADULT, EVEN SO!
CHACHAMARU-SAN, PLEASE—DON'T HOLD BACK! IF I SHOULD PASS BUT YOU WEREN'T TRYING YOUR BEST, IT MEANS NOTHING!
HFF... HFF
B-BUT...
BWOK
BWOOM
...AS YOU WILL.
SMACK
NGAH
N-N-NEGI-KUN~?!
BWAK
NGH!
HE DOESN'T PLAN TO KEEP *GOING*, DOES HE?!
BWAK
BWOK
AWAH
AT THIS RATE...
...HE HAS NO CHANCE TO WIN AT ALL, HAS HE.
BRAKK
BWAK
NEGI-KUN...
BWOK
CLENCH...

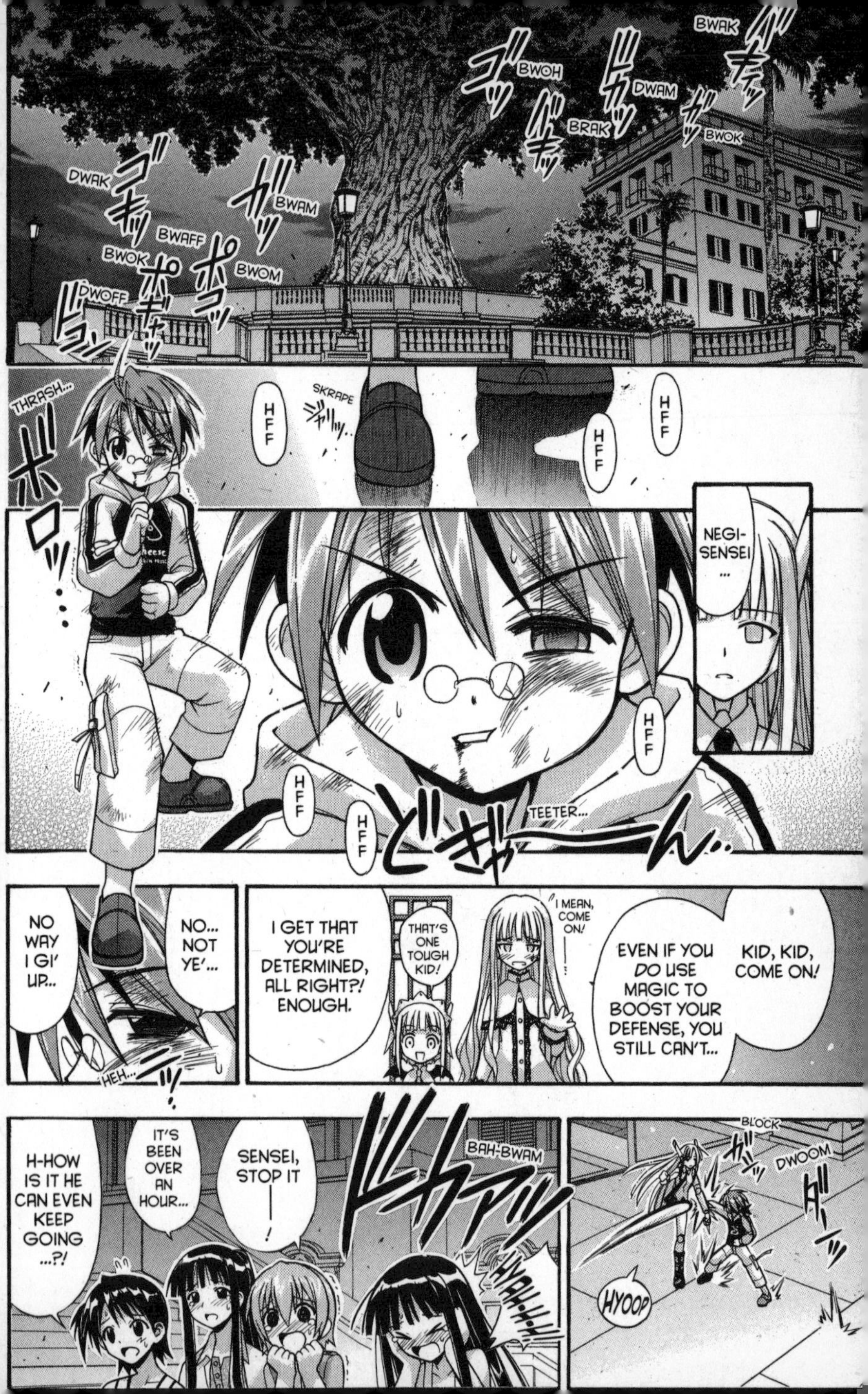
BWAK
DWAM
BWOK
BRAK
BWOH
BWAM
DWAK
BWAFF
BWOK
BWOM
DWOFF
HFF HFF
HFF HFF
SKRAPE
HFF
THRASH...
NEGI-SENSEI...
HFF
TEETER...
HFF
HFF
KID, KID, COME ON!
EVEN IF YOU *DO* USE MAGIC TO BOOST YOUR DEFENSE, YOU STILL CAN'T...
I MEAN, COME ON!
THAT'S ONE TOUGH KID!
I GET THAT YOU'RE DETERMINED, ALL RIGHT?! ENOUGH.
NO... NOT YE'...
NO WAY I GI' UP...
HEH...
BLOCK
DWOOM
HYOOP
BAH-BWAM
HYAH-H-H
SENSEI, STOP IT—!
IT'S BEEN OVER AN HOUR...
H-HOW IS IT HE CAN EVEN KEEP GOING...?!

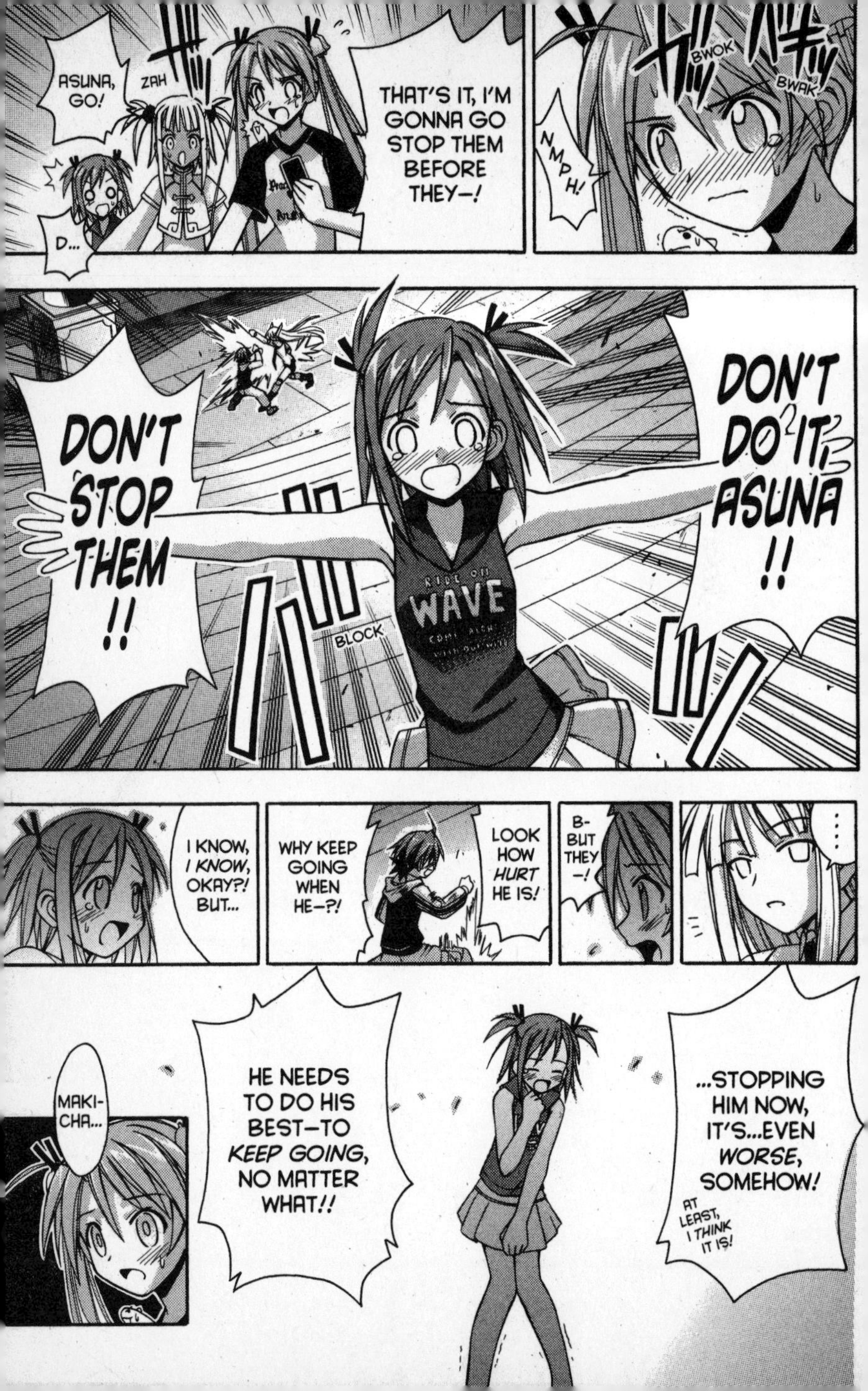
BWOK
BWAK
NMPH!
THAT'S IT, I'M GONNA GO STOP THEM BEFORE THEY—!
ZAH
ASUNA, GO!
D...
DON'T DO IT, ASUNA!!
DON'T STOP THEM!!
BLOCK
WAVE
....
B-BUT THEY—!
LOOK HOW *HURT* HE IS!
WHY KEEP GOING WHEN HE—?!
I KNOW, *I KNOW,* OKAY?! BUT...
...STOPPING HIM NOW, IT'S...EVEN *WORSE,* SOMEHOW!
AT LEAST, I *THINK* IT IS!
HE NEEDS TO DO HIS BEST—TO *KEEP GOING,* NO MATTER WHAT!!
MAKI-CHA...

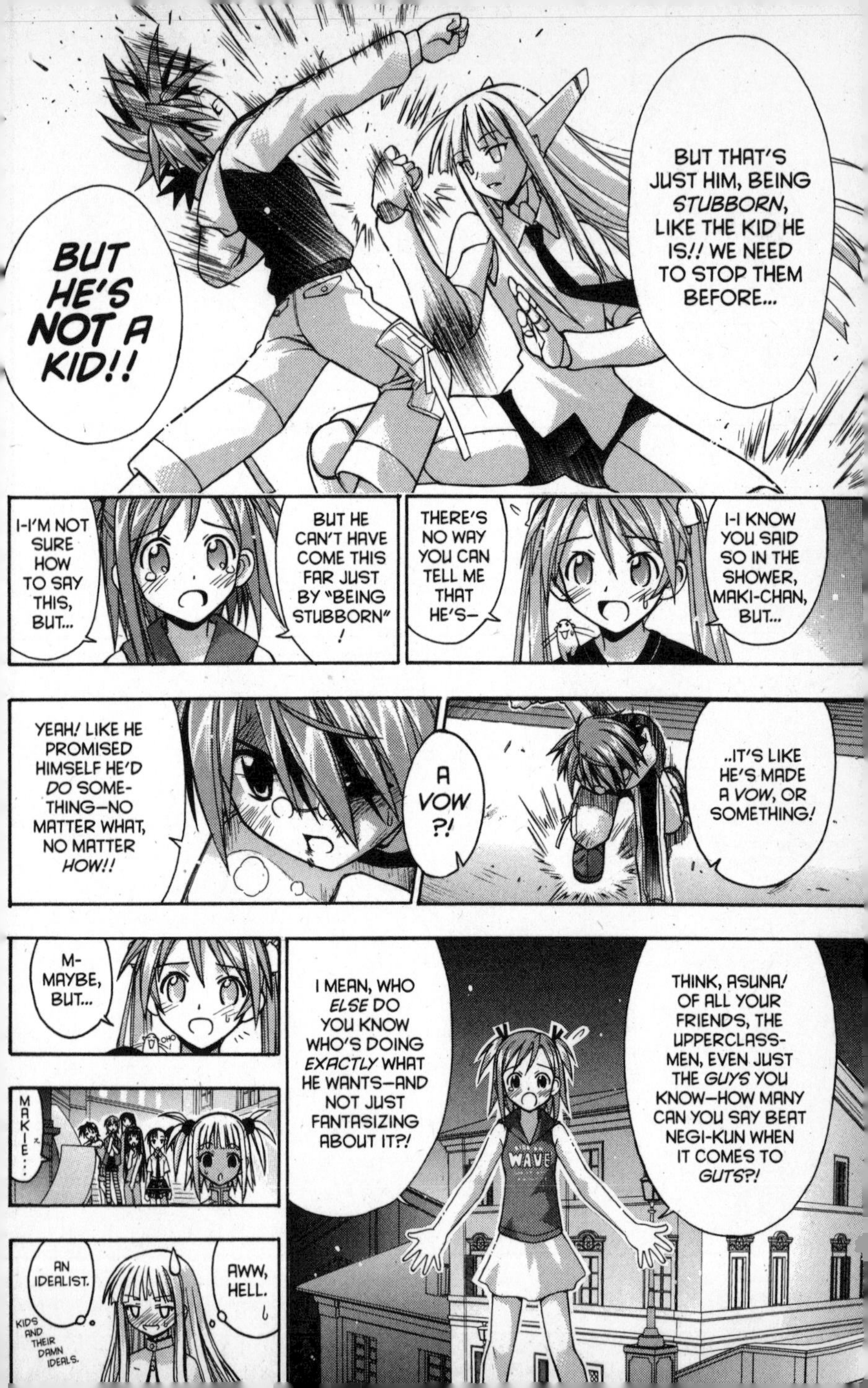
BUT THAT'S JUST HIM, BEING *STUBBORN*, LIKE THE KID HE IS!! WE NEED TO STOP THEM BEFORE...
BUT HE'S NOT A KID!!
I-I KNOW YOU SAID SO IN THE SHOWER, MAKI-CHAN, BUT...
THERE'S NO WAY YOU CAN TELL ME THAT HE'S—
BUT HE CAN'T HAVE COME THIS FAR JUST BY "BEING STUBBORN"!
I-I'M NOT SURE HOW TO SAY THIS, BUT...
..IT'S LIKE HE'S MADE A *VOW*, OR SOMETHING!
A *VOW*?!
YEAH! LIKE HE PROMISED HIMSELF HE'D *DO* SOMETHING—NO MATTER WHAT, NO MATTER *HOW*!!
THINK, ASUNA! OF ALL YOUR FRIENDS, THE UPPERCLASSMEN, EVEN JUST THE *GUYS* YOU KNOW—HOW MANY CAN YOU SAY BEAT NEGI-KUN WHEN IT COMES TO *GUTS*?!
I MEAN, WHO *ELSE* DO YOU KNOW WHO'S DOING *EXACTLY* WHAT HE WANTS—AND NOT JUST FANTASIZING ABOUT IT?!
WAVE
M-MAYBE, BUT...
OHO!
MAKIE...
AWW, HELL.
AN IDEALIST.
KIDS AND THEIR DAMN IDEALS.

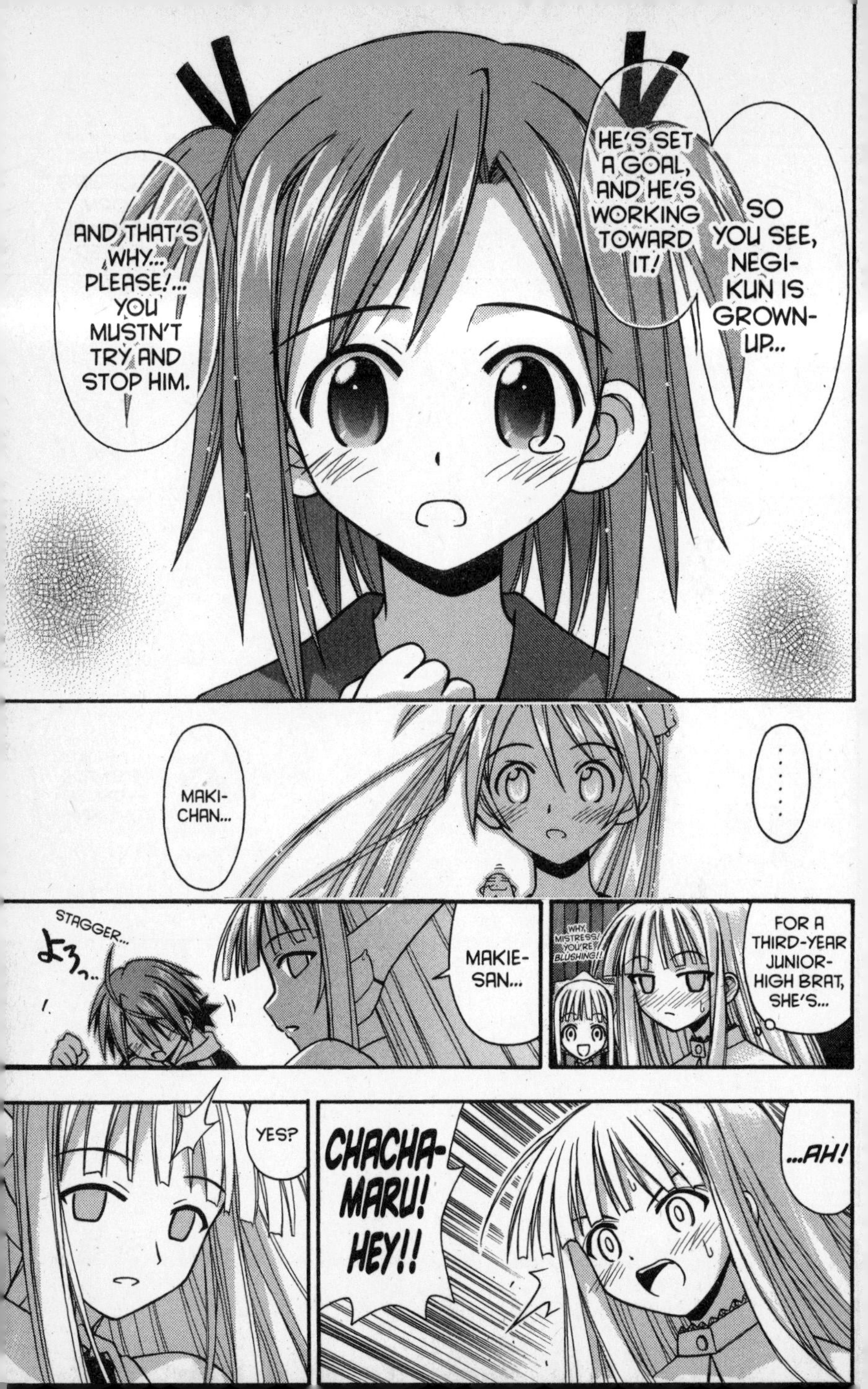
SO YOU SEE, NEGI-KUN IS GROWN-UP...
HE'S SET A GOAL, AND HE'S WORKING TOWARD IT!
AND THAT'S WHY... PLEASE!... YOU MUSTN'T TRY AND STOP HIM.
......
MAKI-CHAN...
FOR A THIRD-YEAR JUNIOR-HIGH BRAT, SHE'S...
WHY, MISTRESS! YOU'RE BLUSHING!!
MAKIE-SAN...
STAGGER...
よろっ
...AH!
CHACHA-MARU! HEY!!
YES?

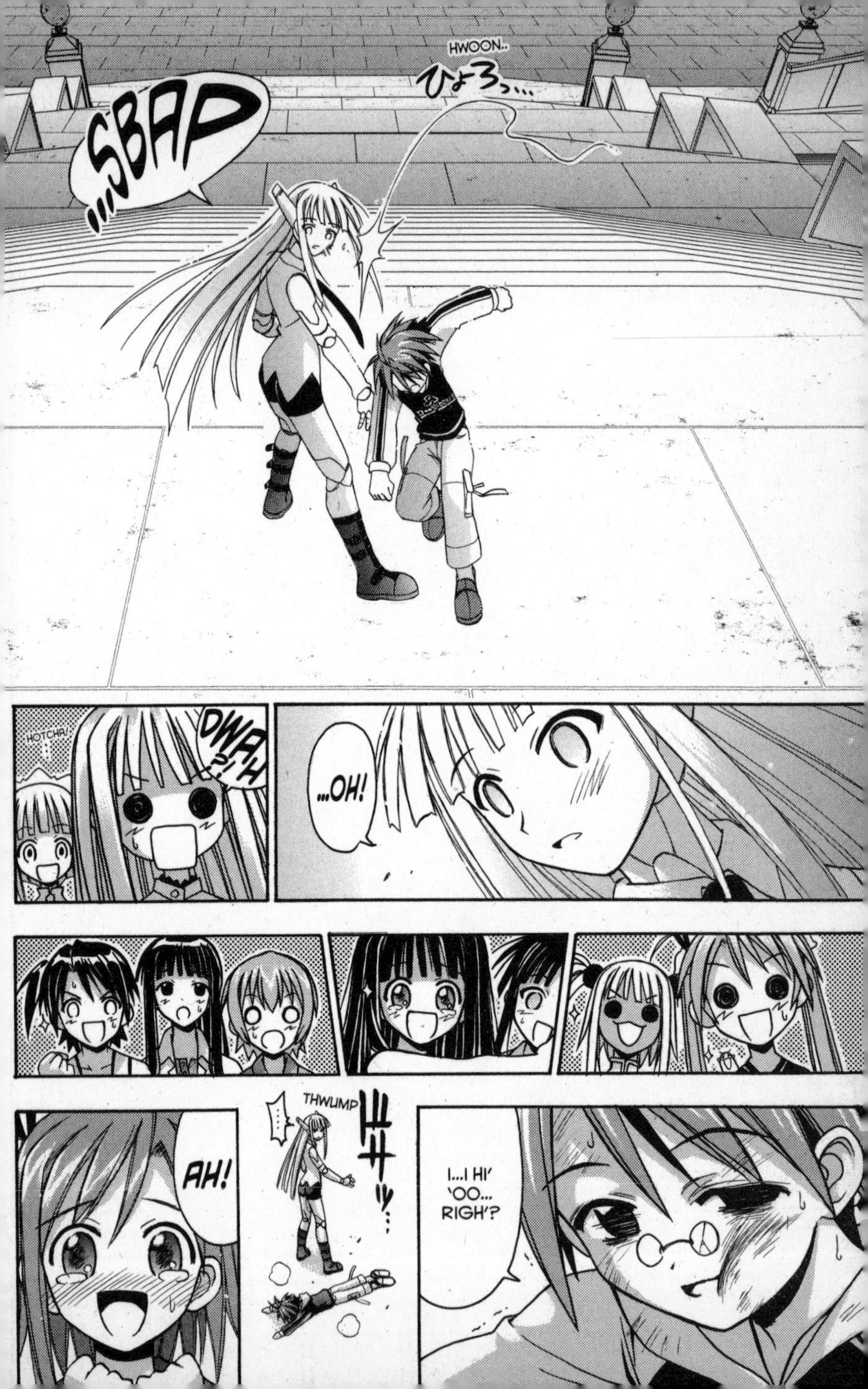

HWOON..
ひょろっ...
...SBAP
...OH!
DWAH?!
HOTCHA!
...
I...I HI' 'OO... RIGH'?
THWUMP
...!
AH!

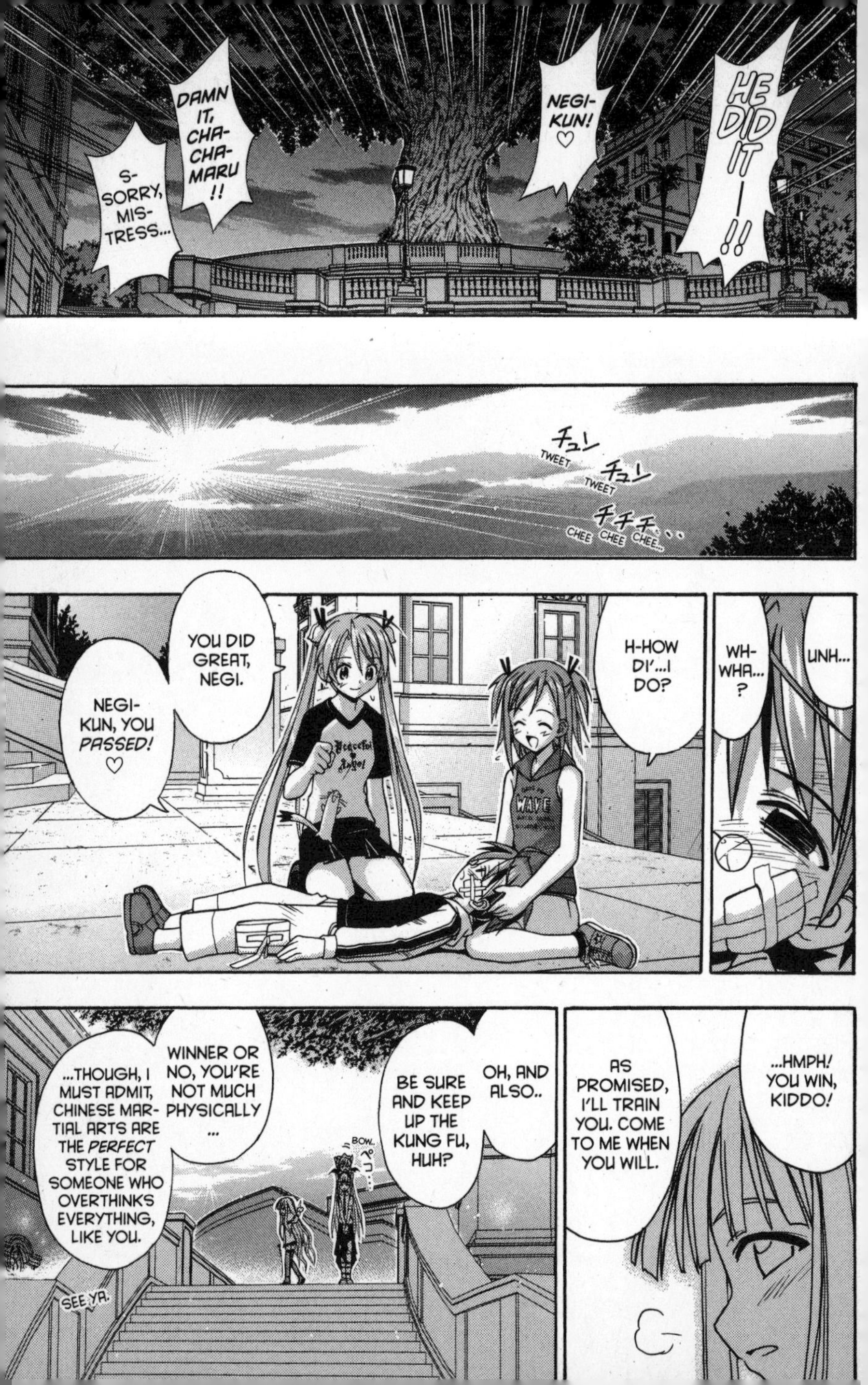
HE DID IT—!!
NEGI-KUN! ♡
DAMN IT, CHACHAMARU!!
S-SORRY, MISTRESS...
チュン TWEET
チュン TWEET
チチチ... CHEE CHEE CHEE...
UNH...
WH-WHA...?
H-HOW DI'...I DO?
YOU DID GREAT, NEGI.
NEGI-KUN, YOU *PASSED!* ♡
...HMPH! YOU WIN, KIDDO!
AS PROMISED, I'LL TRAIN YOU. COME TO ME WHEN YOU WILL.
OH, AND ALSO..
BE SURE AND KEEP UP THE KUNG FU, HUH?
WINNER OR NO, YOU'RE NOT MUCH PHYSICALLY...
...THOUGH, I MUST ADMIT, CHINESE MARTIAL ARTS ARE THE *PERFECT* STYLE FOR SOMEONE WHO OVERTHINKS EVERYTHING, LIKE YOU.
ペコ... BOW..
SEE YA.

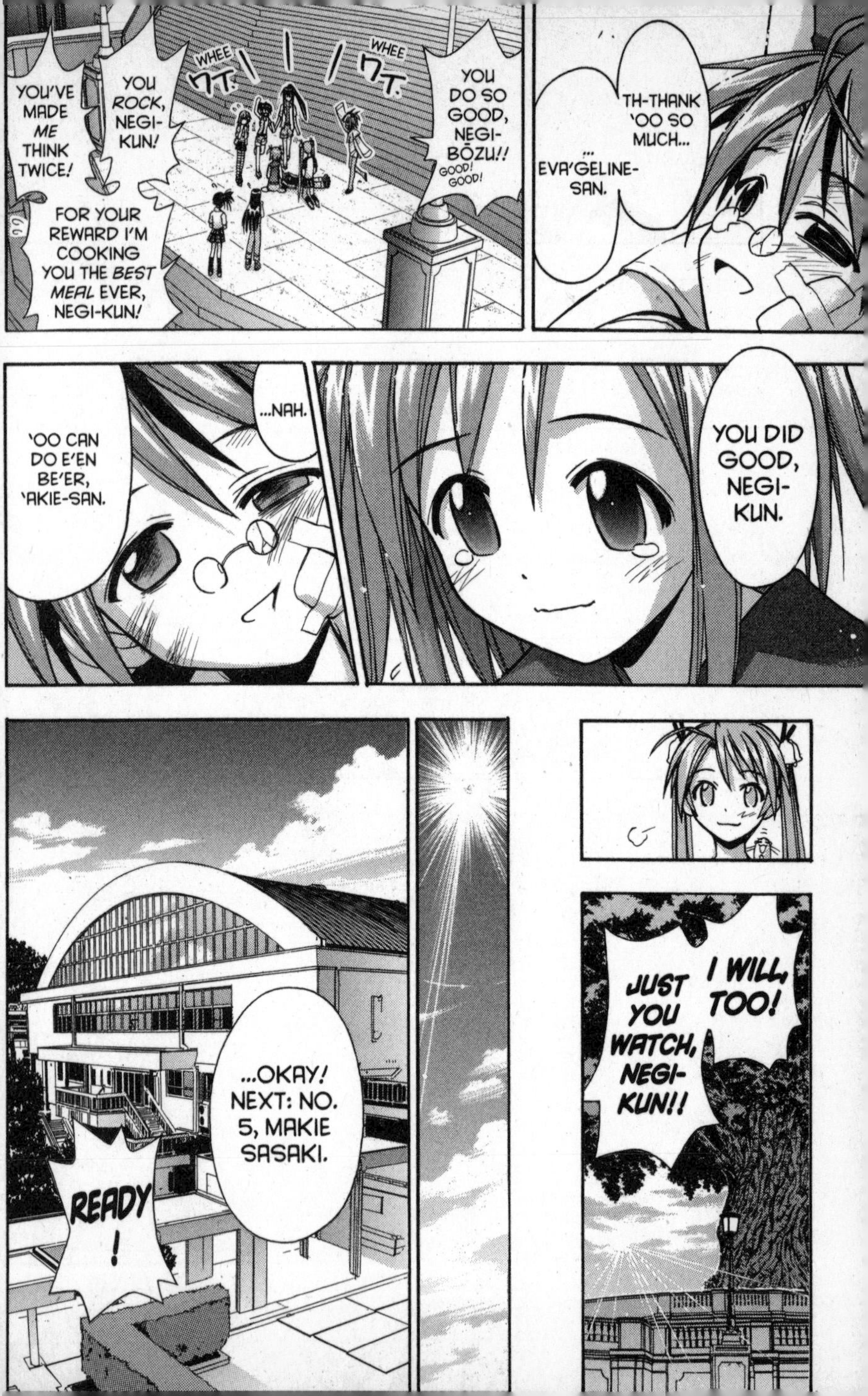
TH-THANK 'OO SO MUCH...
...EVA'GELINE-SAN.
YOU DO SO GOOD, NEGI-BŌZU!!
GOOD! GOOD!
WHEE
WHEE
YOU ROCK, NEGI-KUN!
YOU'VE MADE ME THINK TWICE!
FOR YOUR REWARD I'M COOKING YOU THE BEST MEAL EVER, NEGI-KUN!
YOU DID GOOD, NEGI-KUN.
...NAH.
'OO CAN DO E'EN BE'ER, 'AKIE-SAN.
I WILL, TOO!
JUST YOU WATCH, NEGI-KUN!!
...OKAY! NEXT: NO. 5, MAKIE SASAKI.
READY!

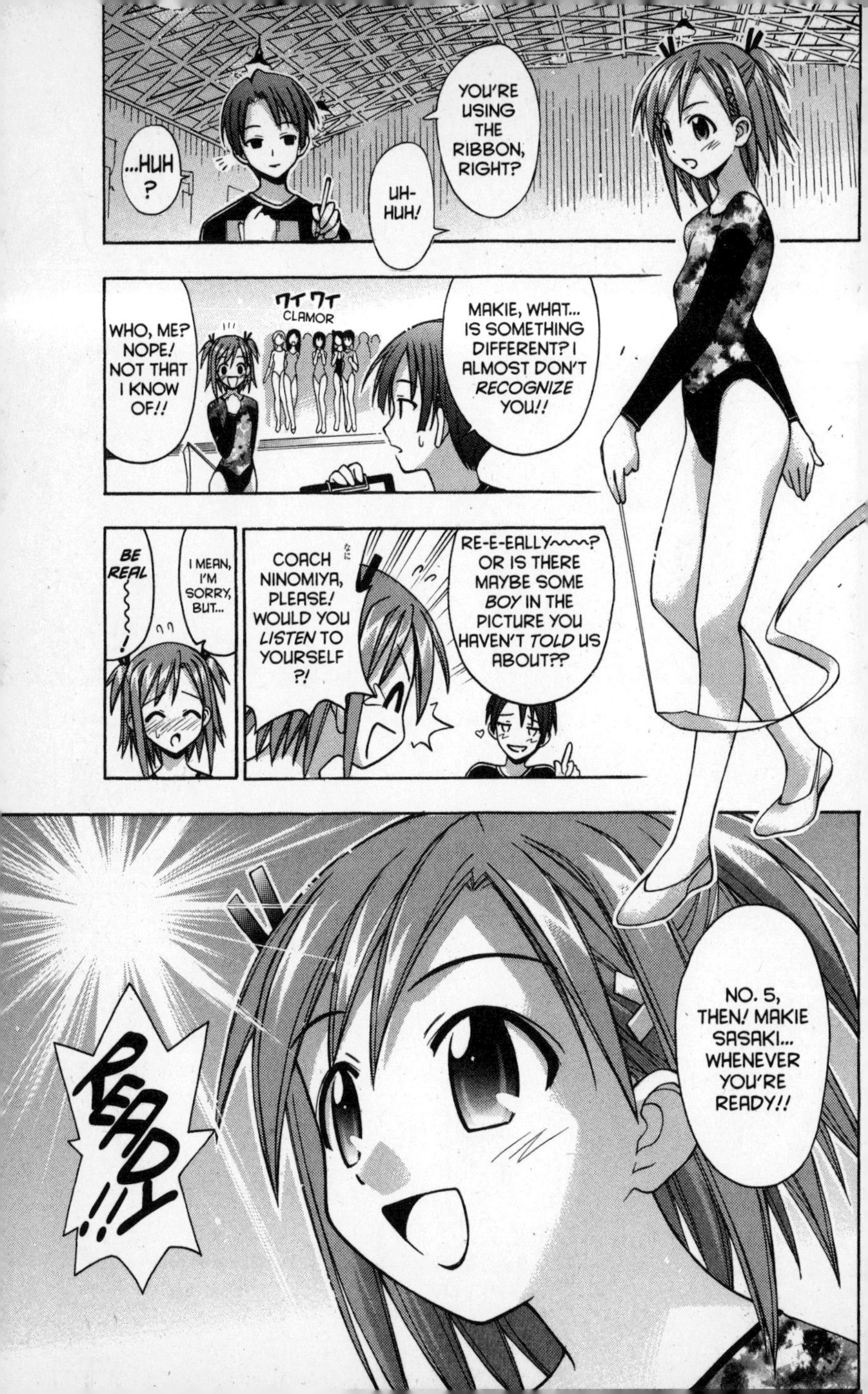
YOU'RE USING THE RIBBON, RIGHT?
UH-HUH!
...HUH?
MAKIE, WHAT... IS SOMETHING DIFFERENT? I ALMOST DON'T *RECOGNIZE* YOU!!
ワイワイ
CLAMOR
WHO, ME? NOPE! NOT THAT I KNOW OF!!
RE-E-EALLY~~~? OR IS THERE MAYBE SOME *BOY* IN THE PICTURE YOU HAVEN'T *TOLD* US ABOUT??
なに
COACH NINOMIYA, PLEASE! WOULD YOU *LISTEN* TO YOURSELF?!
I MEAN, I'M SORRY, BUT...
BE REAL~~!
NO. 5, THEN! MAKIE SASAKI... WHENEVER YOU'RE READY!!
READY!!!

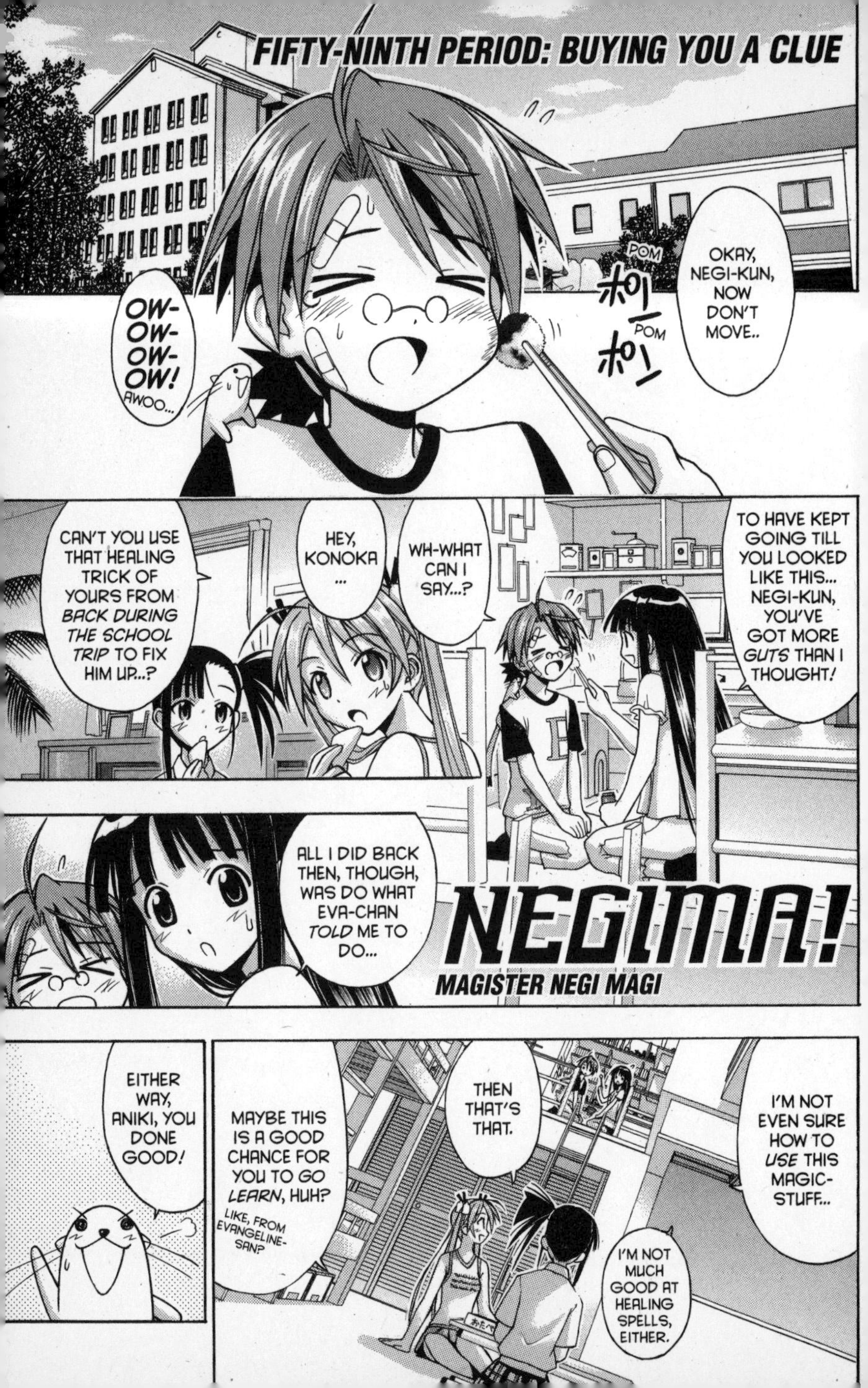
FIFTY-NINTH PERIOD: BUYING YOU A CLUE
OKAY, NEGI-KUN, NOW DON'T MOVE..
POM
POM
OW-OW-OW-OW! AWOO...
TO HAVE KEPT GOING TILL YOU LOOKED LIKE THIS... NEGI-KUN, YOU'VE GOT MORE GUTS THAN I THOUGHT!
WH-WHAT CAN I SAY...?
HEY, KONOKA ...
CAN'T YOU USE THAT HEALING TRICK OF YOURS FROM BACK DURING THE SCHOOL TRIP TO FIX HIM UP...?
ALL I DID BACK THEN, THOUGH, WAS DO WHAT EVA-CHAN TOLD ME TO DO...
NEGIMA!
MAGISTER NEGI MAGI
I'M NOT EVEN SURE HOW TO USE THIS MAGIC-STUFF...
THEN THAT'S THAT.
I'M NOT MUCH GOOD AT HEALING SPELLS, EITHER.
MAYBE THIS IS A GOOD CHANCE FOR YOU TO GO LEARN, HUH?
LIKE, FROM EVANGELINE-SAN?
EITHER WAY, ANIKI, YOU DONE GOOD!

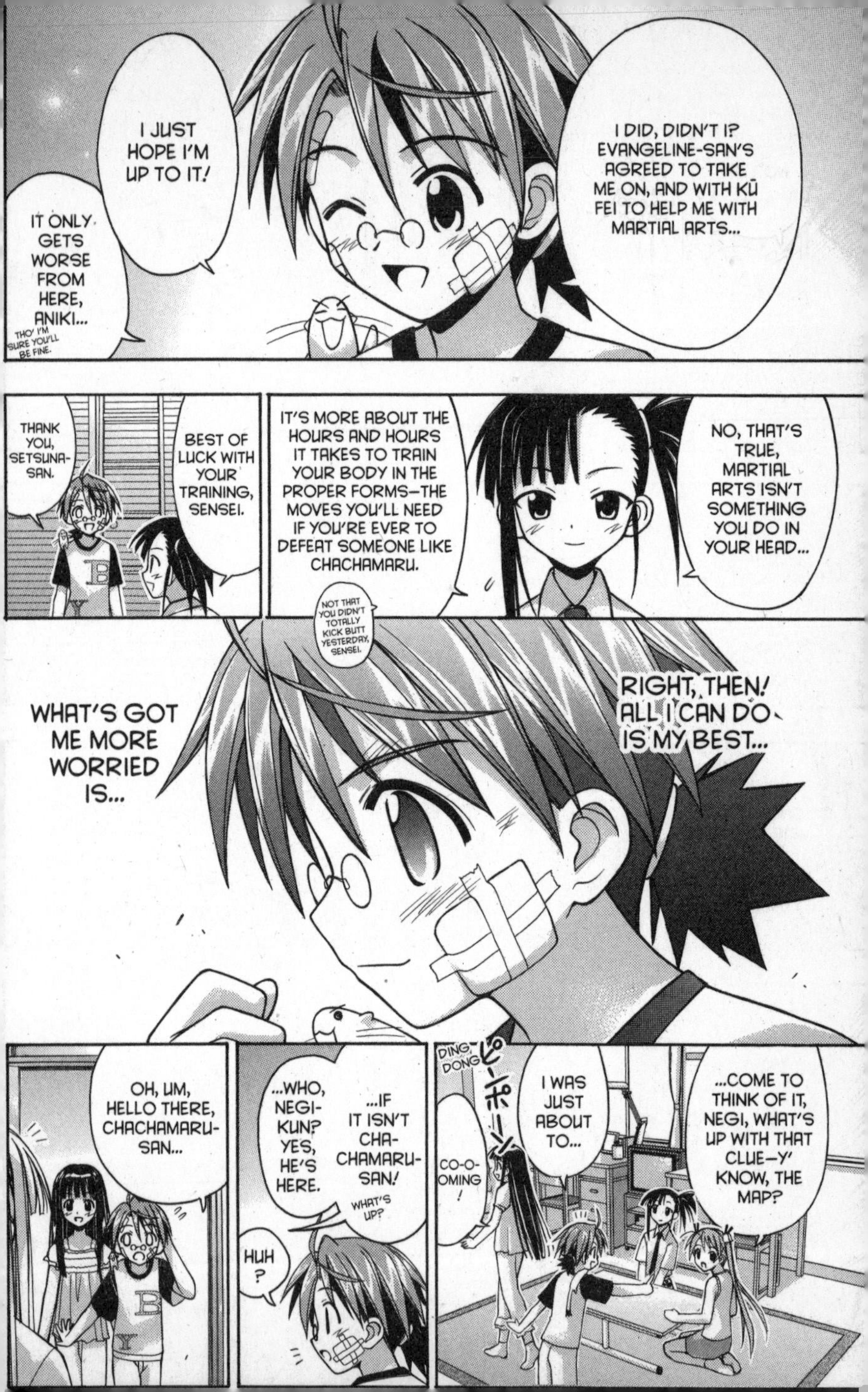
I DID, DIDN'T I? EVANGELINE-SAN'S AGREED TO TAKE ME ON, AND WITH KŪ FEI TO HELP ME WITH MARTIAL ARTS...
I JUST HOPE I'M UP TO IT!
IT ONLY GETS WORSE FROM HERE, ANIKI...
THO' I'M SURE YOU'LL BE FINE.
NO, THAT'S TRUE, MARTIAL ARTS ISN'T SOMETHING YOU DO IN YOUR HEAD...
IT'S MORE ABOUT THE HOURS AND HOURS IT TAKES TO TRAIN YOUR BODY IN THE PROPER FORMS—THE MOVES YOU'LL NEED IF YOU'RE EVER TO DEFEAT SOMEONE LIKE CHACHAMARU.
NOT THAT YOU DIDN'T TOTALLY KICK BUTT YESTERDAY, SENSEI.
BEST OF LUCK WITH YOUR TRAINING, SENSEI.
THANK YOU, SETSUNA-SAN.
RIGHT, THEN! ALL I CAN DO IS MY BEST...
WHAT'S GOT ME MORE WORRIED IS...
...COME TO THINK OF IT, NEGI, WHAT'S UP WITH THAT CLUE—Y' KNOW, THE MAP?
I WAS JUST ABOUT TO...
DING DONG
CO-O-OMING!
...IF IT ISN'T CHA-CHAMARU-SAN!
WHAT'S UP?
...WHO, NEGI-KUN? YES, HE'S HERE.
HUH?
OH, UM, HELLO THERE, CHACHAMARU-SAN...

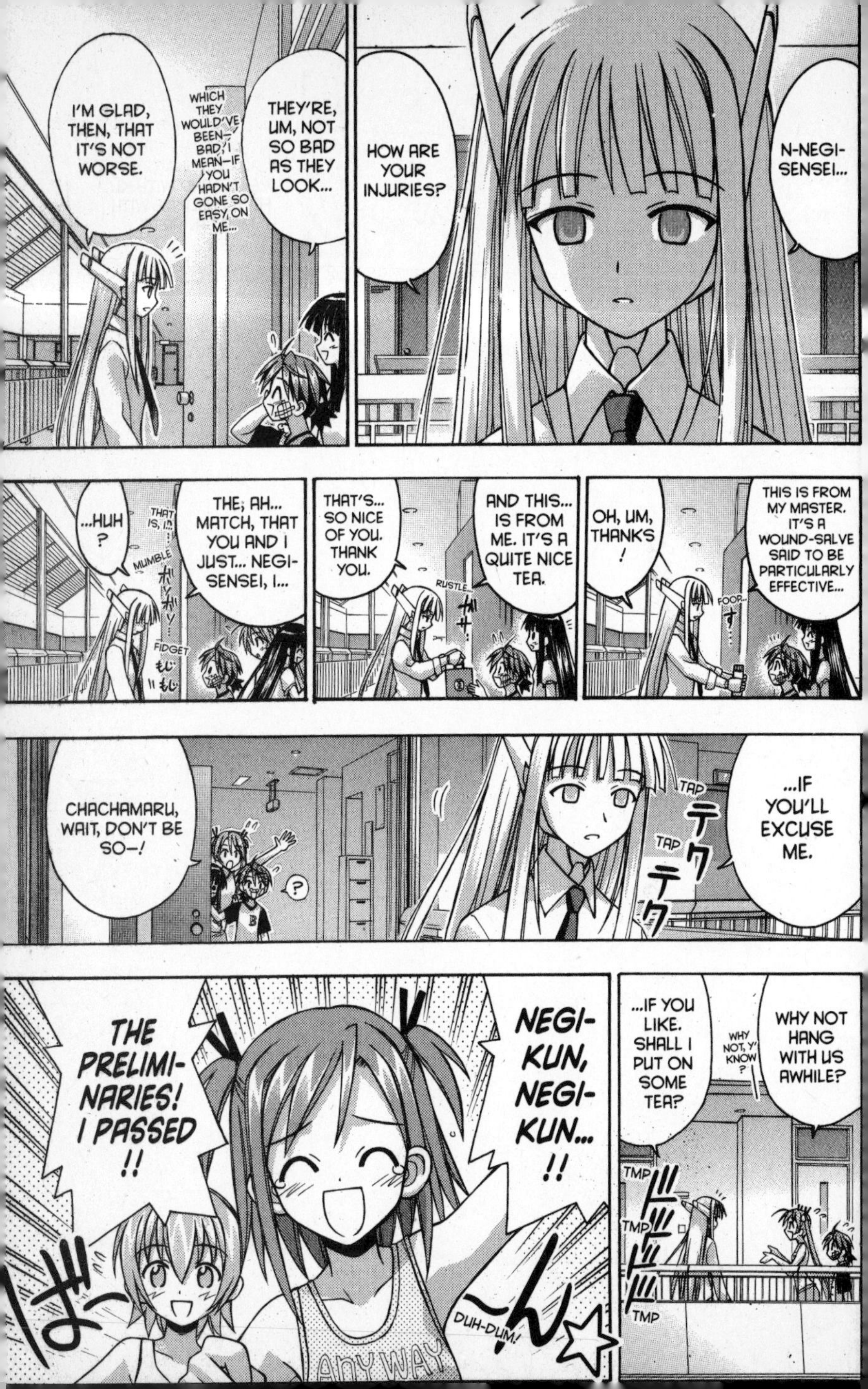
N-NEGI-SENSEI...
HOW ARE YOUR INJURIES?
THEY'RE, UM, NOT SO BAD AS THEY LOOK...
WHICH THEY WOULD'VE BEEN—BAD, I MEAN—IF YOU HADN'T GONE SO EASY ON ME...
I'M GLAD, THEN, THAT IT'S NOT WORSE.
THIS IS FROM MY MASTER. IT'S A WOUND-SALVE SAID TO BE PARTICULARLY EFFECTIVE...
FOOP...
OH, UM, THANKS!
AND THIS... IS FROM ME. IT'S A QUITE NICE TEA.
RUSTLE...
THAT'S... SO NICE OF YOU. THANK YOU.
THE, AH... MATCH, THAT YOU AND I JUST... NEGI-SENSEI, I...
THAT IS, I...
MUMBLE
FIDGET
...HUH?
...IF YOU'LL EXCUSE ME.
TAP
TAP
CHACHAMARU, WAIT, DON'T BE SO—!
WHY NOT HANG WITH US AWHILE?
WHY NOT, Y'KNOW?
...IF YOU LIKE. SHALL I PUT ON SOME TEA?
TMP
TMP
TMP
NEGI-KUN, NEGI-KUN...!!
THE PRELIMINARIES! I PASSED!!
DUH-DUM!
ANY WAY

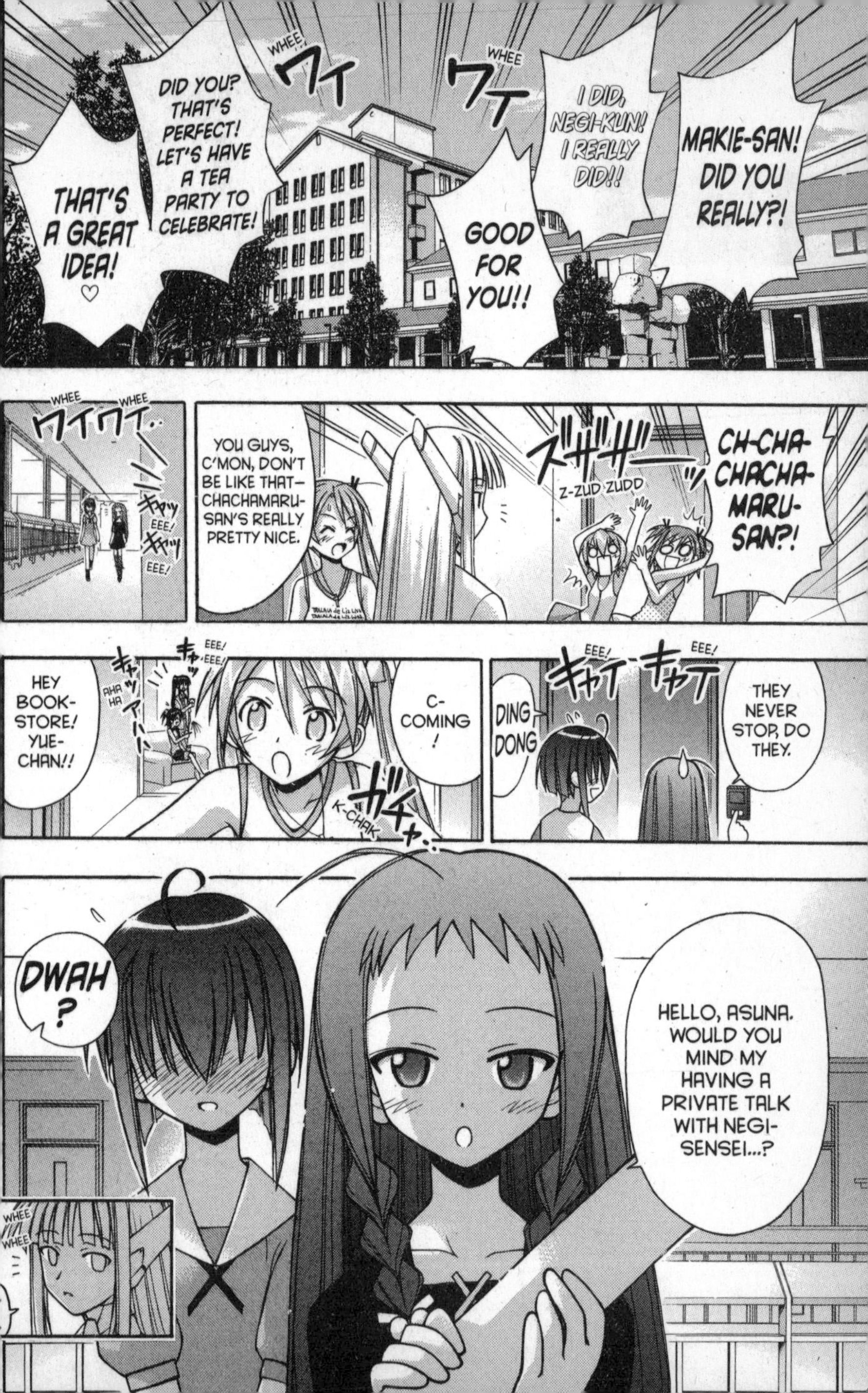
MAKIE-SAN! DID YOU REALLY?!
I DID, NEGI-KUN! I REALLY DID!!
WHEE
GOOD FOR YOU!!
WHEE
DID YOU? THAT'S PERFECT! LET'S HAVE A TEA PARTY TO CELEBRATE!
THAT'S A GREAT IDEA! ♡
CH-CHA-CHACHA-MARU-SAN?!
Z-ZUD ZUDD
YOU GUYS, C'MON, DON'T BE LIKE THAT—CHACHAMARU-SAN'S REALLY PRETTY NICE.
WHEE
WHEE
EEE!
EEE!
THEY NEVER STOP, DO THEY.
EEE!
EEE!
DING DONG
C-COMING!
K-CHAK
EEE!
EEE!
AHA HA
HEY BOOKSTORE! YUE-CHAN!!
HELLO, ASUNA. WOULD YOU MIND MY HAVING A PRIVATE TALK WITH NEGI-SENSEI...?
DWAH?
WHEE
WHEE

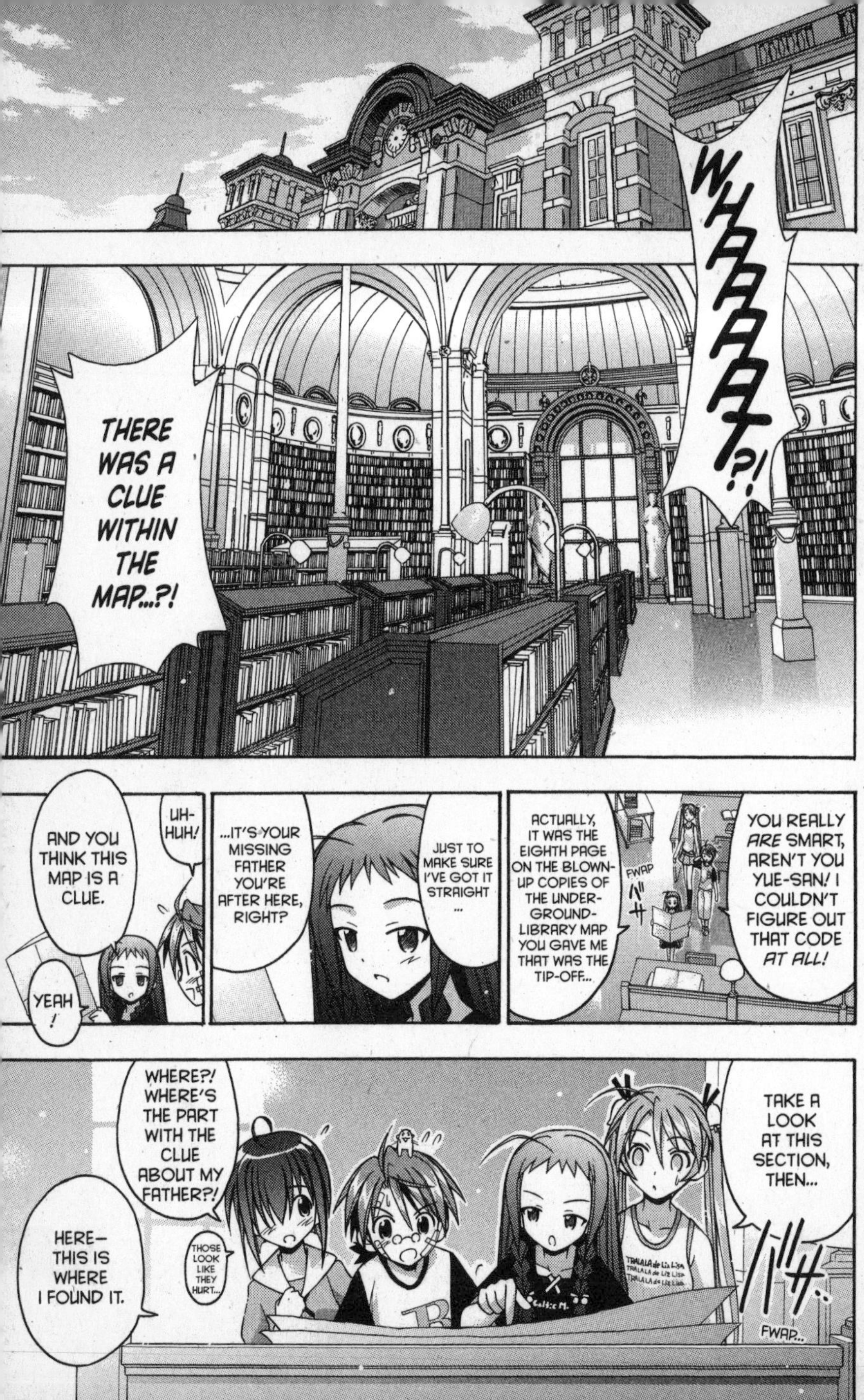
WHAAAAAT?!
THERE WAS A CLUE WITHIN THE MAP...?!
YOU REALLY *ARE* SMART, AREN'T YOU YUE-SAN! I COULDN'T FIGURE OUT THAT CODE *AT ALL!*
ACTUALLY, IT WAS THE EIGHTH PAGE ON THE BLOWN-UP COPIES OF THE UNDER-GROUND-LIBRARY MAP YOU GAVE ME THAT WAS THE TIP-OFF...
FWAP
JUST TO MAKE SURE I'VE GOT IT STRAIGHT ...
...IT'S YOUR MISSING FATHER YOU'RE AFTER HERE, RIGHT?
UH-HUH!
AND YOU THINK THIS MAP IS A CLUE.
YEAH!
TAKE A LOOK AT THIS SECTION, THEN...
FWAP...
WHERE?! WHERE'S THE PART WITH THE CLUE ABOUT MY FATHER?!
THOSE LOOK LIKE THEY HURT...
HERE— THIS IS WHERE I FOUND IT.

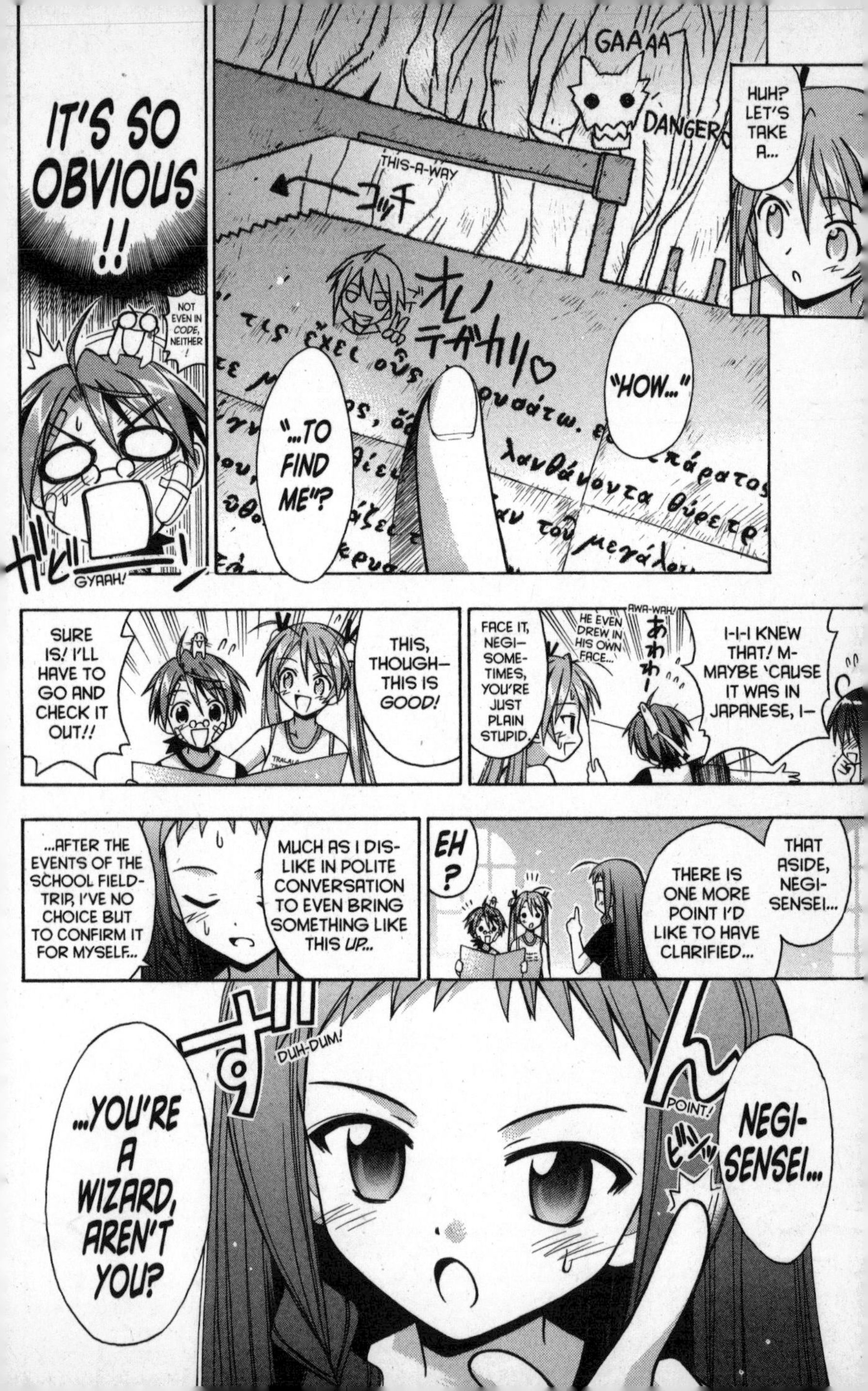
HUH? LET'S TAKE A...
GAAAA
DANGER
THIS-A-WAY
"HOW..."
"...TO FIND ME"?
IT'S SO OBVIOUS!!
NOT EVEN IN CODE, NEITHER!
GYAAH!
I-I-I KNEW THAT! M-MAYBE 'CAUSE IT WAS IN JAPANESE, I—
AWA-WAH!
HE EVEN DREW IN HIS OWN FACE...
FACE IT, NEGI—SOMETIMES, YOU'RE JUST PLAIN STUPID.
THIS, THOUGH—THIS IS GOOD!
SURE IS! I'LL HAVE TO GO AND CHECK IT OUT!!
THAT ASIDE, NEGI-SENSEI...
THERE IS ONE MORE POINT I'D LIKE TO HAVE CLARIFIED...
EH?
MUCH AS I DISLIKE IN POLITE CONVERSATION TO EVEN BRING SOMETHING LIKE THIS UP...
...AFTER THE EVENTS OF THE SCHOOL FIELD-TRIP, I'VE NO CHOICE BUT TO CONFIRM IT FOR MYSELF...
NEGI-SENSEI...
POINT!
DUH-DUM!
...YOU'RE A WIZARD, AREN'T YOU?

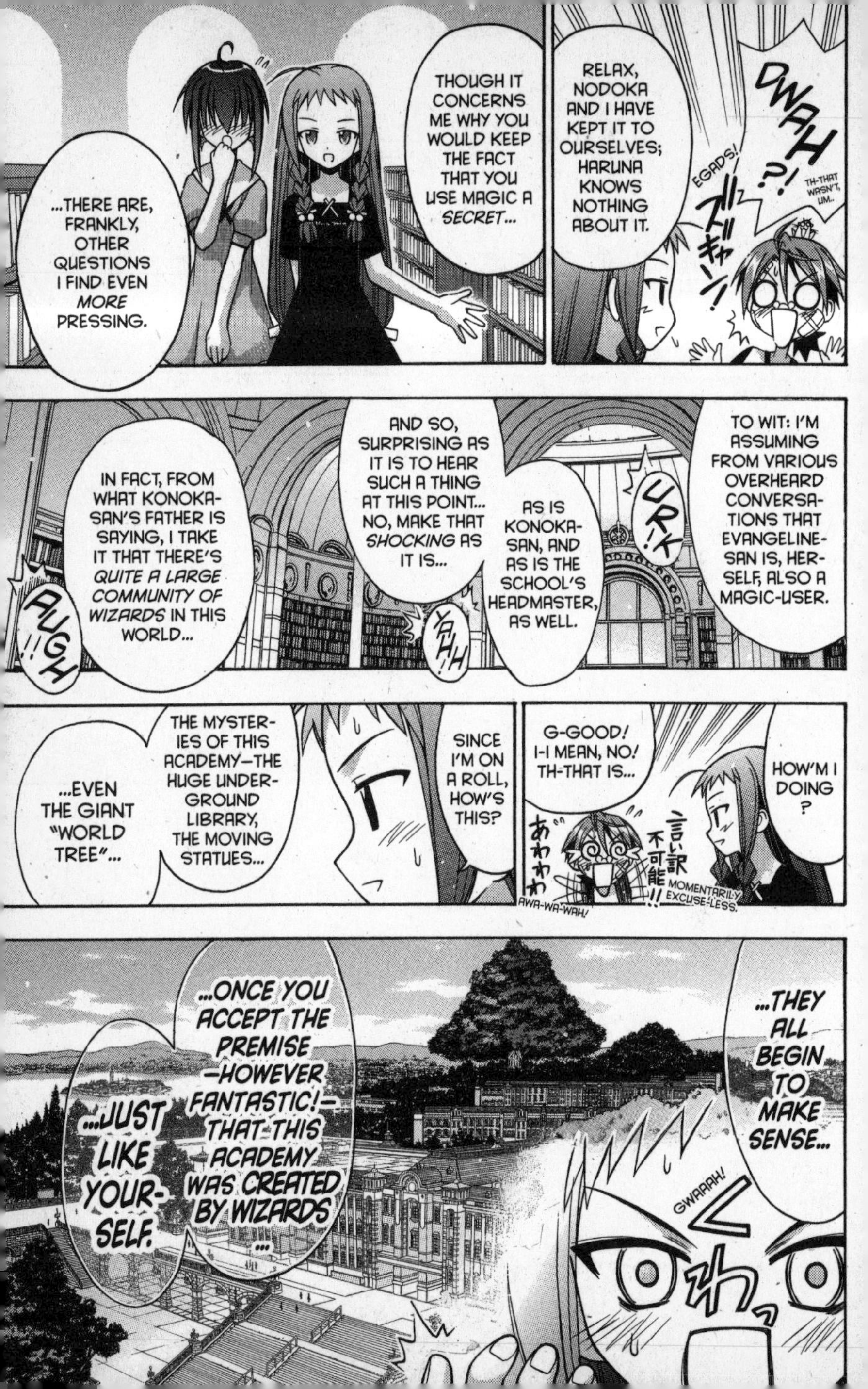
RELAX, NODOKA AND I HAVE KEPT IT TO OURSELVES; HARUNA KNOWS NOTHING ABOUT IT.
DWAH?!
EGADS!
TH-THAT WASN'T, UM..
THOUGH IT CONCERNS ME WHY YOU WOULD KEEP THE FACT THAT YOU USE MAGIC A *SECRET*...
...THERE ARE, FRANKLY, OTHER QUESTIONS I FIND EVEN *MORE* PRESSING.
TO WIT: I'M ASSUMING FROM VARIOUS OVERHEARD CONVERSATIONS THAT EVANGELINE-SAN IS, HERSELF, ALSO A MAGIC-USER.
URK!
AS IS KONOKA-SAN, AND AS IS THE SCHOOL'S HEADMASTER, AS WELL.
YAH!
AND SO, SURPRISING AS IT IS TO HEAR SUCH A THING AT THIS POINT... NO, MAKE THAT *SHOCKING* AS IT IS...
IN FACT, FROM WHAT KONOKA-SAN'S FATHER IS SAYING, I TAKE IT THAT THERE'S *QUITE A LARGE COMMUNITY OF WIZARDS* IN THIS WORLD...
AUGH!!
HOW'M I DOING?
G-GOOD! I-I MEAN, NO! TH-THAT IS...
言い訳不可能!!
MOMENTARILY EXCUSE-LESS.
あわわわ
AWA-WA-WAH!
SINCE I'M ON A ROLL, HOW'S THIS?
THE MYSTERIES OF THIS ACADEMY—THE HUGE UNDERGROUND LIBRARY, THE MOVING STATUES...
...EVEN THE GIANT "WORLD TREE"...
...THEY ALL BEGIN TO MAKE SENSE...
GWAAAH!
わっ
...ONCE YOU ACCEPT THE PREMISE —HOWEVER FANTASTIC!— THAT THIS ACADEMY WAS CREATED BY WIZARDS...
...JUST LIKE YOURSELF.

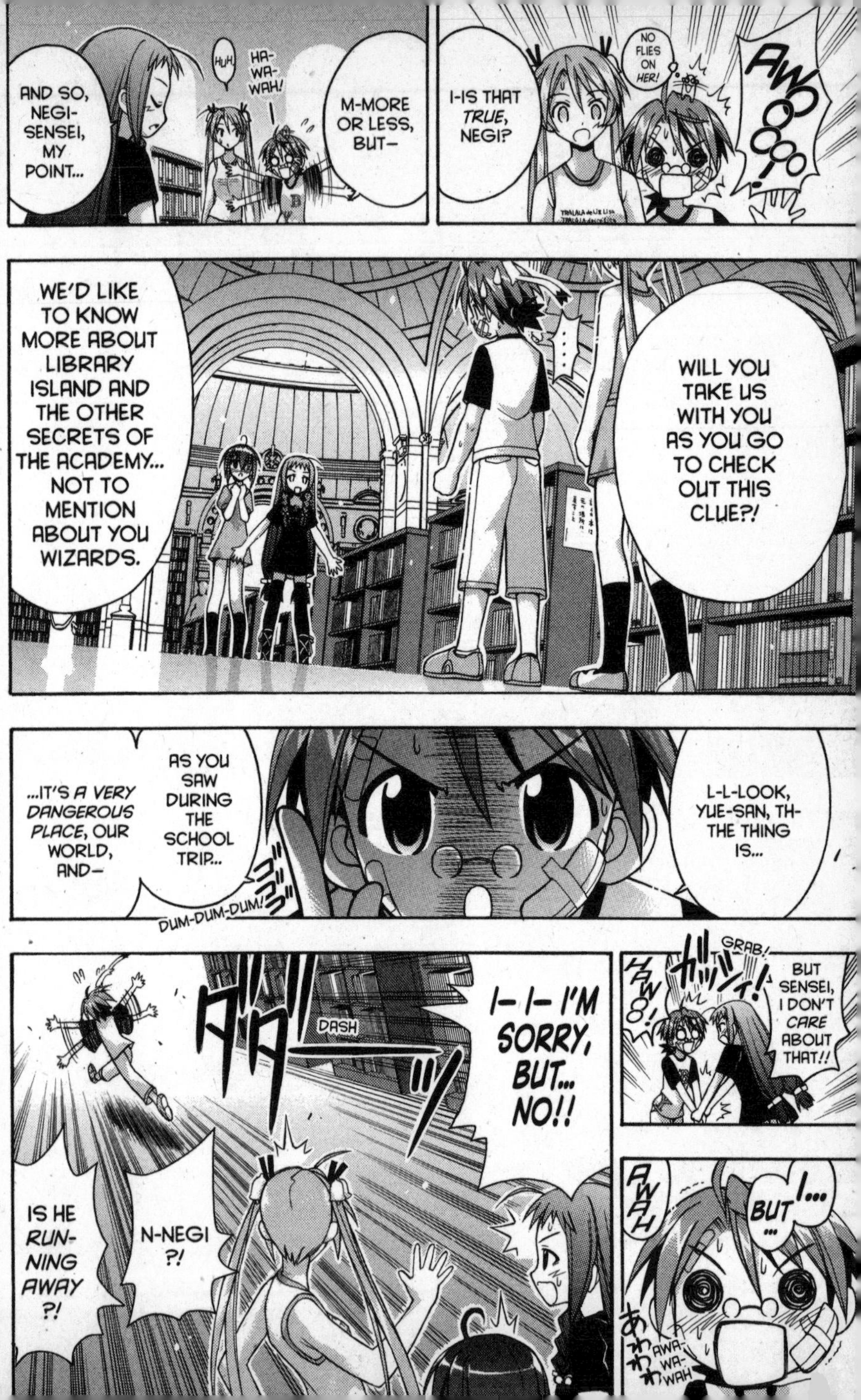
AWOOOOOOO!
NO FLIES ON HER!
I-IS THAT TRUE, NEGI?
M-MORE OR LESS, BUT–
HA-WA-WAH!
HUH
AND SO, NEGI-SENSEI, MY POINT...
WILL YOU TAKE US WITH YOU AS YOU GO TO CHECK OUT THIS CLUE?!
WE'D LIKE TO KNOW MORE ABOUT LIBRARY ISLAND AND THE OTHER SECRETS OF THE ACADEMY... NOT TO MENTION ABOUT YOU WIZARDS.
L-L-LOOK, YUE-SAN, TH-THE THING IS...
AS YOU SAW DURING THE SCHOOL TRIP...
...IT'S A VERY DANGEROUS PLACE, OUR WORLD, AND–
DUM-DUM-DUM!
BUT SENSEI, I DON'T CARE ABOUT THAT!!
GRAB!
HAWA!
I... BUT...
AWAH
AWA-WA-WAH
I-I-I'M SORRY, BUT... NO!!
DASH
N-NEGI?!
IS HE RUNNING AWAY?!

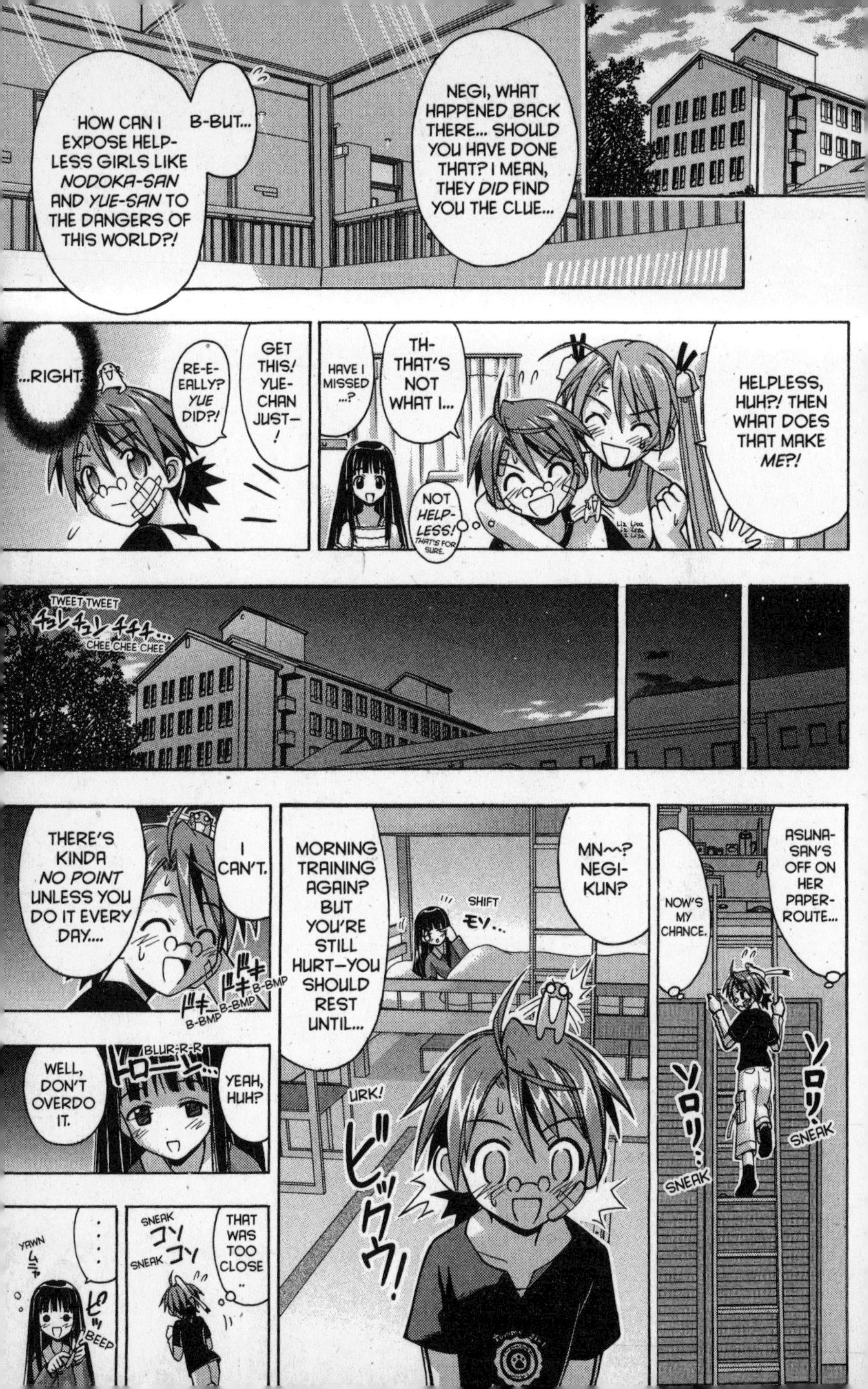
NEGI, WHAT HAPPENED BACK THERE... SHOULD YOU HAVE DONE THAT? I MEAN, THEY *DID* FIND YOU THE CLUE...
B-BUT...
HOW CAN I EXPOSE HELP-LESS GIRLS LIKE *NODOKA-SAN* AND *YUE-SAN* TO THE DANGERS OF THIS WORLD?!
HELPLESS, HUH?! THEN WHAT DOES THAT MAKE *ME*?!
TH-THAT'S NOT WHAT I...
HAVE I MISSED ...?
NOT *HELP-LESS!* THAT'S FOR SURE.
GET THIS! YUE-CHAN JUST—!
RE-E-EALLY? *YUE* DID?!
...RIGHT.
TWEET TWEET
CHEE CHEE CHEE
ASUNA-SAN'S OFF ON HER PAPER-ROUTE...
NOW'S MY CHANCE.
SNEAK
SNEAK
MN~~? NEGI-KUN?
SHIFT
MORNING TRAINING AGAIN? BUT YOU'RE STILL HURT—YOU SHOULD REST UNTIL...
URK!
I CAN'T.
THERE'S KINDA *NO POINT* UNLESS YOU DO IT EVERY DAY....
B-BMP
B-BMP
B-BMP
YEAH, HUH?
WELL, DON'T OVERDO IT.
BLUR-R-R
THAT WAS TOO CLOSE ..
SNEAK
SNEAK
. . . .
YAWN
BEEP

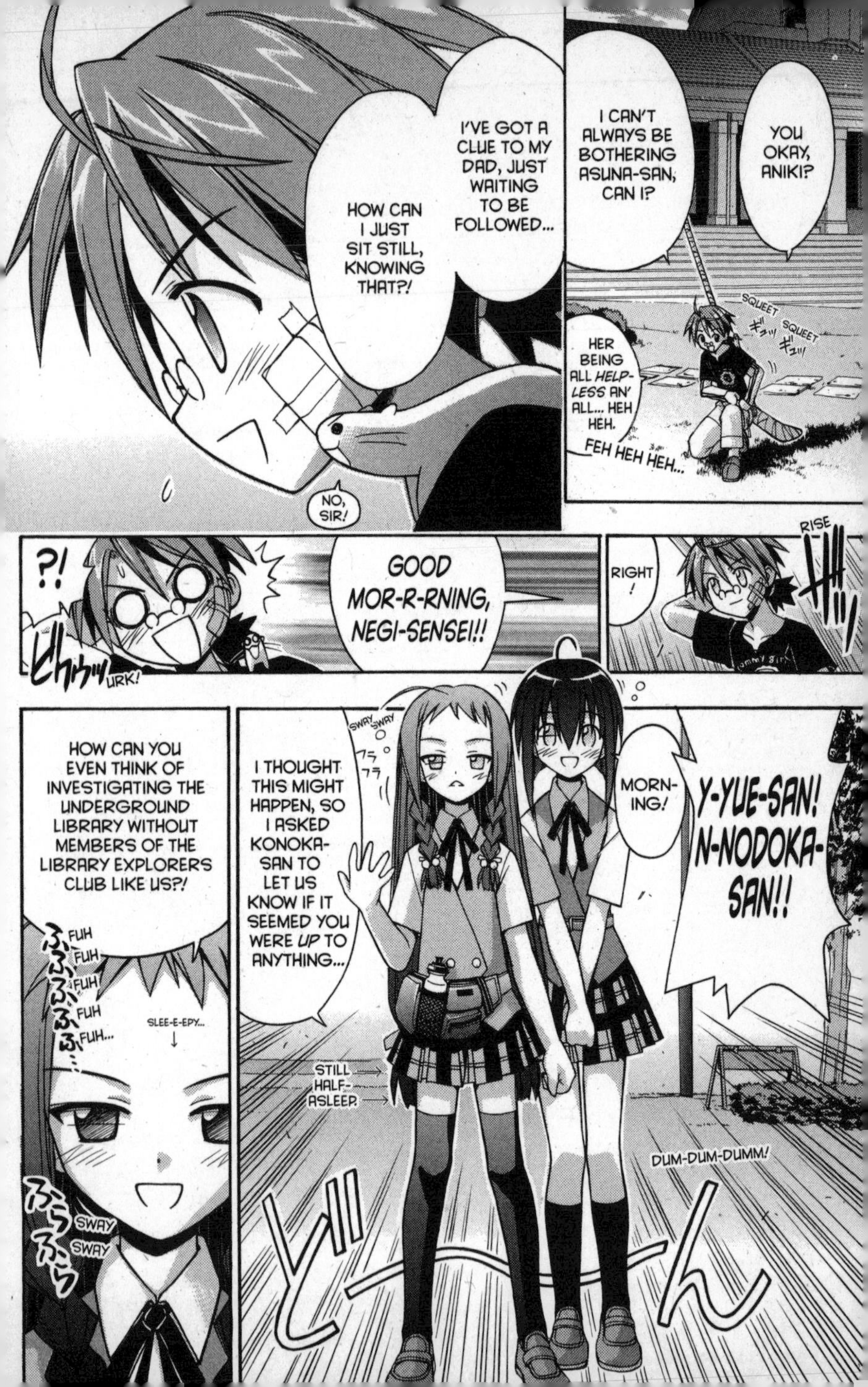
YOU OKAY, ANIKI?
I CAN'T ALWAYS BE BOTHERING ASUNA-SAN, CAN I?
SQUEET
SQUEET
HER BEING ALL *HELP-LESS* AN' ALL... HEH HEH.
FEH HEH HEH...
I'VE GOT A CLUE TO MY DAD, JUST WAITING TO BE FOLLOWED...
HOW CAN I JUST SIT STILL, KNOWING THAT?!
NO, SIR!
RIGHT!
RISE
GOOD MOR-R-RNING, NEGI-SENSEI!!
?!
URK!
Y-YUE-SAN! N-NODOKA-SAN!!
MORNING!
SWAY SWAY
I THOUGHT THIS MIGHT HAPPEN, SO I ASKED KONOKA-SAN TO LET US KNOW IF IT SEEMED YOU WERE *UP* TO ANYTHING...
STILL HALF-ASLEEP.
DUM-DUM-DUMM!
HOW CAN YOU EVEN THINK OF INVESTIGATING THE UNDERGROUND LIBRARY WITHOUT MEMBERS OF THE LIBRARY EXPLORERS CLUB LIKE US?!
FUH FUH FUH FUH FUH...
SLEE-E-EPY...
SWAY SWAY

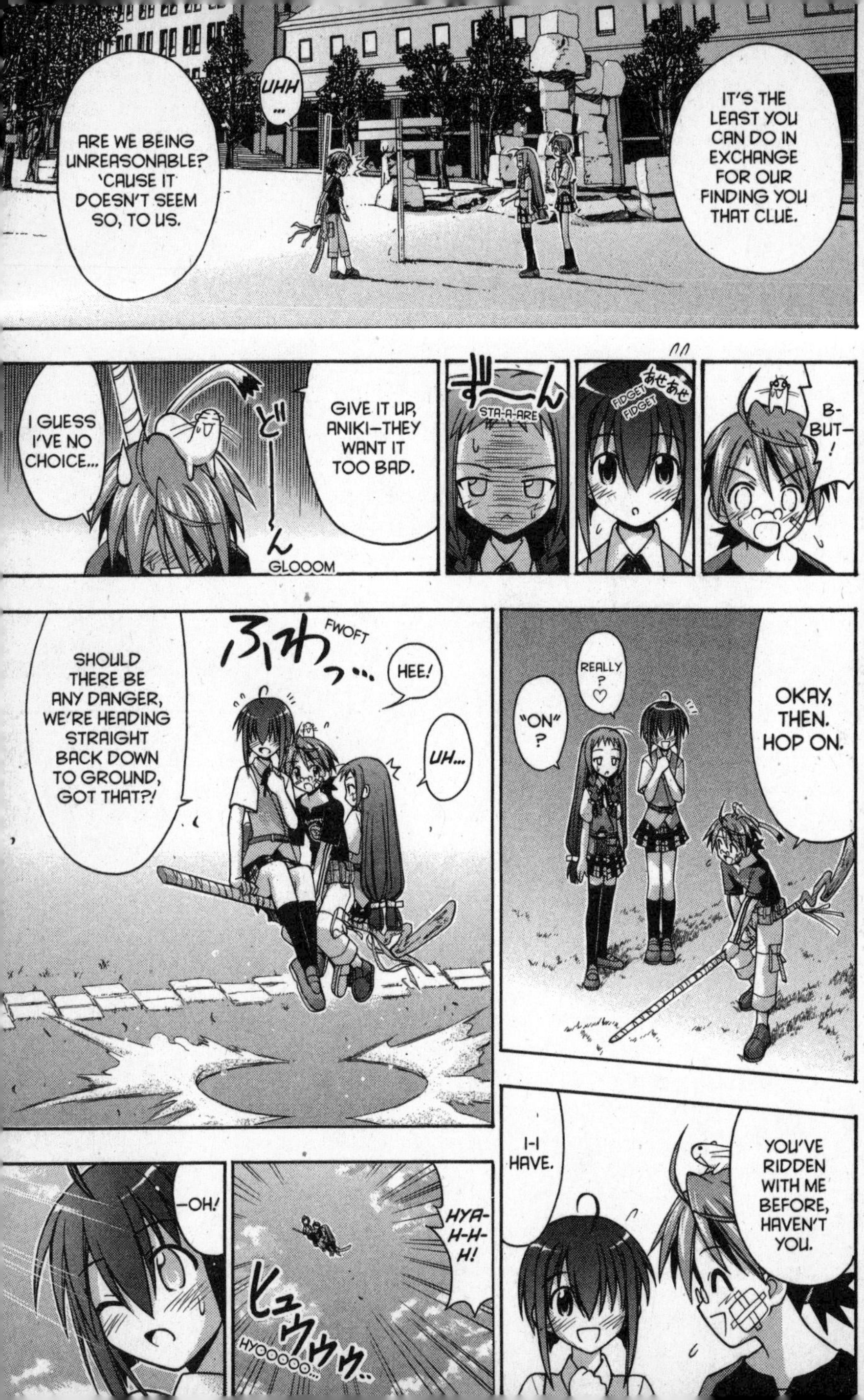
IT'S THE LEAST YOU CAN DO IN EXCHANGE FOR OUR FINDING YOU THAT CLUE.
UHH...
ARE WE BEING UNREASONABLE? 'CAUSE IT DOESN'T SEEM SO, TO US.
B-BUT-!
あせあせ
FIDGET FIDGET
ずーん
STA-A-ARE
GIVE IT UP, ANIKI—THEY WANT IT TOO BAD.
どーん
GLOOOM
I GUESS I'VE NO CHOICE...
OKAY, THEN. HOP ON.
REALLY? ♡
"ON"?
ふわっ...
FWOFT
HEE!
UH...
SHOULD THERE BE ANY DANGER, WE'RE HEADING STRAIGHT BACK DOWN TO GROUND, GOT THAT?!
YOU'VE RIDDEN WITH ME BEFORE, HAVEN'T YOU.
I-I HAVE.
HYA-H-H-H!
ヒュウウウ...
HYOOOOOO...
-OH!

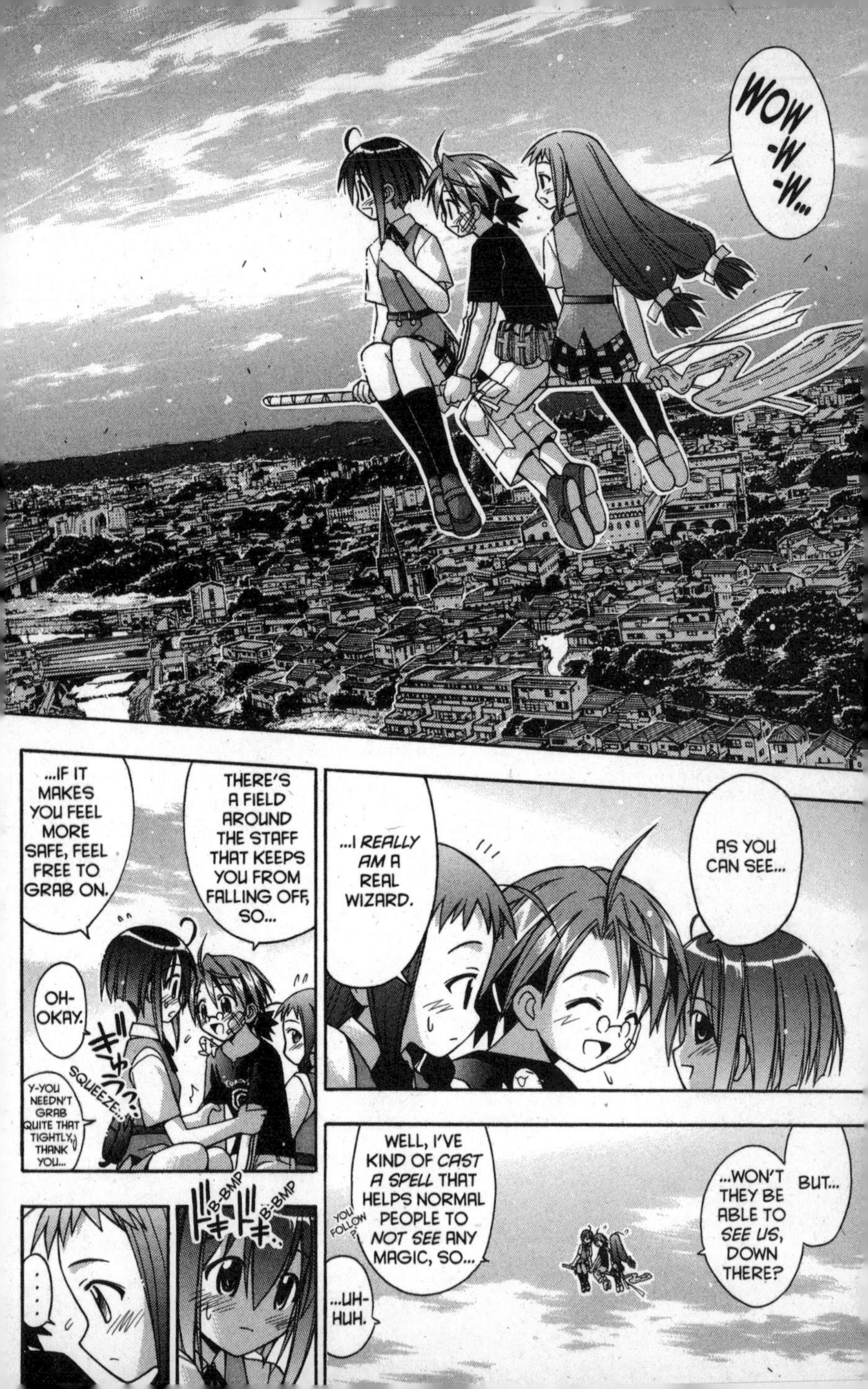
WOW-W-W...
AS YOU CAN SEE...
...I *REALLY AM* A REAL WIZARD.
THERE'S A FIELD AROUND THE STAFF THAT KEEPS YOU FROM FALLING OFF, SO...
...IF IT MAKES YOU FEEL MORE SAFE, FEEL FREE TO GRAB ON.
OH-OKAY.
SQUEEZE...
Y-YOU NEEDN'T GRAB QUITE THAT TIGHTLY, THANK YOU...
BUT...
...WON'T THEY BE ABLE TO *SEE US,* DOWN THERE?
WELL, I'VE KIND OF *CAST A SPELL* THAT HELPS NORMAL PEOPLE TO *NOT SEE* ANY MAGIC, SO...
YOU FOLLOW?
...UH-HUH.
B-BMP
B-BMP
.....

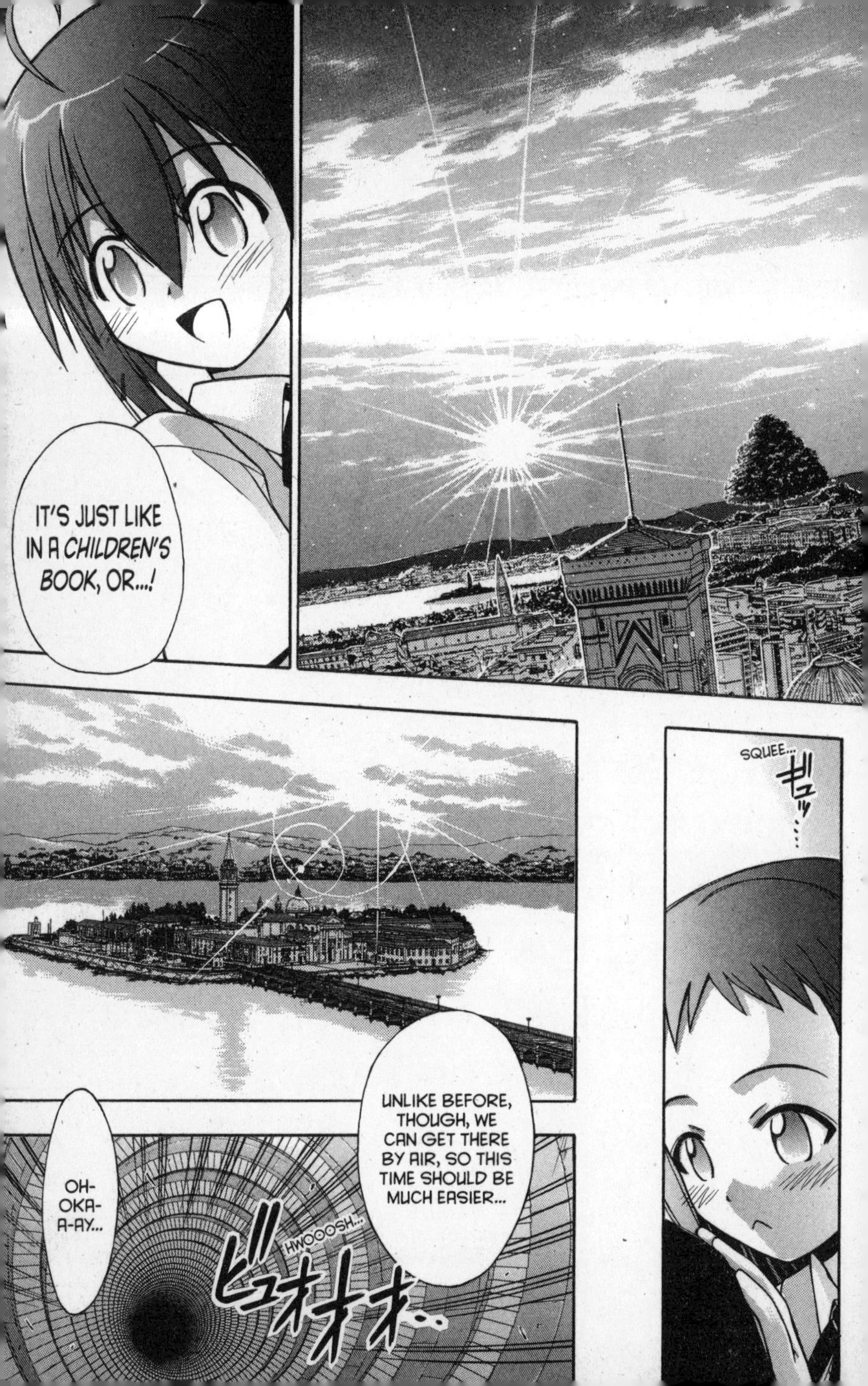
IT'S JUST LIKE IN A CHILDREN'S BOOK, OR...!
SQUEE...
ギュッ…
UNLIKE BEFORE, THOUGH, WE CAN GET THERE BY AIR, SO THIS TIME SHOULD BE MUCH EASIER...
OH-OKA-A-AY...
HWOOOSH...
ビュオオオ…

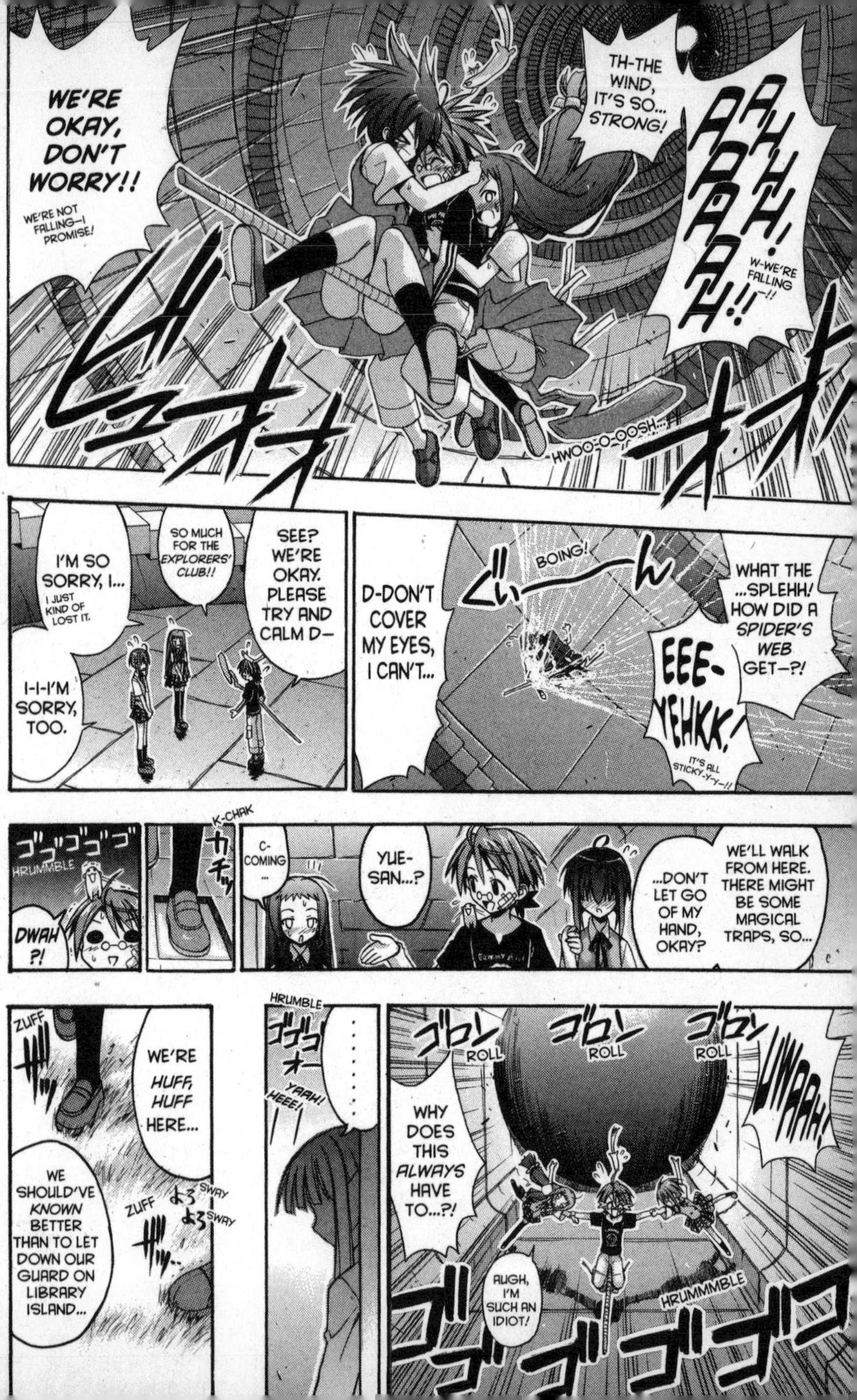
TH-THE WIND, IT'S SO... STRONG!
AAHHH! AAAAAAH!!
W-WE'RE FALLING—!!
WE'RE OKAY, DON'T WORRY!!
WE'RE NOT FALLING—I PROMISE!
HWOO-O-OOSH...
BOING!
WHAT THE ...SPLEHH! HOW DID A SPIDER'S WEB GET—?!
EEE-YEHKK!
IT'S ALL STICKY-Y-Y—!!
D-DON'T COVER MY EYES, I CAN'T...
SEE? WE'RE OKAY. PLEASE TRY AND CALM D—
SO MUCH FOR THE EXPLORERS' CLUB!!
I'M SO SORRY, I...
I JUST KIND OF LOST IT.
I-I-I'M SORRY, TOO.
WE'LL WALK FROM HERE. THERE MIGHT BE SOME MAGICAL TRAPS, SO...
...DON'T LET GO OF MY HAND, OKAY?
YUE-SAN...?
C-COMING...
K-CHAK
HRUMMBLE
DWAH?!
ROLL
ROLL
ROLL
UWAAH!
WHY DOES THIS ALWAYS HAVE TO...?!
AUGH, I'M SUCH AN IDIOT!
HRUMMMBLE
HRUMBLE
YAAH! HEEE!
......
ZUFF
WE'RE HUFF, HUFF HERE...
SWAY
SWAY
ZUFF
WE SHOULD'VE KNOWN BETTER THAN TO LET DOWN OUR GUARD ON LIBRARY ISLAND...

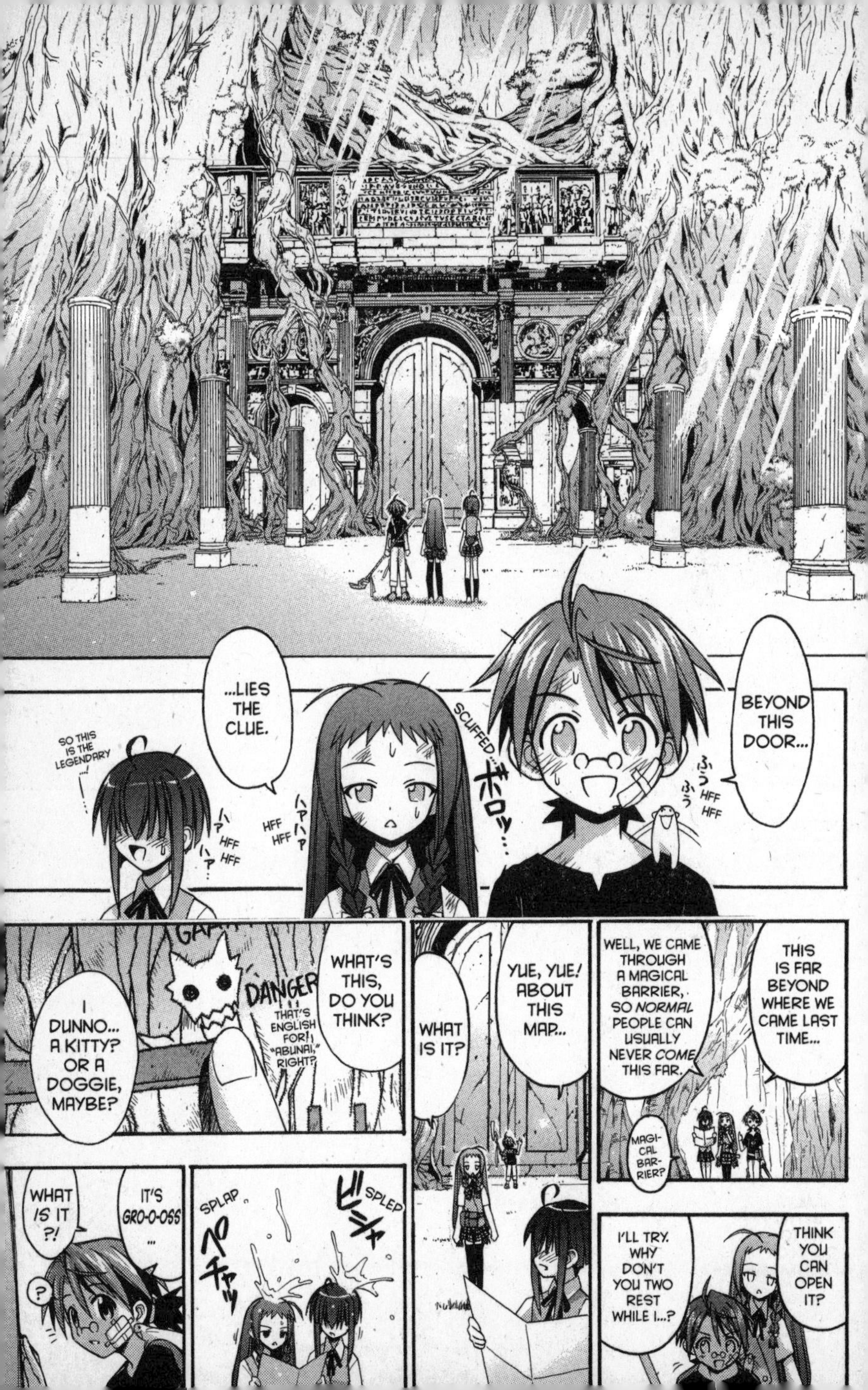
BEYOND THIS DOOR...
ふう ふう HFF HFF
...LIES THE CLUE.
SCUFFED... ボロッ...
ハァハァ HFF HFF
SO THIS IS THE LEGENDARY ...!
ハァ HFF ハァ HFF
THIS IS FAR BEYOND WHERE WE CAME LAST TIME...
WELL, WE CAME THROUGH A MAGICAL BARRIER, SO *NORMAL* PEOPLE CAN USUALLY NEVER *COME* THIS FAR.
MAGICAL BARRIER?
THINK YOU CAN OPEN IT?
I'LL TRY. WHY DON'T YOU TWO REST WHILE I...?
YUE, YUE! ABOUT THIS MAP...
WHAT IS IT?
WHAT'S THIS, DO YOU THINK?
DANGER
THAT'S ENGLISH FOR "ABUNAI," RIGHT?
I DUNNO... A KITTY? OR A DOGGIE, MAYBE?
ビシャ SPLEP
SPLAP ペチャッ
IT'S *GRO-O-OSS* ...
WHAT *IS* IT ?!
?

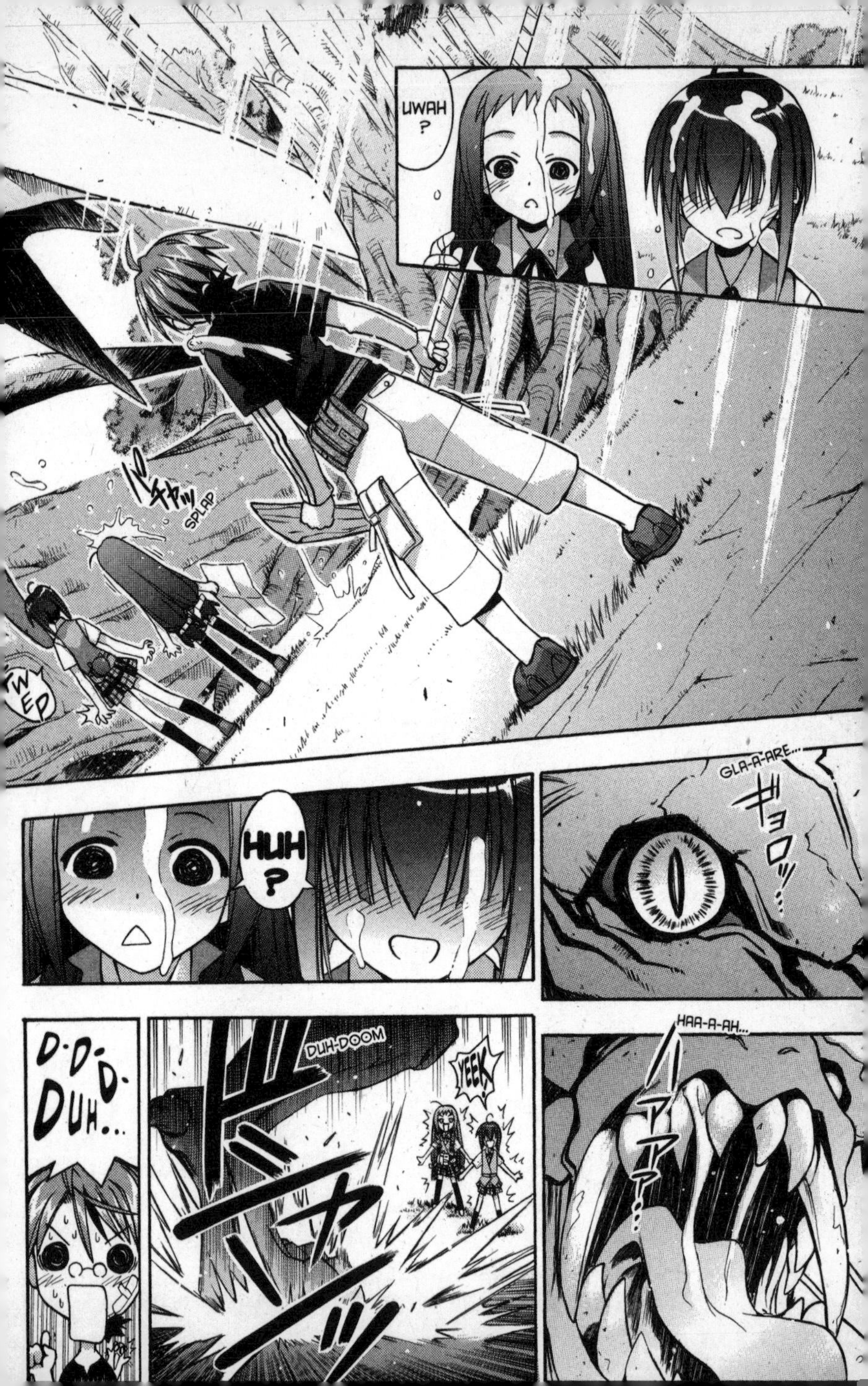

UWAH ?
SPLAP
WEP
GLA-A-ARE...
HUH ?
HAA-A-AH...
DUH-DOOM
YEEK
D-D-D-DUH...

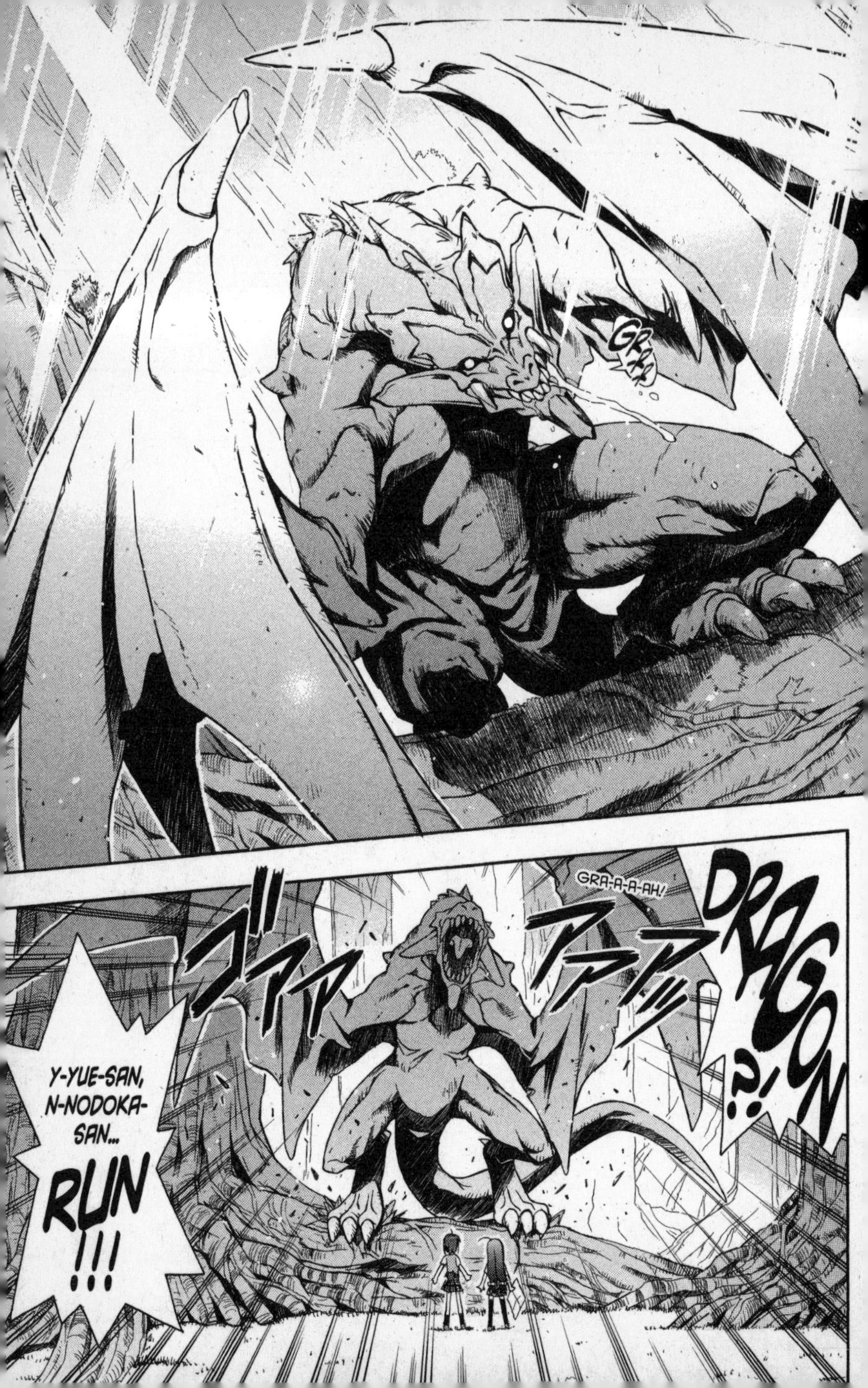
DRAGON?!
GRA-A-A-AH!
ゴァァァ
ァァァ!!
Y-YUE-SAN, N-NODOKA-SAN... RUN!!!

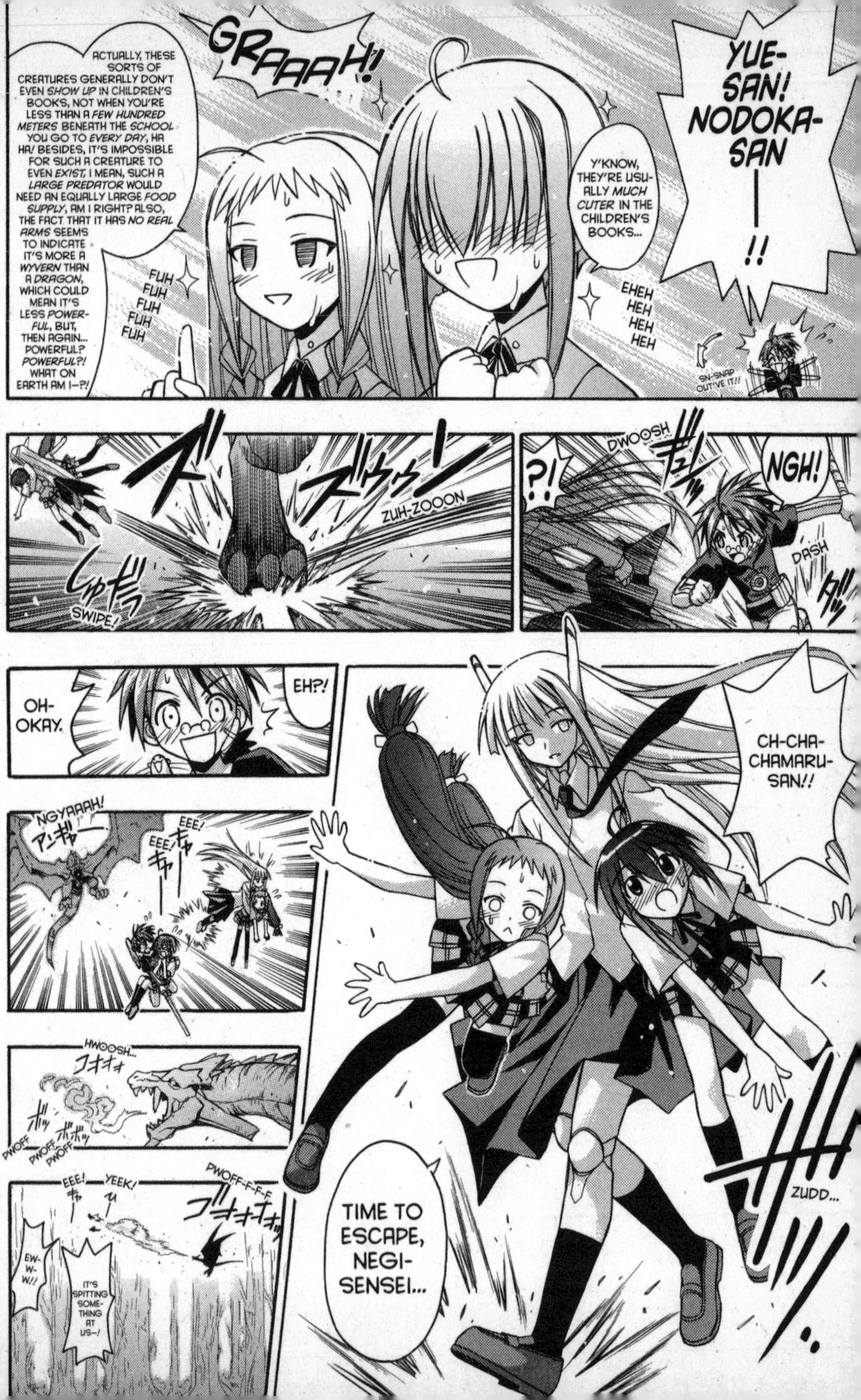
YUE-SAN! NODOKA-SAN—!!
GRAAAH!
Y'KNOW, THEY'RE USUALLY *MUCH CUTER* IN THE CHILDREN'S BOOKS...
EHEH HEH HEH HEH
SN-SNAP OUT'VE IT!!
ACTUALLY, THESE SORTS OF CREATURES GENERALLY DON'T EVEN *SHOW UP* IN CHILDREN'S BOOKS, NOT WHEN YOU'RE LESS THAN A *FEW HUNDRED METERS* BENEATH THE *SCHOOL* YOU GO TO *EVERY DAY*, HA HA! BESIDES, IT'S IMPOSSIBLE FOR SUCH A CREATURE TO EVEN *EXIST*, I MEAN, SUCH A *LARGE PREDATOR* WOULD NEED AN EQUALLY LARGE *FOOD SUPPLY*, AM I RIGHT? ALSO, THE FACT THAT IT HAS *NO REAL ARMS* SEEMS TO INDICATE IT'S MORE A *WYVERN* THAN A *DRAGON*, WHICH COULD MEAN IT'S LESS *POWERFUL*, BUT, THEN AGAIN... POWERFUL? *POWERFUL?!* WHAT ON EARTH AM I—?!
FUH FUH FUH FUH FUH
NGH!
DWOOSH
?!
DASH
ZUH-ZOOON
SWIPE!
CH-CHA-CHAMARU-SAN!!
ZUDD...
TIME TO ESCAPE, NEGI-SENSEI...
EH?!
OH-OKAY.
EEE! EEE!
NGYAAAH!
HWOOSH...
PWOFF PWOFF PWOFF PWOFF
PWOFF-F-F-F
YEEK!
EEE!
EW-W-W!!
IT'S SPITTING SOMETHING AT US—!

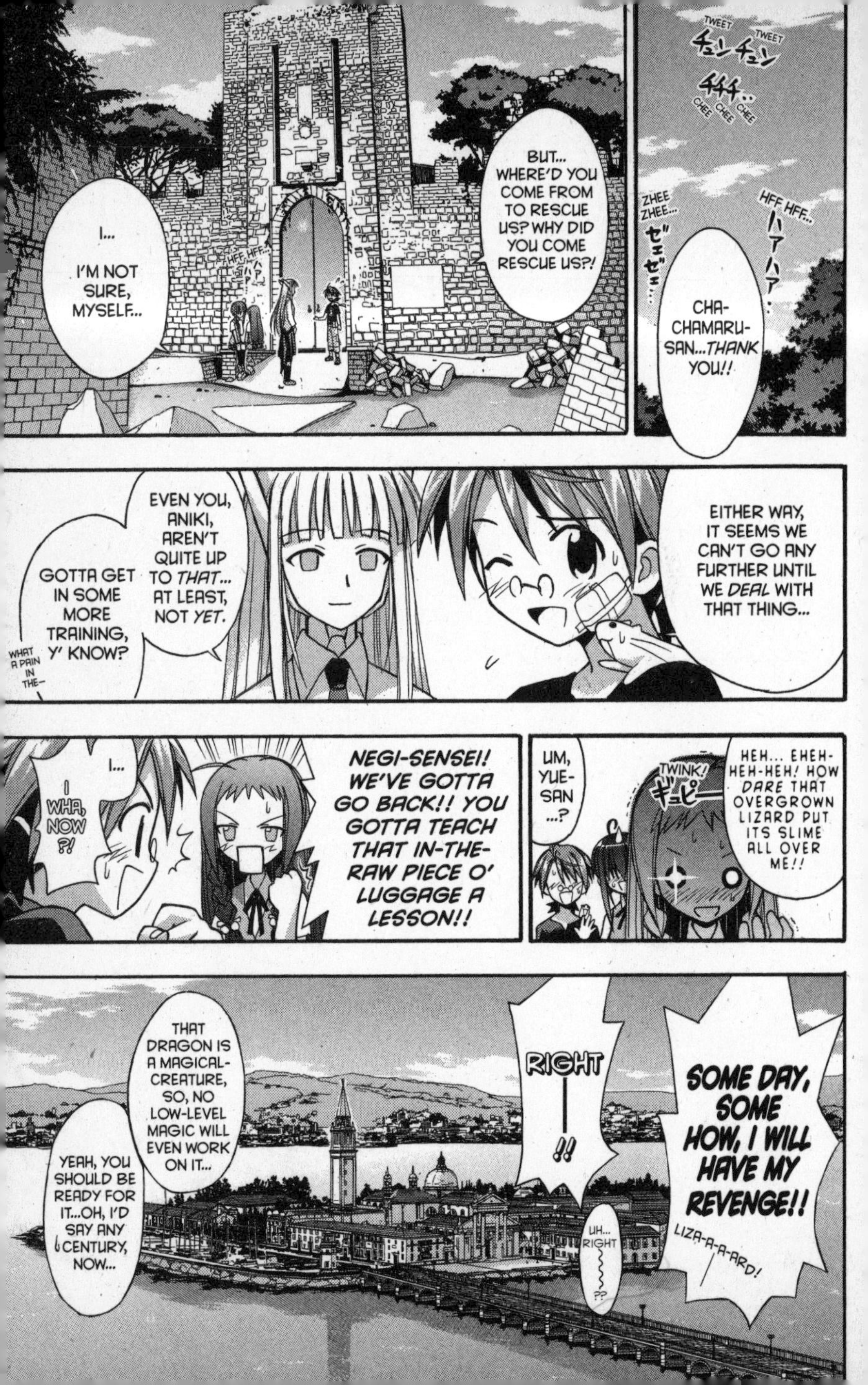
TWEET TWEET
チュンチュン
CHEE CHEE CHEE
チチチ..
ZHEE ZHEE...
ゼェゼェ...
HFF HFF...
ハァハァ...
CHA-CHAMARU-SAN...THANK YOU!!
BUT... WHERE'D YOU COME FROM TO RESCUE US? WHY DID YOU COME RESCUE US?!
HFF HFF...
I... I'M NOT SURE, MYSELF...
EITHER WAY, IT SEEMS WE CAN'T GO ANY FURTHER UNTIL WE DEAL WITH THAT THING...
EVEN YOU, ANIKI, AREN'T QUITE UP TO THAT... AT LEAST, NOT YET.
GOTTA GET IN SOME MORE TRAINING, Y' KNOW?
WHAT A PAIN IN THE—
HEH... EHEH-HEH-HEH! HOW DARE THAT OVERGROWN LIZARD PUT ITS SLIME ALL OVER ME!!
TWINK!
UM, YUE-SAN ...?
NEGI-SENSEI! WE'VE GOTTA GO BACK!! YOU GOTTA TEACH THAT IN-THE-RAW PIECE O' LUGGAGE A LESSON!!
I...
I WHA, NOW ?!
SOME DAY, SOME HOW, I WILL HAVE MY REVENGE!!
LIZA-A-A-ARD!
RIGHT—!!
UH... RIGHT ~~~??
THAT DRAGON IS A MAGICAL-CREATURE, SO, NO LOW-LEVEL MAGIC WILL EVEN WORK ON IT...
YEAH, YOU SHOULD BE READY FOR IT...OH, I'D SAY ANY CENTURY, NOW...

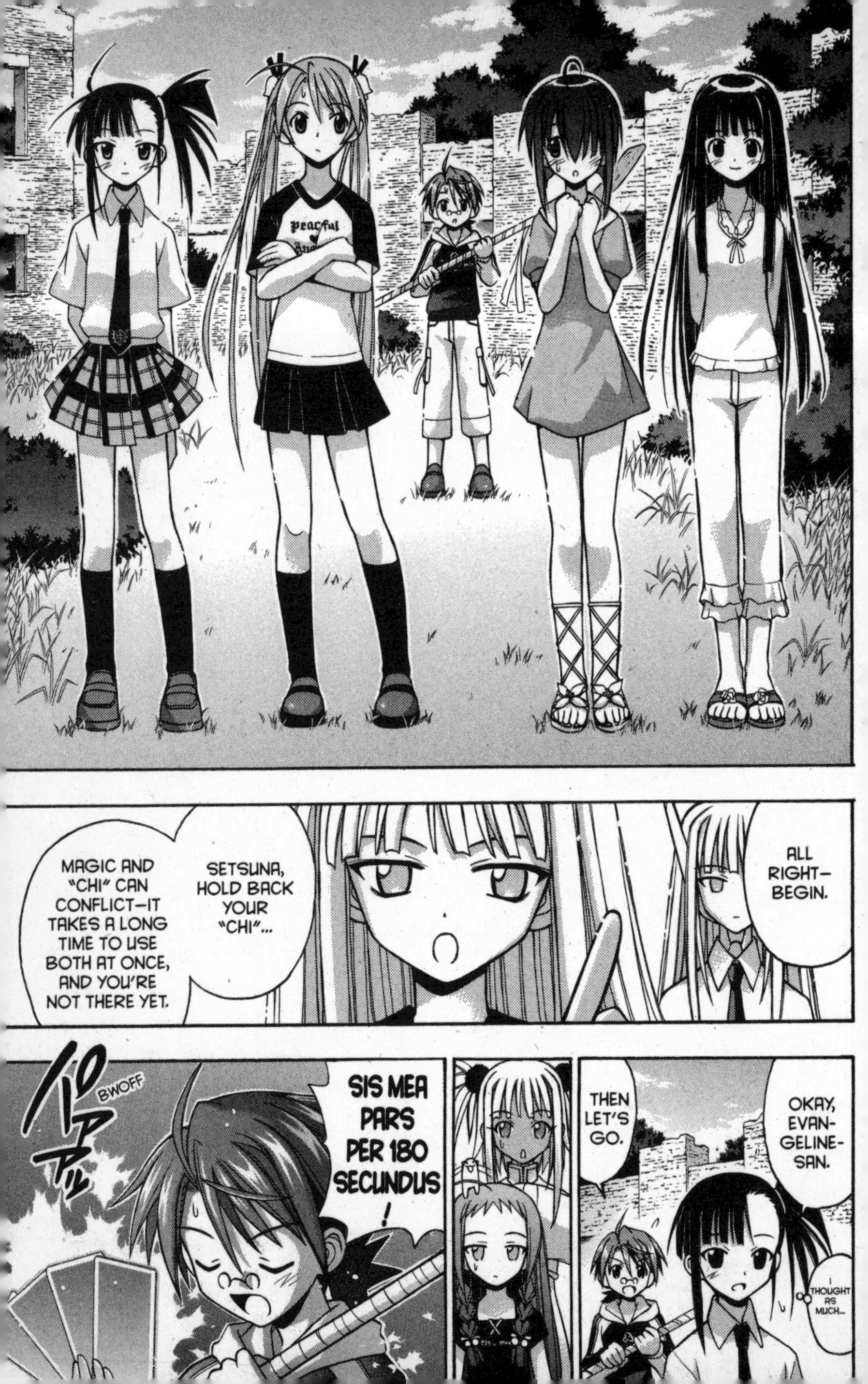
ALL RIGHT—BEGIN.
SETSUNA, HOLD BACK YOUR "CHI"...
MAGIC AND "CHI" CAN CONFLICT—IT TAKES A LONG TIME TO USE BOTH AT ONCE, AND YOU'RE NOT THERE YET.
OKAY, EVAN-GELINE-SAN.
THEN LET'S GO.
I THOUGHT AS MUCH...
SIS MEA PARS PER 180 SECUNDUS!
BWOFF

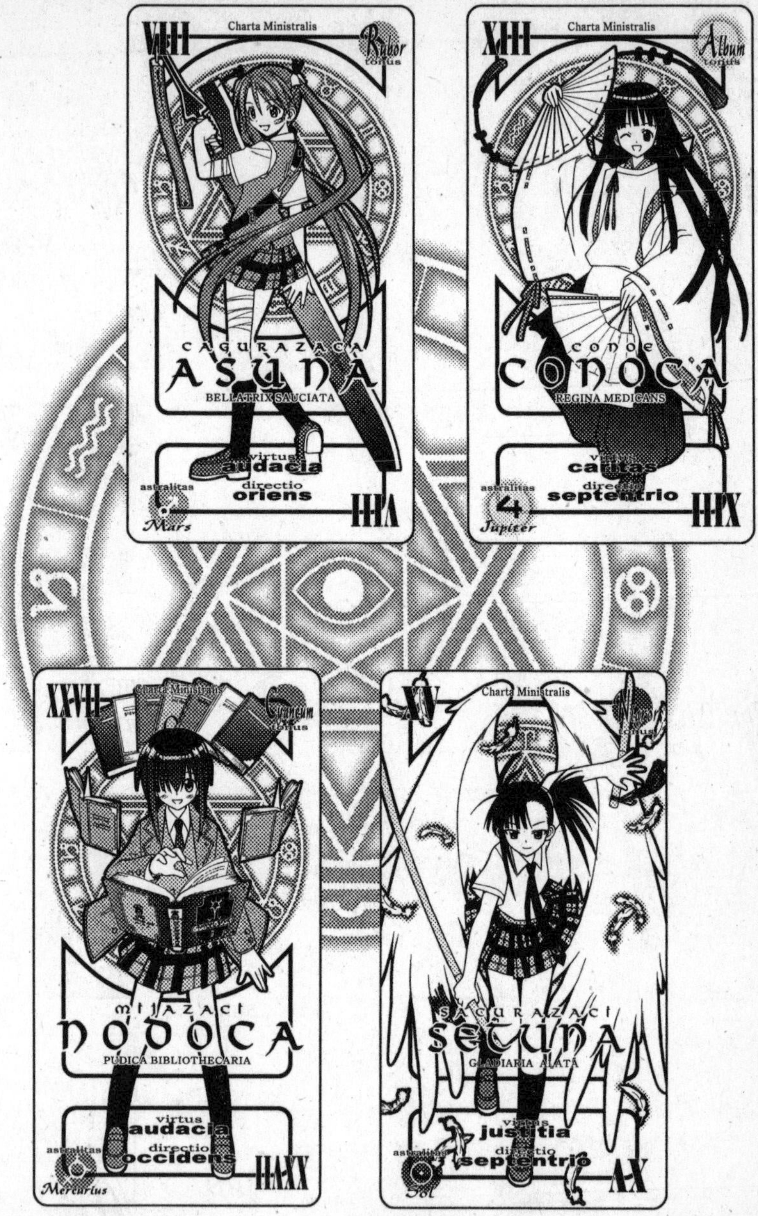
XIII
Charta Ministralis
Album tonus
CONOE
CONOCA
REGINA MEDICANS
virtus caritas
astralitas
directio septentrio
4
Jupiter
VIII
Charta Ministralis
Rubor tonus
CAGURAZACA
ASUNA
BELLATRIX SAUCIATA
virtus audacia
astralitas
directio oriens
Mars
XV
Charta Ministralis
Niger tonus
SACURAZACI
SETUNA
GLADIARIA ALATA
virtus justitia
astralitas
directio septentrio
Sol
XXVII
Charta Ministralis
Cyaneum tonus
MIJAZACI
NODOCA
PUDICA BIBLIOTHECARIA
virtus audacia
astralitas
directio occidens
Mercurius

SIXTIETH PERIOD: CARDS, HOW TO USE

NEGIMA!

MAGISTER NEGI MAGI

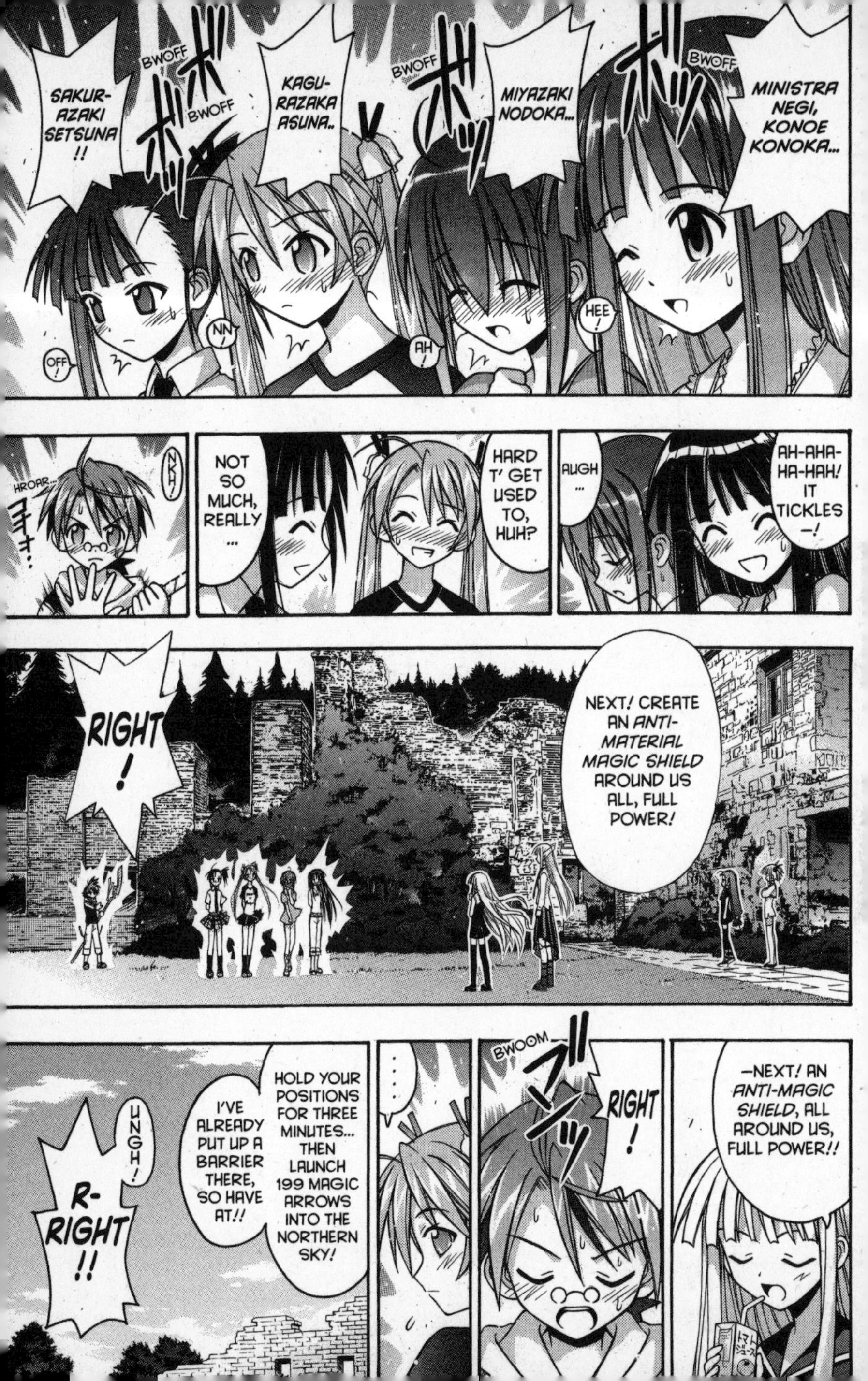
MINISTRA NEGI, KONOE KONOKA...
BWOFF
HEE!
MIYAZAKI NODOKA...
BWOFF
AH!
KAGURAZAKA ASUNA..
BWOFF
NN!
SAKURAZAKI SETSUNA !!
BWOFF
BWOFF
OFF!
AH-AHA-HA-HAH! IT TICKLES—!
AUGH ...
HARD T' GET USED TO, HUH?
NOT SO MUCH, REALLY ...
NKH!
HROAR...
NEXT! CREATE AN ANTI-MATERIAL MAGIC SHIELD AROUND US ALL, FULL POWER!
RIGHT!
—NEXT! AN ANTI-MAGIC SHIELD, ALL AROUND US, FULL POWER!!
BWOOM
RIGHT!
....
HOLD YOUR POSITIONS FOR THREE MINUTES... THEN LAUNCH 199 MAGIC ARROWS INTO THE NORTHERN SKY!
I'VE ALREADY PUT UP A BARRIER THERE, SO HAVE AT!!
UNGH!
R-RIGHT!!

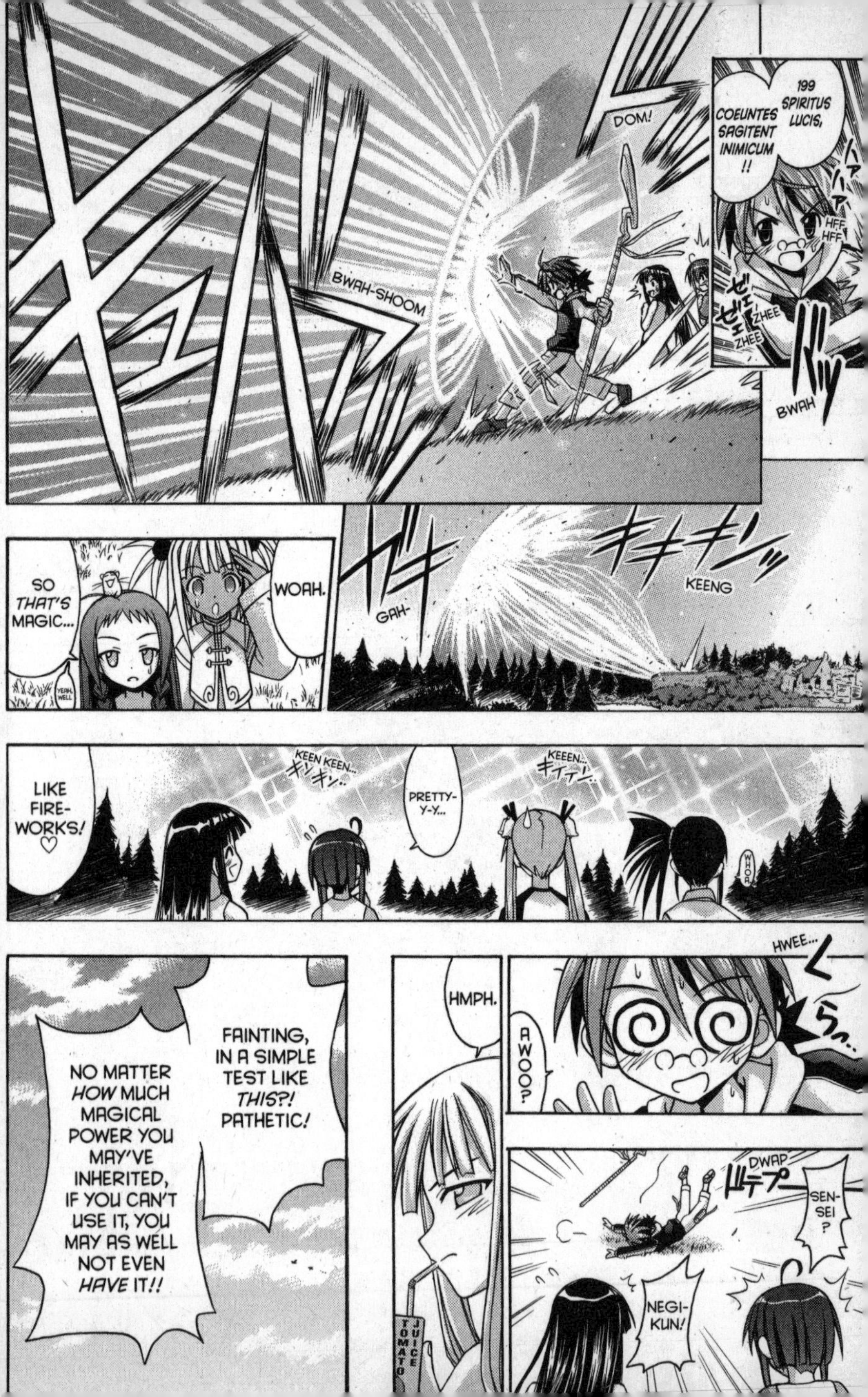
199 SPIRITUS LUCIS, COEUNTES SAGITENT INIMICUM!!
HFF HFF
ZHEE ZHEE
BWAH
DOM!
BWAH-SHOOM
KEENG
GAH-
WOAH.
SO THAT'S MAGIC...
YEAH, WELL
KEEEN...
PRETTY-Y-Y...
KEEN KEEN...
LIKE FIRE-WORKS! ♡
WHOA
HWEE...
AWOO?
DWAP
SEN-SEI?
NEGI-KUN!
HMPH.
FAINTING, IN A SIMPLE TEST LIKE THIS?! PATHETIC!
NO MATTER HOW MUCH MAGICAL POWER YOU MAY'VE INHERITED, IF YOU CAN'T USE IT, YOU MAY AS WELL NOT EVEN HAVE IT!!
TOMATO JUICE

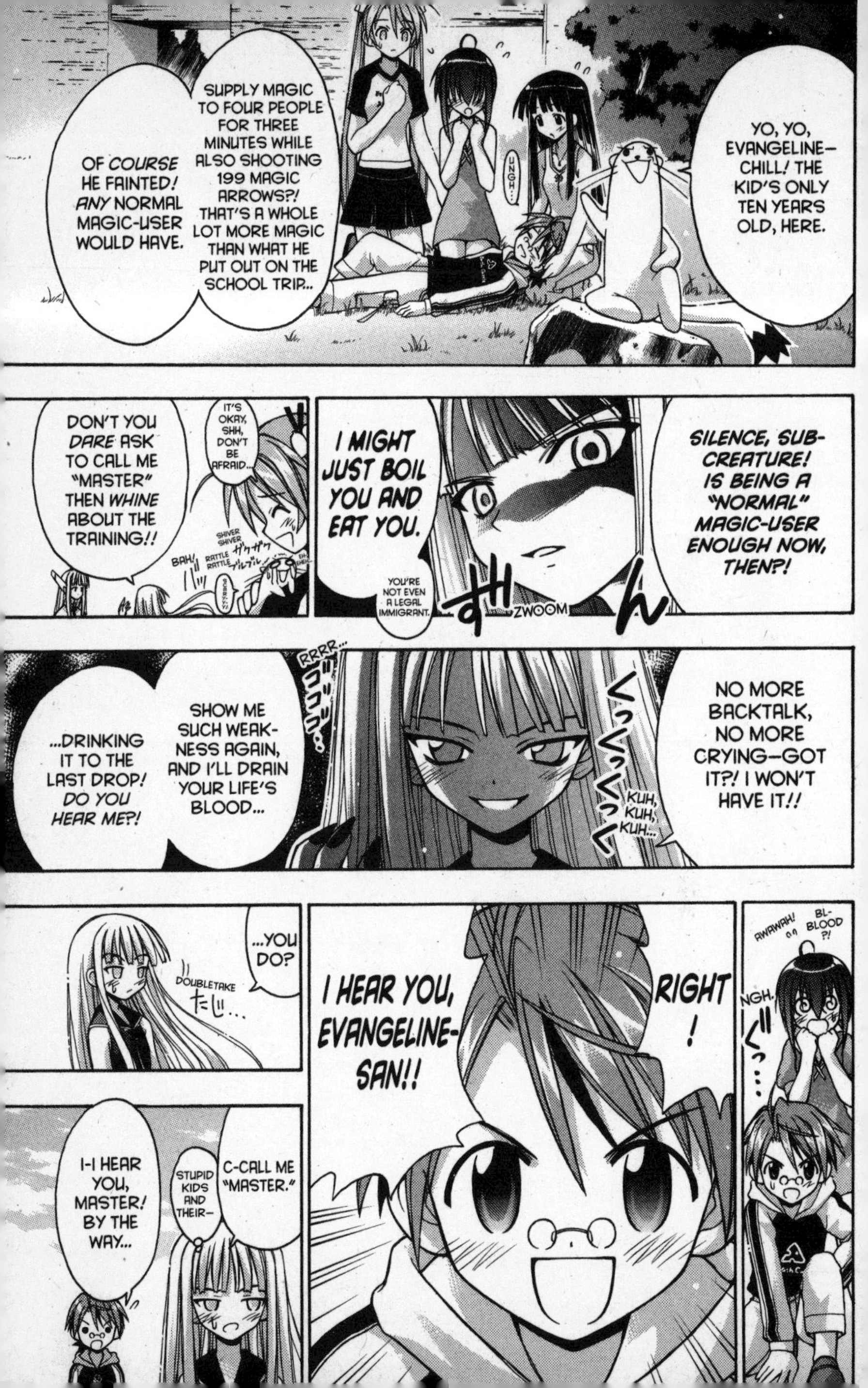
YO, YO, EVANGELINE-CHILL! THE KID'S ONLY TEN YEARS OLD, HERE.
UNGH...
SUPPLY MAGIC TO FOUR PEOPLE FOR THREE MINUTES WHILE ALSO SHOOTING 199 MAGIC ARROWS?! THAT'S A WHOLE LOT MORE MAGIC THAN WHAT HE PUT OUT ON THE SCHOOL TRIP...
OF *COURSE* HE FAINTED! *ANY* NORMAL MAGIC-USER WOULD HAVE.
SILENCE, SUB-CREATURE! IS BEING A "NORMAL" MAGIC-USER ENOUGH NOW, THEN?!
I MIGHT JUST BOIL YOU AND EAT YOU.
ZWOOM
YOU'RE NOT EVEN A LEGAL IMMIGRANT.
IT'S OKAY, SHH, DON'T BE AFRAID...
DON'T YOU *DARE* ASK TO CALL ME "MASTER" THEN *WHINE* ABOUT THE TRAINING!!
SHIVER SHIVER
RATTLE RATTLE
BAH!
NO MORE BACKTALK, NO MORE CRYING—GOT IT?! I WON'T HAVE IT!!
KUH, KUH, KUH...
RRRR...
SHOW ME SUCH WEAK-NESS AGAIN, AND I'LL DRAIN YOUR LIFE'S BLOOD...
...DRINKING IT TO THE LAST DROP! *DO YOU HEAR ME?!*
BL-BLOOD?!
AWAWAH!
NGH.
RIGHT!
I HEAR YOU, EVANGELINE-SAN!!
...YOU DO?
DOUBLETAKE
C-CALL ME "MASTER."
STUPID KIDS AND THEIR—
I-I HEAR YOU, MASTER! BY THE WAY...

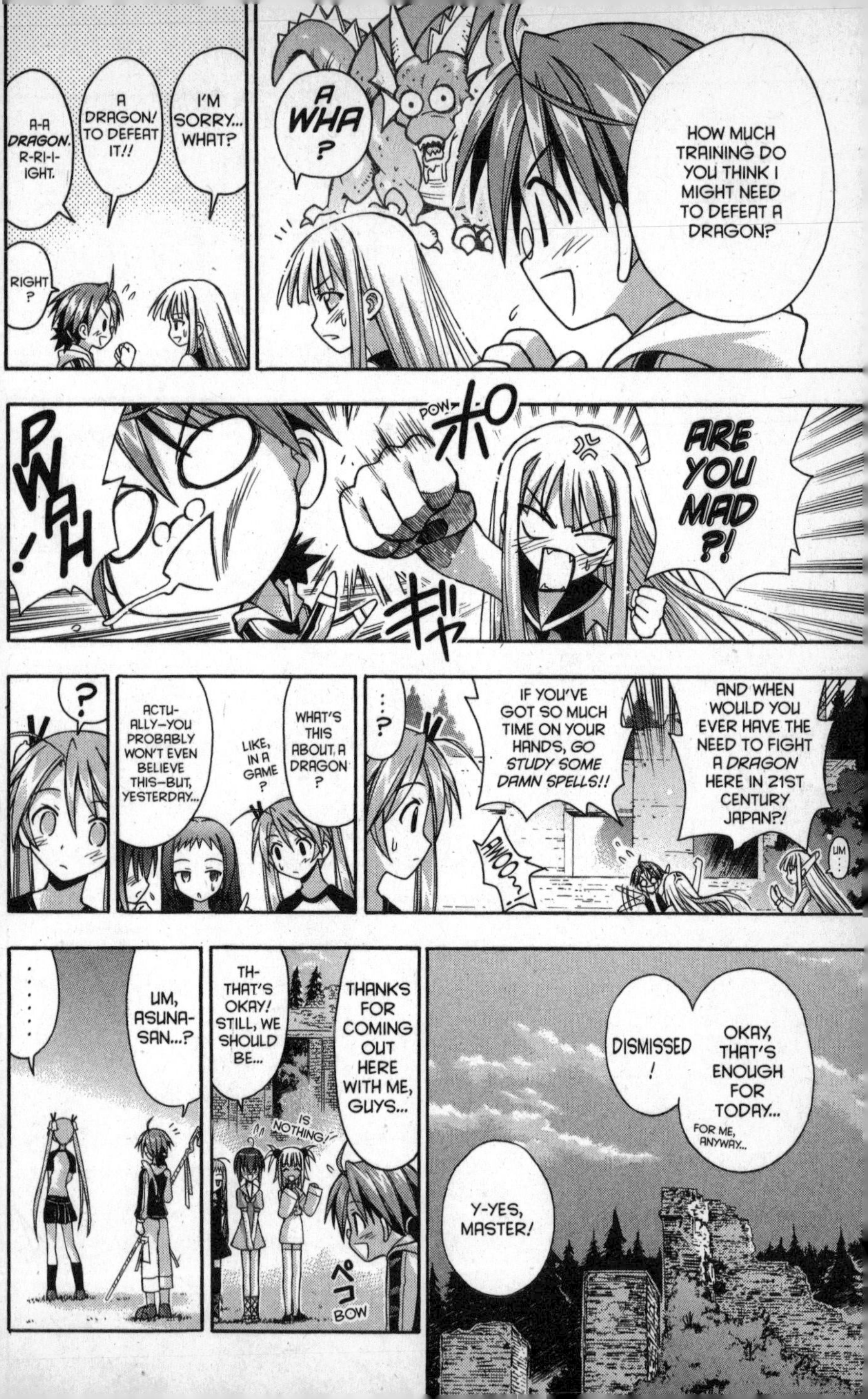

HOW MUCH TRAINING DO YOU THINK I MIGHT NEED TO DEFEAT A DRAGON?
A WHA?
I'M SORRY... WHAT?
A DRAGON! TO DEFEAT IT!!
A-A DRAGON. R-RI-I-IGHT.
RIGHT?
ARE YOU MAD?!
POW
PWAH!
AND WHEN WOULD YOU EVER HAVE THE NEED TO FIGHT A DRAGON HERE IN 21ST CENTURY JAPAN?!
IF YOU'VE GOT SO MUCH TIME ON YOUR HANDS, GO STUDY SOME DAMN SPELLS!!
UM...
AWOO~!
...?
WHAT'S THIS ABOUT A DRAGON?
LIKE, IN A GAME?
ACTU-ALLY—YOU PROBABLY WON'T EVEN BELIEVE THIS—BUT, YESTERDAY...
?
OKAY, THAT'S ENOUGH FOR TODAY...
FOR ME, ANYWAY...
DISMISSED!
Y-YES, MASTER!
THANKS FOR COMING OUT HERE WITH ME, GUYS...
TH-THAT'S OKAY! STILL, WE SHOULD BE...
IS NOTHING!
BOW
UM, ASUNA-SAN...?
......

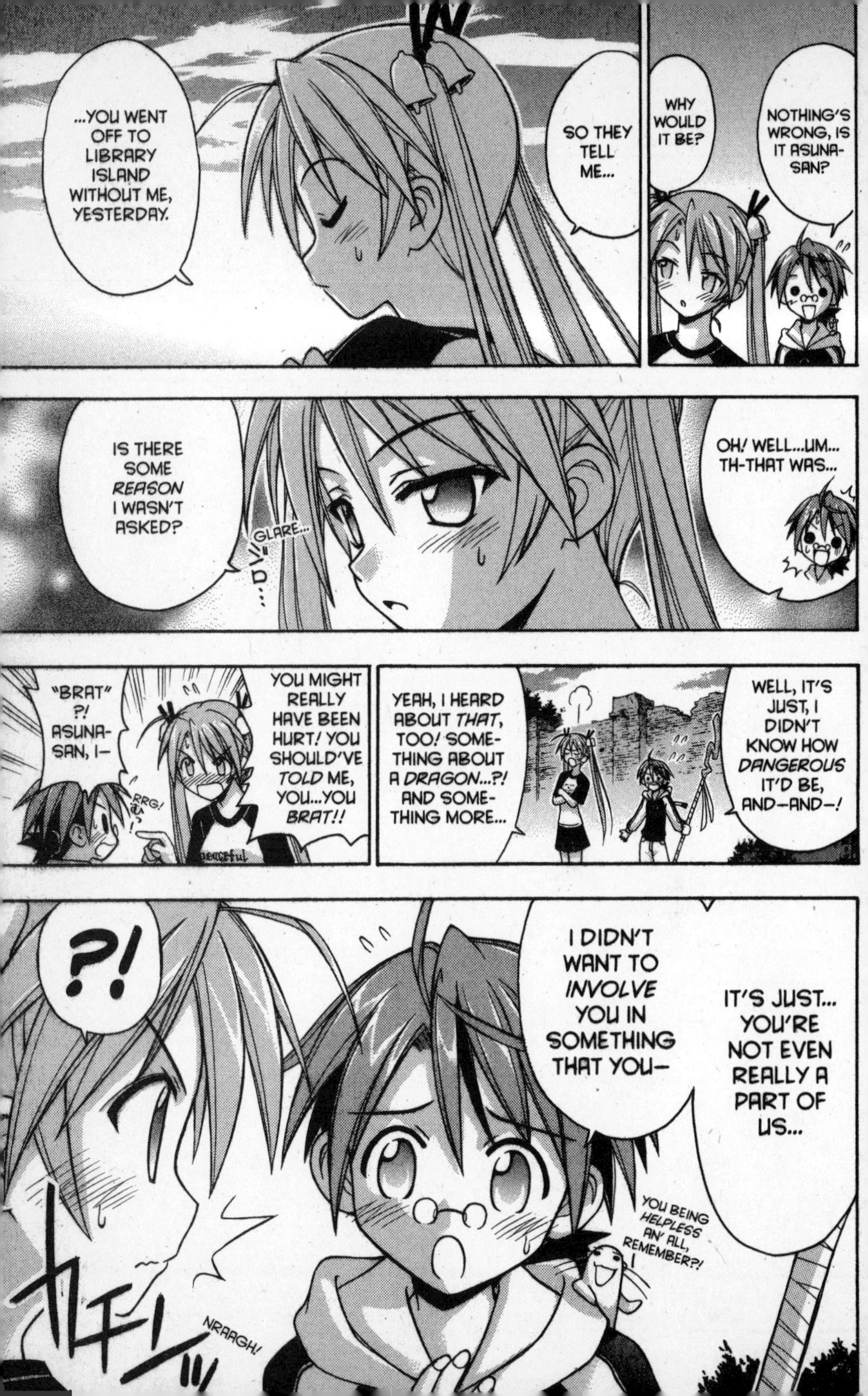
NOTHING'S WRONG, IS IT ASUNA-SAN?
WHY WOULD IT BE?
SO THEY TELL ME...
...YOU WENT OFF TO LIBRARY ISLAND WITHOUT ME, YESTERDAY.
OH! WELL...UM... TH-THAT WAS...
GLARE...
IS THERE SOME *REASON* I WASN'T ASKED?
WELL, IT'S JUST, I DIDN'T KNOW HOW *DANGEROUS* IT'D BE, AND—AND—!
YEAH, I HEARD ABOUT *THAT*, TOO! SOME-THING ABOUT A *DRAGON*...?! AND SOME-THING MORE...
YOU MIGHT REALLY HAVE BEEN HURT! YOU SHOULD'VE *TOLD* ME, YOU...YOU *BRAT*!!
RRG!
"BRAT" ?! ASUNA-SAN, I—
IT'S JUST... YOU'RE NOT EVEN REALLY A PART OF US...
I DIDN'T WANT TO *INVOLVE* YOU IN SOMETHING THAT YOU—
YOU BEING *HELPLESS* AN' ALL, REMEMBER?!
?!
NRAAGH!

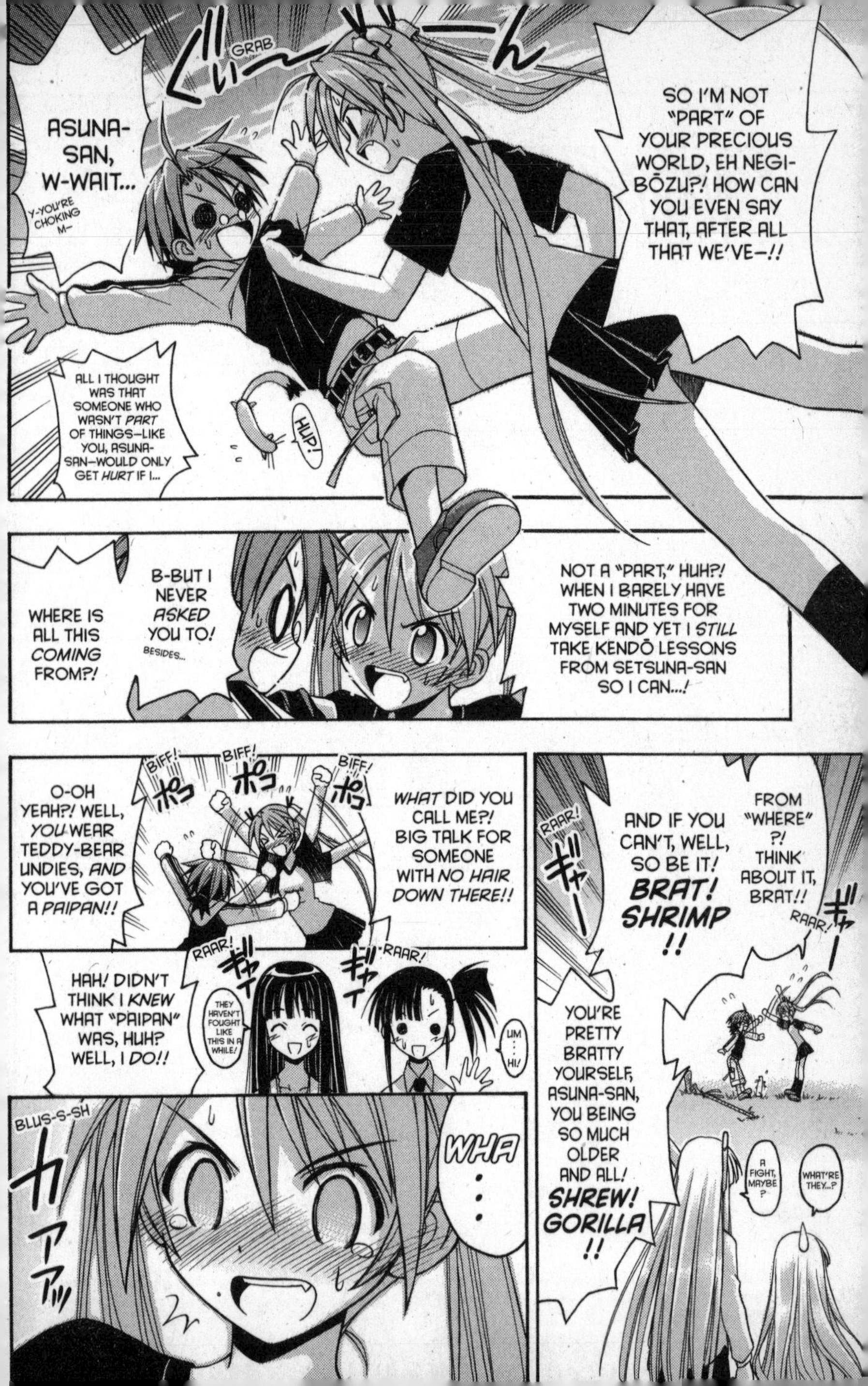
GRAB
SO I'M NOT "PART" OF YOUR PRECIOUS WORLD, EH NEGI-BŌZU?! HOW CAN YOU EVEN SAY THAT, AFTER ALL THAT WE'VE—!!
ASUNA-SAN, W-WAIT...
Y-YOU'RE CHOKING M—
HUP!
ALL I THOUGHT WAS THAT SOMEONE WHO WASN'T PART OF THINGS—LIKE YOU, ASUNA-SAN—WOULD ONLY GET HURT IF I...
NOT A "PART," HUH?! WHEN I BARELY HAVE TWO MINUTES FOR MYSELF AND YET I STILL TAKE KENDŌ LESSONS FROM SETSUNA-SAN SO I CAN...!
B-BUT I NEVER ASKED YOU TO!
BESIDES...
WHERE IS ALL THIS COMING FROM?!
FROM "WHERE"?! THINK ABOUT IT, BRAT!!
RAAR!
AND IF YOU CAN'T, WELL, SO BE IT! BRAT! SHRIMP!!
RAAR!
YOU'RE PRETTY BRATTY YOURSELF, ASUNA-SAN, YOU BEING SO MUCH OLDER AND ALL! SHREW! GORILLA!!
WHAT'RE THEY...?
A FIGHT, MAYBE?
BIFF!
BIFF!
BIFF!
WHAT DID YOU CALL ME?! BIG TALK FOR SOMEONE WITH NO HAIR DOWN THERE!!
O-OH YEAH?! WELL, YOU WEAR TEDDY-BEAR UNDIES, AND YOU'VE GOT A PAIPAN!!
RAAR!
RAAR!
UM ... HI!
THEY HAVEN'T FOUGHT LIKE THIS IN A WHILE!
HAH! DIDN'T THINK I KNEW WHAT "PAIPAN" WAS, HUH? WELL, I DO!!
WHA...
BLUS-S-SH

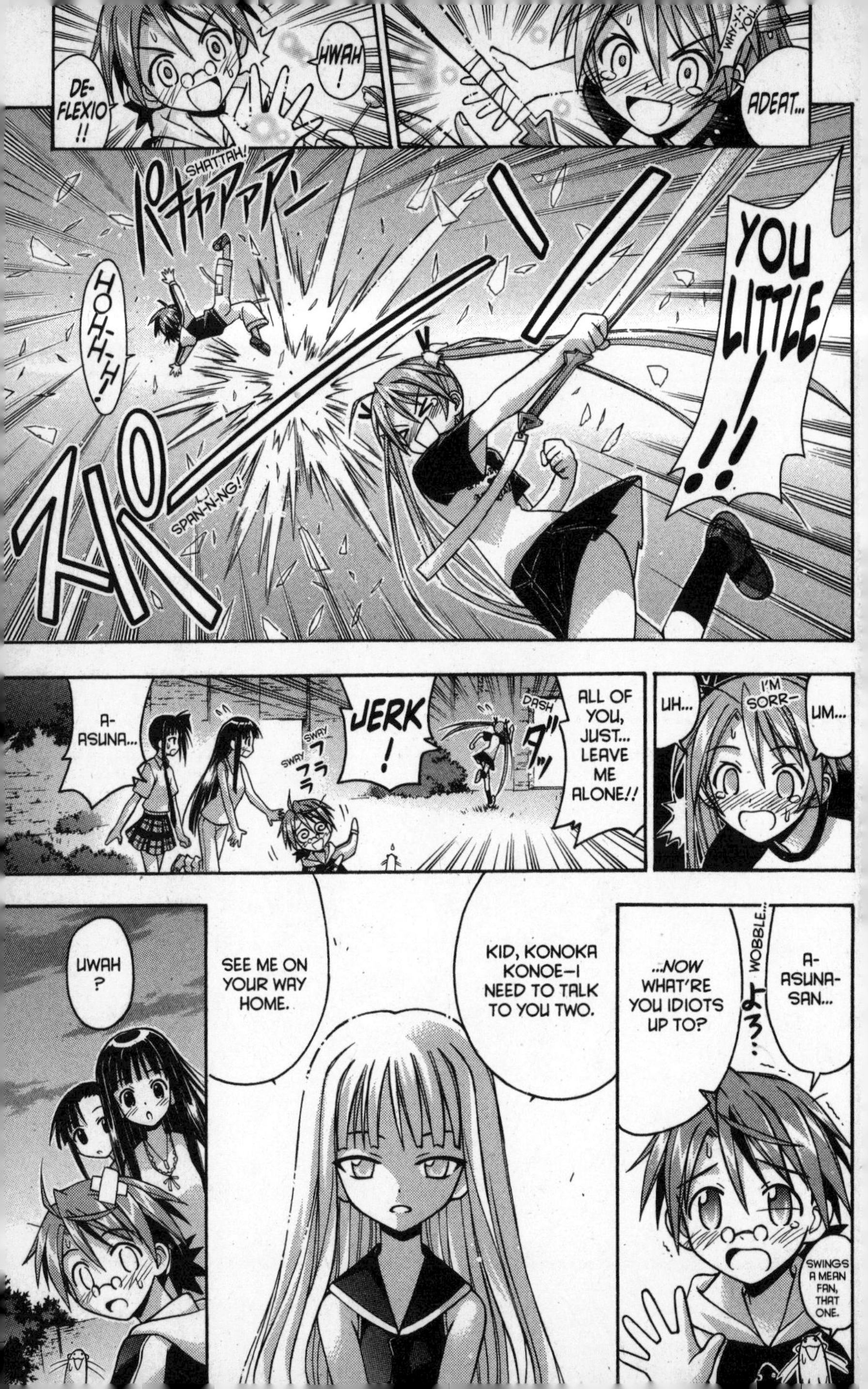
WHY-Y-Y, YOU...
ADEAT...
HWAH!
DE-FLEXIO!!
YOU LITTLE!!!
SHATTAH!
パキャァァン
HOH-H-H-!
スパーン
SPAN-N-NG!
I'M SORR—
UM...
UH...
ALL OF YOU, JUST... LEAVE ME ALONE!!
DASH
ダッ
JERK!
SWAY SWAY
フラフラ
A-ASUNA...
A-ASUNA-SAN...
WOBBLE...
よろ…
...NOW WHAT'RE YOU IDIOTS UP TO?
SWINGS A MEAN FAN, THAT ONE.
KID, KONOKA KONOE—I NEED TO TALK TO YOU TWO.
SEE ME ON YOUR WAY HOME.
UWAH?

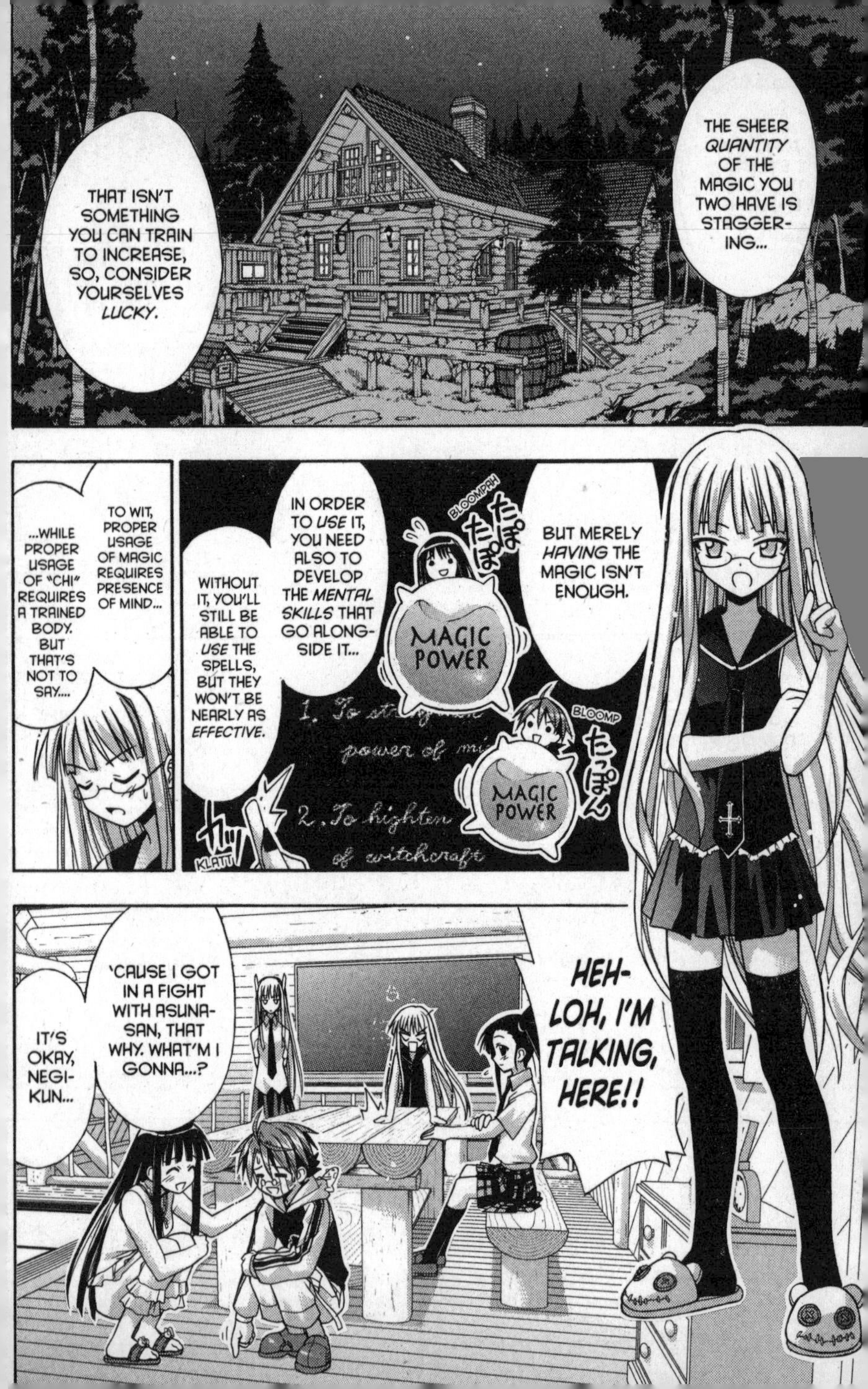
THE SHEER QUANTITY OF THE MAGIC YOU TWO HAVE IS STAGGER-ING...
THAT ISN'T SOMETHING YOU CAN TRAIN TO INCREASE, SO, CONSIDER YOURSELVES LUCKY.
BUT MERELY HAVING THE MAGIC ISN'T ENOUGH.
たぷたぷ BLOOMPAH
MAGIC POWER
たっぽん BLOOMP
MAGIC POWER
IN ORDER TO USE IT, YOU NEED ALSO TO DEVELOP THE MENTAL SKILLS THAT GO ALONG-SIDE IT...
WITHOUT IT, YOU'LL STILL BE ABLE TO USE THE SPELLS, BUT THEY WON'T BE NEARLY AS EFFECTIVE.
2. To highten
of witchcraft
カッ KLATT
TO WIT, PROPER USAGE OF MAGIC REQUIRES PRESENCE OF MIND...
...WHILE PROPER USAGE OF "CHI" REQUIRES A TRAINED BODY. BUT THAT'S NOT TO SAY...
'CAUSE I GOT IN A FIGHT WITH ASUNA-SAN, THAT WHY. WHAT'M I GONNA...?
IT'S OKAY, NEGI-KUN...
HEH-LOH, I'M TALKING, HERE!!

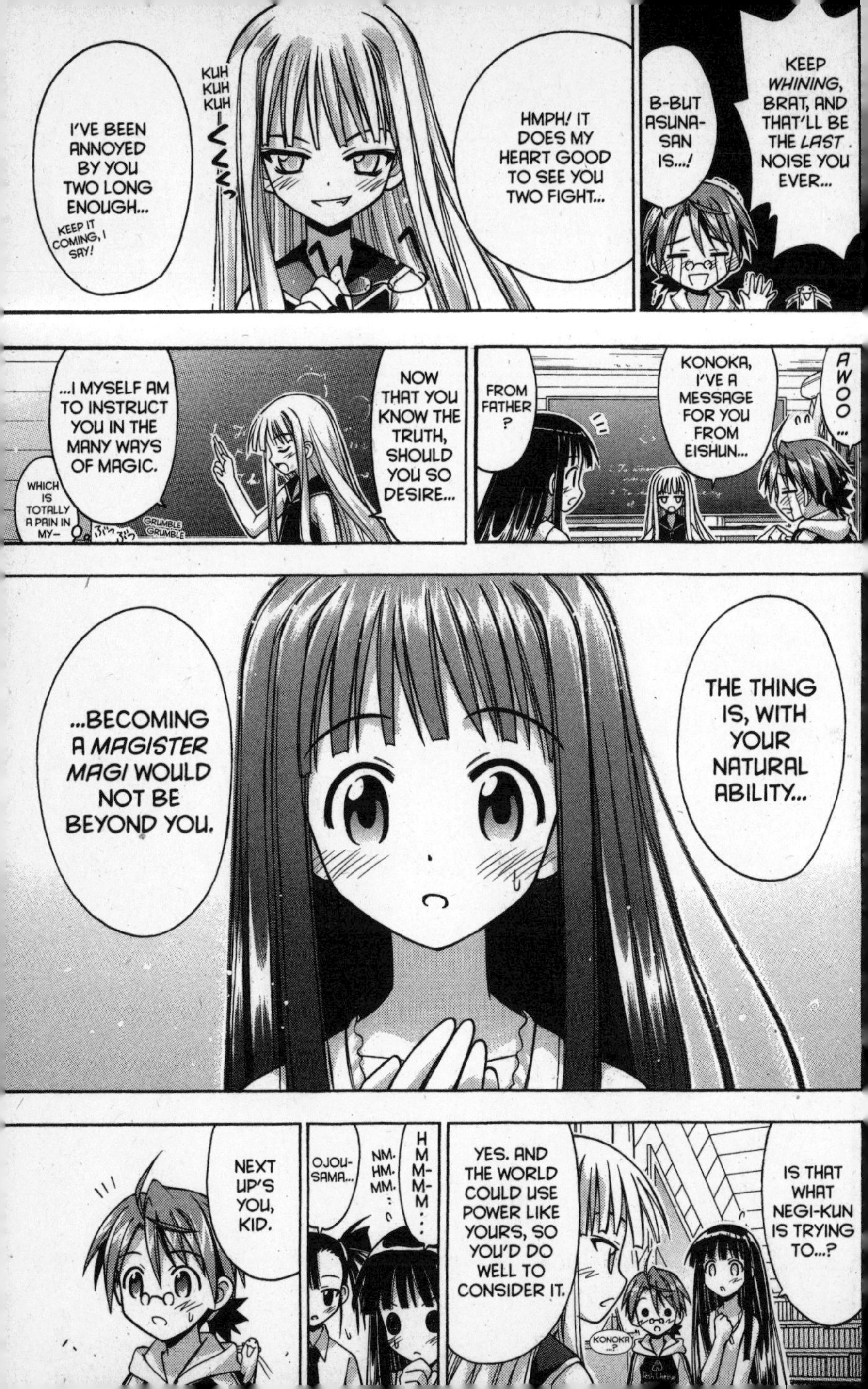
KEEP *WHINING*, BRAT, AND THAT'LL BE THE *LAST* NOISE YOU EVER...
B-BUT ASUNA-SAN IS...!
HMPH! IT DOES MY HEART GOOD TO SEE YOU TWO FIGHT...
KUH KUH KUH
I'VE BEEN ANNOYED BY YOU TWO LONG ENOUGH...
KEEP IT COMING, I SAY!
AWOO...
KONOKA, I'VE A MESSAGE FOR YOU FROM EISHUN...
FROM FATHER?
NOW THAT YOU KNOW THE TRUTH, SHOULD YOU SO DESIRE...
...I MYSELF AM TO INSTRUCT YOU IN THE MANY WAYS OF MAGIC.
WHICH IS TOTALLY A PAIN IN MY—
GRUMBLE GRUMBLE
THE THING IS, WITH YOUR NATURAL ABILITY...
...BECOMING A *MAGISTER MAGI* WOULD NOT BE BEYOND YOU.
IS THAT WHAT NEGI-KUN IS TRYING TO...?
YES. AND THE WORLD COULD USE POWER LIKE YOURS, SO YOU'D DO WELL TO CONSIDER IT.
KONOKA...?
HMMM-M...
NM. HM. MM.
OJOU-SAMA...
NEXT UP'S YOU, KID.

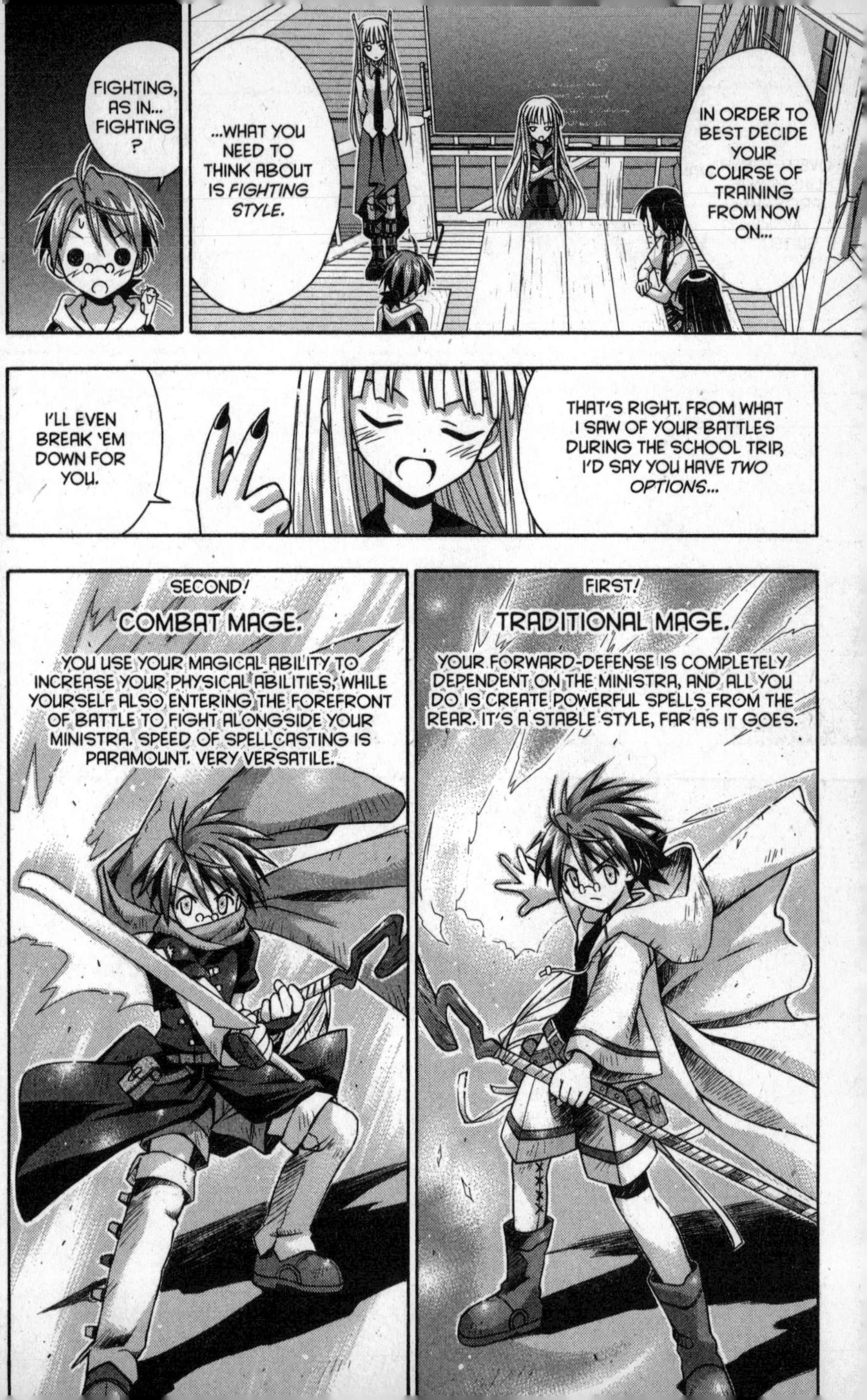
IN ORDER TO BEST DECIDE YOUR COURSE OF TRAINING FROM NOW ON...
...WHAT YOU NEED TO THINK ABOUT IS *FIGHTING STYLE.*
FIGHTING, AS IN... FIGHTING?
THAT'S RIGHT. FROM WHAT I SAW OF YOUR BATTLES DURING THE SCHOOL TRIP, I'D SAY YOU HAVE *TWO OPTIONS*...
I'LL EVEN BREAK 'EM DOWN FOR YOU.
FIRST!
TRADITIONAL MAGE.
YOUR FORWARD-DEFENSE IS COMPLETELY DEPENDENT ON THE MINISTRA, AND ALL YOU DO IS CREATE POWERFUL SPELLS FROM THE REAR. IT'S A STABLE STYLE, FAR AS IT GOES.
SECOND!
COMBAT MAGE.
YOU USE YOUR MAGICAL ABILITY TO INCREASE YOUR PHYSICAL ABILITIES, WHILE YOURSELF ALSO ENTERING THE FOREFRONT OF BATTLE TO FIGHT ALONGSIDE YOUR MINISTRA. SPEED OF SPELLCASTING IS PARAMOUNT. VERY VERSATILE.

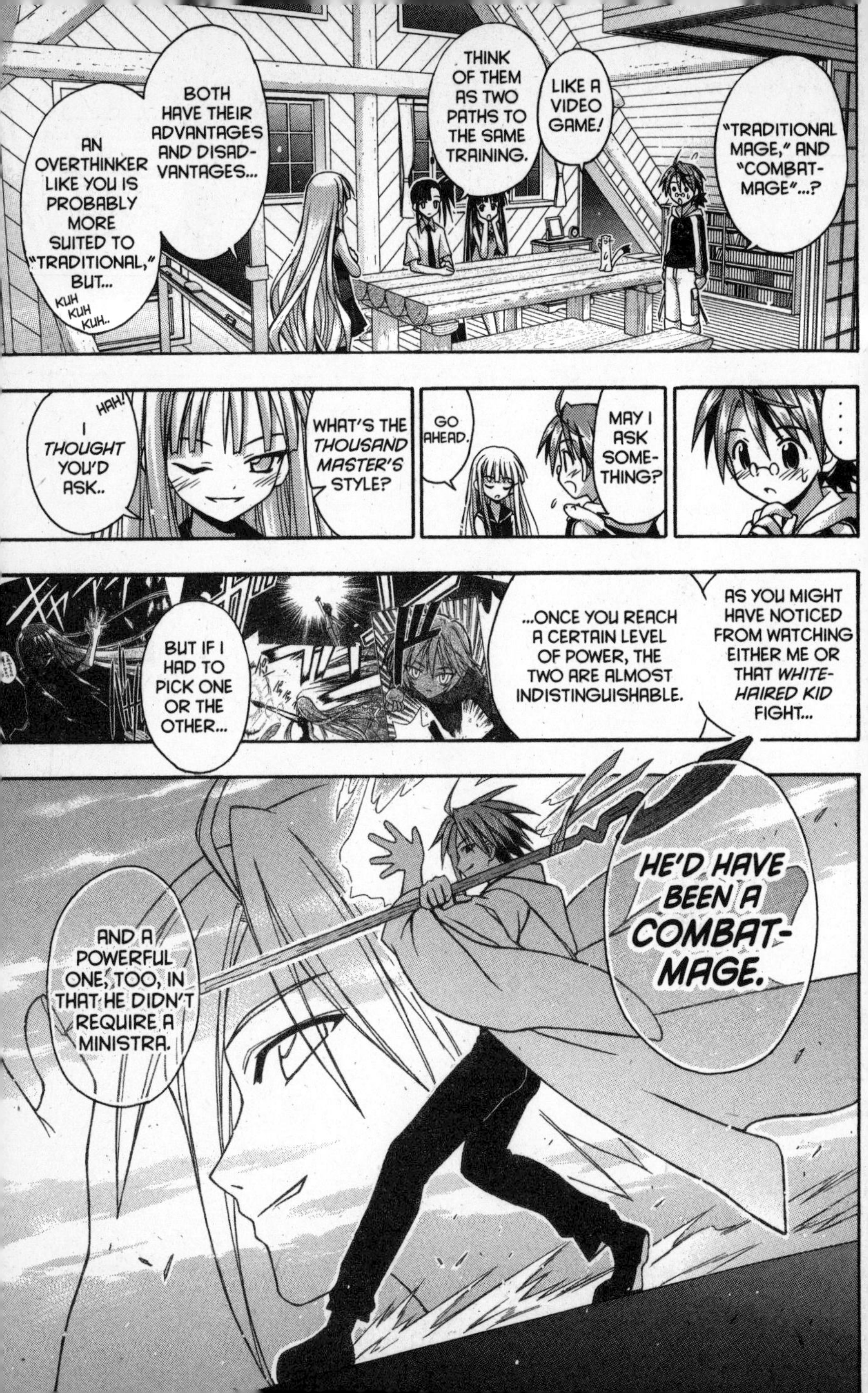
"TRADITIONAL MAGE," AND "COMBAT-MAGE"...?
LIKE A VIDEO GAME!
THINK OF THEM AS TWO PATHS TO THE SAME TRAINING.
BOTH HAVE THEIR ADVANTAGES AND DISAD-VANTAGES...
AN OVERTHINKER LIKE YOU IS PROBABLY MORE SUITED TO "TRADITIONAL," BUT...
KUH KUH KUH..
....
MAY I ASK SOME-THING?
GO AHEAD.
WHAT'S THE *THOUSAND MASTER'S* STYLE?
HAH!
I *THOUGHT* YOU'D ASK..
AS YOU MIGHT HAVE NOTICED FROM WATCHING EITHER ME OR THAT *WHITE-HAIRED KID* FIGHT...
...ONCE YOU REACH A CERTAIN LEVEL OF POWER, THE TWO ARE ALMOST INDISTINGUISHABLE.
BUT IF I HAD TO PICK ONE OR THE OTHER...
HE'D HAVE BEEN A COMBAT-MAGE.
AND A POWERFUL ONE, TOO, IN THAT HE DIDN'T REQUIRE A MINISTRA.

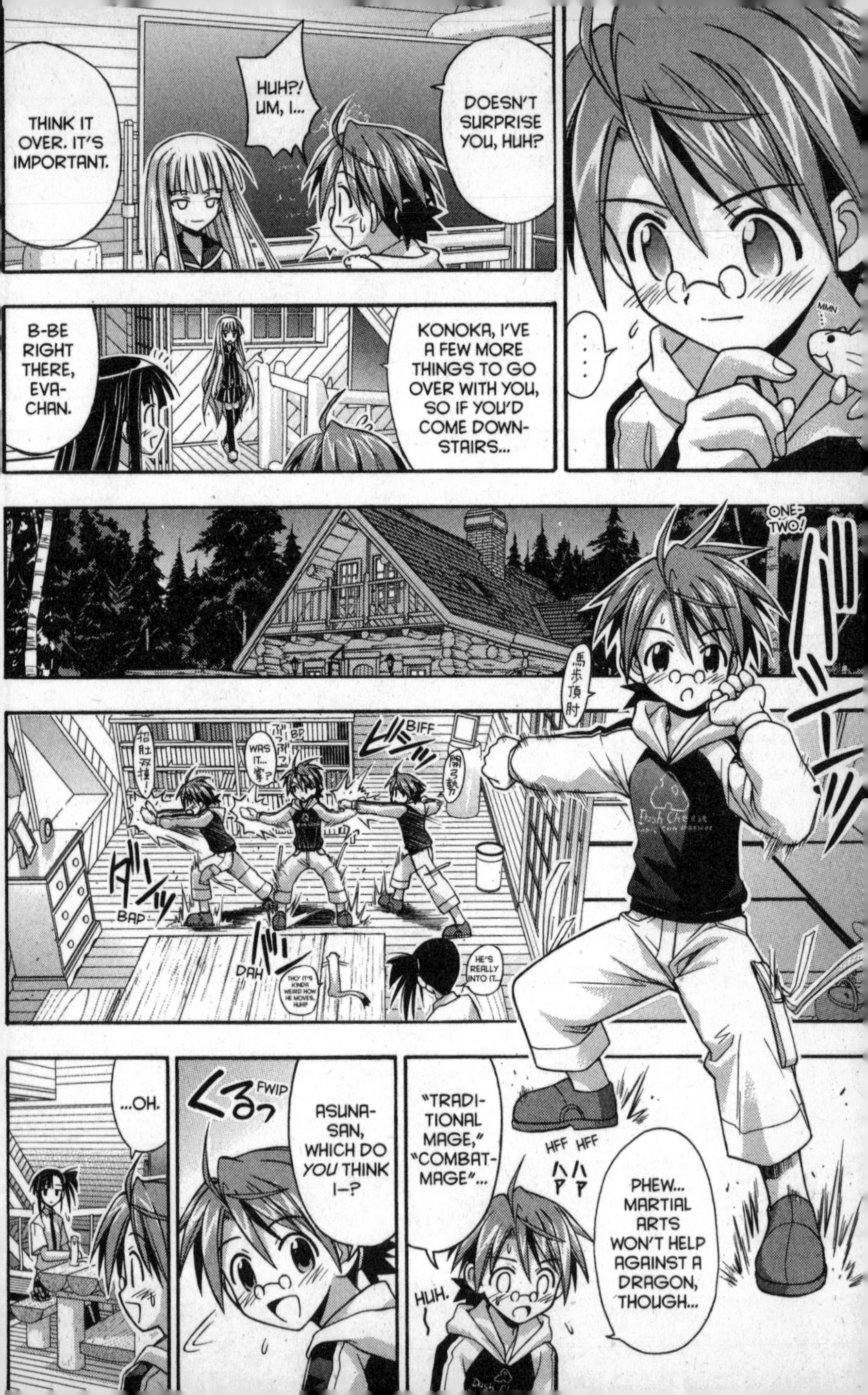
...
MMN
DOESN'T SURPRISE YOU, HUH?
HUH?! UM, I...
THINK IT OVER. IT'S IMPORTANT.
KONOKA, I'VE A FEW MORE THINGS TO GO OVER WITH YOU, SO IF YOU'D COME DOWN-STAIRS...
B-BE RIGHT THERE, EVA-CHAN.
ONE-TWO!
馬歩頂肘
BIFF
開之勢
WAS IT... 掌?
BP
招肚双撞!
BAP
DAH
HE'S REALLY INTO IT...
THO' IT'S KINDA WEIRD HOW HE MOVES, HUH?
HFF HFF
PHEW... MARTIAL ARTS WON'T HELP AGAINST A DRAGON, THOUGH...
HUH.
"TRADI-TIONAL MAGE," "COMBAT-MAGE"...
ASUNA-SAN, WHICH DO *YOU* THINK I-?
FWIP
...OH.

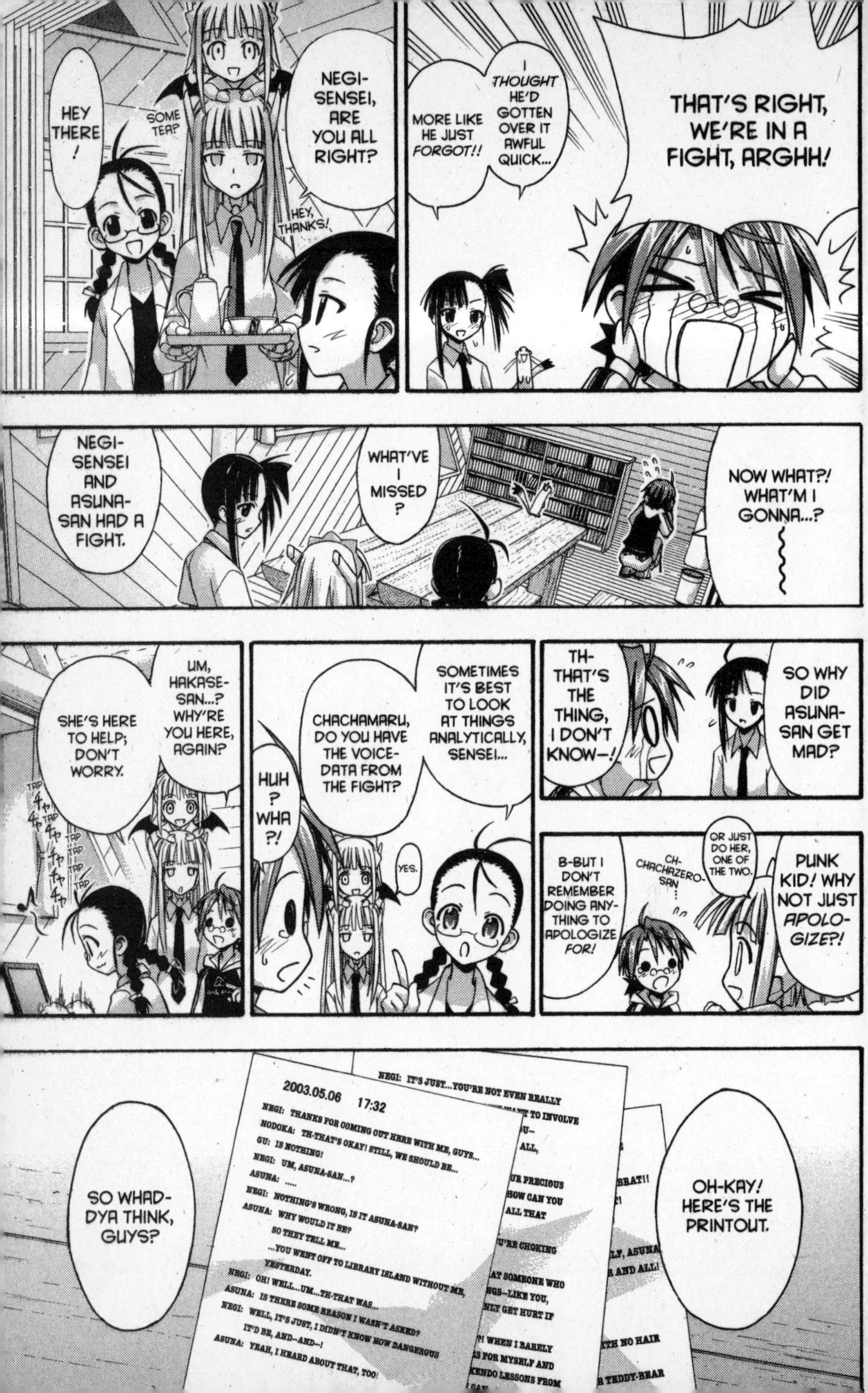
THAT'S RIGHT, WE'RE IN A FIGHT, ARGHH!
I THOUGHT HE'D GOTTEN OVER IT AWFUL QUICK...
MORE LIKE HE JUST FORGOT!!
NEGI-SENSEI, ARE YOU ALL RIGHT?
HEY, THANKS!
SOME TEA?
HEY THERE!
NOW WHAT?! WHAT'M I GONNA...?
WHAT'VE I MISSED?
NEGI-SENSEI AND ASUNA-SAN HAD A FIGHT.
SO WHY DID ASUNA-SAN GET MAD?
TH-THAT'S THE THING, I DON'T KNOW—!
PUNK KID! WHY NOT JUST APOLOGIZE?!
OR JUST DO HER, ONE OF THE TWO.
CH-CHACHAZERO-SAN...
B-BUT I DON'T REMEMBER DOING ANYTHING TO APOLOGIZE FOR!
SOMETIMES IT'S BEST TO LOOK AT THINGS ANALYTICALLY, SENSEI...
CHACHAMARU, DO YOU HAVE THE VOICE-DATA FROM THE FIGHT?
YES.
HUH? WHA?!
UM, HAKASE-SAN...? WHY'RE YOU HERE, AGAIN?
SHE'S HERE TO HELP; DON'T WORRY.
TAP TAP TAP TAP TAP TAP
OH-KAY! HERE'S THE PRINTOUT.
NEGI: IT'S JUST...YOU'RE NOT EVEN REALLY
2003.05.06 17:32
NEGI: THANKS FOR COMING OUT HERE WITH ME, GUYS...
NODOKA: TH-THAT'S OKAY! STILL, WE SHOULD BE...
GU: IS NOTHING!
NEGI: UM, ASUNA-SAN...?
ASUNA: .....
NEGI: NOTHING'S WRONG, IS IT ASUNA-SAN?
ASUNA: WHY WOULD IT BE?
SO THEY TELL ME...
...YOU WENT OFF TO LIBRARY ISLAND WITHOUT ME, YESTERDAY.
NEGI: OH! WELL...UM...TH-THAT WAS...
ASUNA: IS THERE SOME REASON I WASN'T ASKED?
NEGI: WELL, IT'S JUST, I DIDN'T KNOW HOW DANGEROUS IT'D BE, AND—AND—!
ASUNA: YEAH, I HEARD ABOUT THAT, TOO!
SO WHADDYA THINK, GUYS?

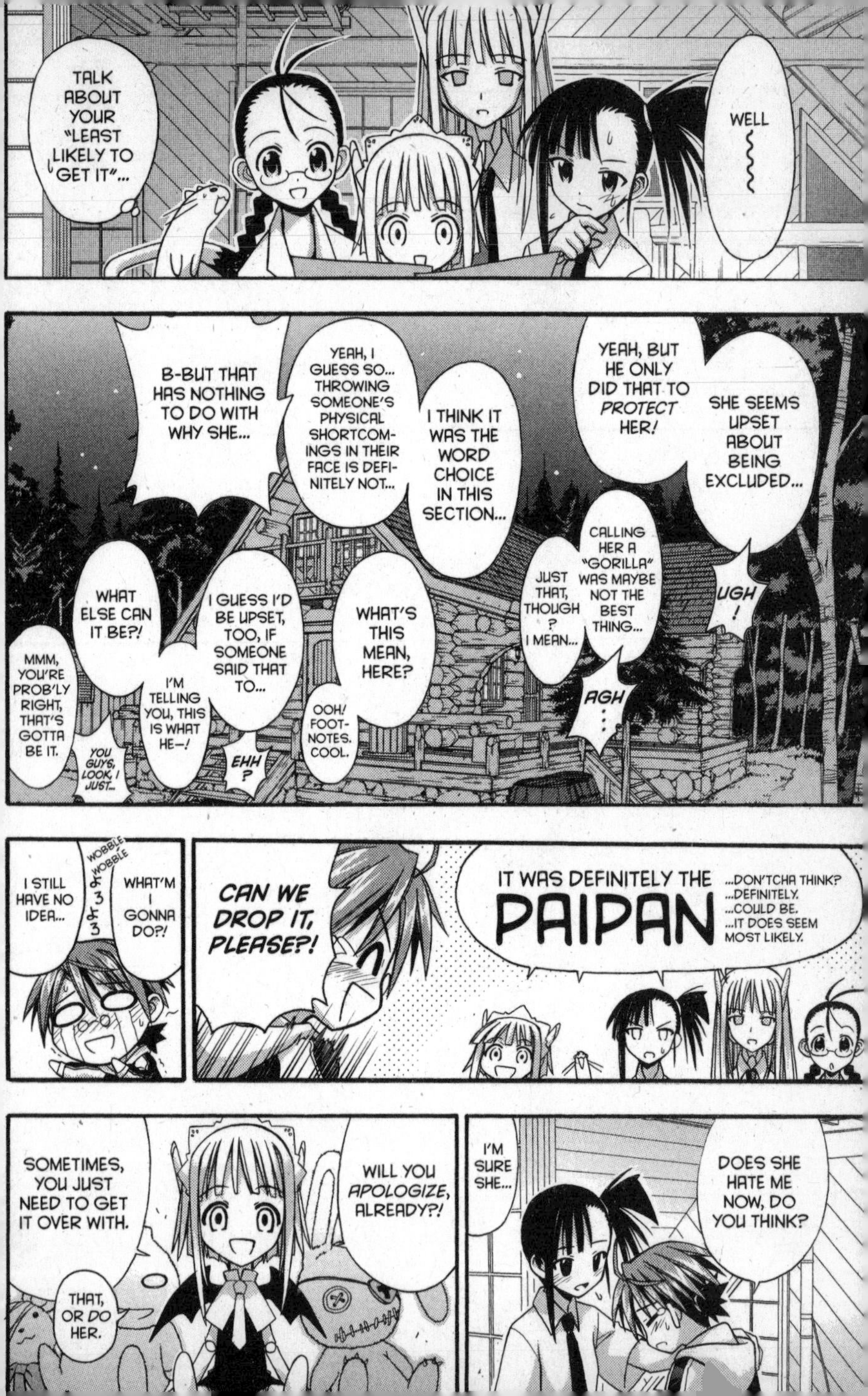
WELL ~~~
TALK ABOUT YOUR "LEAST LIKELY TO GET IT"...
SHE SEEMS UPSET ABOUT BEING EXCLUDED...
YEAH, BUT HE ONLY DID THAT TO *PROTECT* HER!
I THINK IT WAS THE WORD CHOICE IN THIS SECTION...
YEAH, I GUESS SO... THROWING SOMEONE'S PHYSICAL SHORTCOMINGS IN THEIR FACE IS DEFINITELY NOT...
B-BUT THAT HAS NOTHING TO DO WITH WHY SHE...
UGH!
CALLING HER A "GORILLA" WAS MAYBE NOT THE BEST THING...
JUST THAT, THOUGH? I MEAN...
AGH...
WHAT'S THIS MEAN, HERE?
OOH! FOOTNOTES. COOL.
I GUESS I'D BE UPSET, TOO, IF SOMEONE SAID THAT TO...
EHH?
I'M TELLING YOU, THIS IS WHAT HE—!
WHAT ELSE CAN IT BE?!
MMM, YOU'RE PROB'LY RIGHT, THAT'S GOTTA BE IT.
YOU GUYS, LOOK, I JUST...
IT WAS DEFINITELY THE PAIPAN
...DON'TCHA THINK? ...DEFINITELY. ...COULD BE. ...IT DOES SEEM MOST LIKELY.
CAN WE DROP IT, PLEASE?!
WHAT'M I GONNA DO?!
WOBBLE WOBBLE
I STILL HAVE NO IDEA...
DOES SHE HATE ME NOW, DO YOU THINK?
I'M SURE SHE...
WILL YOU *APOLOGIZE*, ALREADY?!
SOMETIMES, YOU JUST NEED TO GET IT OVER WITH.
THAT, OR *DO* HER.

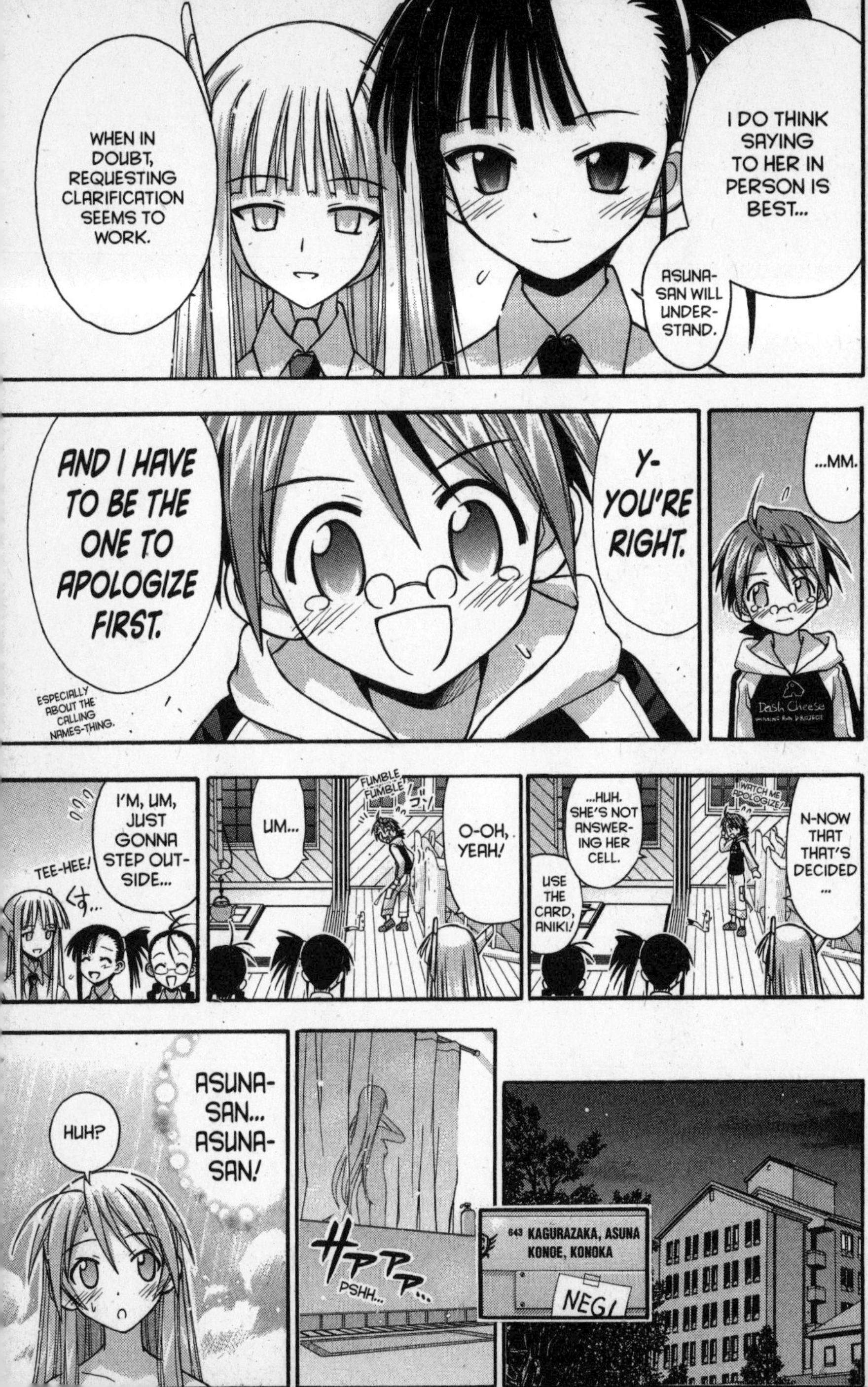
I DO THINK SAYING TO HER IN PERSON IS BEST...
ASUNA-SAN WILL UNDERSTAND.
WHEN IN DOUBT, REQUESTING CLARIFICATION SEEMS TO WORK.
...MM.
Y- YOU'RE RIGHT.
AND I HAVE TO BE THE ONE TO APOLOGIZE FIRST.
ESPECIALLY ABOUT THE CALLING NAMES-THING.
N-NOW THAT THAT'S DECIDED ...
WATCH ME APOLOGIZE!
...HUH. SHE'S NOT ANSWERING HER CELL.
USE THE CARD, ANIKI!
FUMBLE FUMBLE
O-OH, YEAH!
UM...
I'M, UM, JUST GONNA STEP OUTSIDE...
TEE-HEE!
くす...
643 KAGURAZAKA, ASUNA
KONOE, KONOKA
NEGI
HPPP...
PSHH...
ASUNA-SAN... ASUNA-SAN!
HUH?

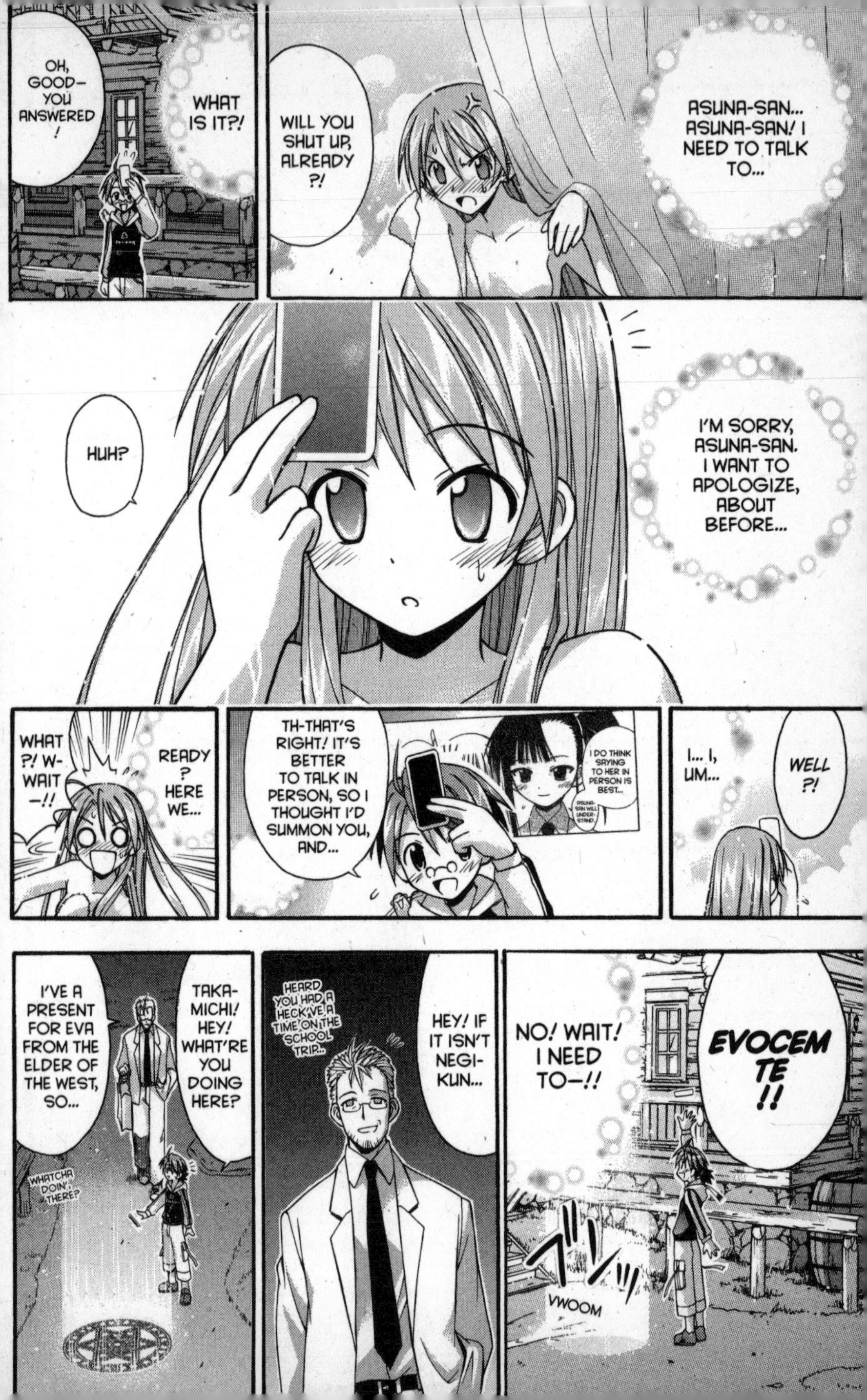
ASUNA-SAN... ASUNA-SAN! I NEED TO TALK TO...
WILL YOU SHUT UP, ALREADY?!
WHAT IS IT?!
OH, GOOD—YOU ANSWERED!
I'M SORRY, ASUNA-SAN. I WANT TO APOLOGIZE, ABOUT BEFORE...
HUH?
WELL?!
I... I, UM...
TH-THAT'S RIGHT! IT'S BETTER TO TALK IN PERSON, SO I THOUGHT I'D SUMMON YOU, AND...
I DO THINK SAYING TO HER IN PERSON IS BEST...
ASUNA-SAN WILL UNDERSTAND.
READY? HERE WE...
WHAT?! W-WAIT—!!
EVOCEMTE!!
NO! WAIT! I NEED TO—!!
VWOOM
HEY! IF IT ISN'T NEGI-KUN...
HEARD YOU HAD A HECK'VE A TIME ON THE SCHOOL TRIP...
TAKA-MICHI! HEY! WHAT'RE YOU DOING HERE?
I'VE A PRESENT FOR EVA FROM THE ELDER OF THE WEST, SO...
WHATCHA DOIN' THERE?

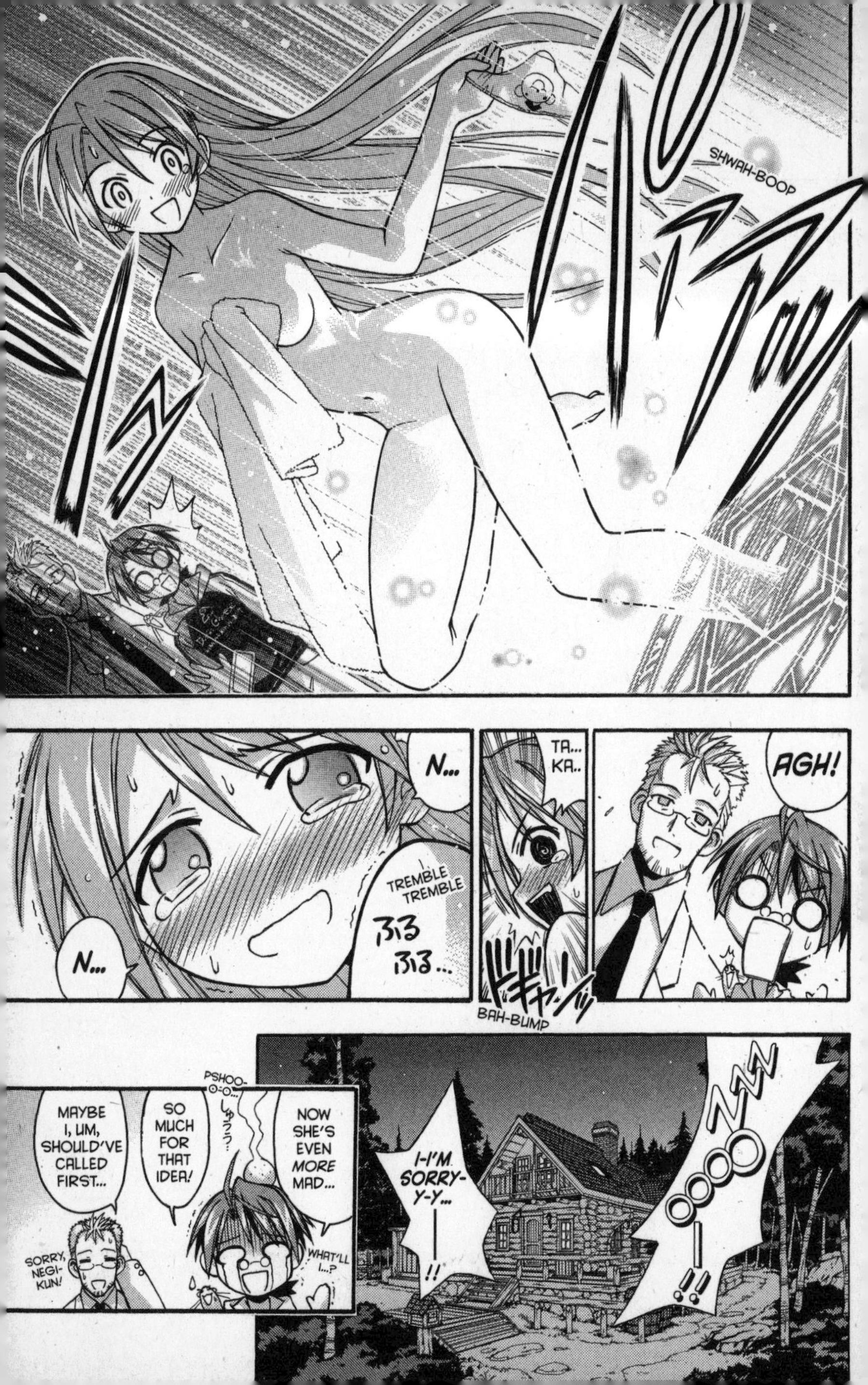
SHWAH-BOOP
AGH!
TA... KA...
BAH-BUMP
N...
TREMBLE TREMBLE
ふるふる...
N...
I-I'M SORRY-Y-Y...!!
NOW SHE'S EVEN MORE MAD...
PSHOO-O-O...
SO MUCH FOR THAT IDEA!
MAYBE I, UM, SHOULD'VE CALLED FIRST...
WHAT'LL I...?
SORRY, NEGI-KUN!

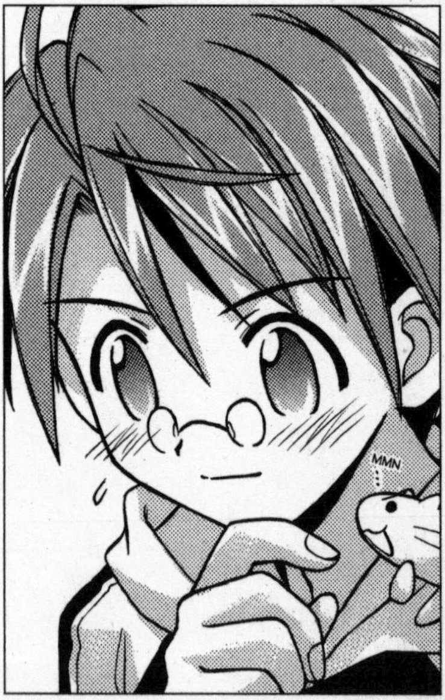
MMN
...

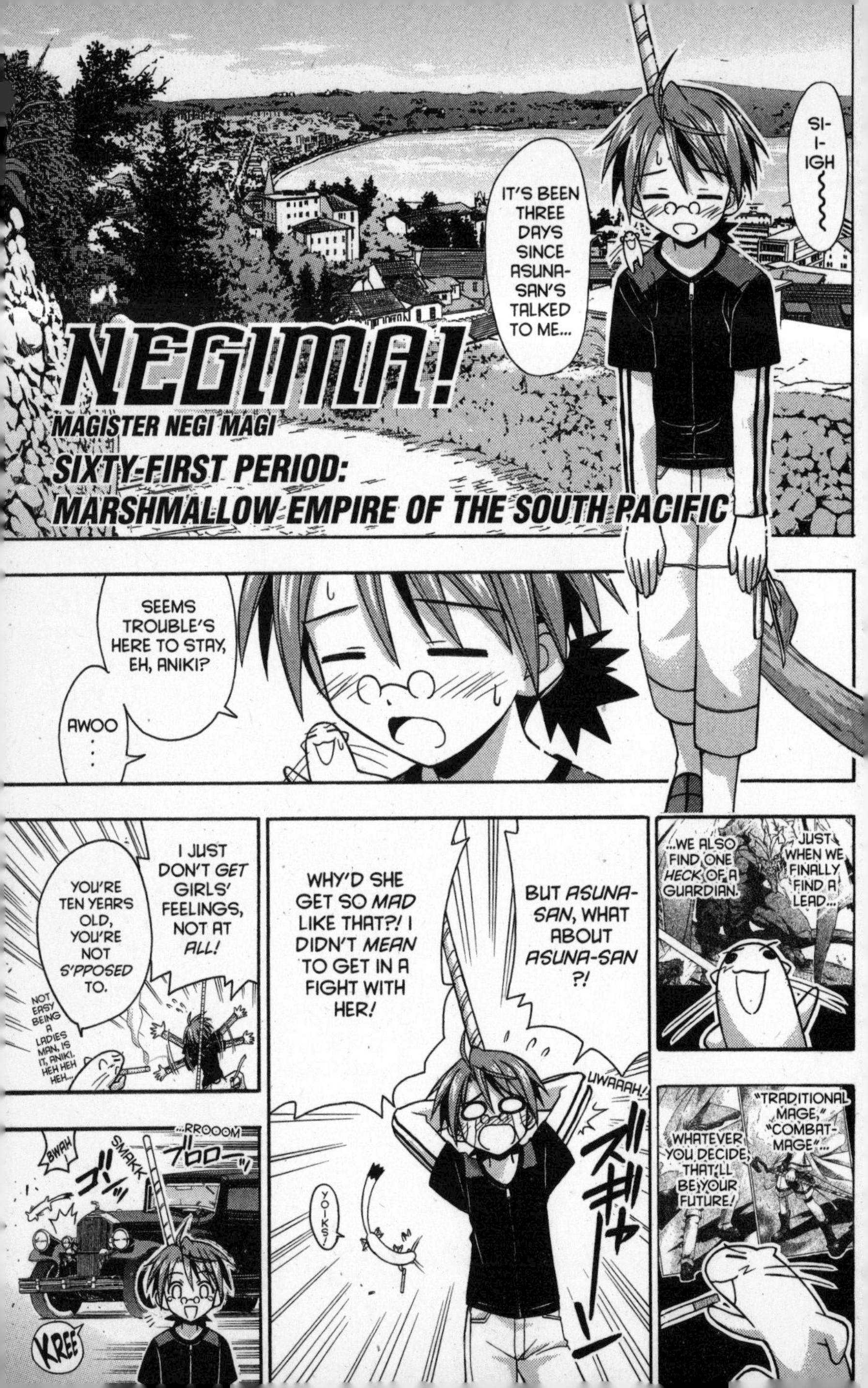
SI-I-IGH
IT'S BEEN THREE DAYS SINCE ASUNA-SAN'S TALKED TO ME...
NEGIMA!
MAGISTER NEGI MAGI
SIXTY-FIRST PERIOD: MARSHMALLOW EMPIRE OF THE SOUTH PACIFIC
SEEMS TROUBLE'S HERE TO STAY, EH, ANIKI?
AWOO...
JUST WHEN WE FINALLY FIND A LEAD...
...WE ALSO FIND ONE HECK OF A GUARDIAN.
"TRADITIONAL MAGE," "COMBAT-MAGE"...
WHATEVER YOU DECIDE, THAT'LL BE YOUR FUTURE!
BUT ASUNA-SAN, WHAT ABOUT ASUNA-SAN?!
WHY'D SHE GET SO MAD LIKE THAT?! I DIDN'T MEAN TO GET IN A FIGHT WITH HER!
UWAAAH!
YOIKS!
I JUST DON'T GET GIRLS' FEELINGS, NOT AT ALL!
YOU'RE TEN YEARS OLD, YOU'RE NOT S'PPOSED TO.
NOT EASY BEING A LADIES MAN, IS IT, ANIKI. HEH HEH HEH...
...RROOOM
SMAKK
BWAH
KREE

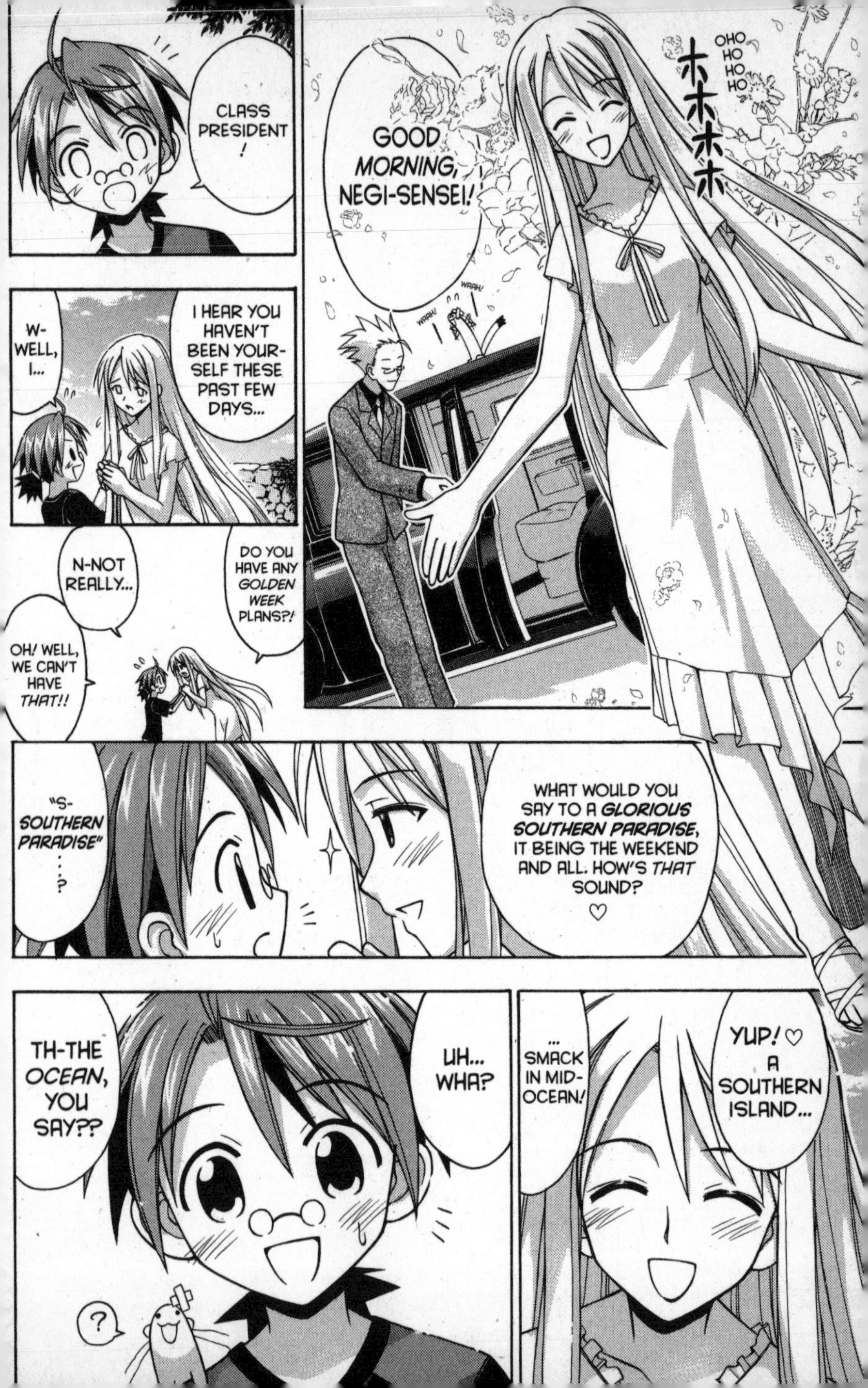
OHO HO HO HO
ホホホホ
GOOD MORNING, NEGI-SENSEI!
WAAH!
WAAH!
CLASS PRESIDENT!
I HEAR YOU HAVEN'T BEEN YOURSELF THESE PAST FEW DAYS...
W-WELL, I...
DO YOU HAVE ANY GOLDEN WEEK PLANS?!
N-NOT REALLY...
OH! WELL, WE CAN'T HAVE THAT!!
WHAT WOULD YOU SAY TO A GLORIOUS SOUTHERN PARADISE, IT BEING THE WEEKEND AND ALL. HOW'S THAT SOUND? ♡
"S-SOUTHERN PARADISE"...?
YUP! ♡ A SOUTHERN ISLAND...
...SMACK IN MID-OCEAN!
UH... WHA?
TH-THE OCEAN, YOU SAY??
?

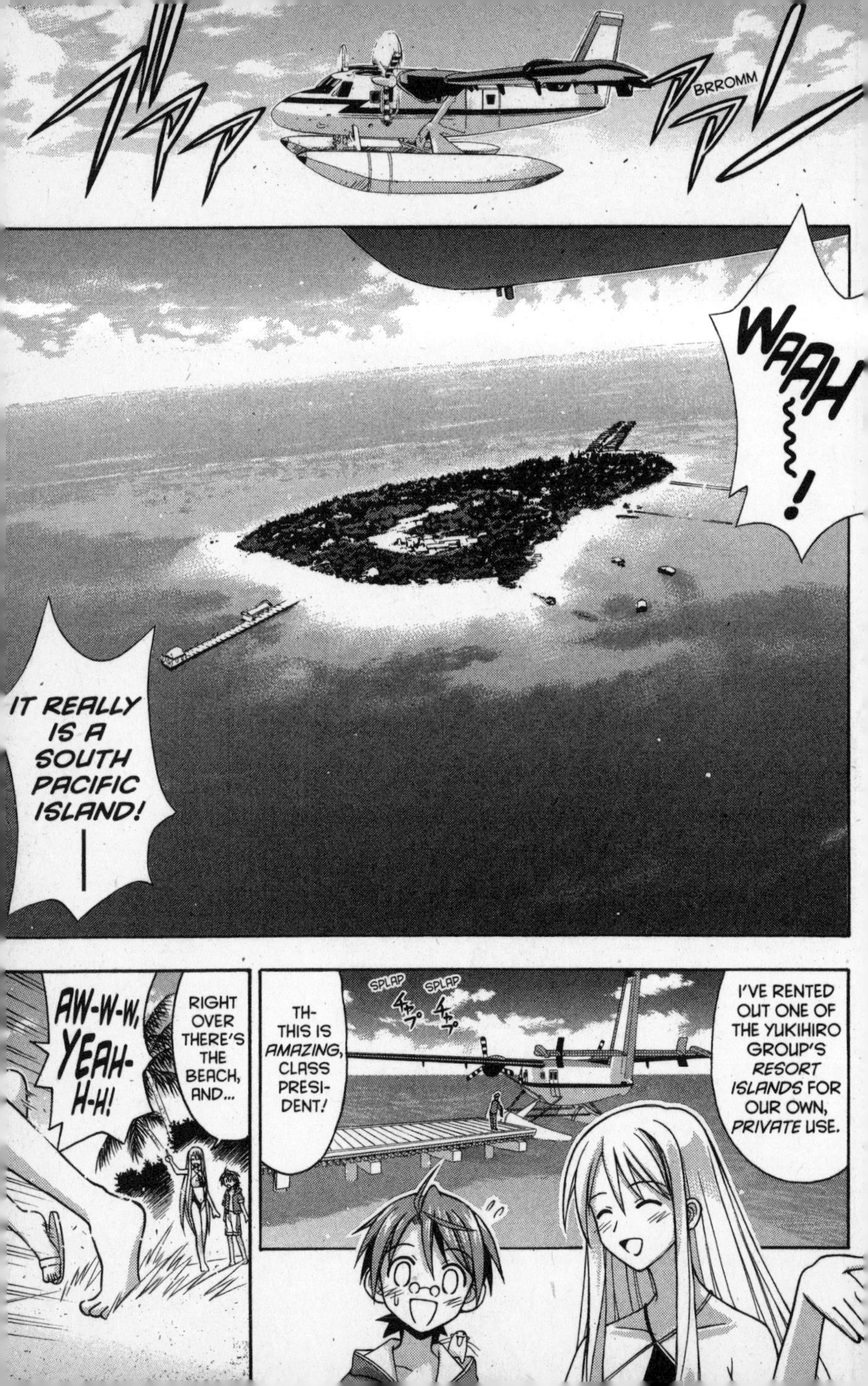
BRROMM
WAAH~!
IT REALLY IS A SOUTH PACIFIC ISLAND!
I'VE RENTED OUT ONE OF THE YUKIHIRO GROUP'S *RESORT ISLANDS* FOR OUR OWN, *PRIVATE* USE.
SPLAP SPLAP
TH- THIS IS *AMAZING*, CLASS PRESIDENT!
RIGHT OVER THERE'S THE BEACH, AND...
AW-W-W, YEAH-H-H!

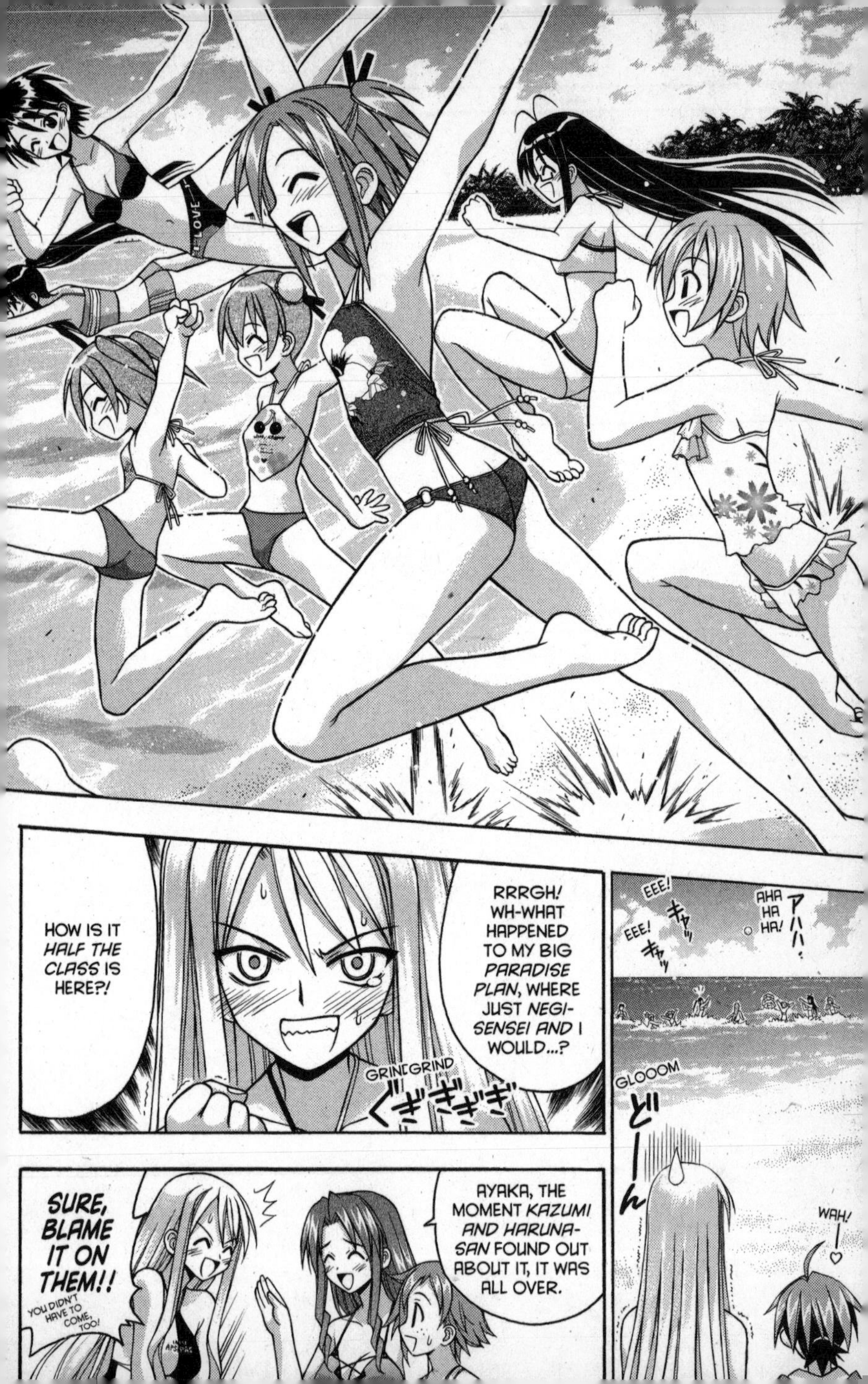
AHA HA HA!
アハハ
EEE!
キャッ
EEE!
キャッ
GLOOOM
どーん
WAH!
RRRGH! WH-WHAT HAPPENED TO MY BIG *PARADISE PLAN*, WHERE JUST *NEGI-SENSEI AND* I WOULD...?
GRINDGRIND
ぐぎぎぎ
HOW IS IT *HALF THE CLASS* IS HERE?!
AYAKA, THE MOMENT *KAZUMI AND HARUNA-SAN* FOUND OUT ABOUT IT, IT WAS ALL OVER.
SURE, BLAME IT ON THEM!!
YOU DIDN'T HAVE TO COME, TOO!

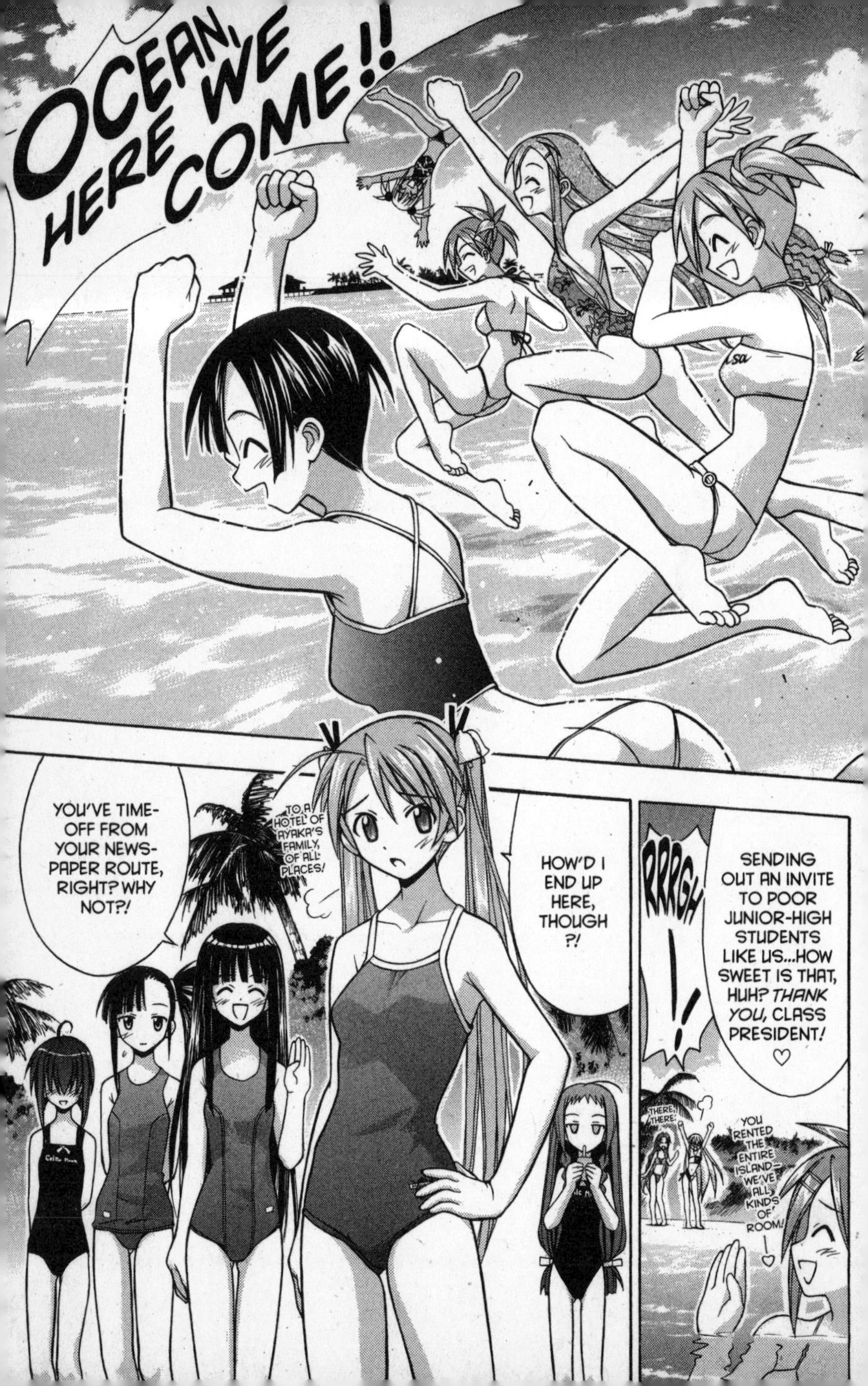
OCEAN, HERE WE COME!!
SENDING OUT AN INVITE TO POOR JUNIOR-HIGH STUDENTS LIKE US...HOW SWEET IS THAT, HUH? THANK YOU, CLASS PRESIDENT! ♥
RRRGH!!
YOU RENTED THE ENTIRE ISLAND—WE'VE ALL KINDS OF ROOM! ♥
THERE, THERE.
HOW'D I END UP HERE, THOUGH?!
TO A HOTEL OF AYAKA'S FAMILY, OF ALL PLACES!
YOU'VE TIME-OFF FROM YOUR NEWS-PAPER ROUTE, RIGHT? WHY NOT?!

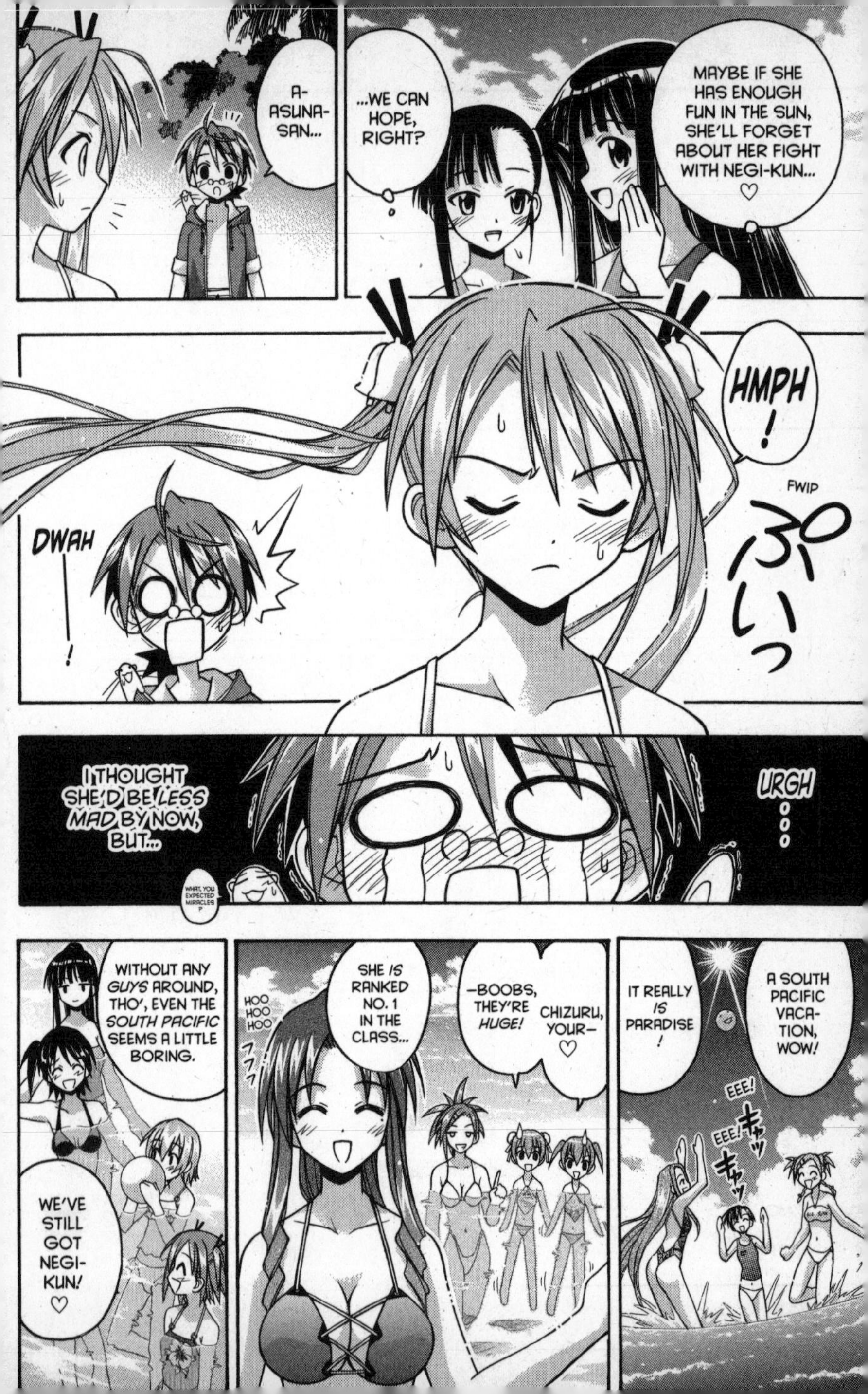

MAYBE IF SHE HAS ENOUGH FUN IN THE SUN, SHE'LL FORGET ABOUT HER FIGHT WITH NEGI-KUN... ♡
...WE CAN HOPE, RIGHT?
A-ASUNA-SAN...
HMPH!
FWIP
ぷいっ
DWAH!
URGH...
I THOUGHT SHE'D BE *LESS* MAD BY NOW, BUT...
WHAT, YOU EXPECTED MIRACLES?
A SOUTH PACIFIC VACATION, WOW!
IT REALLY *IS* PARADISE!
EEE!
キャッ
EEE!
キャッ
CHIZURU, YOUR—♡
—BOOBS, THEY'RE *HUGE*!
SHE *IS* RANKED NO. 1 IN THE CLASS...
HOO HOO HOO
フフフ
WITHOUT ANY *GUYS* AROUND, THO', EVEN THE *SOUTH PACIFIC* SEEMS A LITTLE BORING.
WE'VE STILL GOT NEGI-KUN! ♡

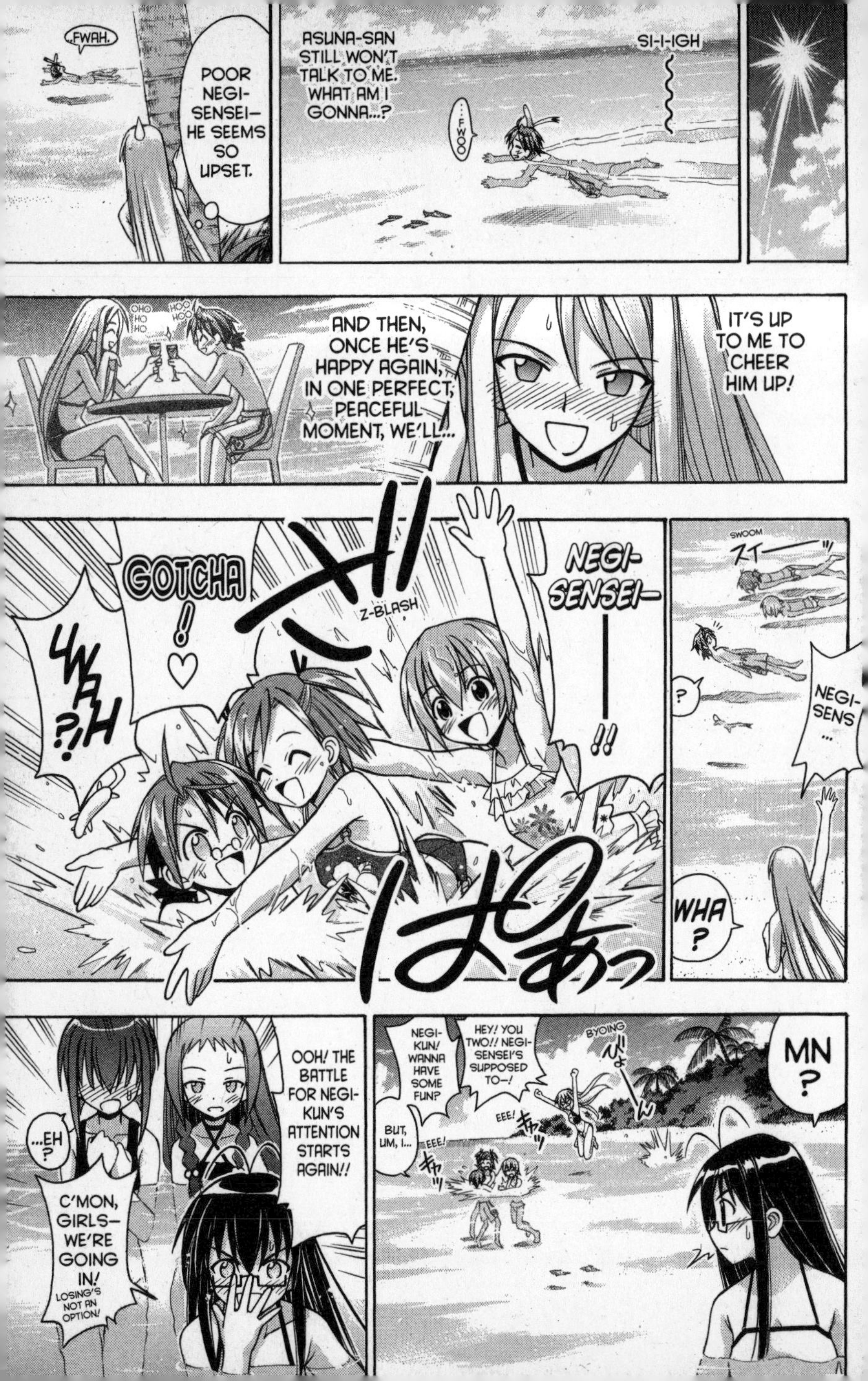
SI-I-IGH
ASUNA-SAN STILL WON'T TALK TO ME. WHAT AM I GONNA...?
...FWOO
POOR NEGI-SENSEI— HE SEEMS SO UPSET.
FWAH.
IT'S UP TO ME TO CHEER HIM UP!
AND THEN, ONCE HE'S HAPPY AGAIN, IN ONE PERFECT, PEACEFUL MOMENT, WE'LL...
OHO HO HO
HOO HOO
SWOOM
スイー
?
NEGI-SENS...
WHA?
NEGI-SENSEI—!!
Z-BLASH
GOTCHA! ♥
UWAH?!
MN?
BYOING
HEY! YOU TWO!! NEGI-SENSEI'S SUPPOSED TO—!
NEGI-KUN! WANNA HAVE SOME FUN?
BUT, UM, I...
EEE!
EEE!
OOH! THE BATTLE FOR NEGI-KUN'S ATTENTION STARTS AGAIN!!
...EH?
C'MON, GIRLS— WE'RE GOING IN!
LOSING'S NOT AN OPTION!

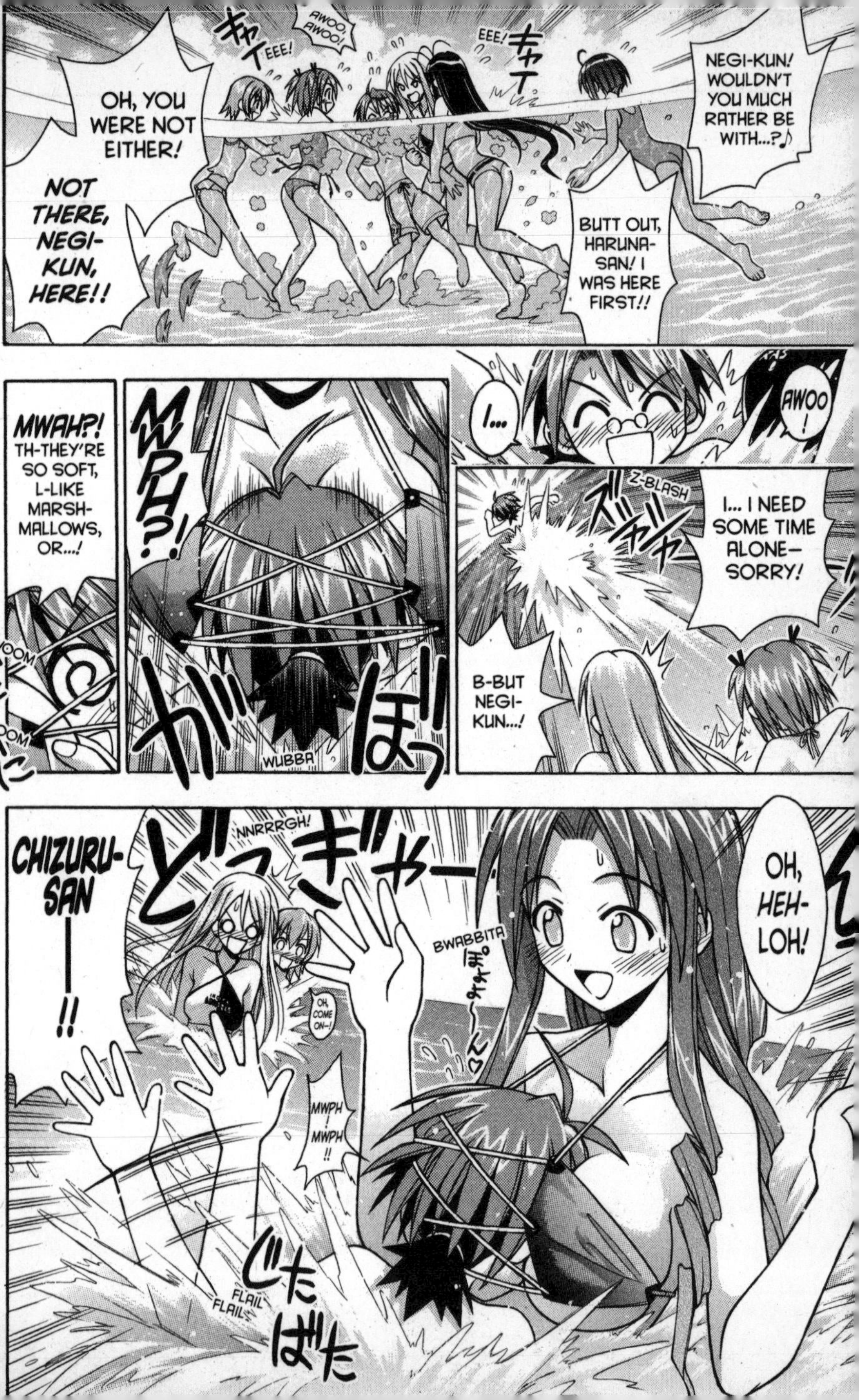
NEGI-KUN! WOULDN'T YOU MUCH RATHER BE WITH...?♪
EEE!
AWOO, AWOO!
EEE!
BUTT OUT, HARUNA-SAN! I WAS HERE FIRST!!
OH, YOU WERE NOT EITHER!
NOT THERE, NEGI-KUN, HERE!!
AWOO!
I...
Z-BLASH
I... I NEED SOME TIME ALONE— SORRY!
B-BUT NEGI-KUN...!
MWPH?!
WUBBA
MWAH?! TH-THEY'RE SO SOFT, L-LIKE MARSH-MALLOWS, OR...!
WOOM
WOOM
OH, HEH-LOH!
BWABBITA
NNRRRGH!
CHIZURU-SAN——!!
OH, COME ON—!
MWPH! MWPH!!
FLAIL FLAIL

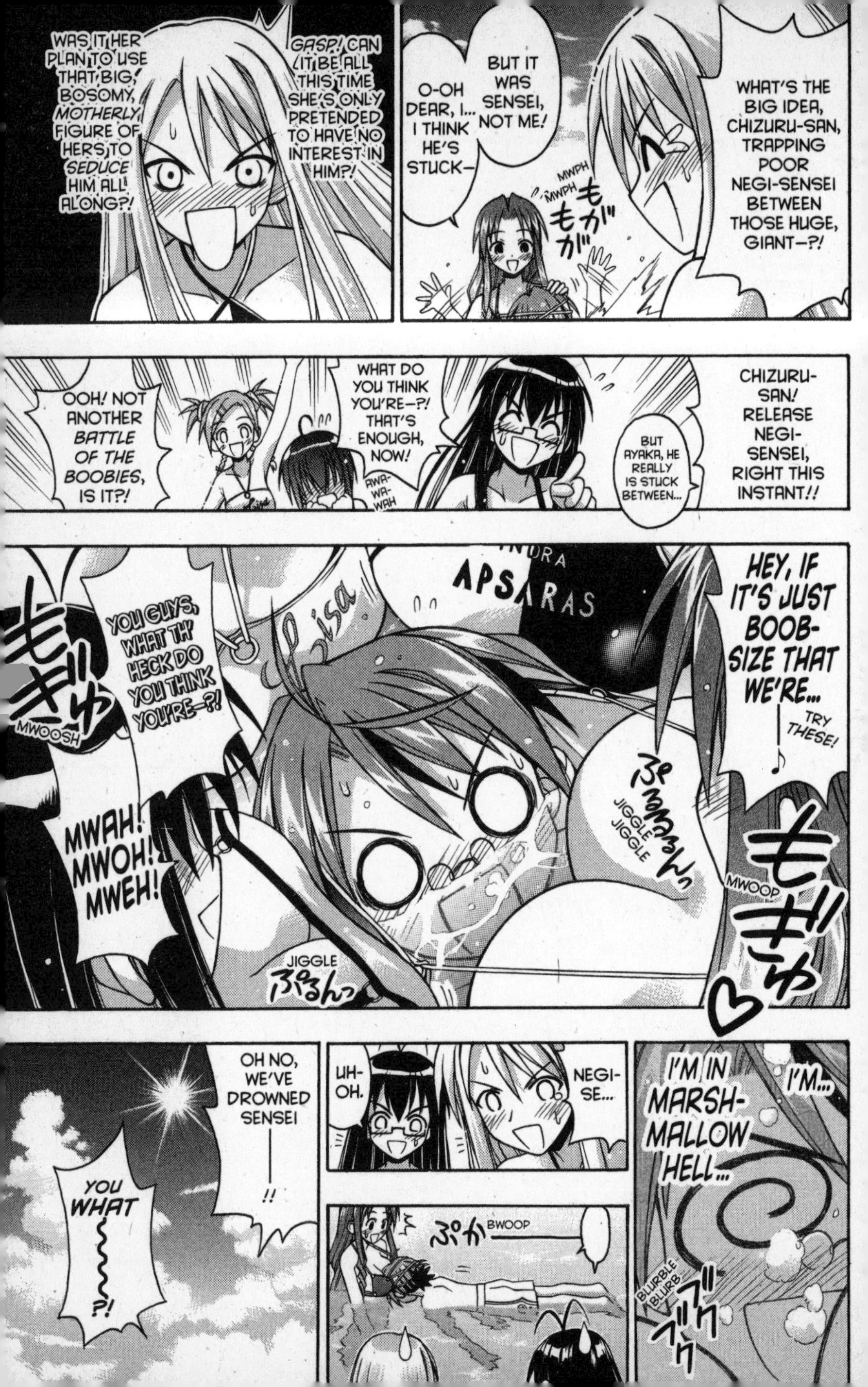
WHAT'S THE BIG IDEA, CHIZURU-SAN, TRAPPING POOR NEGI-SENSEI BETWEEN THOSE HUGE, GIANT–?!
BUT IT WAS SENSEI, NOT ME!
O-OH DEAR, I... I THINK HE'S STUCK–
もがもが MWPH MWPH
GASP! CAN IT BE ALL THIS TIME SHE'S ONLY PRETENDED TO HAVE NO INTEREST IN HIM?!
WAS IT HER PLAN TO USE THAT BIG, BOSOMY, MOTHERLY FIGURE OF HERS TO SEDUCE HIM ALL ALONG?!
CHIZURU-SAN! RELEASE NEGI-SENSEI, RIGHT THIS INSTANT!!
BUT AYAKA, HE REALLY IS STUCK BETWEEN...
WHAT DO YOU THINK YOU'RE–?! THAT'S ENOUGH, NOW!
AWA-WA-WAH
OOH! NOT ANOTHER BATTLE OF THE BOOBIES, IS IT?!
HEY, IF IT'S JUST BOOB-SIZE THAT WE'RE...
TRY THESE! ♪
もぎゅ MWOOP
ぷるるるるんっ JIGGLE JIGGLE
APSARAS
Lisa
ぷるんっ JIGGLE
YOU GUYS, WHAT TH' HECK DO YOU THINK YOU'RE–?!
もぎゅ MWOOSH
MWAH! MWOH! MWEH!
I'M...
I'M IN MARSH-MALLOW HELL...
ブクブク BLURBLE BLURB
NEGI-SE...
UH-OH.
ぷか BWOOP
OH NO, WE'VE DROWNED SENSEI —!!
YOU WHAT ~~~~?!

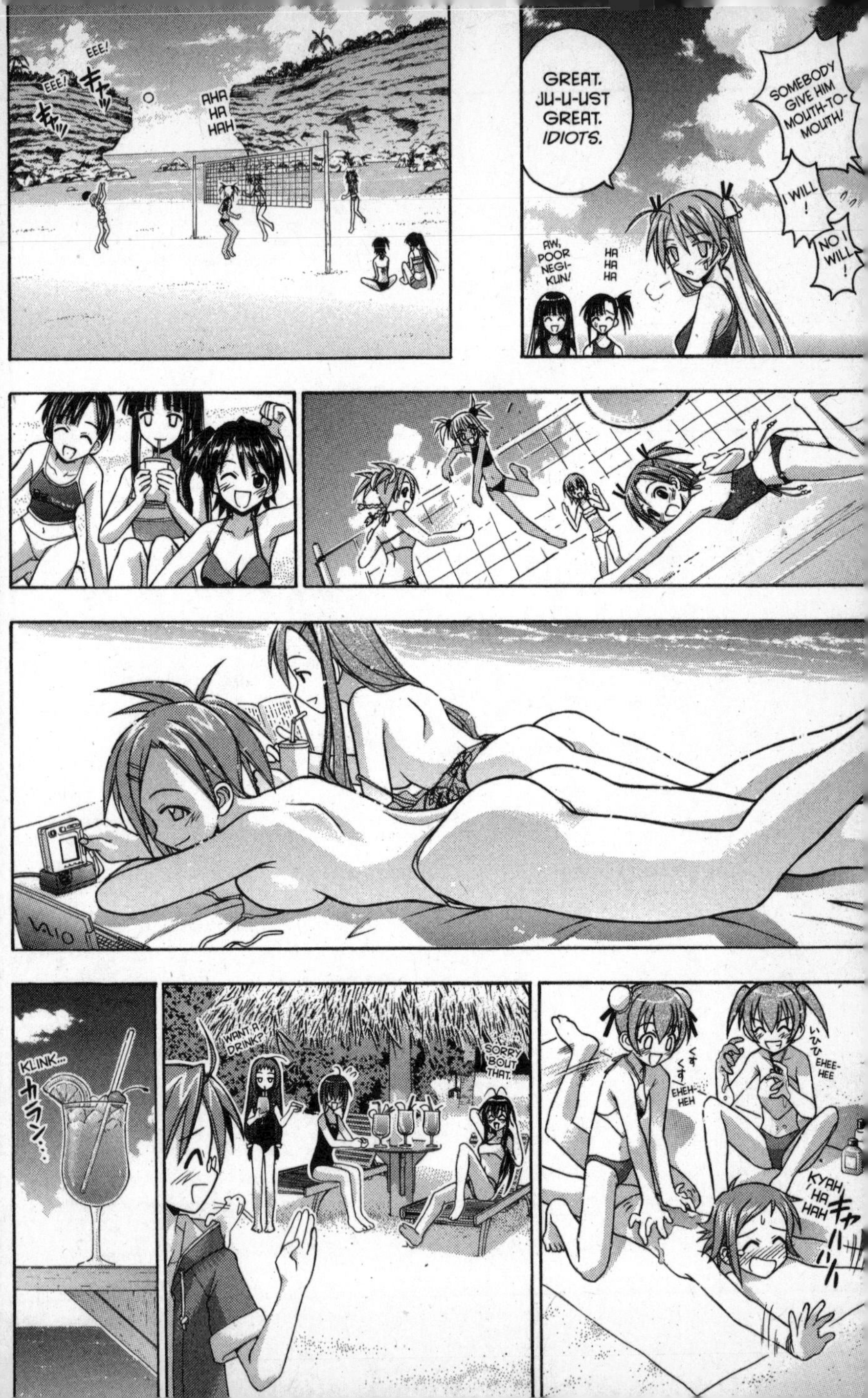
SOMEBODY GIVE HIM MOUTH-TO-MOUTH!
I WILL!
NO! I WILL!
GREAT. JU-U-UST GREAT. IDIOTS.
HA HA HA
AW, POOR NEGI-KUN!
AHA HA HAH
EEE! キャッ
EEE! キャッ
VAIO
いひひ EHEE-HEE
くすくす EHEH-HEH
KYAH HA HAH キャハハハ
SORRY 'BOUT THAT.
WANT A DRINK?
KLINK... カラン...

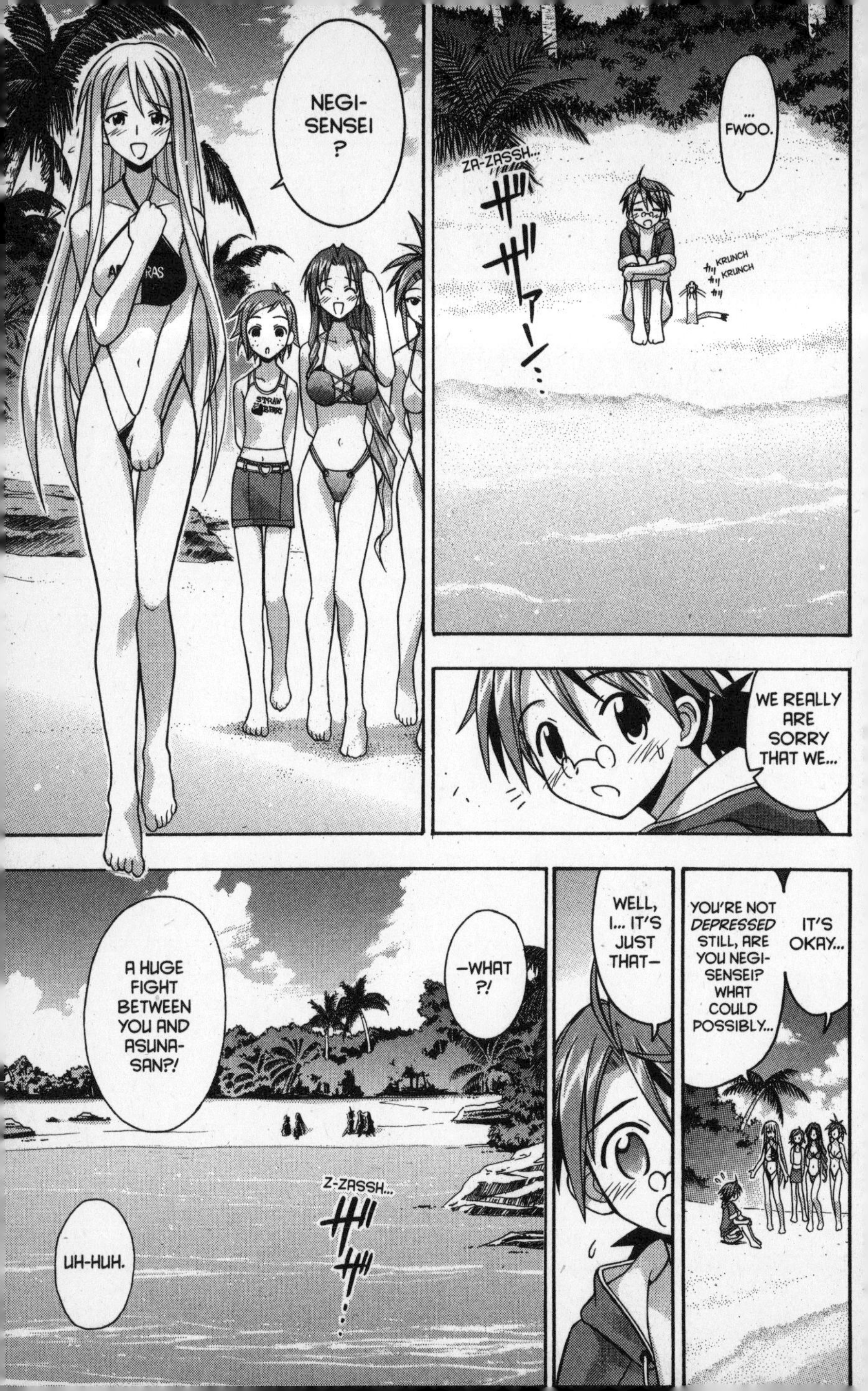
... FWOO.
ZA-ZASSH...
ザザァーン…
KRUNCH KRUNCH
WE REALLY ARE SORRY THAT WE...
NEGI-SENSEI?
IT'S OKAY...
YOU'RE NOT *DEPRESSED* STILL, ARE YOU NEGI-SENSEI? WHAT COULD POSSIBLY...
WELL, I... IT'S JUST THAT—
—WHAT?!
A HUGE FIGHT BETWEEN YOU AND ASUNA-SAN?!
UH-HUH.
Z-ZASSH...

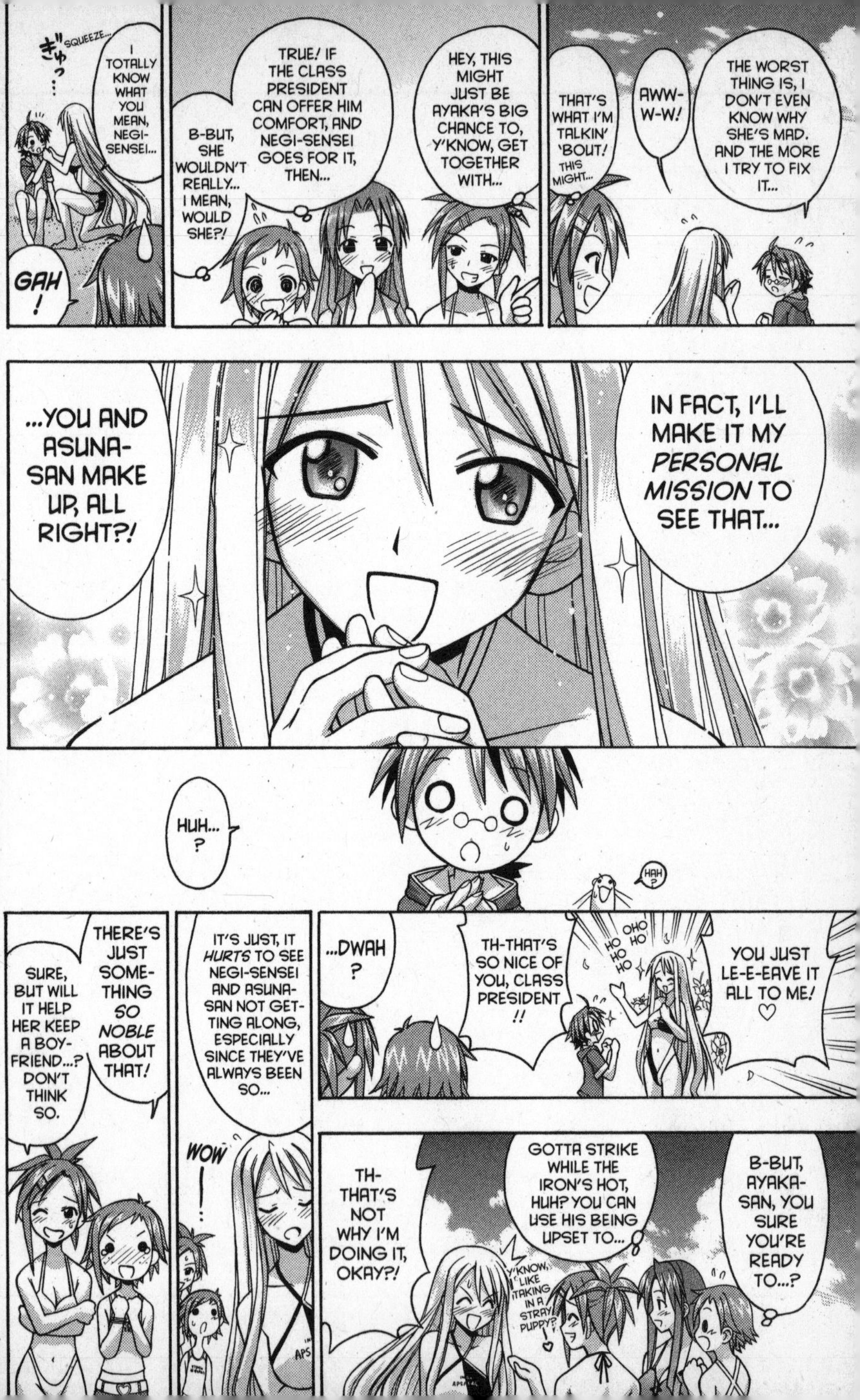
THE WORST THING IS, I DON'T EVEN KNOW WHY SHE'S MAD. AND THE MORE I TRY TO FIX IT...
AWW-W-W!
THAT'S WHAT I'M TALKIN' 'BOUT! THIS MIGHT...
HEY, THIS MIGHT JUST BE AYAKA'S BIG CHANCE TO, Y'KNOW, GET TOGETHER WITH...
TRUE! IF THE CLASS PRESIDENT CAN OFFER HIM COMFORT, AND NEGI-SENSEI GOES FOR IT, THEN...
B-BUT, SHE WOULDN'T REALLY... I MEAN, WOULD SHE?!
I TOTALLY KNOW WHAT YOU MEAN, NEGI-SENSEI...
ぎゅっ... SQUEEZE...
GAH!
IN FACT, I'LL MAKE IT MY *PERSONAL MISSION* TO SEE THAT...
...YOU AND ASUNA-SAN MAKE UP, ALL RIGHT?!
HAH?
HUH...?
YOU JUST LE-E-EAVE IT ALL TO ME! ♡
OHO HO HO HO HO
TH-THAT'S SO NICE OF YOU, CLASS PRESIDENT!!
...DWAH?
B-BUT, AYAKA-SAN, YOU SURE YOU'RE READY TO...?
GOTTA STRIKE WHILE THE IRON'S HOT, HUH? YOU CAN USE HIS BEING UPSET TO...
Y'KNOW, LIKE TAKING IN A STRAY PUPPY?! ♡
TH-THAT'S NOT WHY I'M DOING IT, OKAY?!
IT'S JUST, IT *HURTS* TO SEE NEGI-SENSEI AND ASUNA-SAN NOT GETTING ALONG, ESPECIALLY SINCE THEY'VE ALWAYS BEEN SO...
WOW!
THERE'S JUST SOMETHING *SO NOBLE* ABOUT THAT!
SURE, BUT WILL IT HELP HER KEEP A BOYFRIEND...? DON'T THINK SO.

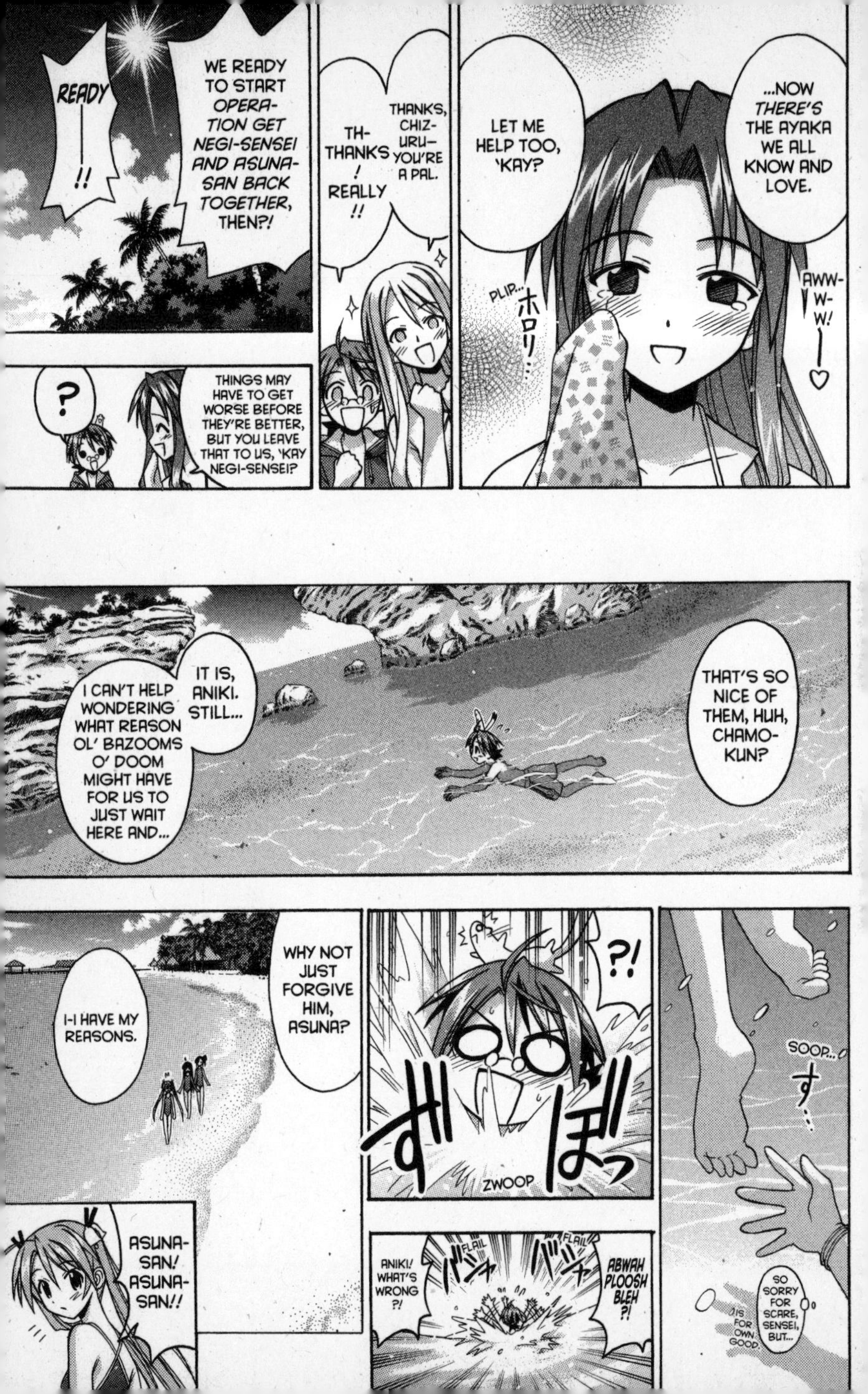
...NOW THERE'S THE AYAKA WE ALL KNOW AND LOVE.
LET ME HELP TOO, 'KAY?
PLIP... ホロリ...
AWWW-W-W!—♡
THANKS, CHIZURU— YOU'RE A PAL.
TH-THANKS! REALLY!!
WE READY TO START OPERATION GET NEGI-SENSEI AND ASUNA-SAN BACK TOGETHER, THEN?!
READY—!!
THINGS MAY HAVE TO GET WORSE BEFORE THEY'RE BETTER, BUT YOU LEAVE THAT TO US, 'KAY NEGI-SENSEI?
?
THAT'S SO NICE OF THEM, HUH, CHAMO-KUN?
IT IS, ANIKI. STILL...
I CAN'T HELP WONDERING WHAT REASON OL' BAZOOMS O' DOOM MIGHT HAVE FOR US TO JUST WAIT HERE AND...
SOOP... す...
SO SORRY FOR SCARE, SENSEI, BUT... IS FOR OWN GOOD.
?!
ずぽっ
ZWOOP
WHY NOT JUST FORGIVE HIM, ASUNA?
I-I HAVE MY REASONS.
ABWAH PLOOSH BLEH?!
FLAIL バシャ
FLAIL バシャ
ANIKI! WHAT'S WRONG?!
ASUNA-SAN! ASUNA-SAN!!

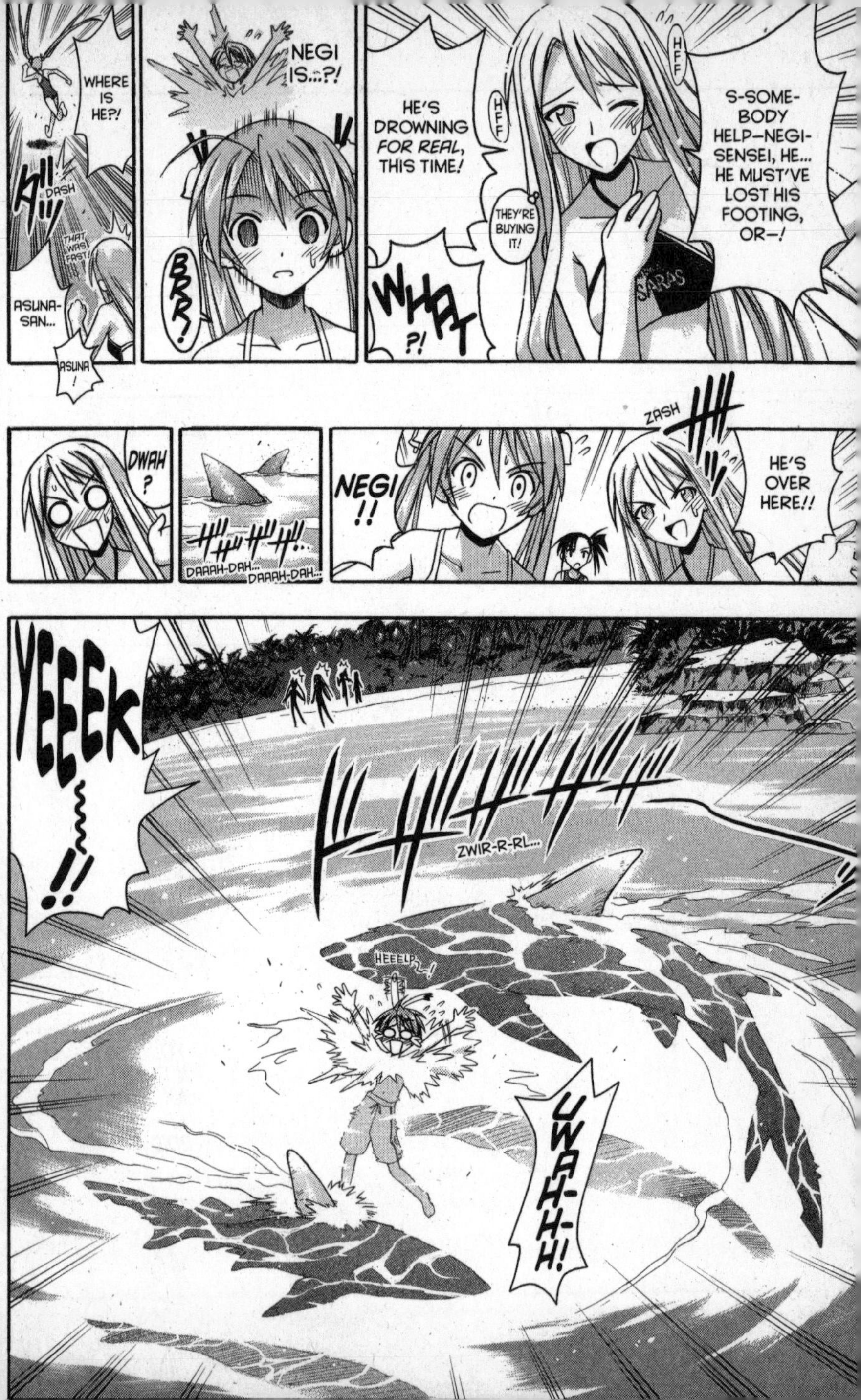
HFF
S-SOMEBODY HELP—NEGI-SENSEI, HE... HE MUST'VE LOST HIS FOOTING, OR—!
HFF
THEY'RE BUYING IT!
HE'S DROWNING FOR REAL, THIS TIME!
WHAT ?!
NEGI IS...?!
BRR!
WHERE IS HE?!
DASH
THAT WAS FAST!
ASUNA-SAN...
ASUNA!
ZASH
HE'S OVER HERE!!
NEGI !!
DAAAH-DAH... DAAAH-DAH...
DWAH ?
YEEEK!!
ZWIR-R-RL...
HEEELP!
UWAH-H-H-H!

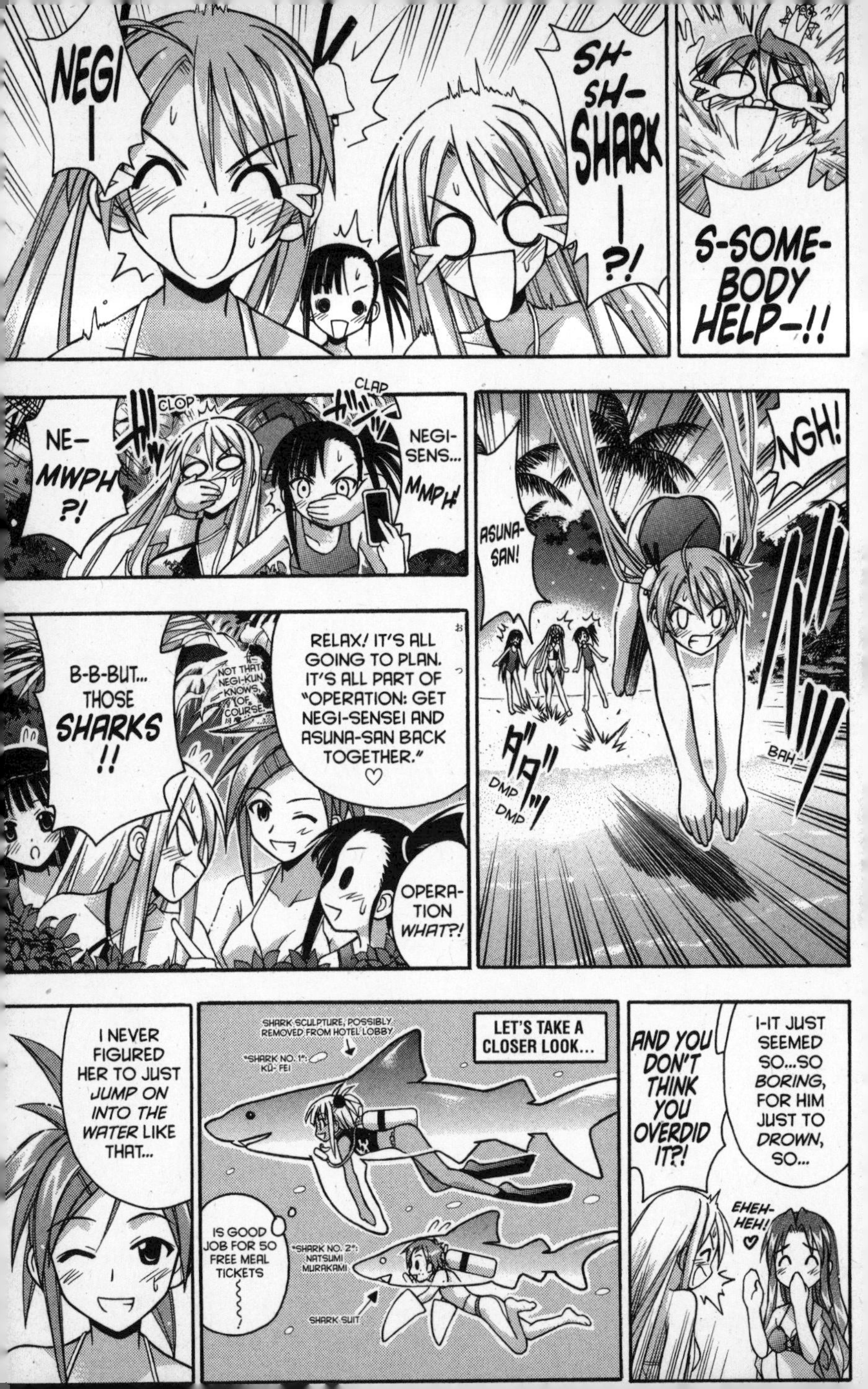
S-SOME-BODY HELP—!!
SH-SH-SHARK—?!
NEGI—
NGH!
ASUNA-SAN!
BAH—
DMP DMP
NEGI-SENS... MMPH!
CLAP
CLOP
NE—MWPH?!
RELAX! IT'S ALL GOING TO PLAN. IT'S ALL PART OF "OPERATION: GET NEGI-SENSEI AND ASUNA-SAN BACK TOGETHER." ♡
NOT THAT NEGI-KUN KNOWS, OF COURSE.
B-B-BUT... THOSE SHARKS!!
OPERATION WHAT?!
I-IT JUST SEEMED SO...SO BORING, FOR HIM JUST TO DROWN, SO...
AND YOU DON'T THINK YOU OVERDID IT?!
EHEH-HEH! ♡
LET'S TAKE A CLOSER LOOK...
SHARK SCULPTURE, POSSIBLY REMOVED FROM HOTEL LOBBY
"SHARK NO. 1": KŪ FEI
"SHARK NO. 2": NATSUMI MURAKAMI
SHARK SUIT
IS GOOD JOB FOR 50 FREE MEAL TICKETS~!
I NEVER FIGURED HER TO JUST JUMP ON INTO THE WATER LIKE THAT...

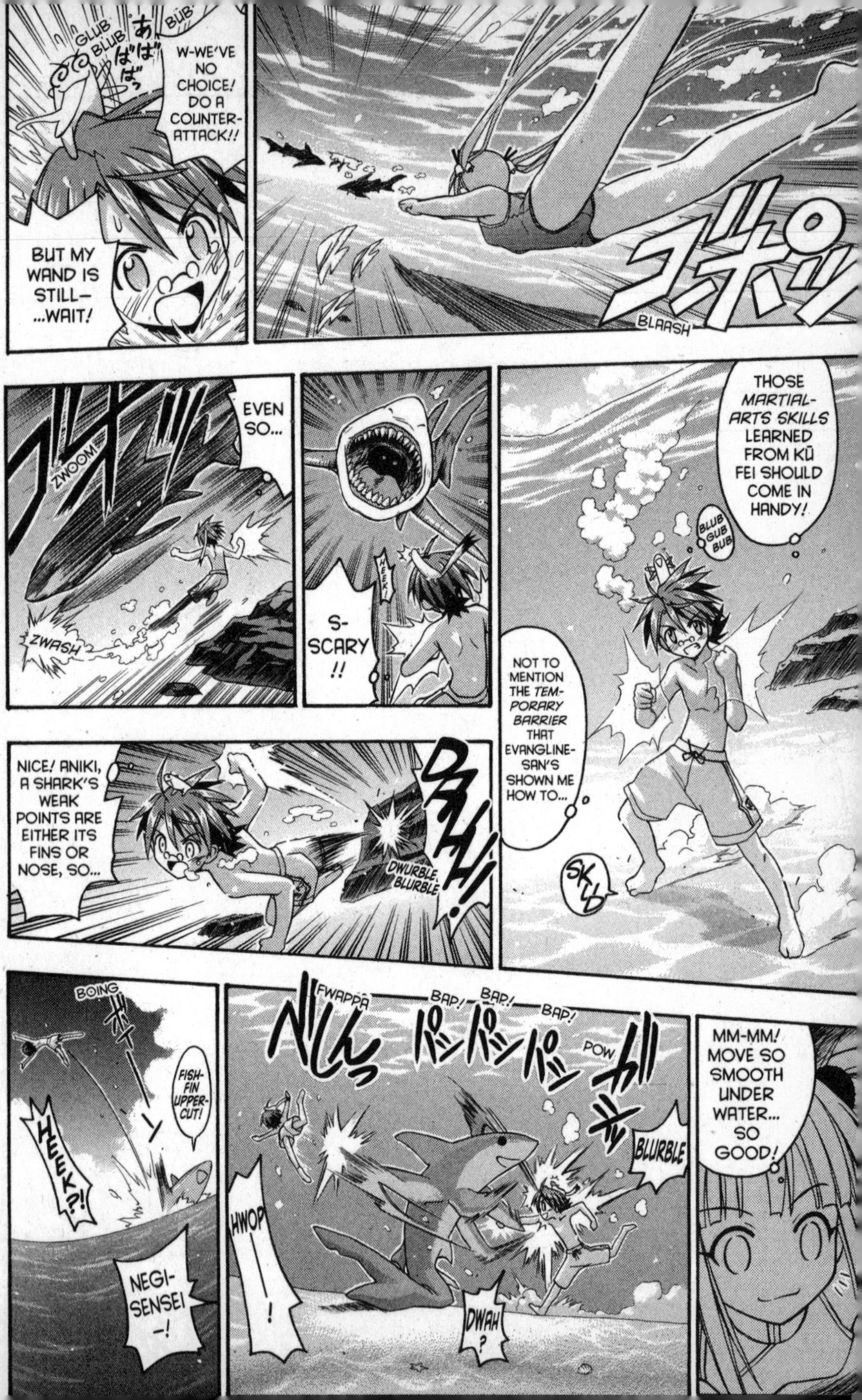

コポッ
BLAASH
GLUB
BLUB
BUB
あばばっ
W-WE'VE NO CHOICE! DO A COUNTER-ATTACK!!
BUT MY WAND IS STILL— ...WAIT!
THOSE MARTIAL-ARTS SKILLS LEARNED FROM KŪ FEI SHOULD COME IN HANDY!
BLUB GUB BUB
NOT TO MENTION THE TEMPORARY BARRIER THAT EVANGLINE-SAN'S SHOWN ME HOW TO...
SKID
HEEK!
S-SCARY!!
EVEN SO...
ZWOOM
ZWASH
DAAH!!
DWURBLE BLURBLE
NICE! ANIKI, A SHARK'S WEAK POINTS ARE EITHER ITS FINS OR NOSE, SO...
MM-MM! MOVE SO SMOOTH UNDER WATER... SO GOOD!
FWAPPA
BAP!
BAP!
BAP!
POW
BLURBLE
HWOP—!
DWAH?
BOING
FISH-FIN UPPERCUT!
HEEEK?!
NEGI-SENSEI—!

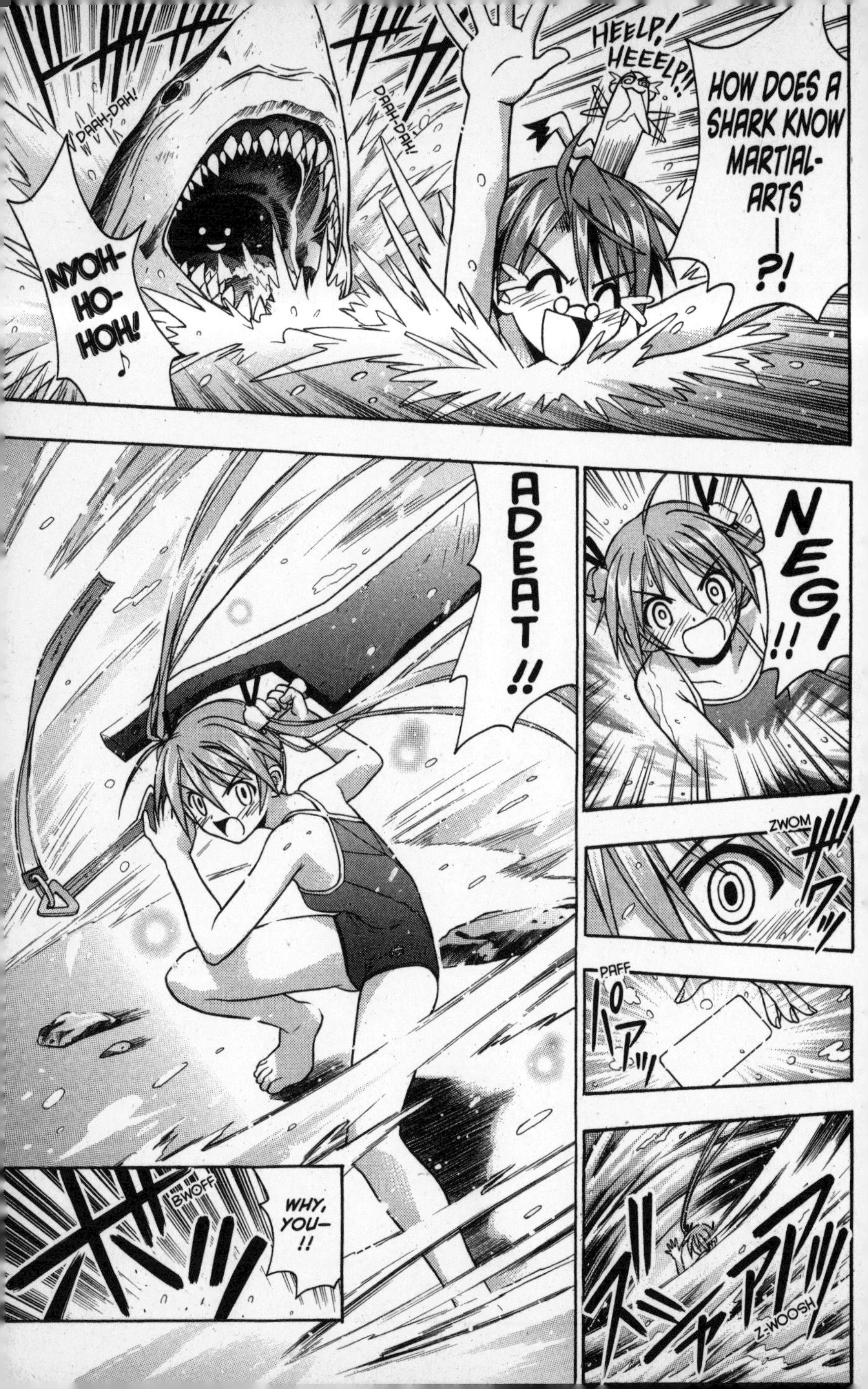
HOW DOES A SHARK KNOW MARTIAL-ARTS—?!
HEELP! HEEELP!!
DAAH-DAH!
DAAH-DAH!
NYOH-HO-HOH! ♪
NEGI!!
ZWOM
PAFF
Z-WOOSH
ADEAT!!
BWOFF
WHY, YOU—!!

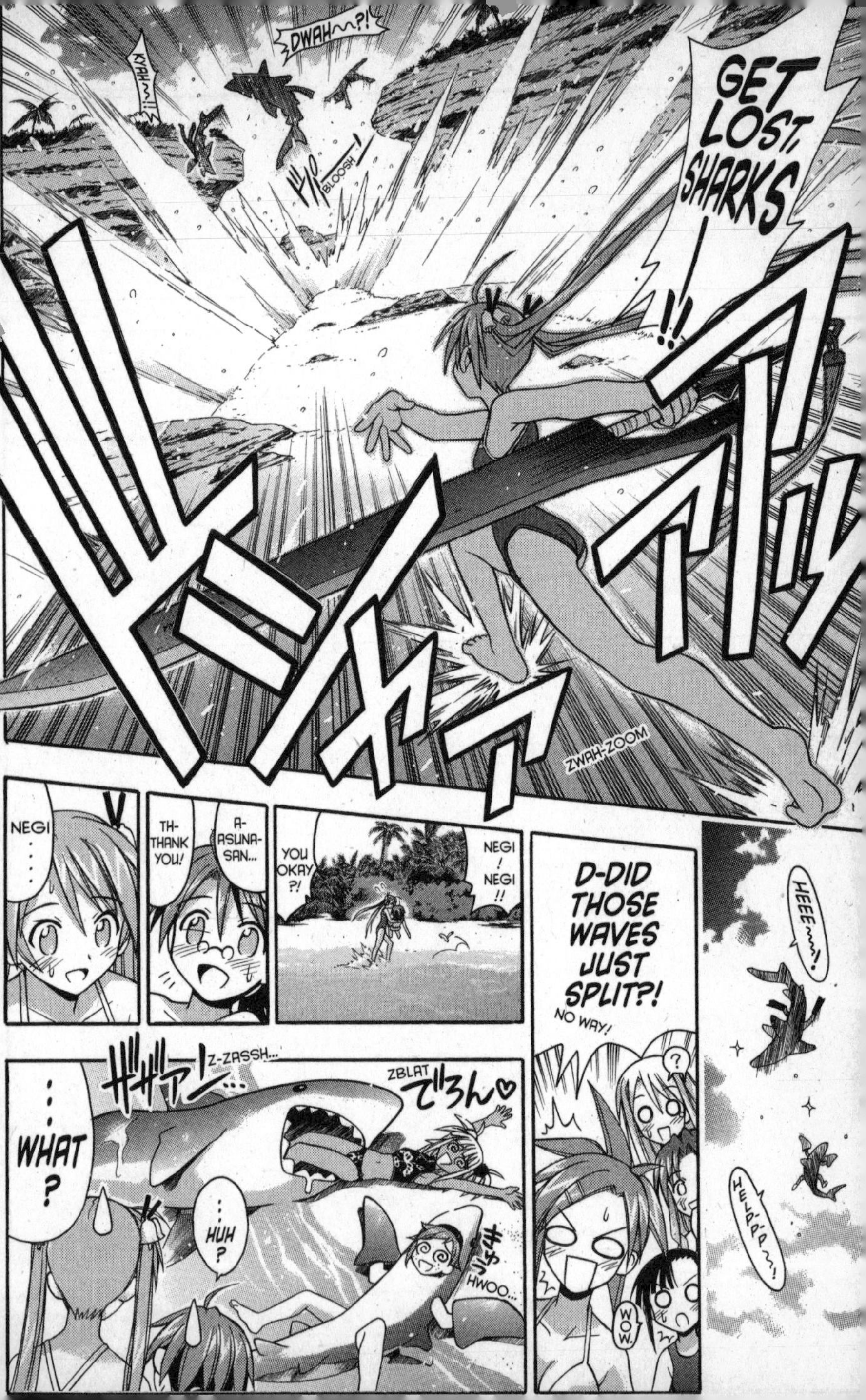
GET LOST, SHARKS!!!
DWAH~?!
KYAH~!!
BLOOSH
ZWAH-ZOOM
HEEE~!
HELP-P-P~?!
D-DID THOSE WAVES JUST SPLIT?!
NO WAY!
WOW.
NEGI! NEGI!!
YOU OKAY?!
A-ASUNA-SAN...
TH-THANK YOU!
NEGI...
Z-ZASSH...
ZBLAT
...WHAT?
...HUH?
HWOO...

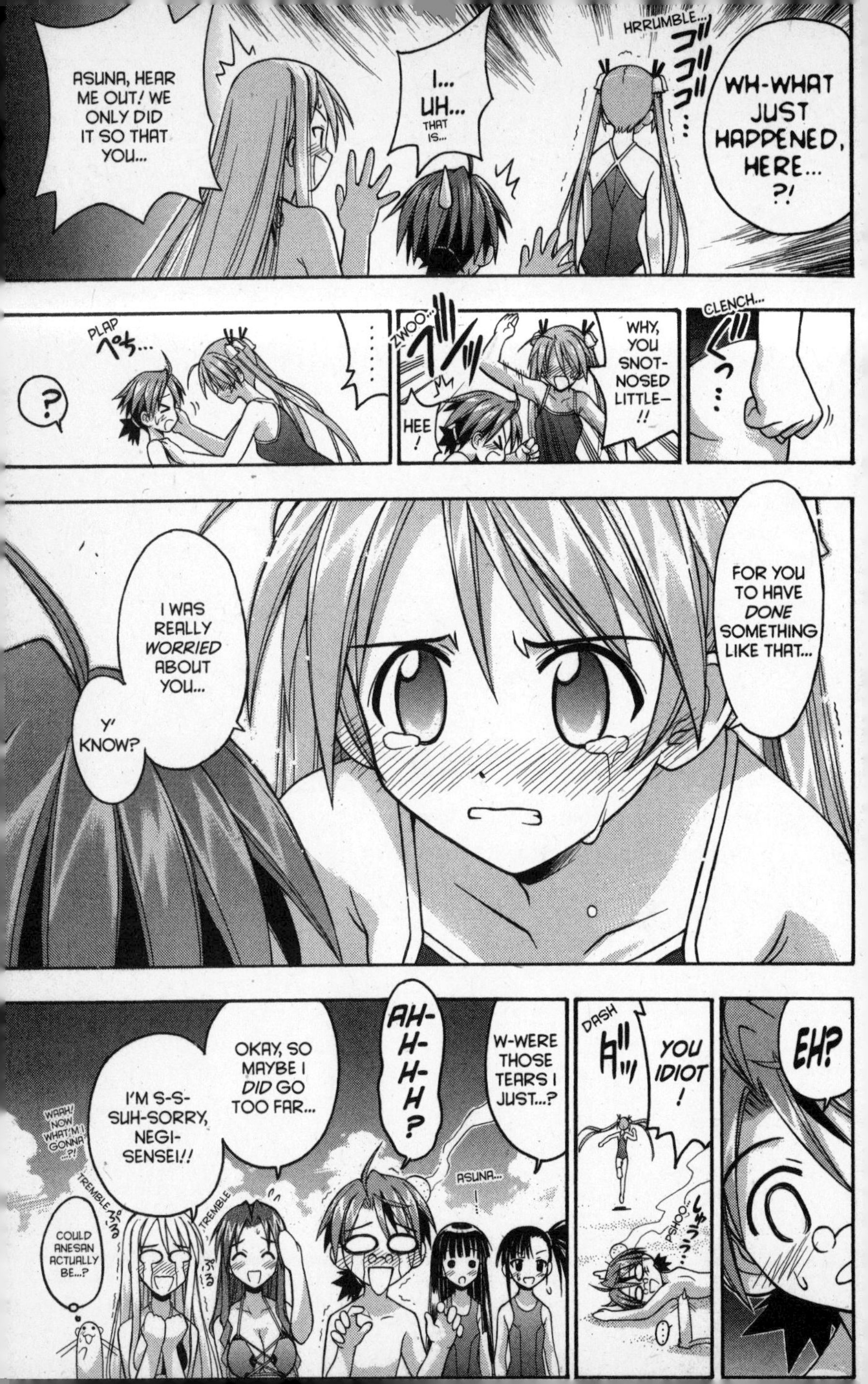
HRRUMBLE...
WH-WHAT JUST HAPPENED, HERE...?!
I... UH... THAT IS...
ASUNA, HEAR ME OUT! WE ONLY DID IT SO THAT YOU...
CLENCH...
...
WHY, YOU SNOT-NOSED LITTLE—!!
ZWOO...
HEE!
......
PLAP
?
FOR YOU TO HAVE *DONE* SOMETHING LIKE THAT...
I WAS REALLY *WORRIED* ABOUT YOU...
Y' KNOW?
EH?
DASH
YOU IDIOT!
PSHOO...
...
W-WERE THOSE TEARS I JUST...?
AH-H-H-H?
ASUNA...
!
OKAY, SO MAYBE I *DID* GO TOO FAR...
I'M S-S-SUH-SORRY, NEGI-SENSEI!!
WAAH! NOW WHAT'M I GONNA ...?!
TREMBLE
TREMBLE
COULD ANESAN ACTUALLY BE...?

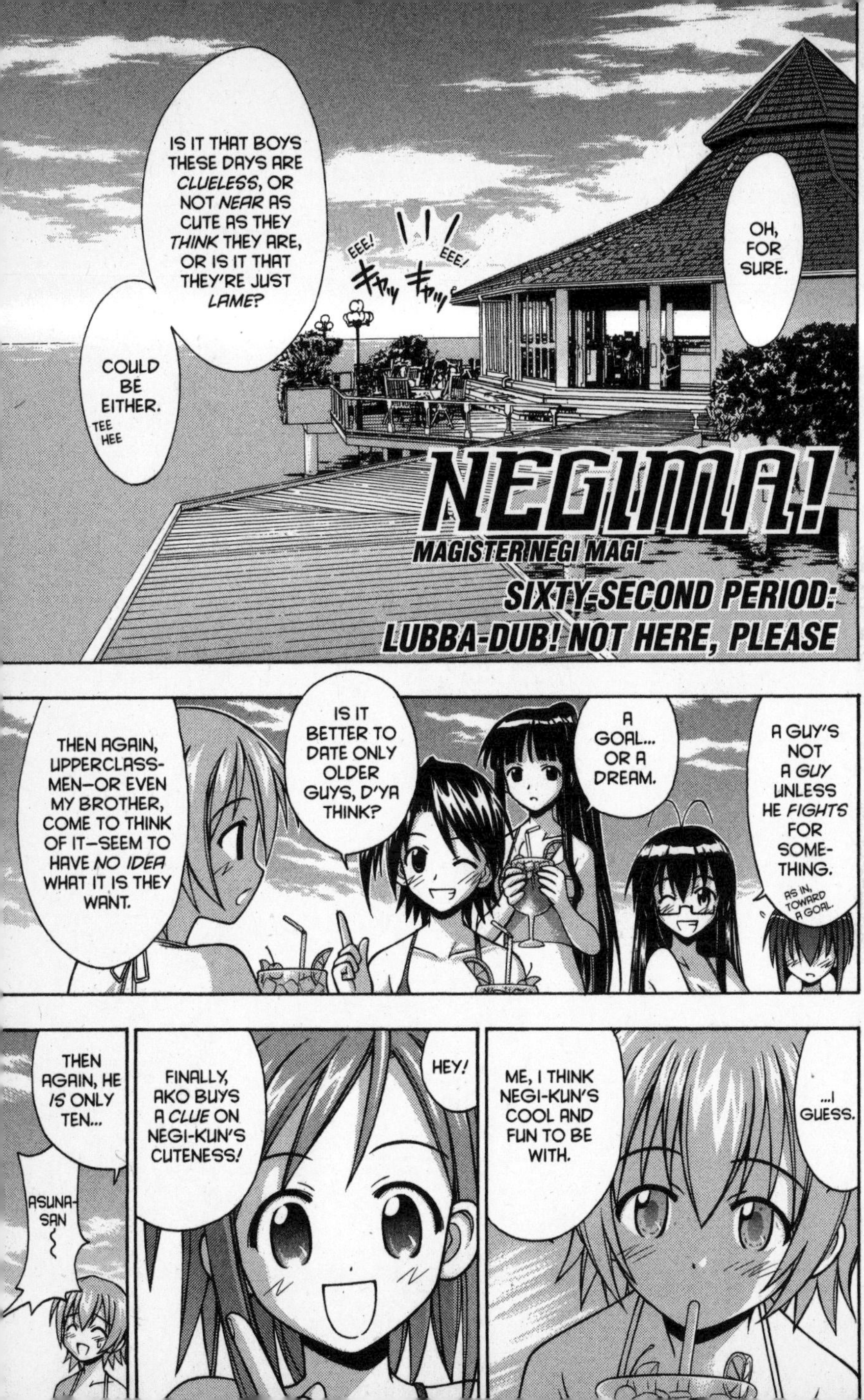
IS IT THAT BOYS THESE DAYS ARE *CLUELESS*, OR NOT *NEAR* AS CUTE AS THEY *THINK* THEY ARE, OR IS IT THAT THEY'RE JUST *LAME*?
EEE! キャッ
EEE! キャッ
OH, FOR SURE.
COULD BE EITHER.
TEE HEE
NEGIMA!
MAGISTER NEGI MAGI
SIXTY-SECOND PERIOD:
LUBBA-DUB! NOT HERE, PLEASE
A GUY'S NOT A *GUY* UNLESS HE *FIGHTS* FOR SOMETHING.
AS IN, TOWARD A GOAL.
A GOAL... OR A DREAM.
IS IT BETTER TO DATE ONLY OLDER GUYS, D'YA THINK?
THEN AGAIN, UPPERCLASSMEN—OR EVEN MY BROTHER, COME TO THINK OF IT—SEEM TO HAVE *NO IDEA* WHAT IT IS THEY WANT.
ME, I THINK NEGI-KUN'S COOL AND FUN TO BE WITH.
...I GUESS.
HEY!
FINALLY, AKO BUYS A *CLUE* ON NEGI-KUN'S CUTENESS!
THEN AGAIN, HE *IS* ONLY TEN...
ASUNA-SAN ~

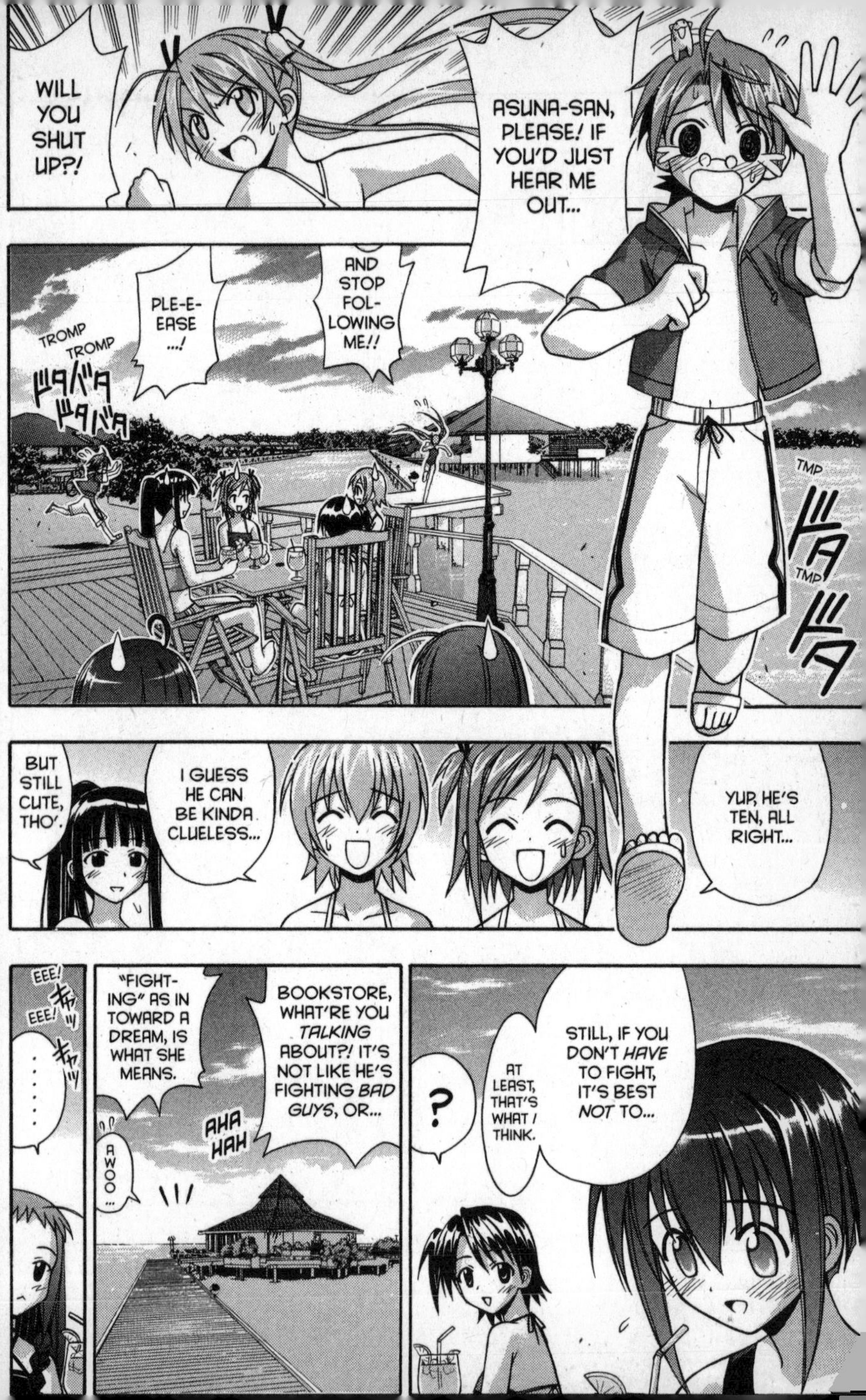
ASUNA-SAN, PLEASE! IF YOU'D JUST HEAR ME OUT...
WILL YOU SHUT UP?!
AND STOP FOL-LOWING ME!!
PLE-E-EASE ...!
TROMP TROMP
ドタバタ ドタバタ
TMP TMP
YUP, HE'S TEN, ALL RIGHT...
I GUESS HE CAN BE KINDA CLUELESS...
BUT STILL CUTE, THO'.
STILL, IF YOU DON'T *HAVE* TO FIGHT, IT'S BEST *NOT* TO...
AT LEAST, THAT'S WHAT *I* THINK.
?
BOOKSTORE, WHAT'RE YOU *TALKING* ABOUT?! IT'S NOT LIKE HE'S FIGHTING *BAD GUYS*, OR...
"FIGHT-ING" AS IN TOWARD A DREAM, IS WHAT SHE MEANS.
AHA HAH
AWOO...
EEE! EEE!
......

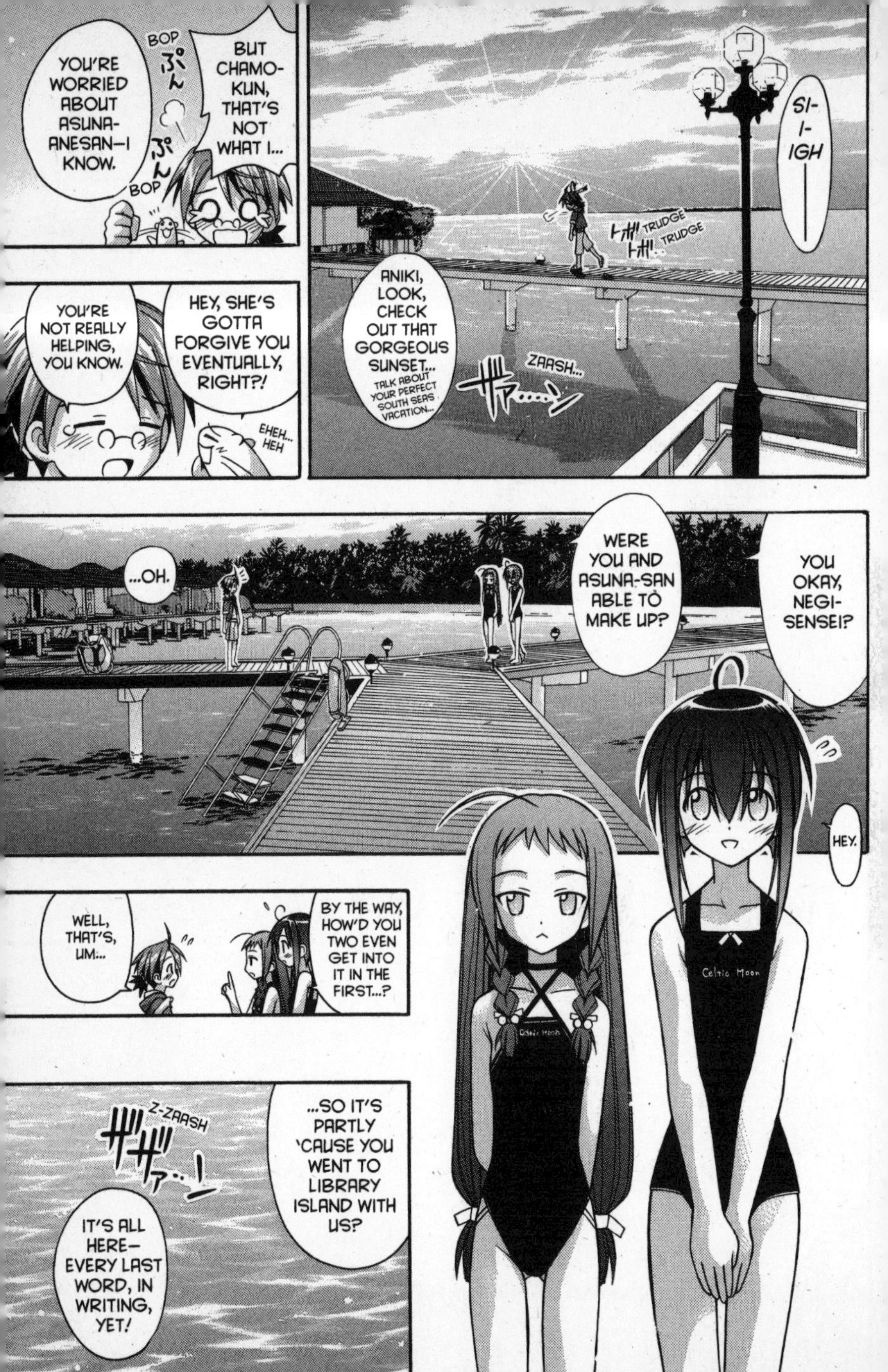
SI-I-IGH—
トボ TRUDGE
トボ… TRUDGE
ANIKI, LOOK, CHECK OUT THAT GORGEOUS SUNSET... TALK ABOUT YOUR PERFECT SOUTH SEAS VACATION...
ザァ……ン ZAASH...
BUT CHAMO-KUN, THAT'S NOT WHAT I...
BOP ぷん
ぷん BOP
YOU'RE WORRIED ABOUT ASUNA-ANESAN—I KNOW.
HEY, SHE'S GOTTA FORGIVE YOU EVENTUALLY, RIGHT?!
YOU'RE NOT REALLY HELPING, YOU KNOW.
EHEH... HEH
YOU OKAY, NEGI-SENSEI?
WERE YOU AND ASUNA-SAN ABLE TO MAKE UP?
...OH.
HEY.
Celtic Moon
BY THE WAY, HOW'D YOU TWO EVEN GET INTO IT IN THE FIRST...?
WELL, THAT'S, UM...
...SO IT'S PARTLY 'CAUSE YOU WENT TO LIBRARY ISLAND WITH US?
ザザァ…! Z-ZAASH
IT'S ALL HERE—EVERY LAST WORD, IN WRITING, YET!

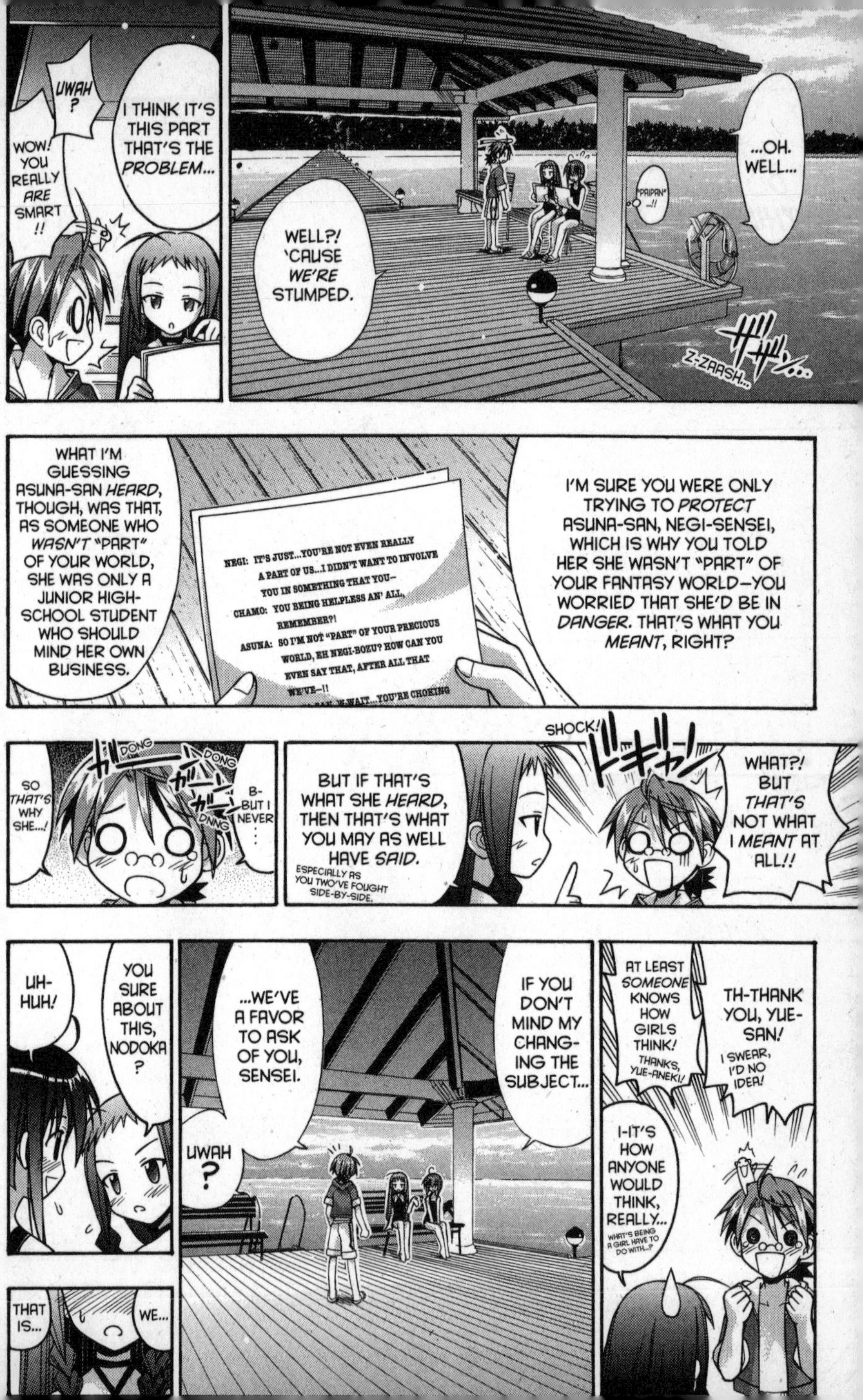
...OH. WELL...
"PAIPAN" ...!!
WELL?! 'CAUSE WE'RE STUMPED.
Z-ZAASH...
I THINK IT'S THIS PART THAT'S THE PROBLEM...
UWAH?
WOW! YOU REALLY ARE SMART!!
I'M SURE YOU WERE ONLY TRYING TO PROTECT ASUNA-SAN, NEGI-SENSEI, WHICH IS WHY YOU TOLD HER SHE WASN'T "PART" OF YOUR FANTASY WORLD—YOU WORRIED THAT SHE'D BE IN DANGER. THAT'S WHAT YOU MEANT, RIGHT?
NEGI: IT'S JUST...YOU'RE NOT EVEN REALLY A PART OF US...I DIDN'T WANT TO INVOLVE YOU IN SOMETHING THAT YOU—
CHAMO: YOU BEING HELPLESS AN' ALL, REMEMBER?!
ASUNA: SO I'M NOT "PART" OF YOUR PRECIOUS WORLD, EH NEGI-BOZU? HOW CAN YOU EVEN SAY THAT, AFTER ALL THAT WE'VE—!!
WHAT I'M GUESSING ASUNA-SAN HEARD, THOUGH, WAS THAT, AS SOMEONE WHO WASN'T "PART" OF YOUR WORLD, SHE WAS ONLY A JUNIOR HIGH-SCHOOL STUDENT WHO SHOULD MIND HER OWN BUSINESS.
SHOCK!
WHAT?! BUT THAT'S NOT WHAT I MEANT AT ALL!!
BUT IF THAT'S WHAT SHE HEARD, THEN THAT'S WHAT YOU MAY AS WELL HAVE SAID.
ESPECIALLY AS YOU TWO'VE FOUGHT SIDE-BY-SIDE.
DONG
DONG
DNNG
B-BUT I NEVER...
SO THAT'S WHY SHE...!
TH-THANK YOU, YUE-SAN!
I SWEAR, I'D NO IDEA!
AT LEAST SOMEONE KNOWS HOW GIRLS THINK!
THANKS, YUE-ANEKI!
I-IT'S HOW ANYONE WOULD THINK, REALLY...
WHAT'S BEING A GIRL HAVE TO DO WITH...?
IF YOU DON'T MIND MY CHANGING THE SUBJECT...
...WE'VE A FAVOR TO ASK OF YOU, SENSEI.
UWAH?
YOU SURE ABOUT THIS, NODOKA?
UH-HUH!
WE...
THAT IS...

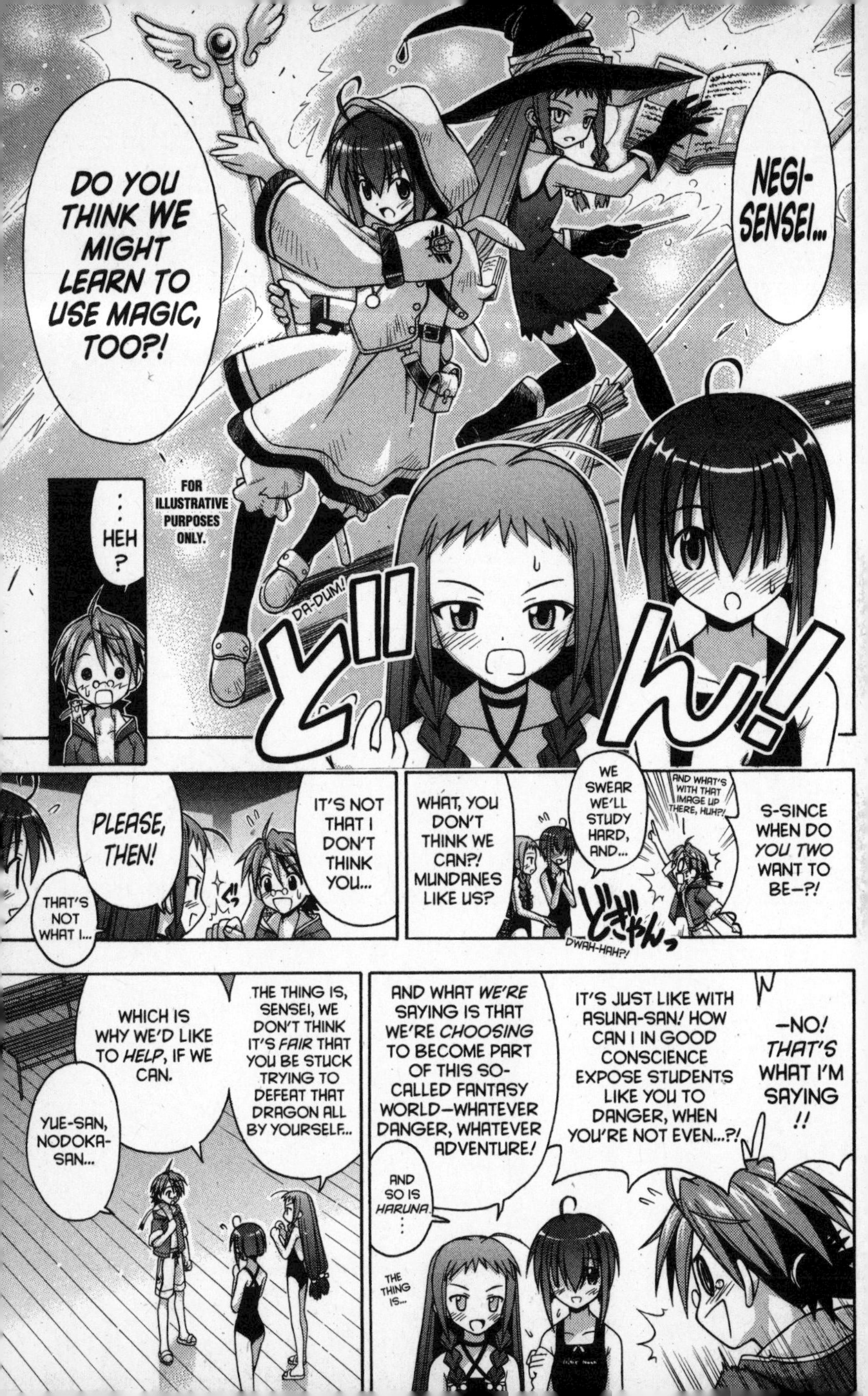
NEGI-SENSEI...
DO YOU THINK WE MIGHT LEARN TO USE MAGIC, TOO?!
DA-DUM!
どーん!
FOR ILLUSTRATIVE PURPOSES ONLY.
...HEH?
S-SINCE WHEN DO YOU TWO WANT TO BE—?!
AND WHAT'S WITH THAT IMAGE UP THERE, HUH?!
WE SWEAR WE'LL STUDY HARD, AND...
どぎゃんっ
DWAH-HAH?!
WHAT, YOU DON'T THINK WE CAN?! MUNDANES LIKE US?
IT'S NOT THAT I DON'T THINK YOU...
PLEASE, THEN!
THAT'S NOT WHAT I...
—NO! THAT'S WHAT I'M SAYING!!
IT'S JUST LIKE WITH ASUNA-SAN! HOW CAN I IN GOOD CONSCIENCE EXPOSE STUDENTS LIKE YOU TO DANGER, WHEN YOU'RE NOT EVEN...?!
AND WHAT WE'RE SAYING IS THAT WE'RE CHOOSING TO BECOME PART OF THIS SO-CALLED FANTASY WORLD—WHATEVER DANGER, WHATEVER ADVENTURE!
AND SO IS HARUNA...
THE THING IS...
THE THING IS, SENSEI, WE DON'T THINK IT'S FAIR THAT YOU BE STUCK TRYING TO DEFEAT THAT DRAGON ALL BY YOURSELF...
WHICH IS WHY WE'D LIKE TO HELP, IF WE CAN.
YUE-SAN, NODOKA-SAN...

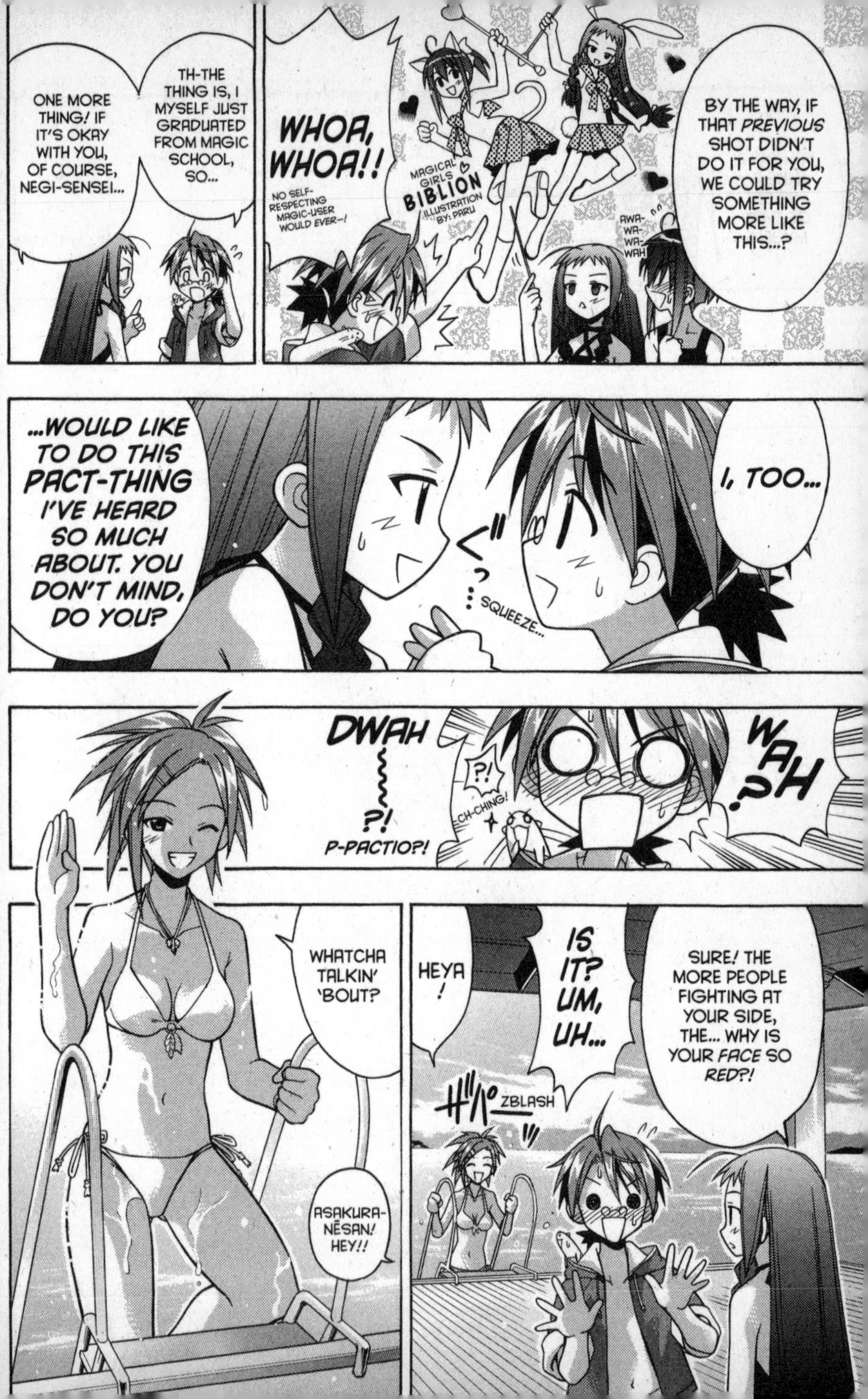
BY THE WAY, IF THAT *PREVIOUS* SHOT DIDN'T DO IT FOR YOU, WE COULD TRY SOMETHING MORE LIKE THIS...?
AWA-WA-WA-WAH
WHOA, WHOA!!
NO SELF-RESPECTING MAGIC-USER WOULD *EVER*—!
MAGICAL GIRLS BIBLION ILLUSTRATION BY: PARU
TH-THE THING IS, I MYSELF JUST GRADUATED FROM MAGIC SCHOOL, SO...
ONE MORE THING! IF IT'S OKAY WITH YOU, OF COURSE, NEGI-SENSEI...
I, TOO...
...WOULD LIKE TO DO THIS PACT-THING I'VE HEARD SO MUCH ABOUT. YOU DON'T MIND, DO YOU?
SQUEEZE...
WAH?
?!
CH-CHING!
DWAH~?!
P-PACTIO?!
SURE! THE MORE PEOPLE FIGHTING AT YOUR SIDE, THE... WHY IS YOUR *FACE* SO *RED*?!
IS IT? UM, UH...
HEYA!
ZBLASH
WHATCHA TALKIN' 'BOUT?
ASAKURA-NĒSAN! HEY!!

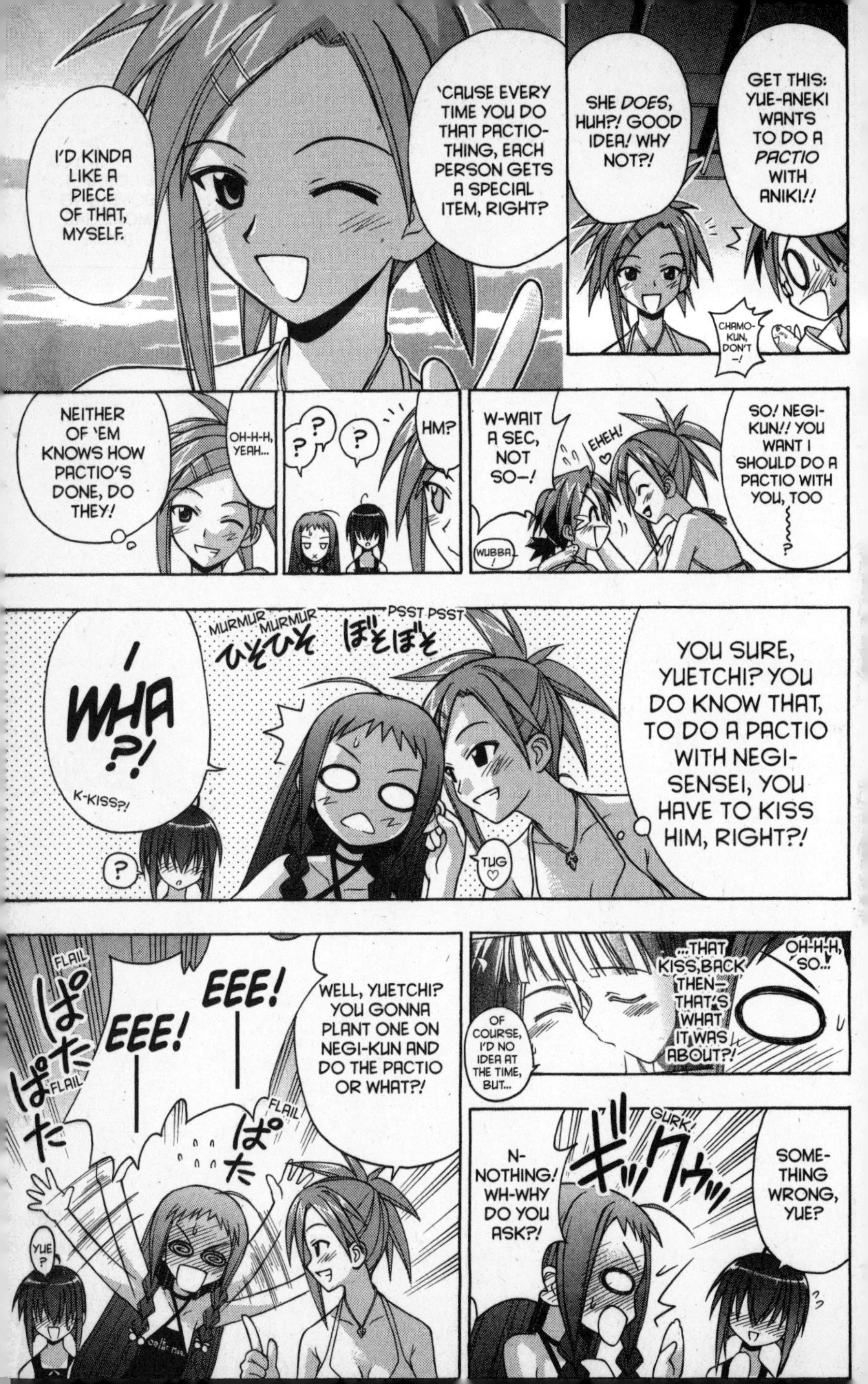
GET THIS: YUE-ANEKI WANTS TO DO A PACTIO WITH ANIKI!!
SHE DOES, HUH?! GOOD IDEA! WHY NOT?!
CHAMO-KUN, DON'T —!
'CAUSE EVERY TIME YOU DO THAT PACTIO-THING, EACH PERSON GETS A SPECIAL ITEM, RIGHT?
I'D KINDA LIKE A PIECE OF THAT, MYSELF.
SO! NEGI-KUN!! YOU WANT I SHOULD DO A PACTIO WITH YOU, TOO ~~~?
EHEH! ♡
W-WAIT A SEC, NOT SO—!
WUBBA!
HM?
? ? ?
OH-H-H, YEAH...
NEITHER OF 'EM KNOWS HOW PACTIO'S DONE, DO THEY!
YOU SURE, YUETCHI? YOU DO KNOW THAT, TO DO A PACTIO WITH NEGI-SENSEI, YOU HAVE TO KISS HIM, RIGHT?!
PSST PSST
ぼそぼそ
MURMUR MURMUR
ひそひそ
TUG ♡
WHA?!
K-KISS?!
?
OH-H-H, SO..!
...THAT KISS, BACK THEN— THAT'S WHAT IT WAS ABOUT?!
OF COURSE, I'D NO IDEA AT THE TIME, BUT...
SOME-THING WRONG, YUE?
GURK!
ギクゥッ
N-NOTHING! WH-WHY DO YOU ASK?!
WELL, YUETCHI? YOU GONNA PLANT ONE ON NEGI-KUN AND DO THE PACTIO OR WHAT?!
EEE!
EEE!
FLAIL
ぱた
FLAIL
ぱた
FLAIL
ぱた
YUE?

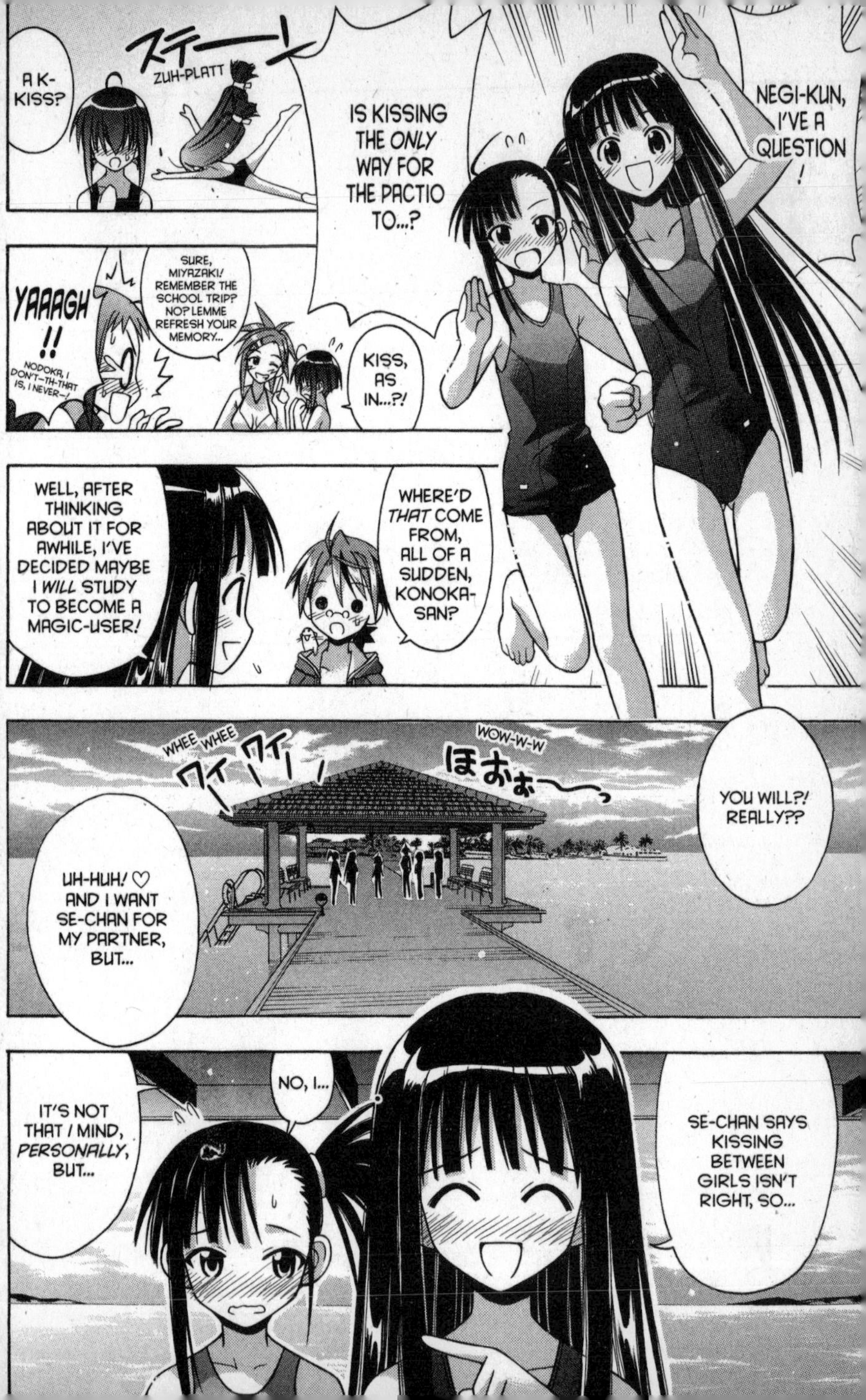
NEGI-KUN, I'VE A QUESTION!
IS KISSING THE ONLY WAY FOR THE PACTIO TO...?
ス テー ン
ZUH-PLATT
A K-KISS?
KISS, AS IN...?!
SURE, MIYAZAKI! REMEMBER THE SCHOOL TRIP? NO? LEMME REFRESH YOUR MEMORY...
YAAAGH!!
NODOKA, I DON'T—TH-THAT IS, I NEVER—!
WHERE'D THAT COME FROM, ALL OF A SUDDEN, KONOKA-SAN?
WELL, AFTER THINKING ABOUT IT FOR AWHILE, I'VE DECIDED MAYBE I WILL STUDY TO BECOME A MAGIC-USER!
YOU WILL?! REALLY??
ほぉぉ~
WOW-W-W
ワイ ワイ
WHEE WHEE
UH-HUH! ♡ AND I WANT SE-CHAN FOR MY PARTNER, BUT...
SE-CHAN SAYS KISSING BETWEEN GIRLS ISN'T RIGHT, SO...
NO, I...
IT'S NOT THAT I MIND, PERSONALLY, BUT...

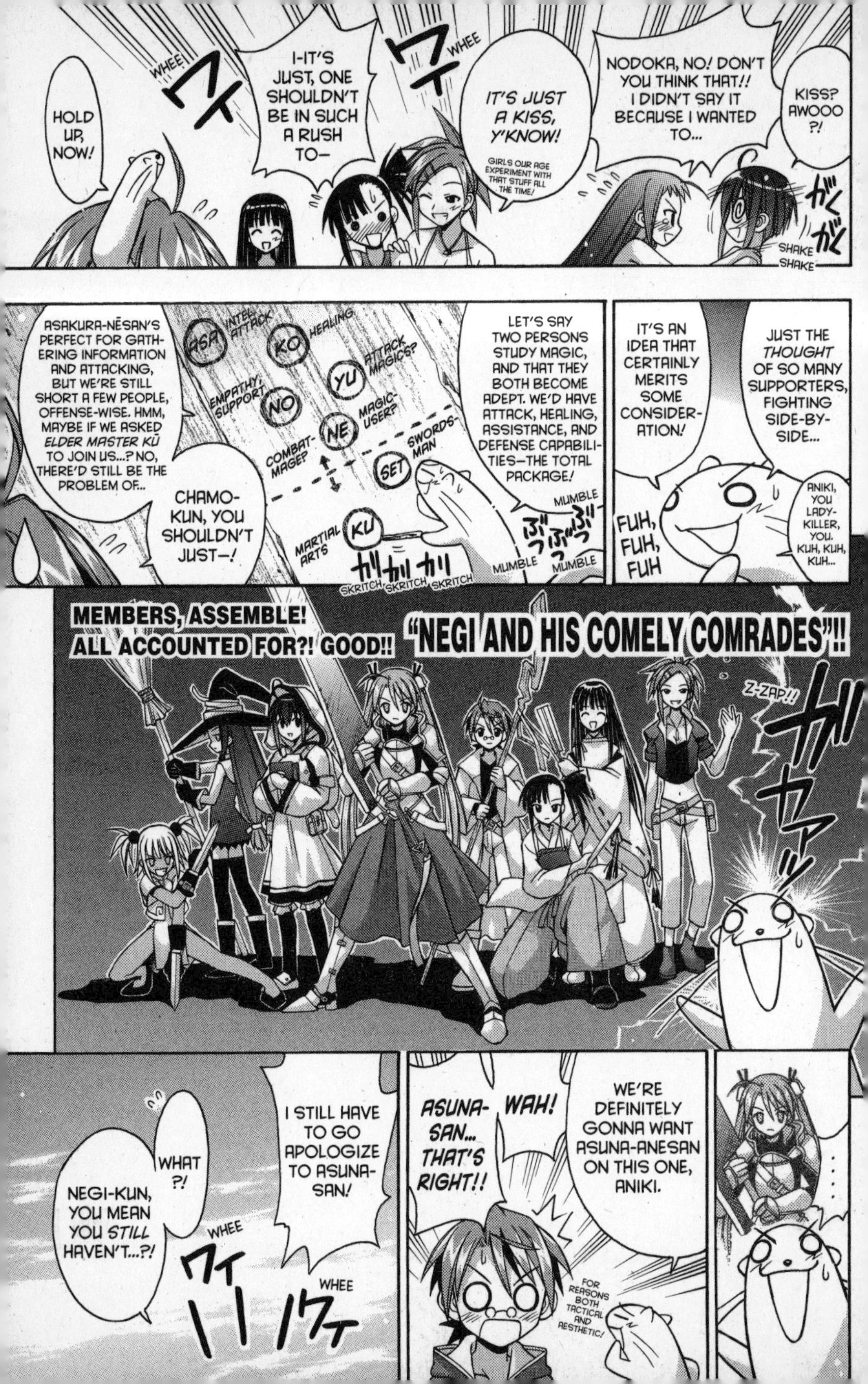
KISS? AWOOO?!
NODOKA, NO! DON'T YOU THINK THAT!! I DIDN'T SAY IT BECAUSE I WANTED TO...
がくがく SHAKE SHAKE
IT'S JUST A KISS, Y'KNOW!
GIRLS OUR AGE EXPERIMENT WITH THAT STUFF ALL THE TIME!
ワイ WHEE
I-IT'S JUST, ONE SHOULDN'T BE IN SUCH A RUSH TO—
ワイ WHEE
HOLD UP, NOW!
JUST THE THOUGHT OF SO MANY SUPPORTERS, FIGHTING SIDE-BY-SIDE...
IT'S AN IDEA THAT CERTAINLY MERITS SOME CONSIDERATION!
ANIKI, YOU LADY-KILLER, YOU. KUH, KUH, KUH...
FUH, FUH, FUH
LET'S SAY TWO PERSONS STUDY MAGIC, AND THAT THEY BOTH BECOME ADEPT. WE'D HAVE ATTACK, HEALING, ASSISTANCE, AND DEFENSE CAPABILITIES—THE TOTAL PACKAGE!
ぶつぶつぶつ MUMBLE MUMBLE MUMBLE
ASA INTEL ATTACK
KO HEALING
YU ATTACK MAGICS?
NO EMPATHY, SUPPORT
NE MAGIC-USER? COMBAT-MAGE?
SET SWORDSMAN
KU MARTIAL ARTS
ASAKURA-NĒSAN'S PERFECT FOR GATHERING INFORMATION AND ATTACKING, BUT WE'RE STILL SHORT A FEW PEOPLE, OFFENSE-WISE. HMM, MAYBE IF WE ASKED ELDER MASTER KŪ TO JOIN US...? NO, THERE'D STILL BE THE PROBLEM OF...
CHAMO-KUN, YOU SHOULDN'T JUST—!
カリカリカリ SKRITCH SKRITCH SKRITCH
MEMBERS, ASSEMBLE! ALL ACCOUNTED FOR?! GOOD!!
"NEGI AND HIS COMELY COMRADES"!!
ガシャァッ Z-ZAP!!
...
WE'RE DEFINITELY GONNA WANT ASUNA-ANESAN ON THIS ONE, ANIKI.
WAH!
ASUNA-SAN... THAT'S RIGHT!!
FOR REASONS BOTH TACTICAL AND AESTHETIC!
I STILL HAVE TO GO APOLOGIZE TO ASUNA-SAN!
WHAT?!
NEGI-KUN, YOU MEAN YOU STILL HAVEN'T...?!
ワイ WHEE
ワイ WHEE

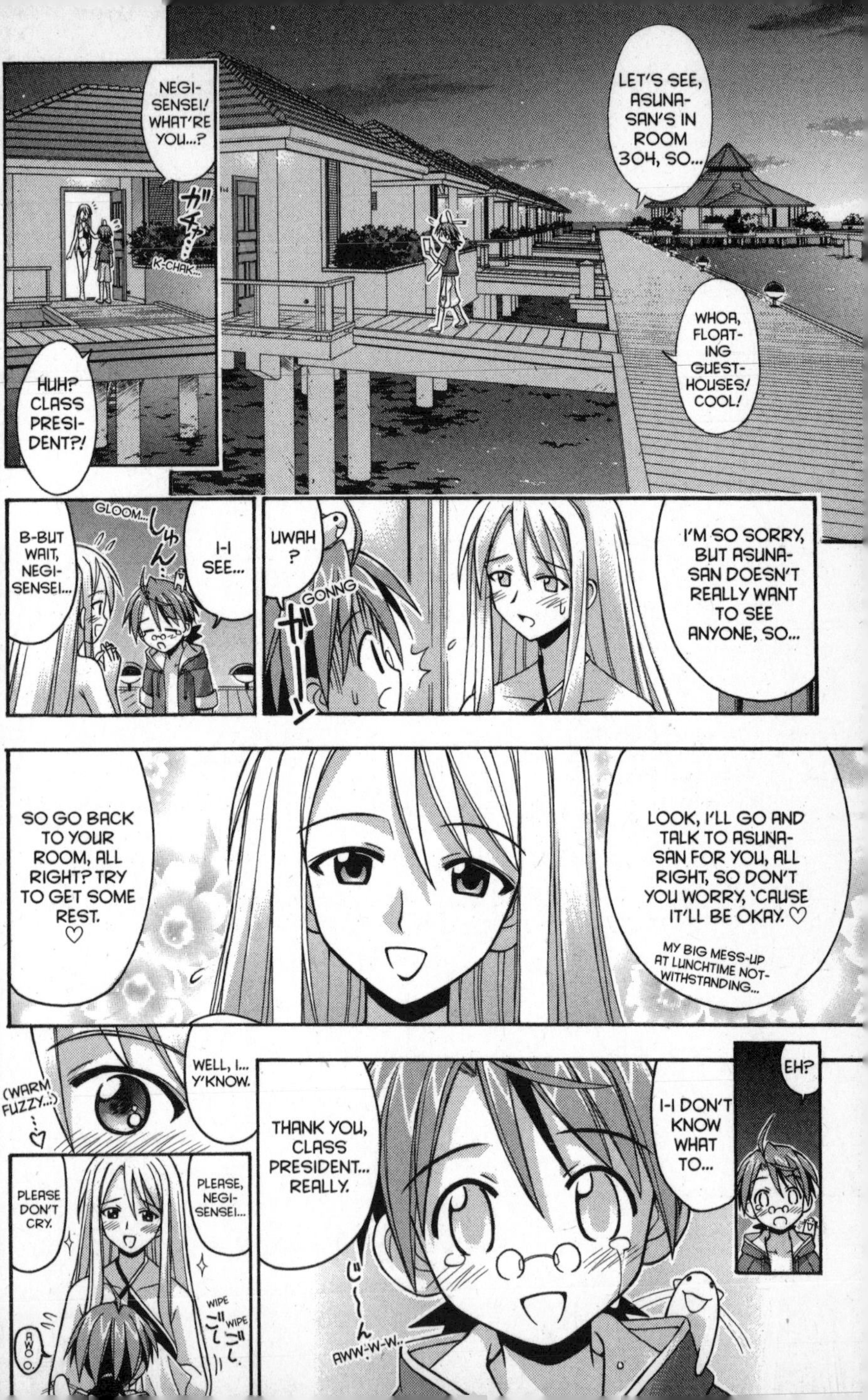

LET'S SEE, ASUNA-SAN'S IN ROOM 304, SO...
WHOA, FLOATING GUEST-HOUSES! COOL!
NEGI-SENSEI! WHAT'RE YOU...?
ガチャ
K-CHAK...
HUH? CLASS PRESIDENT?!
I'M SO SORRY, BUT ASUNA-SAN DOESN'T REALLY WANT TO SEE ANYONE, SO...
UWAH?
GONNG
I-I SEE...
GLOOM...
B-BUT WAIT, NEGI-SENSEI...
LOOK, I'LL GO AND TALK TO ASUNA-SAN FOR YOU, ALL RIGHT, SO DON'T YOU WORRY, 'CAUSE IT'LL BE OKAY. ♡
MY BIG MESS-UP AT LUNCHTIME NOT-WITHSTANDING...
SO GO BACK TO YOUR ROOM, ALL RIGHT? TRY TO GET SOME REST. ♡
EH?
I-I DON'T KNOW WHAT TO...
THANK YOU, CLASS PRESIDENT... REALLY.
AWW-W-W...
WELL, I... Y'KNOW.
(WARM FUZZY...)
PLEASE, NEGI-SENSEI...
PLEASE DON'T CRY.
WIPE WIPE
AWOO.

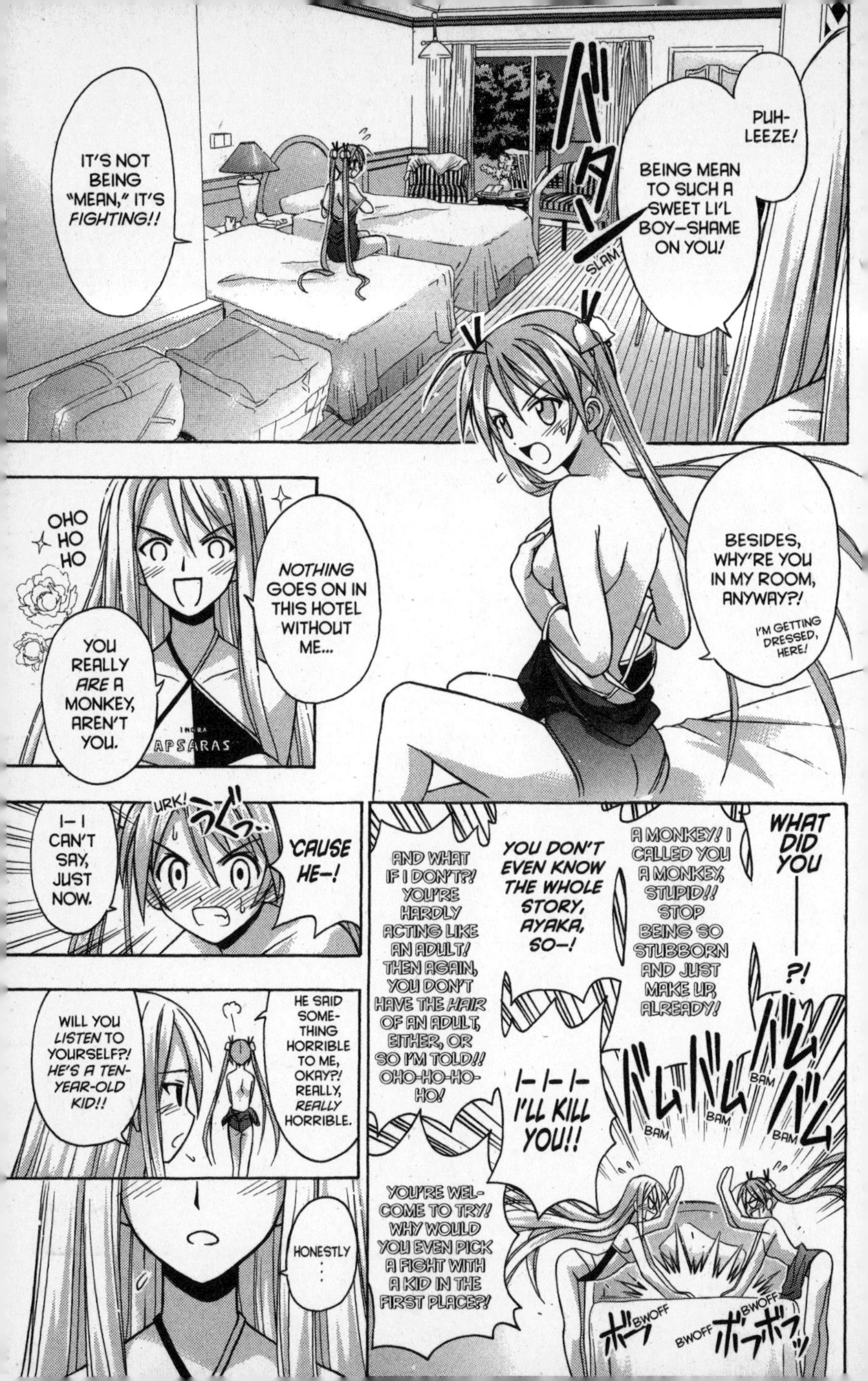
PUH-LEEZE!
BEING MEAN TO SUCH A SWEET LI'L BOY—SHAME ON YOU!
SLAM!
IT'S NOT BEING "MEAN," IT'S *FIGHTING!!*
BESIDES, WHY'RE YOU IN MY ROOM, ANYWAY?!
I'M GETTING DRESSED, HERE!
OHO HO HO
NOTHING GOES ON IN THIS HOTEL WITHOUT ME...
YOU REALLY *ARE* A MONKEY, AREN'T YOU.
APSARAS
WHAT DID YOU—?!
A MONKEY! I CALLED YOU A MONKEY, STUPID!! STOP BEING SO STUBBORN AND JUST MAKE UP, ALREADY!
YOU DON'T EVEN KNOW THE WHOLE STORY, AYAKA, SO—!
AND WHAT IF I DON'T?! YOU'RE HARDLY ACTING LIKE AN ADULT! THEN AGAIN, YOU DON'T HAVE THE *HAIR* OF AN ADULT, EITHER, OR SO I'M TOLD!! OHO-HO-HO-HO!
I-I-I-I'LL KILL YOU!!
BAM BAM BAM BAM
YOU'RE WEL-COME TO TRY! WHY WOULD YOU EVEN PICK A FIGHT WITH A KID IN THE FIRST PLACE?!
BWOFF BWOFF BWOFF
URK!
I—I CAN'T SAY, JUST NOW.
'CAUSE HE—!
HE SAID SOME-THING HORRIBLE TO ME, OKAY?! REALLY, *REALLY* HORRIBLE.
WILL YOU *LISTEN* TO YOURSELF?! HE'S A TEN-YEAR-OLD KID!!
HONESTLY...

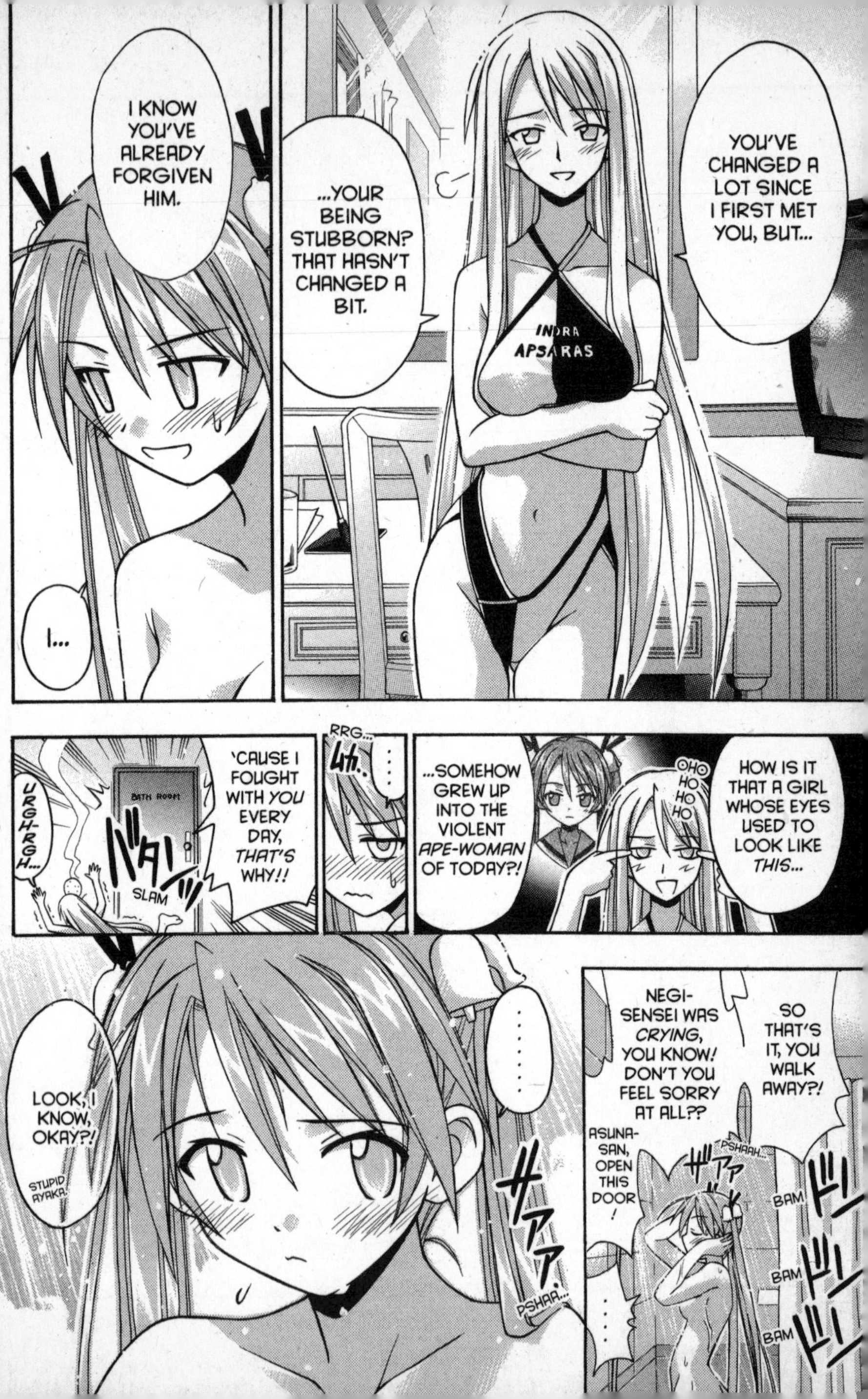

YOU'VE CHANGED A LOT SINCE I FIRST MET YOU, BUT...
INDRA APSARAS
...YOUR BEING STUBBORN? THAT HASN'T CHANGED A BIT.
I KNOW YOU'VE ALREADY FORGIVEN HIM.
I...
HOW IS IT THAT A GIRL WHOSE EYES USED TO LOOK LIKE *THIS*...
OHO HO HO HO
...SOMEHOW GREW UP INTO THE VIOLENT *APE-WOMAN* OF TODAY?!
RRG...
ムカ
. . . .
'CAUSE I FOUGHT WITH *YOU* EVERY DAY, *THAT'S* WHY!!
BATH ROOM
バタン
SLAM
URGHRGH...
SO THAT'S IT, YOU WALK AWAY?!
NEGI-SENSEI WAS *CRYING*, YOU KNOW! DON'T YOU FEEL SORRY AT ALL??
ASUNA-SAN, OPEN THIS DOOR!
ドン
BAM
ドン
BAM
ドン
BAM
ザァ
PSHAAH...
. . .
. . . . . .
ザアア
PSHAA...
LOOK, I KNOW, OKAY?!
STUPID AYAKA.

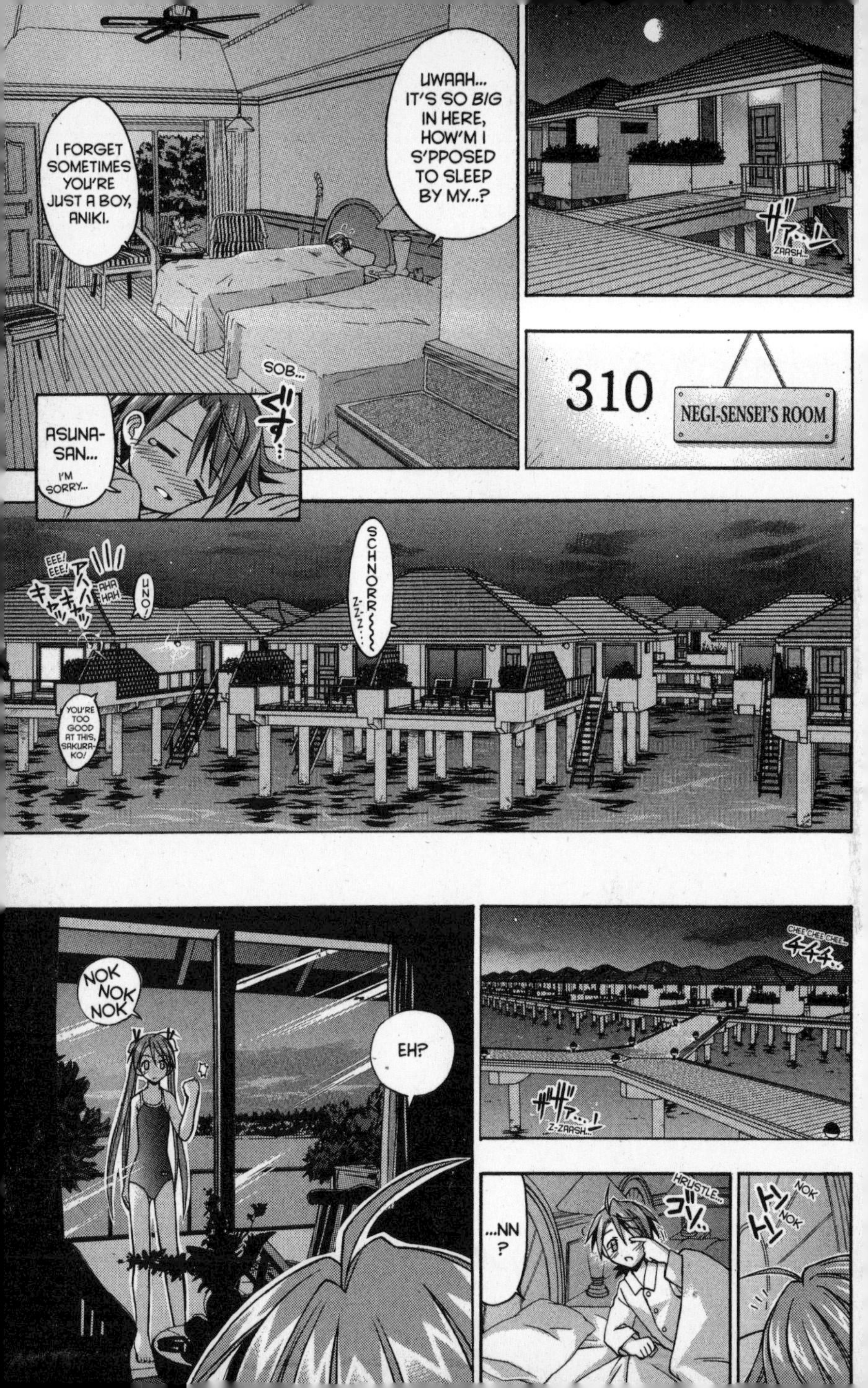
ZAASH...
310
NEGI-SENSEI'S ROOM
UWAAH... IT'S SO *BIG* IN HERE, HOW'M I S'PPOSED TO SLEEP BY MY...?
I FORGET SOMETIMES YOU'RE JUST A BOY, ANIKI.
SOB...
ASUNA-SAN...
I'M SORRY...
SCHNORR~~~
Z-Z-Z...
UNO!
AHA HAH
EEE! EEE!
YOU'RE TOO GOOD AT THIS, SAKURA-KO!
CHEE CHEE CHEE...
Z-ZAASH...!
NOK NOK
HRUSTLE...
...NN?
NOK NOK NOK
EH?

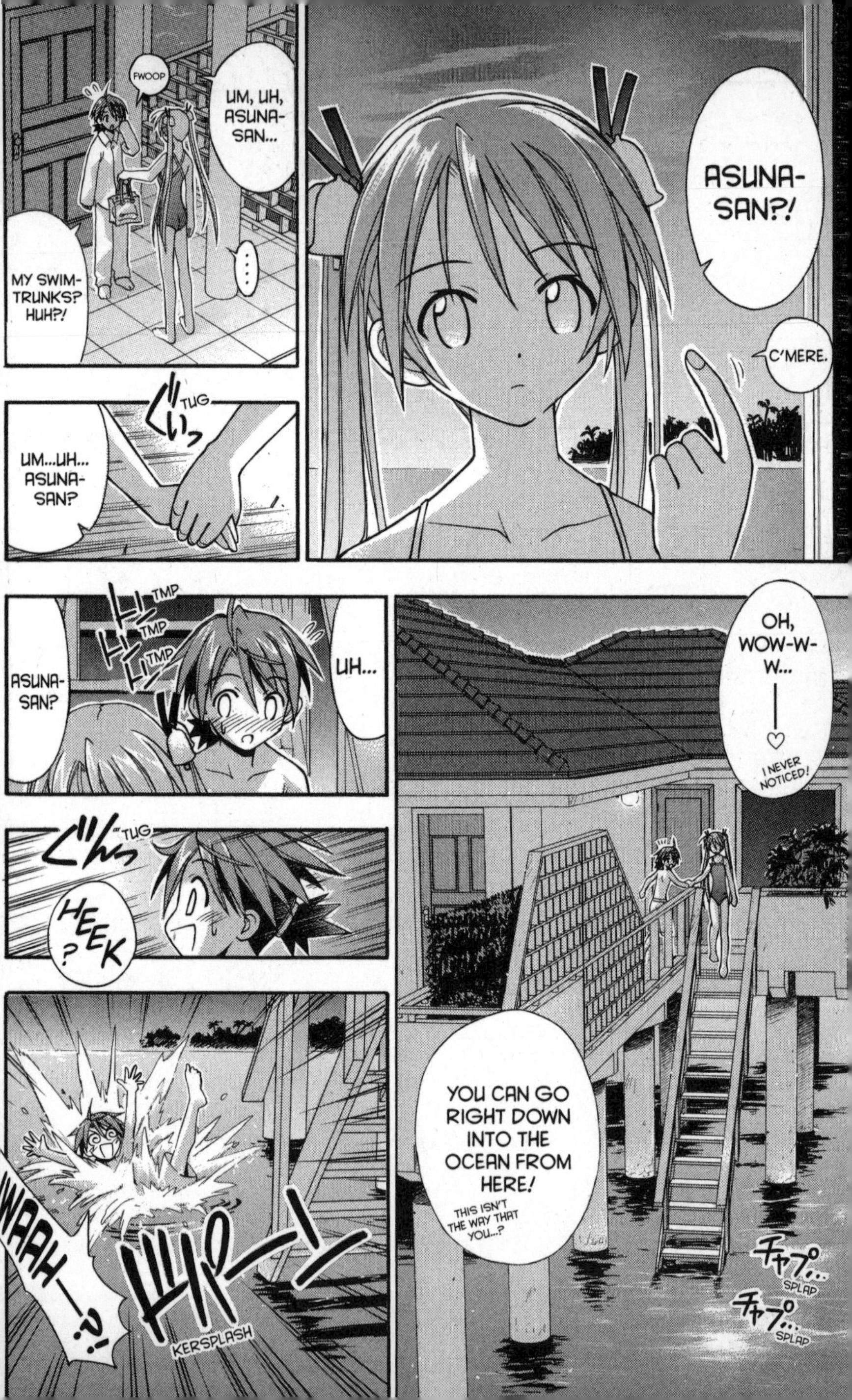
ASUNA-SAN?!
C'MERE.
UM, UH, ASUNA-SAN...
FWOOP
...
MY SWIM-TRUNKS? HUH?!
TUG
UM...UH... ASUNA-SAN?
OH, WOW-W-W... ♡
I NEVER NOTICED!
YOU CAN GO RIGHT DOWN INTO THE OCEAN FROM HERE!
THIS ISN'T THE WAY THAT YOU...?
チャプ… SPLAP
チャプ… SPLAP
UH...
TMP TMP TMP
ASUNA-SAN?
TUG
HEEK?
KERSPLASH
WAAH--?!

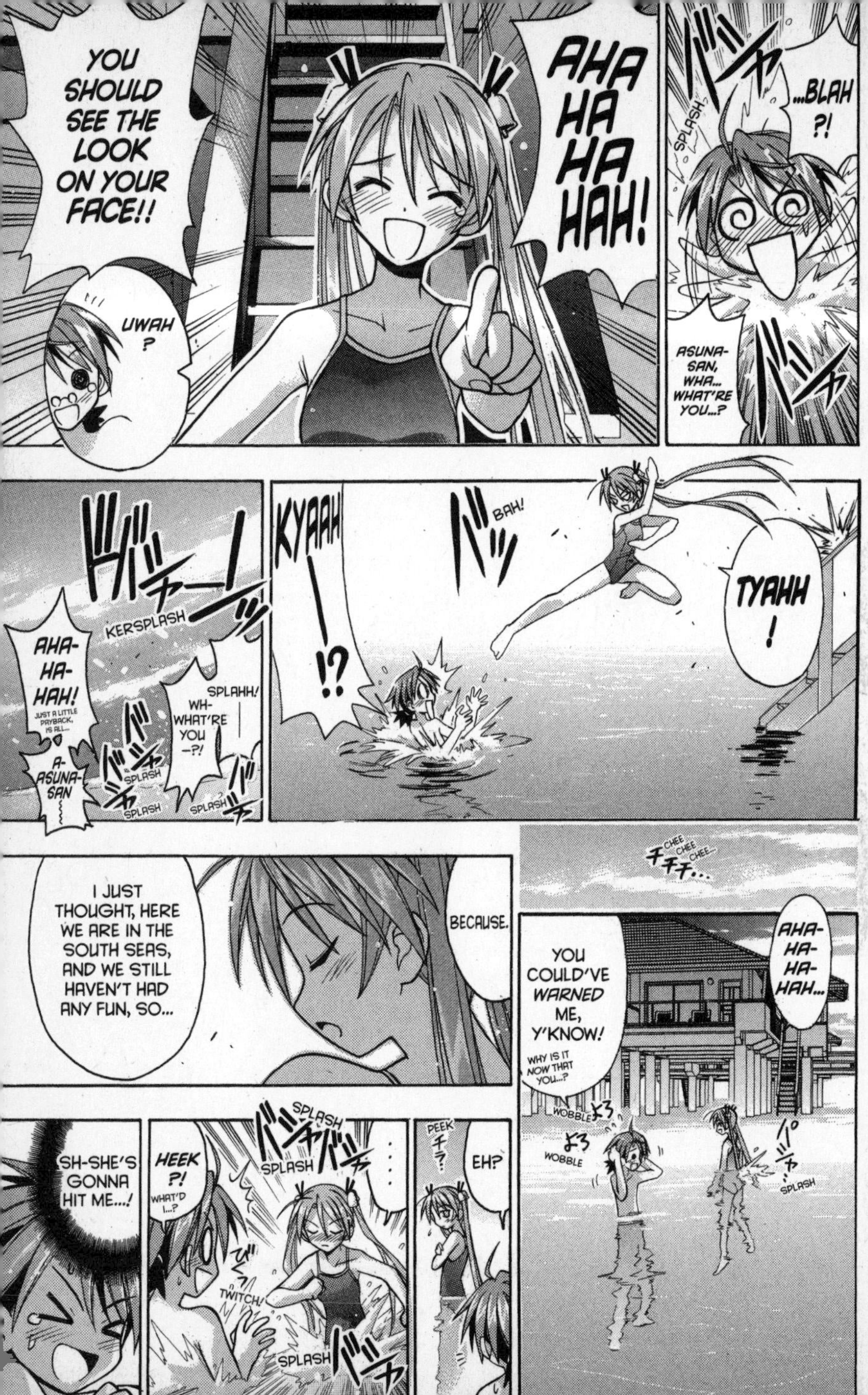
SPLASH
…BLAH ?!
ASUNA-SAN, WHA… WHAT'RE YOU…?
AHA HA HA HAH!
YOU SHOULD SEE THE LOOK ON YOUR FACE!!
UWAH ?
BAH!
TYAHH !
KYAAH !?
KERSPLASH
SPLAHH!
WH-WHAT'RE YOU—?!
AHA-HA-HAH!
JUST A LITTLE PAYBACK, IS ALL…
A-ASUNA-SAN
SPLASH
SPLASH
SPLASH
チチチ…
CHEE CHEE CHEE…
AHA-HA-HA-HAH…
YOU COULD'VE WARNED ME, Y'KNOW!
WHY IS IT NOW THAT YOU…?
WOBBLE
WOBBLE
SPLASH
BECAUSE.
I JUST THOUGHT, HERE WE ARE IN THE SOUTH SEAS, AND WE STILL HAVEN'T HAD ANY FUN, SO…
EH?
チラ
PEEK
SPLASH
SPLASH
HEEK ?!
WHAT'D I…?
TWITCH!
SPLASH
SH-SHE'S GONNA HIT ME…!

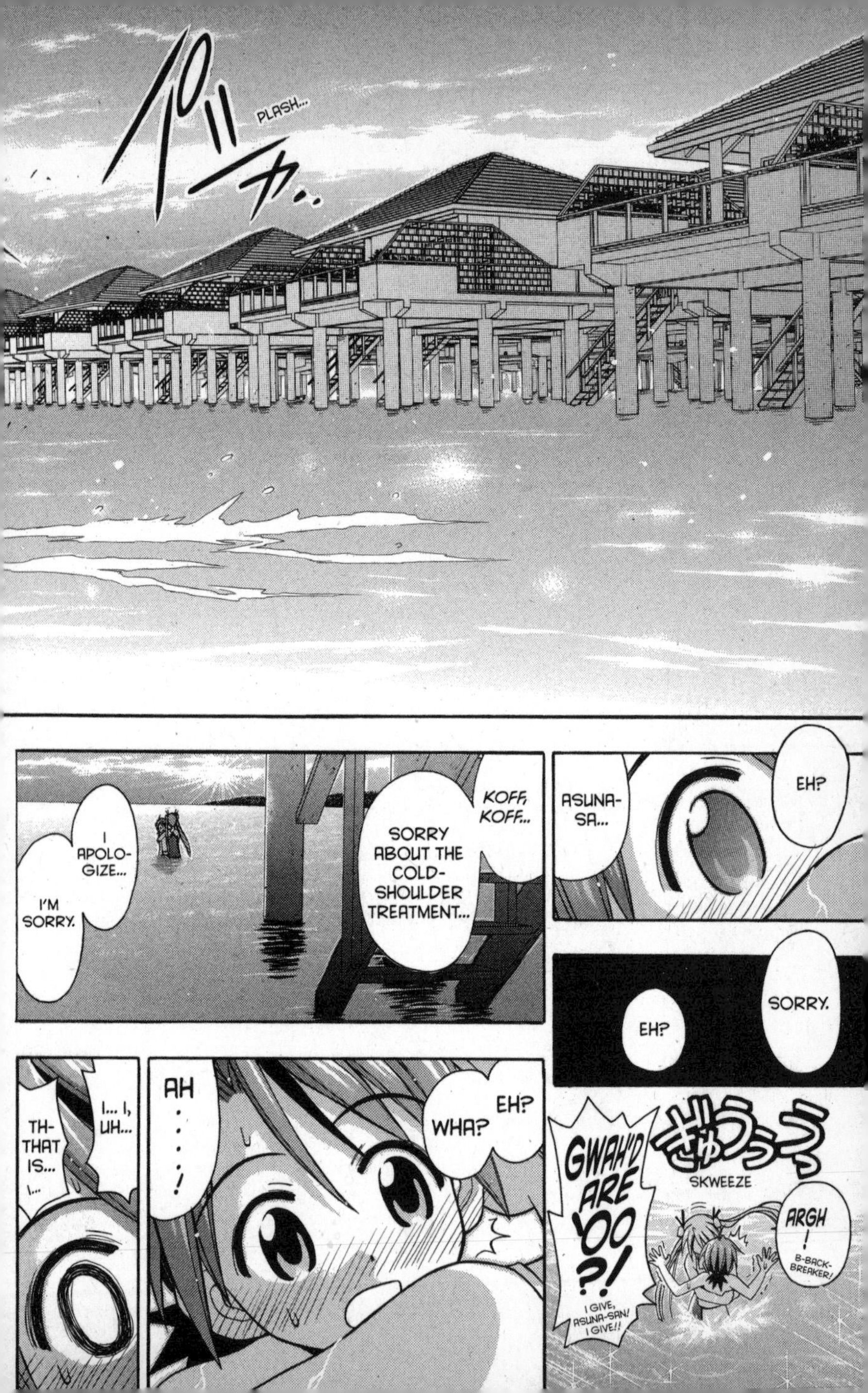

PLASH...
EH?
ASUNA-SA...
KOFF, KOFF...
SORRY ABOUT THE COLD-SHOULDER TREATMENT...
I APOLOGIZE...
I'M SORRY.
SORRY.
EH?
SKWEEZE
GWAH'D ARE YOO?!
ARGH!
B-BACK-BREAKER!
I GIVE, ASUNA-SAN! I GIVE!!
EH?
WHA?
AH.....!
I... I, UH...
TH-THAT IS... I...

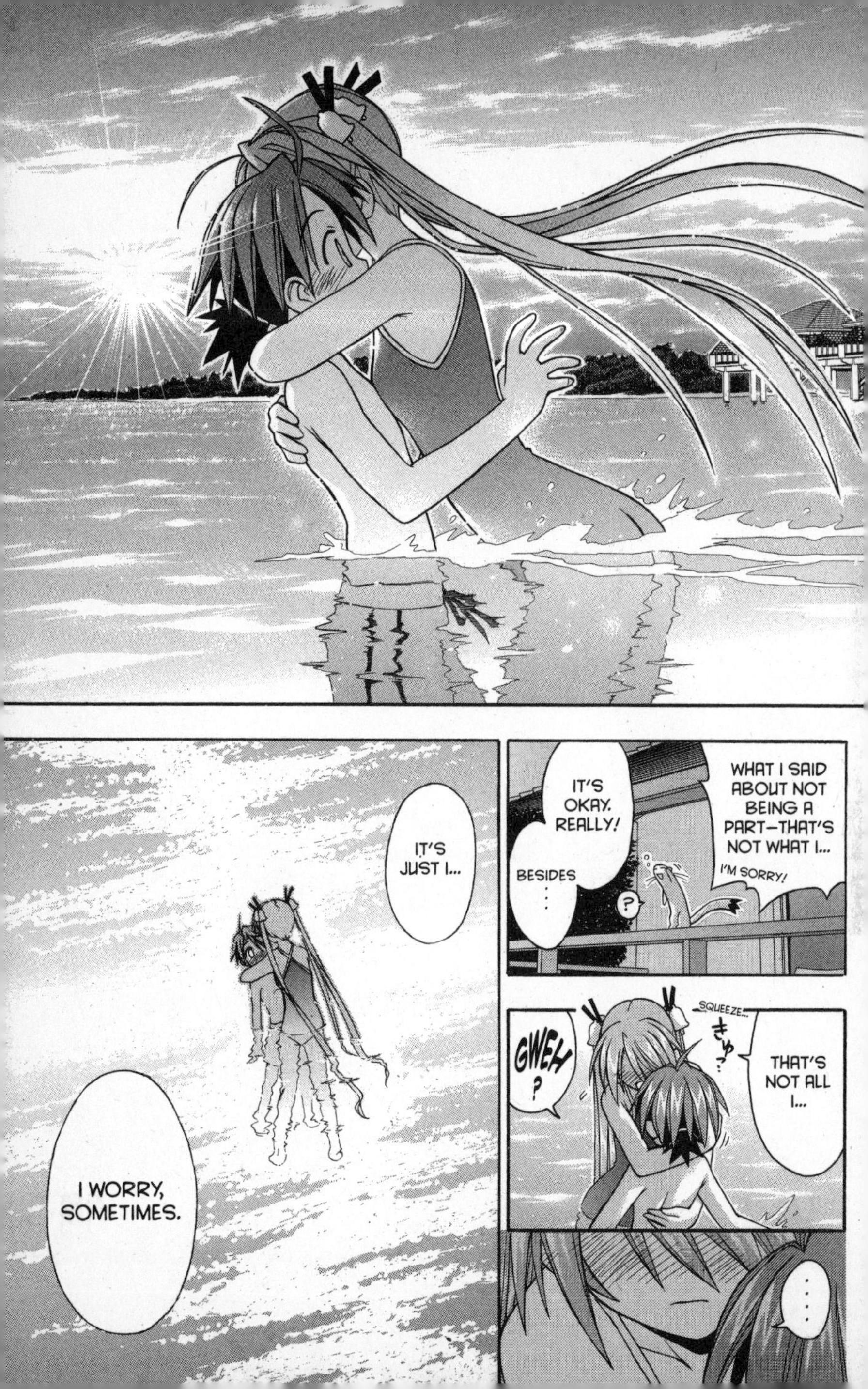
WHAT I SAID ABOUT NOT BEING A PART—THAT'S NOT WHAT I...
I'M SORRY!
IT'S OKAY. REALLY!
BESIDES . . .
?
THAT'S NOT ALL I...
SQUEEZE...
きゅっ
GWEH?
. . . .
IT'S JUST I...
I WORRY, SOMETIMES.

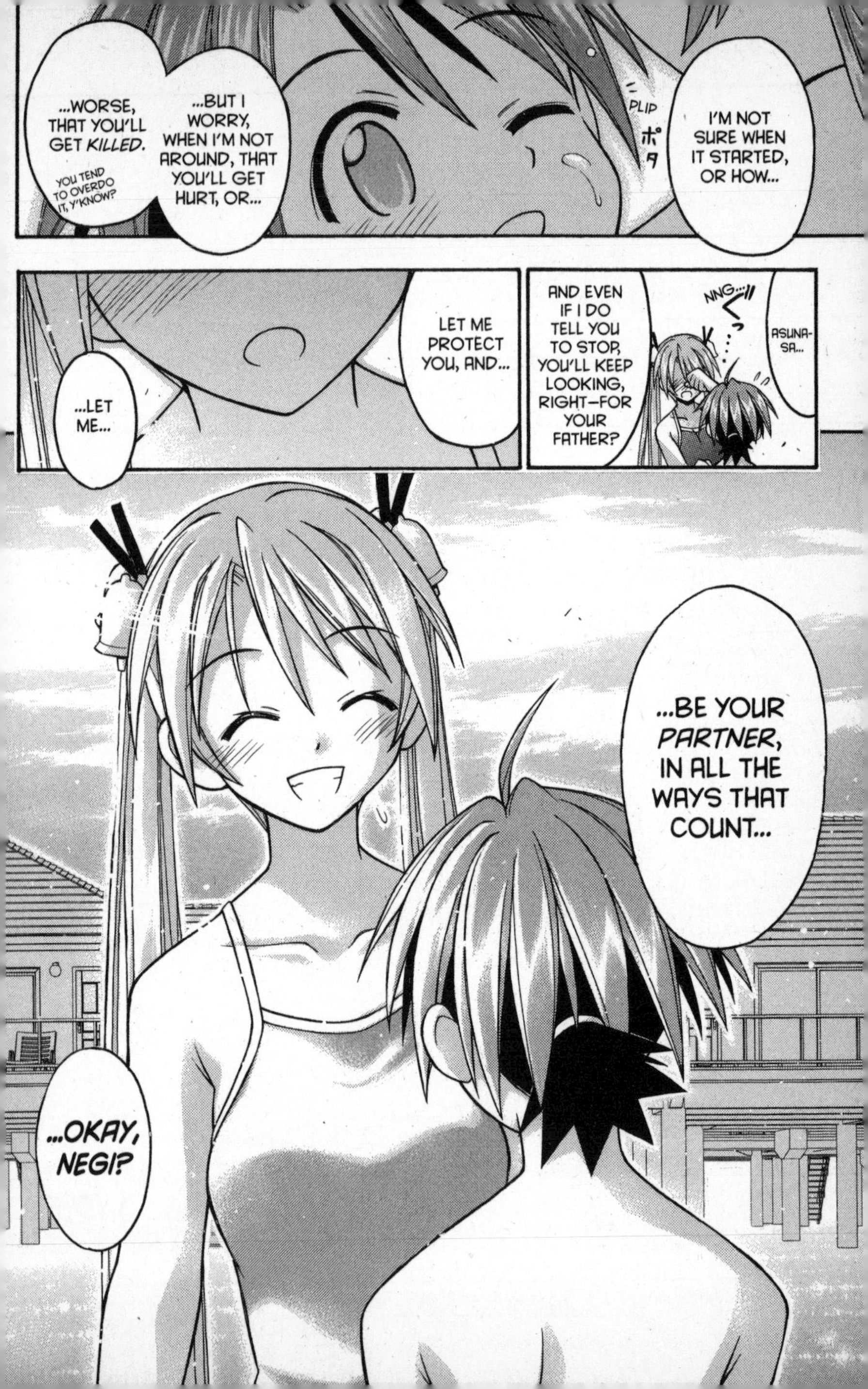
I'M NOT SURE WHEN IT STARTED, OR HOW...
PLIP
ポタ
...BUT I WORRY, WHEN I'M NOT AROUND, THAT YOU'LL GET HURT, OR...
...WORSE, THAT YOU'LL GET *KILLED*.
YOU TEND TO OVERDO IT, Y'KNOW?
ASUNA-SA...
NNG...
AND EVEN IF I DO TELL YOU TO STOP, YOU'LL KEEP LOOKING, RIGHT—FOR YOUR FATHER?
LET ME PROTECT YOU, AND...
...LET ME...
...BE YOUR *PARTNER*, IN ALL THE WAYS THAT COUNT...
...OKAY, NEGI?

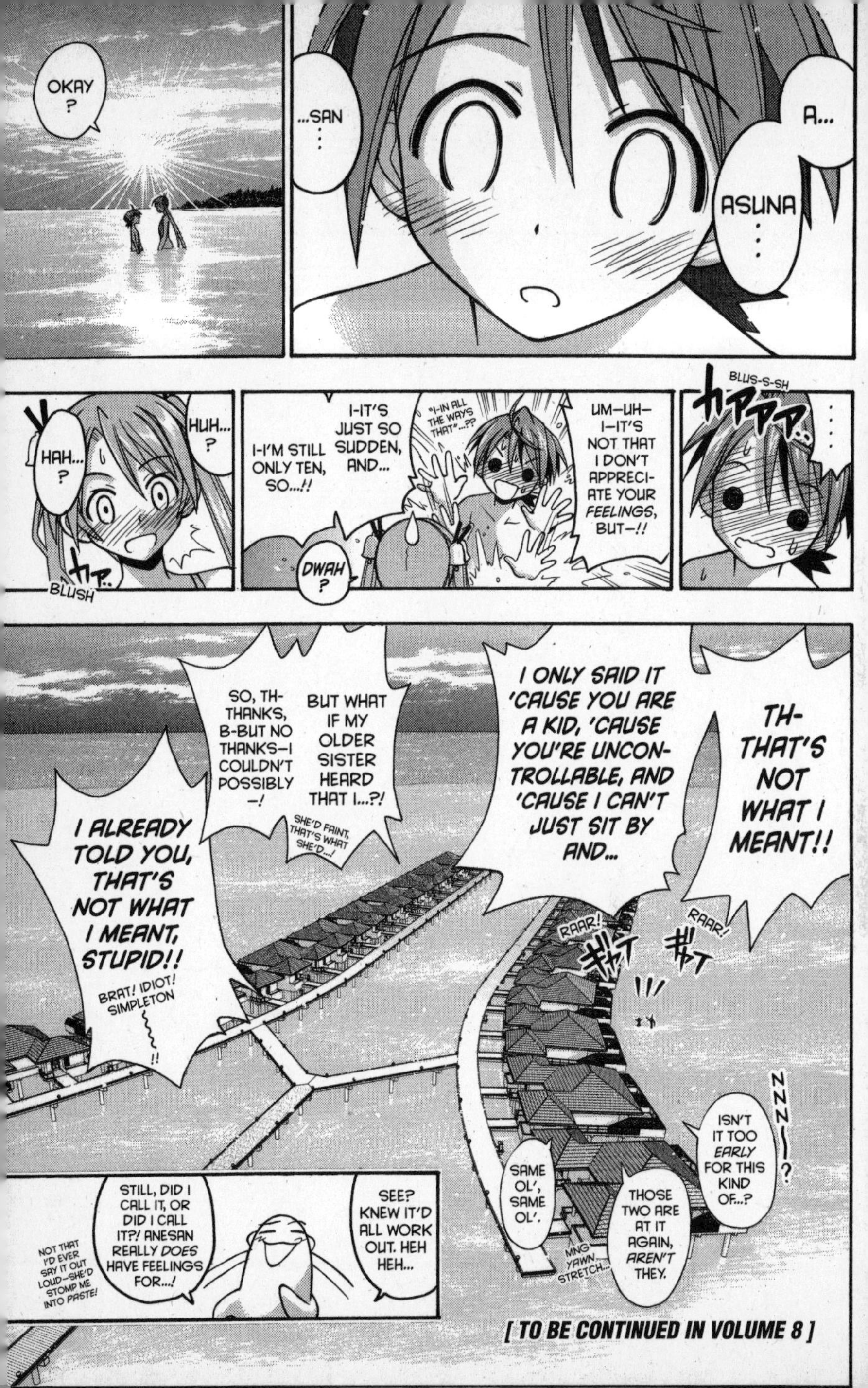
A... ASUNA...
...SAN...
OKAY?
BLUS-S-SH
...
UM—UH— I-IT'S NOT THAT I DON'T APPRECIATE YOUR FEELINGS, BUT—!!
"I-IN ALL THE WAYS THAT"...??
I-IT'S JUST SO SUDDEN, AND...
I-I'M STILL ONLY TEN, SO...!!
DWAH?
HUH...?
HAH...?
BLUSH
TH-THAT'S NOT WHAT I MEANT!!
I ONLY SAID IT 'CAUSE YOU ARE A KID, 'CAUSE YOU'RE UNCONTROLLABLE, AND 'CAUSE I CAN'T JUST SIT BY AND...
BUT WHAT IF MY OLDER SISTER HEARD THAT I...?!
SHE'D FAINT, THAT'S WHAT SHE'D...!
SO, TH-THANKS, B-BUT NO THANKS—I COULDN'T POSSIBLY—!
I ALREADY TOLD YOU, THAT'S NOT WHAT I MEANT, STUPID!!
BRAT! IDIOT! SIMPLETON!!
RAAR!
RAAR!
NNNI—?
ISN'T IT TOO *EARLY* FOR THIS KIND OF...?
THOSE TWO ARE AT IT AGAIN, *AREN'T* THEY.
SAME OL', SAME OL'.
MNG YAWN STRETCH...
SEE? KNEW IT'D ALL WORK OUT. HEH HEH...
STILL, DID I CALL IT, OR DID I CALL IT?! ANESAN REALLY *DOES* HAVE FEELINGS FOR...!
NOT THAT I'D EVER SAY IT OUT LOUD—SHE'D STOMP ME INTO *PASTE*!
[TO BE CONTINUED IN VOLUME 8]

NEGIMA!
PRELIMINARY DESIGN SPECS —ORIGINAL ROUGH CHARACTER SKETCHES—(ADDENDUM)

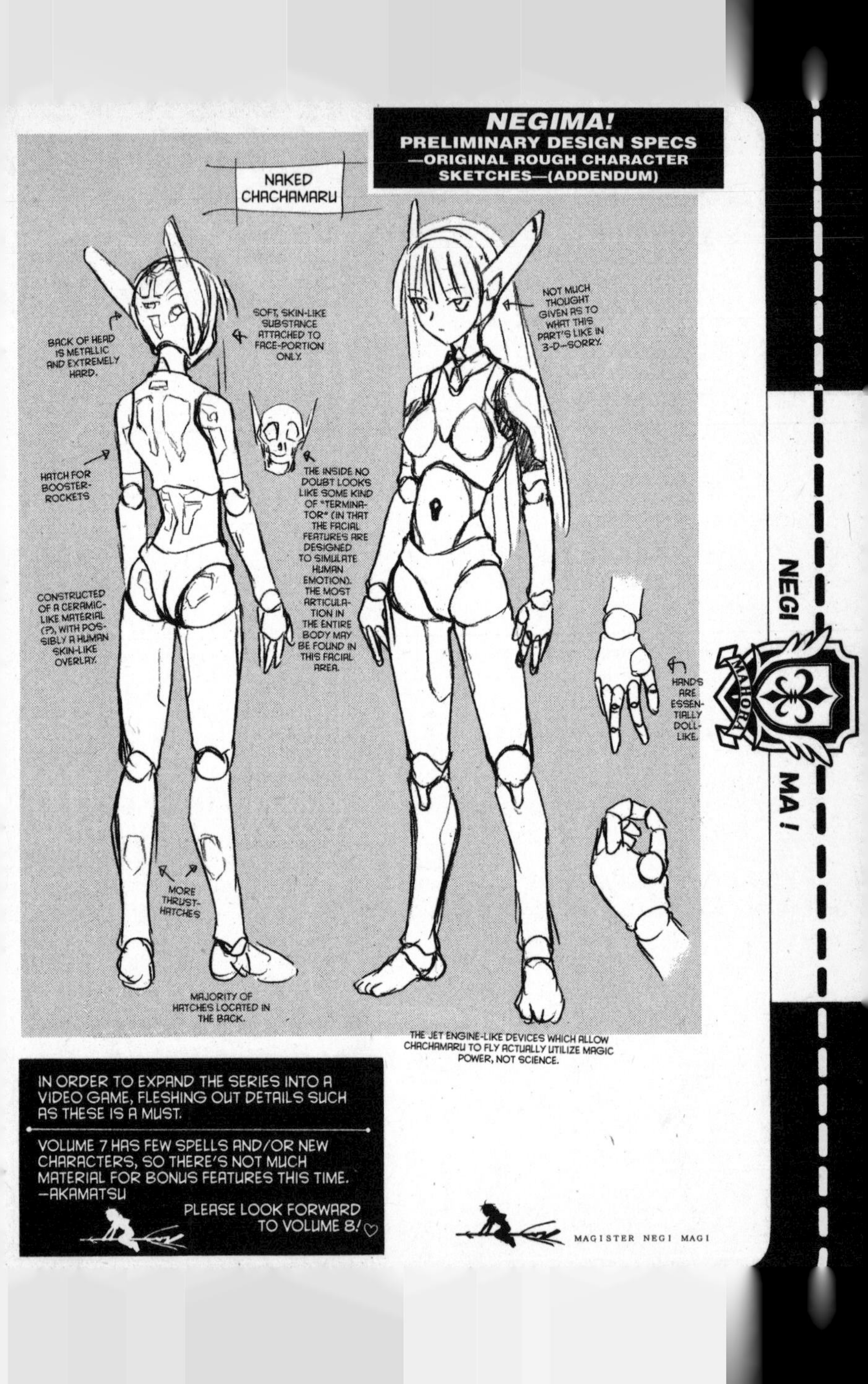
NAKED CHACHAMARU
BACK OF HEAD IS METALLIC AND EXTREMELY HARD.
SOFT, SKIN-LIKE SUBSTANCE ATTACHED TO FACE-PORTION ONLY.
NOT MUCH THOUGHT GIVEN AS TO WHAT THIS PART'S LIKE IN 3-D—SORRY.
HATCH FOR BOOSTER-ROCKETS
THE INSIDE NO DOUBT LOOKS LIKE SOME KIND OF "TERMINATOR" (IN THAT THE FACIAL FEATURES ARE DESIGNED TO SIMULATE HUMAN EMOTION). THE MOST ARTICULATION IN THE ENTIRE BODY MAY BE FOUND IN THIS FACIAL AREA.
CONSTRUCTED OF A CERAMIC-LIKE MATERIAL (?), WITH POSSIBLY A HUMAN SKIN-LIKE OVERLAY.
HANDS ARE ESSENTIALLY DOLL-LIKE.
MORE THRUST-HATCHES
MAJORITY OF HATCHES LOCATED IN THE BACK.

THE JET ENGINE-LIKE DEVICES WHICH ALLOW CHACHAMARU TO FLY ACTUALLY UTILIZE MAGIC POWER, NOT SCIENCE.

IN ORDER TO EXPAND THE SERIES INTO A VIDEO GAME, FLESHING OUT DETAILS SUCH AS THESE IS A MUST.

VOLUME 7 HAS FEW SPELLS AND/OR NEW CHARACTERS, SO THERE'S NOT MUCH MATERIAL FOR BONUS FEATURES THIS TIME. —AKAMATSU

PLEASE LOOK FORWARD TO VOLUME 8! ♡

NEGIMA!

FAN ART CORNER

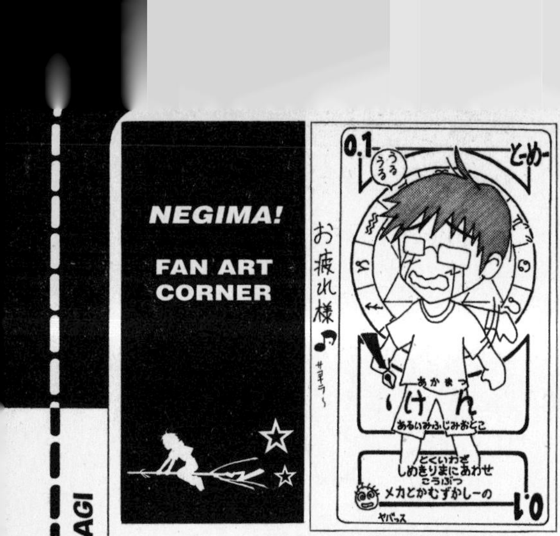
0.1
とめー
お疲れ様♪
あかまつ
いけん
あるいみふじみおとこ
とくいわざ
しめきりまにあわせ
こうぶつ
メカとかむずかしーの
ヤバッス
0.1

NICE IDEA! (HEH.) A BIG HIT AMONG THE STAFF.

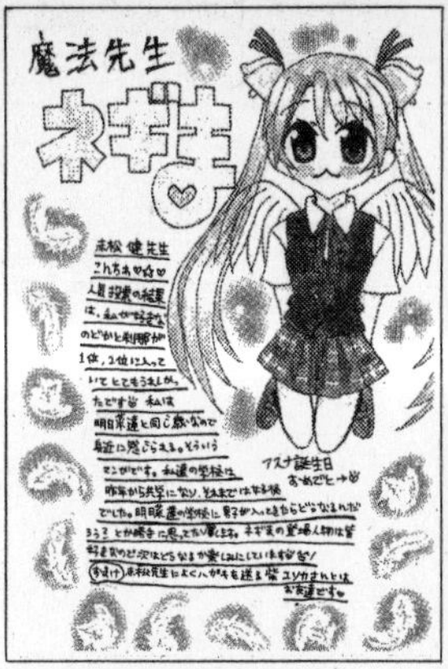
魔法先生
ネギま
赤松 健先生
こんちわ☆

THE LIGHT AND AIRY FEELING IS WELL DONE.

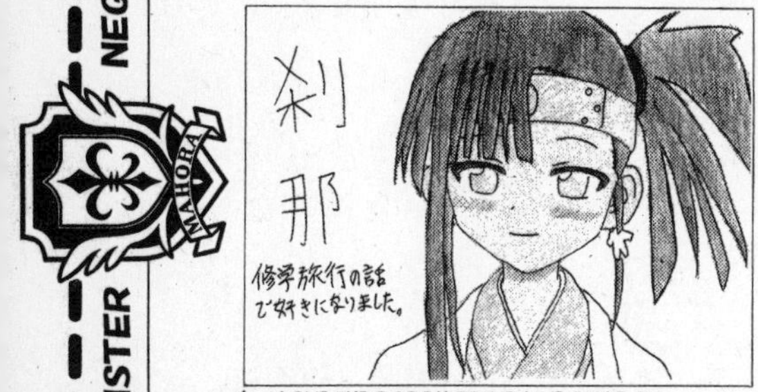
刹那
修学旅行の話で好きになりました。

I LOVE THE BODDHISATVA-LIKE SMILE ON SETSUNA, HERE.

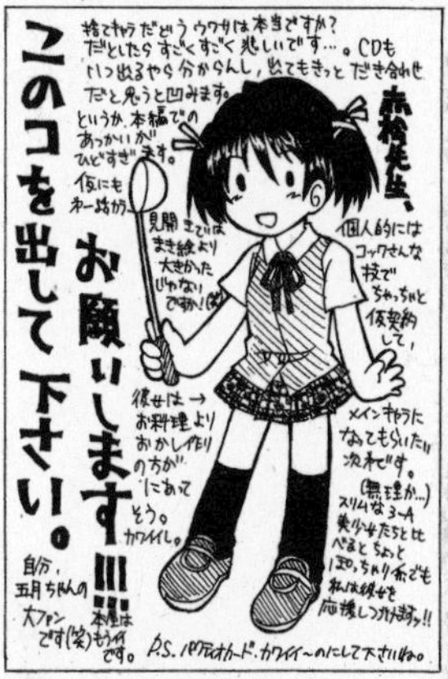
捨てキャラだというウワサは本当ですか?
だとしたらすごくすごく悲しいです…。CDもいつ出るやら分からんし、出てもきっとだき合わせだと思うと凹みます。
このコを出して下さい。
お願いします!!!
赤松先生、
P.S. パクティオカード、カワイイ~のにして下さいね。

YOTSUBA'S CARD MAY PROVE INTERESTING...

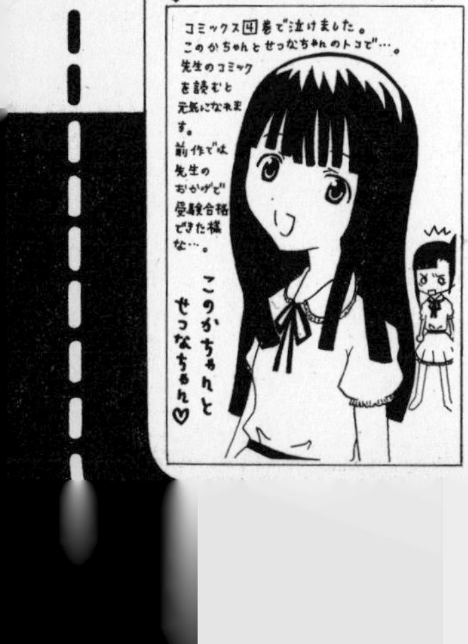
コミックス④巻で泣けました。
このかちゃんとせっなちゃんのトコで…。
先生のコミックを読むと元気になれます。
前作では先生のおかげで受験合格できた様な…。
このかちゃんとせっなちゃん♡

SETSUNA'S EXPRESSION IN THE BACKGROUND IS PRICELESS.

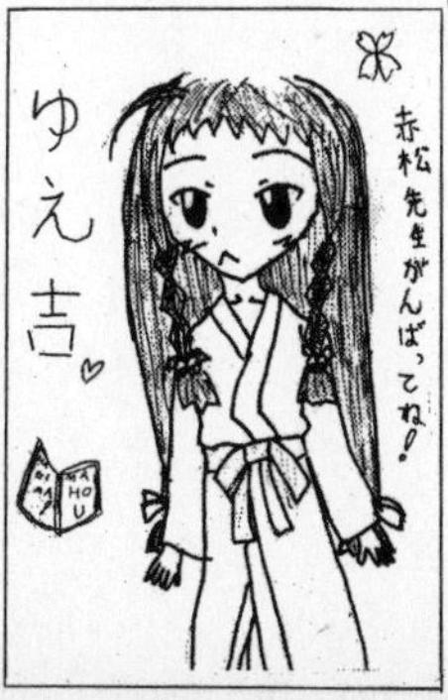
ゆえ吉
赤松先生がんばってね!

"YUEKICHI" IS A FUN TOUCH.

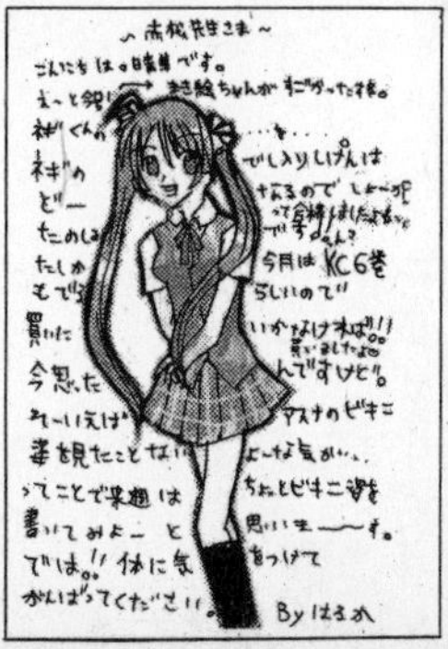
~赤松先生さま~
今月はKC6巻らしいので

ILLUSTRATIONS ALWAYS WELCOME!

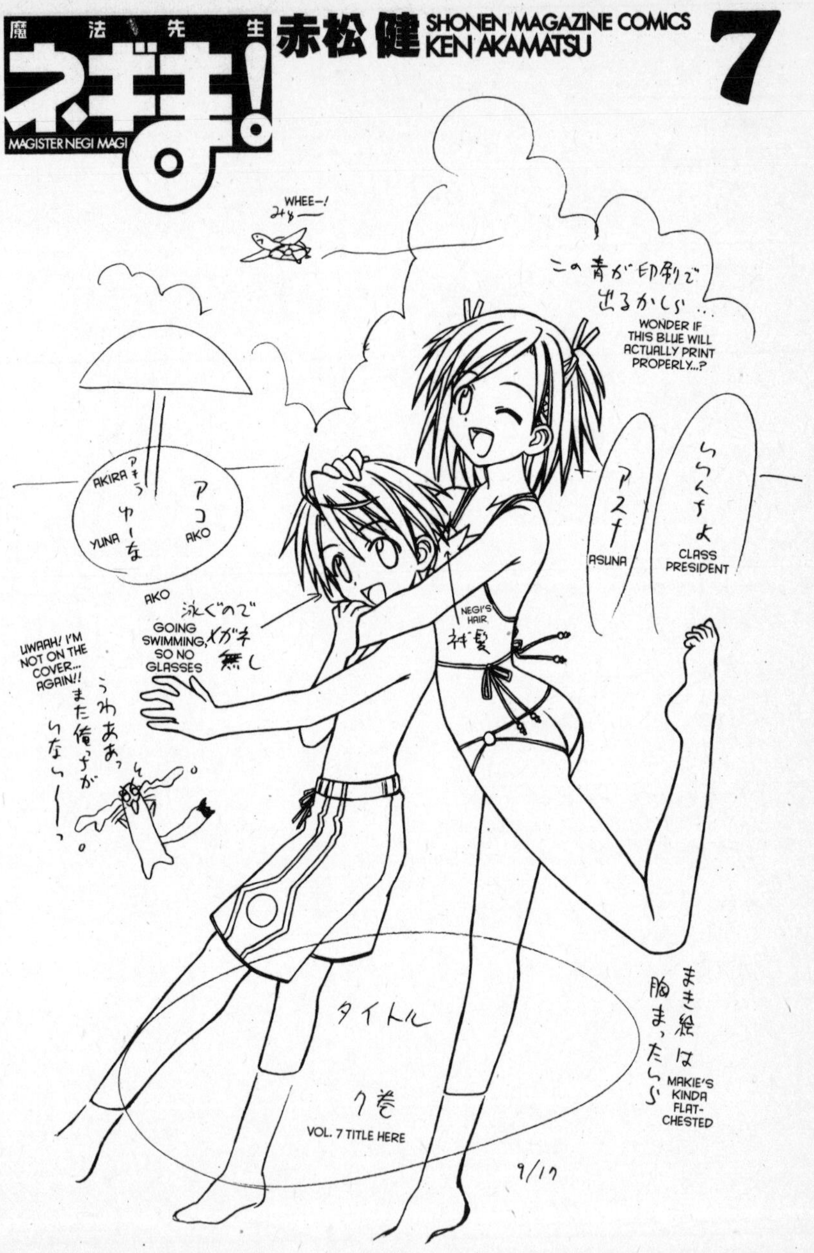

魔法先生
ネギま!
MAGISTER NEGI MAGI
赤松健
SHONEN MAGAZINE COMICS
KEN AKAMATSU
7
みゃー
WHEE—!
この青が印刷で出るかしら…
WONDER IF THIS BLUE WILL ACTUALLY PRINT PROPERLY...?
いいんちょ
CLASS PRESIDENT
アスナ
ASUNA
アコ
AKO
アキラ
AKIRA
ゆーな
YUNA
AKO
泳ぐのでメガネ無し
GOING SWIMMING, SO NO GLASSES
NEGI'S HAIR
ネギ髪
UWAAH! I'M NOT ON THE COVER... AGAIN!!
まき絵は胸まったいら
MAKIE'S KINDA FLAT-CHESTED
タイトル
7巻
VOL. 7 TITLE HERE
9/17

キャラ解説

CHARACTER PROFILE

ゆきひろ

㉙ 雪広 あやか (いいんちょ)

㉙ YUKIHIRO AYAKA (CLASS PRESIDENT)

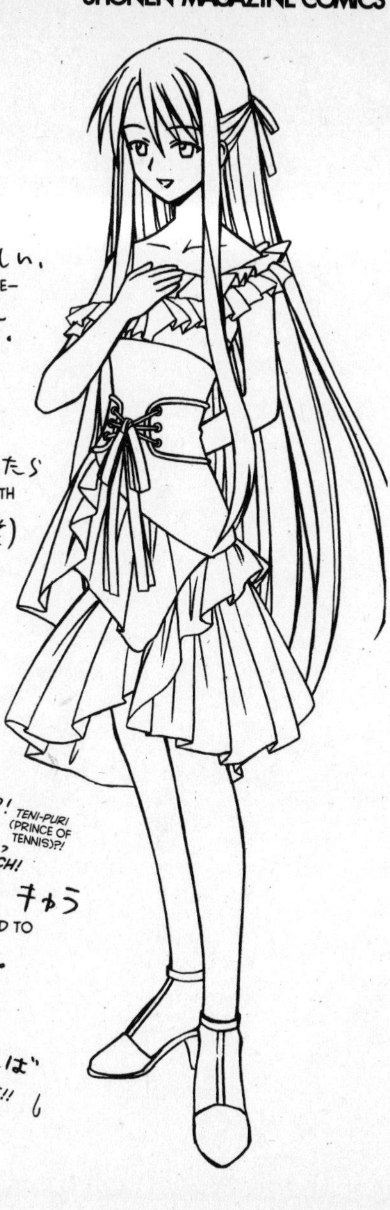

赤松マンガでは 非常にめずらしい。

A RARE CHARACTER TO APPEAR IN AN AKAMATSU TITLE—

高飛車お嬢様タイプの キャラです。

THAT OF THE OVERBEARING RICH GIRL. SLATED IN THE

最初は ヒロインに いじわるをする

BEGINNING TO ACT AS A FOIL FOR THE HEROINE, ONCE I

役の予定だったのですが、描いてみたら

STARTED DRAWING HER SHE BECAME A "NICE" GIRL WITH

正義感の強い「いいひと」に!(笑)

A STRONG SENSE OF RIGHT AND WRONG (HEH).

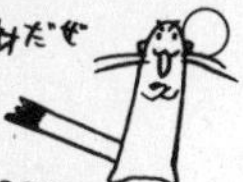
いい素材だぜ
うん
うん
SHE'S GOT IT GOING ON! UH-HUH, UH-HUH
アニキと
パクって
くんねーかなー
WONDER IF SHE'S GONNA *PACTIO* WITH ANIKI!?!

声優さんも ゴージャスに

FOR HER VOICE IN THE ANIME VERSION, WE HAVE THE

皆川純子サマ。

GORGEOUS MINAGAWA JUNKO!

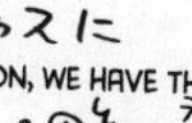
テニプリ?!
TENI-PURI (PRINCE OF TENNIS)?!
びくっ
TWITCH!

今後も活躍が 期待できる キャラ

THIS IS ONE CHARACTER WE CAN LOOK FORWARD TO

ですね〜! いやホント。

IN THE FUTURE. (NO REALLY!)

…ホントだってば

...REALLY! I TOTALLY MEAN IT!!

赤松

AKAMATSU

About the Creator

Negima! is only Ken Akamatsu's third manga, although he started working in the field in 1994 with *AI Ga Tomaranai* (released in the United States with the title *A.I. Love You*). Like all of Akamatsu's work to date, it was published in Kodansha's *Shonen Magazine*. *AI Ga Tomaranai* ran for five years before concluding in 1999. In 1998, however, Akamatsu began the work that would make him one of the most popular manga artists in Japan: *Love Hina*. *Love Hina* ran for four years, and before its conclusion in 2002, it would cause Akamatsu to be granted the prestigious Manga of the Year award from Kodansha, as well as going on to become one of the best-selling manga in the United States.

Translation Notes

Japanese is a tricky language for most Westerners, and translation is often more art than science. For your edification and reading pleasure, here are notes on some of the places where we could have gone in a different direction in our translation of the work, or where a Japanese cultural reference is used.

Arisan Kinsen-cha, page 9

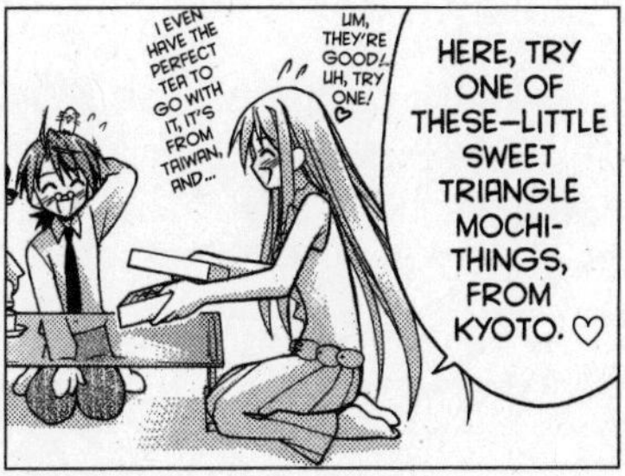
HERE, TRY ONE OF THESE—LITTLE SWEET TRIANGLE MOCHI-THINGS, FROM KYOTO. ♡
UM, THEY'RE GOOD! UH, TRY ONE! ♡
I EVEN HAVE THE PERFECT TEA TO GO WITH IT, IT'S FROM TAIWAN, AND...

Glossed over within the comic itself for reasons of space, the F/X next to Ayaka's head on page 9, panel 3—where she's offering Negi some tea—is a reference to a very expensive and high-end drink. Known as *Arisan Kinsen-cha* (Kinsen tea harvested from Mt. Ari in Taiwan, a well-known tea region), the brew is akin to oolong in that it emits a rich, milk-like, sweet scent once prepared.

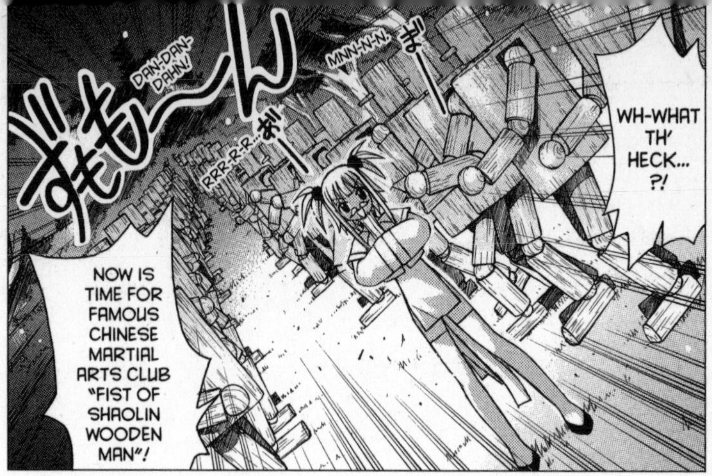
WH-WHAT TH' HECK... ?!
MNN-N-N.
DAN-DAN-DAHN!
RRR-R-R...
NOW IS TIME FOR FAMOUS CHINESE MARTIAL ARTS CLUB "FIST OF SHAOLIN WOODEN MAN"!

Mokujin, page 69

Originally from the obscure seventies Jackie Chan film, *Shaolin Wooden Men,* these wooden soldiers or *mokujin* (from the Japanese *moku*, "wood" + *jin*, "person/people/men") appear only in the movie's first half but apparently made quite an impression. In the film, as part of his marital-arts training, the character Jackie plays must get past a pulley-and chain-operated series of them. (This may be the only film where the actor has no lines until the movie's end.) "Mokujin" also notably appears in the Namco video-game series Tekken, as a playable character.

Paipan, page 130

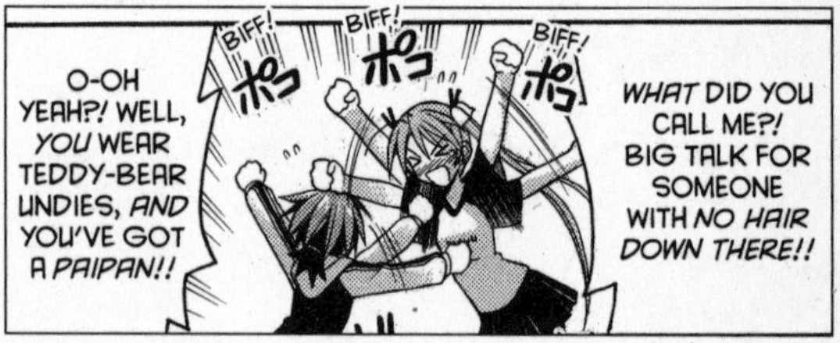
WHAT DID YOU CALL ME?! BIG TALK FOR SOMEONE WITH NO HAIR DOWN THERE!!
BIFF!
BIFF!
BIFF!
O-OH YEAH?! WELL, YOU WEAR TEDDY-BEAR UNDIES, AND YOU'VE GOT A PAIPAN!!

A term that's appeared more than once in the *Negima!* series, it certainly isn't the kind of word one would expect a well-brought-up young lad like Negi to be using. Most recently appearing on page 130 of this volume, the closest translation might be "shorn"...as in what one might do to one's nether regions, were one so inclined. (It can also refer to those prepubescents who've yet to develop...um, certain secondary sexual characteristics.) Naughty Negi!

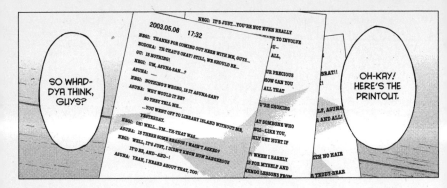

OH-KAY! HERE'S THE PRINTOUT.
NEGI: IT'S JUST...YOU'RE NOT EVEN REALLY
2003.05.06 17:32
NEGI: THANKS FOR COMING OUT HERE WITH ME, GUYS...
NODOKA: TH-THAT'S OKAY! STILL, WE SHOULD BE...
GU: IS NOTHING!
NEGI: UM, ASUNA-SAN...?
ASUNA: .....
NEGI: NOTHING'S WRONG, IS IT ASUNA-SAN?
ASUNA: WHY WOULD IT BE?
SO THEY TELL ME...
...YOU WENT OFF TO LIBRARY ISLAND WITHOUT ME, YESTERDAY.
NEGI: OH! WELL...UM...TH-THAT WAS...
ASUNA: IS THERE SOME REASON I WASN'T ASKED?
NEGI: WELL, IT'S JUST, I DIDN'T KNOW HOW DANGEROUS IT'D BE, AND—AND—!
ASUNA: YEAH, I HEARD ABOUT THAT, TOO!
SO WHAD-DYA THINK, GUYS?

Gu, page 137

In the printout of the infamous conversation between (mostly) Asuna and Negi, each of the speakers is identified. Fei Kū, listed herein as "Gu," appears as such only because that is apparently how the name is properly romanized in Pinyin.

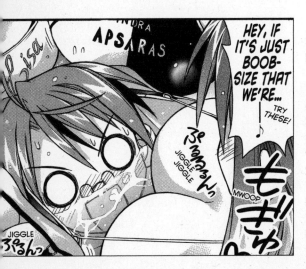

HEY, IF IT'S JUST BOOB-SIZE THAT WE'RE...
TRY THESE!
MWOOP
APSARAS
JIGGLE JIGGLE
JIGGLE

Indra Apsaras, page 151

From text on Ayaka's swimsuit in the "Marshmallow Empire" story. A celestial dancer—one of the beautiful maidens who purportedly delight the inhabitants of paradise—Apsaras is a character from Indian mythology and resident of the celestial realms conceived of as analogous to earthly courts, with palaces, gardens, kings and nobles, dancers and musicians.

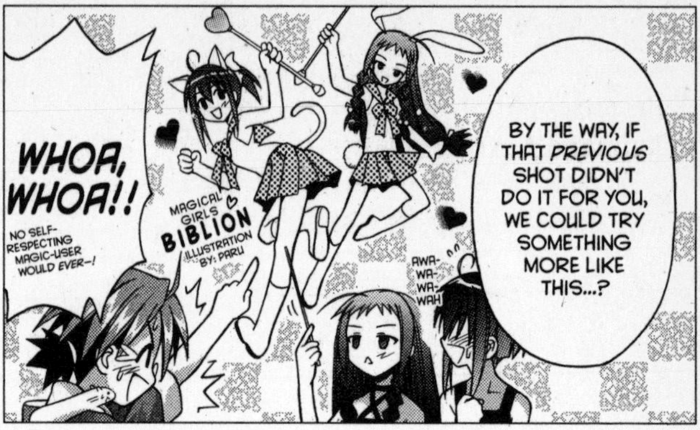
BY THE WAY, IF THAT *PREVIOUS* SHOT DIDN'T DO IT FOR YOU, WE COULD TRY SOMETHING MORE LIKE THIS...?
MAGICAL GIRLS BIBLION ILLUSTRATION BY: PARU
AWA-WA-WA-WAH
WHOA, WHOA!!
NO SELF-RESPECTING MAGIC-USER WOULD *EVER*–!

Magical Girls Biblion, page 168

Fresh from the imagination of Yue, "Magical Girls Biblion" is her version of a Sailor Moon–like magical girl show of the above-mentioned title. (βιβλιον, of course, is "bible" in Greek.)

Preview of Volume Eight

Because we're running about one year behind the release of the Japanese *Negima!* manga, we have the opportunity to present to you a preview from volume eight. This volume will be available in English on December 27, 2005.

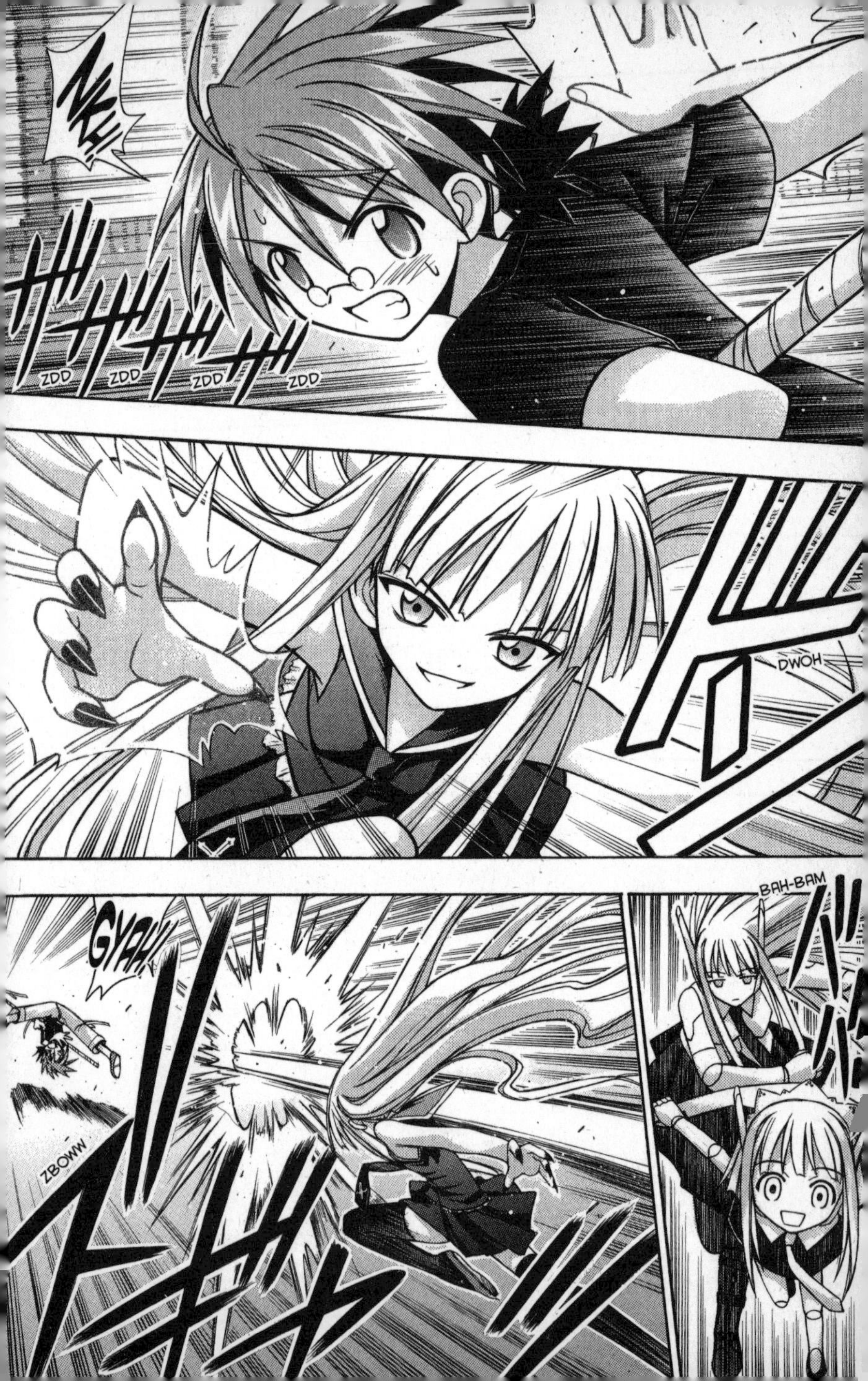
NKH!
ZDD ZDD ZDD ZDD
DWOH
BAH-BAM
GYAH!
ZBOWW

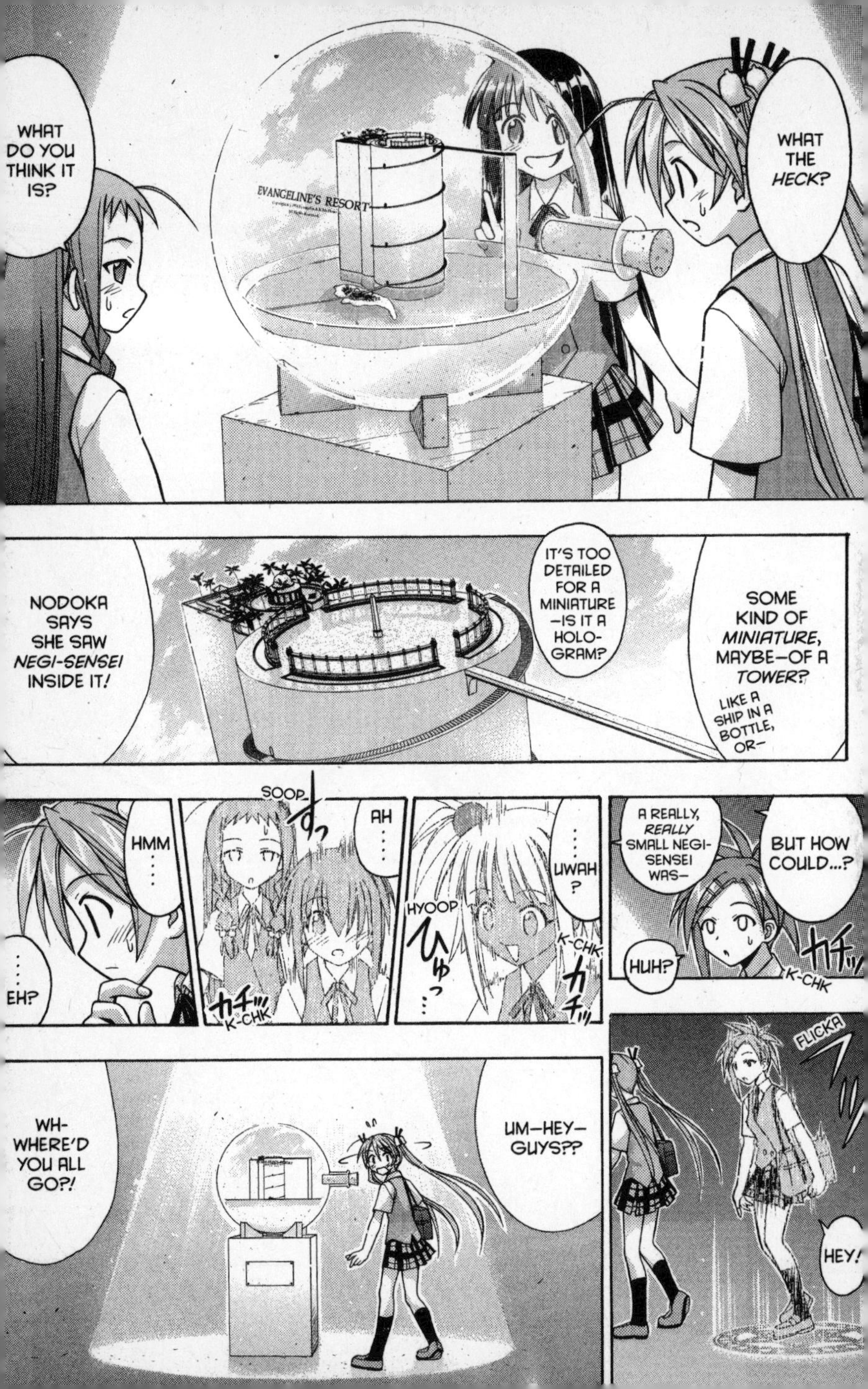
WHAT THE HECK?
EVANGELINE'S RESORT
WHAT DO YOU THINK IT IS?
SOME KIND OF MINIATURE, MAYBE—OF A TOWER?
LIKE A SHIP IN A BOTTLE, OR—
IT'S TOO DETAILED FOR A MINIATURE—IS IT A HOLOGRAM?
NODOKA SAYS SHE SAW NEGI-SENSEI INSIDE IT!
BUT HOW COULD...?
A REALLY, REALLY SMALL NEGI-SENSEI WAS—
HUH?
K-CHK
...UWAH?
HYOOP
K-CHK
AH....
SOOP
K-CHK
HMM....
....EH?
FLICKA
HEY!
UM—HEY—GUYS??
WH-WHERE'D YOU ALL GO?!

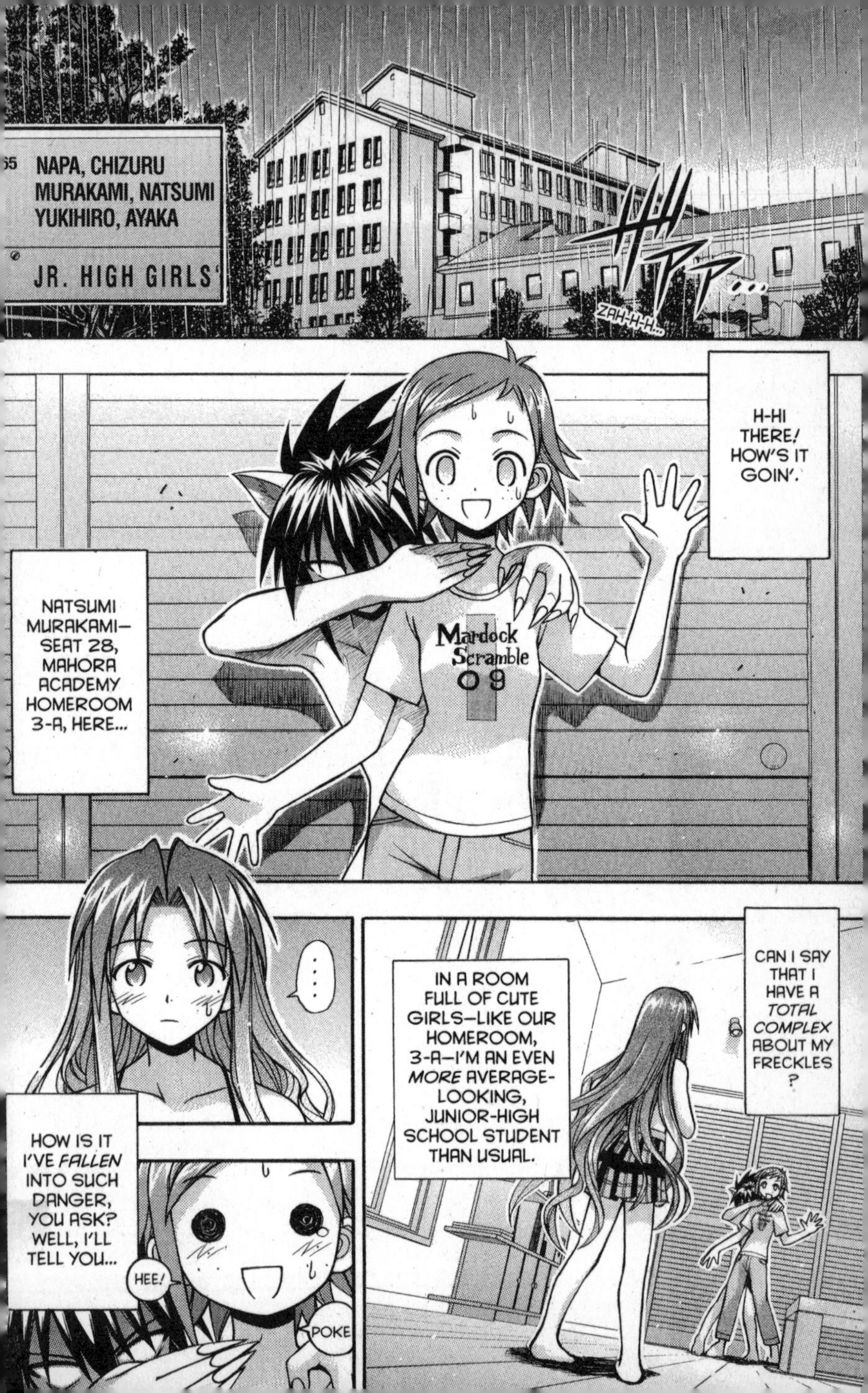
NAPA, CHIZURU
MURAKAMI, NATSUMI
YUKIHIRO, AYAKA
JR. HIGH GIRLS'
ZAHHHH...
H-HI THERE! HOW'S IT GOIN'.
Mardock Scramble 09
NATSUMI MURAKAMI—SEAT 28, MAHORA ACADEMY HOMEROOM 3-A, HERE...
CAN I SAY THAT I HAVE A *TOTAL COMPLEX* ABOUT MY FRECKLES?
IN A ROOM FULL OF CUTE GIRLS—LIKE OUR HOMEROOM, 3-A—I'M AN EVEN *MORE* AVERAGE-LOOKING, JUNIOR-HIGH SCHOOL STUDENT THAN USUAL.
....
HOW IS IT I'VE *FALLEN* INTO SUCH DANGER, YOU ASK? WELL, I'LL TELL YOU...
HEE!
POKE

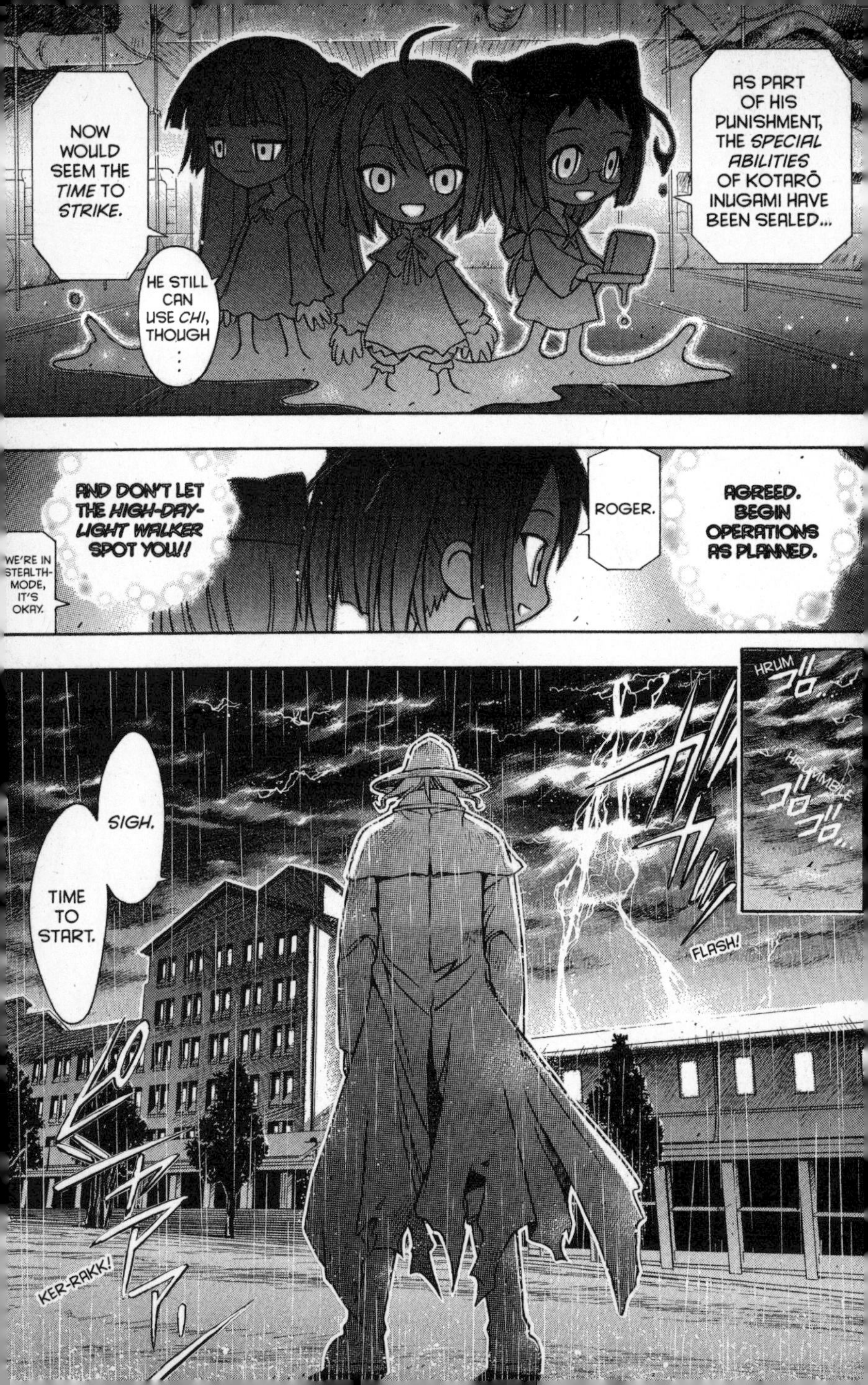
AS PART OF HIS PUNISHMENT, THE *SPECIAL ABILITIES* OF KOTARŌ INUGAMI HAVE BEEN SEALED...
NOW WOULD SEEM THE *TIME* TO *STRIKE*.
HE STILL CAN USE *CHI*, THOUGH...
AGREED. BEGIN OPERATIONS AS PLANNED.
ROGER.
AND DON'T LET THE *HIGH-DAY-LIGHT WALKER* SPOT YOU!!
WE'RE IN STEALTH-MODE, IT'S OKAY.
HRUM
HRUMMBLE
FLASH!
SIGH.
TIME TO START.
KER-RAKK!

Gacha Gacha ①

BY HIROYUKI TAMAKOSHI

SECRET CRUSH

HIROYUKI TAMAKOSHI

Lately, Kouhei can't get his friend Kurara out of his mind. Even though he has known her since elementary school, all of a sudden, ever since she came back from summer vacation, he has been crushing on her . . . hard.

But something is different about Kurara—lately she has been acting very unusual. Sometimes she seems wholesome, pure, and innocent, and other times she is extremely forward and unabashed. Kouhei soon learns that Kurara has multiple personalities—and decides to help her keep her secret from their classmates. But Kouhei soon finds himself struggling between helping her as a friend, and trying to win her heart . . . which is a challenge, since she has many!

Ages: 16+

Includes special extras after the story!

VOLUME 1: On sale August 30, 2005

For more information and to sign up for Del Rey's manga e-newsletter, visit www.delreymanga.com

GHOST HUNT

VOLUME 1

ART BY SHIHO INADA

BASED ON THE NOVEL BY FUYUMI ONO

AUTHOR OF *TWELVE KINGDOMS*

Ages: 16+

The decrepit building was condemned long ago, but every time the owners try to tear it down, "accidents" start to happen—people get hurt, sometimes even killed. Mai Taniyama and her classmates have heard the rumors that the creepy old high school is haunted—possibly by ghosts from the Second World War. So one rainy day they gather at the old school to tell ghost stories, hoping to attract one of the suspected spirits.

No ghosts materialize, but they do meet Kazuya Shibuya, the handsome young owner of Shibuya Psychic Research, hired to investigate paranormal activity at the school. Also at the scene are an exorcist, a Buddhist monk, a woman who can speak with the dead, and an outspoken Shinto priestess. Surely one of them will have the talents to solve this mystery. . . .

Includes special extras after the story!

VOLUME 1: On sale September 27, 2005

For more information and to sign up for Del Rey's manga e-newsletter, visit www.delreymanga.com

Sugar Sugar Rune

BY **MOYOCO ANNO**   *VOLUME 1*

QUEEN OF HEARTS

Little witch-girls Chocolat and Vanilla are best friends, but only one of them can be Queen of the Magic World. To determine who deserves the title, they must go to the Human World and enter a strange competition. Whoever attracts the most human boys wins!

Here's how it works: When a boy falls for a witch-girl, she utters a few mystic words and the boy's heart will be hers in jewel-like form. It may sound simple, but winning hearts is tricky business. While Chocolat had no problem enticing witch-boys with her forthright personality, human boys seem to be drawn to shy and modest girls like Vanilla. And to make matters worse, Chocolat is finding herself increasingly drawn to the cool and mysterious Pierre—who feels nothing for her! The girls had planned to be best friends forever, but both of them want to be Queen. Will their rivalry ruin their friendship?

Ages: 10 +

Includes special extras after the story!

VOLUME 1: On sale September 27, 2005

 For more information and to sign up for Del Rey's manga e-newsletter, visit www.delreymanga.com

LOVE ROMA

VOLUME 1

BY MINORU TOYODA

"We have been telling all the people we meet to read this manga!" —CLAMP creators of Tsubasa

One morning, in front of the entire class, a complete stranger walks right up to Negishi and announces: "I like you. Can we go out on a date sometime?" With these simple words, a surprising journey begins. The forthright boy, Hoshino, is an over-thinker—and much too honest for his own good. He can always be counted on to say exactly what's on his mind. Every time Hoshino plans a date, his innocence and inexperience land him in hot water—much to Negishi's embarrassment!

Yet nothing can keep Hoshino from his destiny with romance—not rival lovers, a school full of prying eyes, horribly mismatched astrological signs, or even a disapproving dad!

Ages: 16 +

Includes special extras after the story!

VOLUME 1: On sale August 30, 2005

For more information and to sign up for Del Rey's manga e-newsletter, visit www.delreymanga.com

A PERFECT DAY FOR LOVE LETTERS

VOLUME 2

BY GEORGE ASAKURA

SIX TANTALIZING TALES OF LOVE

• When Araki finds an old fax machine, he starts corresponding with the only girl who can receive his letters. But there's a twist!

• A brother's dying request: deliver a videotape to his girlfriend . . . someone his sibling didn't even know existed. And there will be other secrets.

• Natsume must attend summer school while her #1 friend takes an exotic vacation. Oh well, best take his advice and "let the wind blow through you!"

• With a move to Alaska imminent, a girl vows to win the heart of her secret crush. Will a swimming pool rendezvous dampen her message?

• **Plus bonus stories!**

Ages: 16+

Love is in the air . . . and in the water . . . and in the mail with these intriguing tales of affection, rejection, miscommunication, and sweet connection!

Includes special extras after the story!

VOLUME 2: On sale November 29, 2005

GENSHIKEN

The Society for the Study of Modern Visual Culture

VOLUME 3
BY KIO SHIMOKU

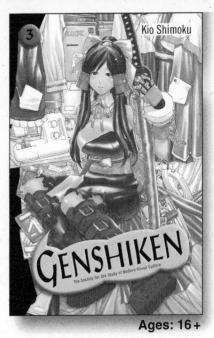

Kanji Sasahara's annoyingly normal little sister, Keiko, has fallen for video game master Kousaka. And now she's willing to do whatever it takes to steal him away from his girl-friend, Saki Kasukabe . . . even if it means becoming a fangirl herself! But as a wise member of the Genshiken once said: "You don't become an otaku by trying." So Saki teaches Keiko-chan what dating a rabid fan truly means . . . and it ain't pretty. Just to add to the craziness, there's plastic modeling mayhem (don't ask), the challenge of Kanji's first PC, and Saki's penchant for pyromania. Looks like things are heating up!

Kio Shimoku

Ages: 16+

Includes special extras after the story!

VOLUME 3: On sale October 25, 2005

For more information and to sign up for Del Rey's manga e-newsletter, visit www.delreymanga.com

TOMARE!

[STOP!]

You're going the wrong way!

Manga is a completely different
type of reading experience.

To start at the *beginning*,
go to the *end*!

That's right! Authentic manga is read the traditional Japanese way—
from right to left. Exactly the *opposite* of how American books are
read. It's easy to follow: Just go to the other end of the book, and read
each page—and each panel—from right side to left side, starting at
the top right. Now you're experiencing manga as it was meant to be.